PRINCETON-PRAGUE SYMPOSIA ！ _SUS

Edited by James H. Charlesworth and Petr Pokorný

I *Jesus Research: An International Perspective*
The First Princeton-Prague Symposium on Jesus Research,
Prague 2005

Jesus Research: An International Perspective

The First Princeton-Prague Symposium on Jesus Research, Prague 2005

Edited by

James H. Charlesworth with Petr Pokorný

and with Brian Rhea, Jan Roskovec, & Jonathan Soyars

WILLIAM B. EERDMANS PUBLISHING COMPANY
GRAND RAPIDS, MICHIGAN / CAMBRIDGE, U.K.

Published 2009 by
Wm. B. Eerdmans Publishing Co.
2140 Oak Industrial Drive N.E., Grand Rapids, Michigan 49505 /
P.O. Box 163, Cambridge CB3 9PU U.K.

Printed in the United States of America

15 14 13 12 11 10 09   7 6 5 4 3 2 1

Library of Congress Cataloging-in-Publication Data

Princeton-Prague Symposium on Jesus Research (1st 2005: Prague, Czech Republic)
    An international look at Jesus research: the first Princeton-Prague Symposium on
Jesus Research, Prague 2005 / edited by James H. Charlesworth and Petr Pokorný.
        p.   cm.   — (Princeton-Prague Symposia series on the historical Jesus)
    Includes bibliographical references and indexes.
    ISBN 978-0-8028-6353-9 (pbk.: alk. paper)
    1. Jesus Christ — Historicity.   2. Jesus Christ — Person and offices.
    I. Charlesworth, James H.   II. Pokorný, Petr.   III. Title.

BT303.2.P755   2005
232.9 — dc22

                                         2009015435

www.eerdmans.com

Contents

APPRECIATIONS — ix

ABBREVIATIONS — xi

CONTRIBUTORS — xix

PREFACE — xxi

   Petr Pokorný

INTRODUCTION: Why Evaluate Twenty-Five Years
of Jesus Research? — 1

   James H. Charlesworth

A Dead End or a New Beginning? Examining the Criteria
for Authenticity in Light of Albert Schweitzer — 16

   Stanley E. Porter

Jesus of Galilee: The Role of Location in Understanding Jesus — 36

   Jens Schröter

From Old to New: Paradigm Shifts concerning Judaism,
the Gospel of John, Jesus, and the Advent of "Christianity" — 56

   James H. Charlesworth

Contents

Turning Water to Wine: Re-reading the Miracle at
the Wedding in Cana   73

    Carsten Claussen

Jesus as an Itinerant Teacher: Reflections from
Social History on Jesus' Roles   98

    Gerd Theissen

Jesus as a Teller of Parables: On Jesus' Self-Interpretation
in His Parables   123

    Michael Wolter

"What Must I Do to Inherit Eternal Life?" Implicit Christology
in Jesus' Sayings about Life and the Kingdom   140

    Klaus Haacker

How Did Jesus Understand His Death?
The Parables in Eschatological Prospect   154

    Rudolf Hoppe

Demoniac and Drunkard: John the Baptist and Jesus
According to Q 7:33-34   170

    Petr Pokorný

"Have You Not Read . . . ?" Jesus' Subversive
Interpretation of Scripture   182

    Craig Evans

A Contagious Purity: Jesus' Inverse Strategy
for Eschatological Cleanliness   199

    Tom Holmén

Founding Christianity: Comparing Jesus and Japanese
"New Religions"   230

    Ulrich Luz

Selected Bibliography   255
     Brian Rhea

INDEX OF MODERN AUTHORS   287

INDEX OF ANCIENT TEXTS   295

Appreciations

Many should receive thanks and deep appreciations for launching the Princeton-Prague Symposia and for making them such a success. The first symposium met in Prague in the Spring of 2005. This volume contains the proceedings. The second symposium was held in April 2007 at Princeton Theological Seminary thanks to the support of President Iain Torrance; those who attended constituted a "Who's Who" in Jesus Research. The proceedings of the second symposium will be sent to W. B. Eerdmans about one year from now.

First and foremost, I wish to express my deep appreciations to Petr Pokorný. He, with some help from me, initiated these Symposia and invited distinguished specialists in Jesus Research to Prague. He graciously allowed me to live in his guest room, and Vera, his wife, warmly welcomed all to her home.

I am most grateful to all those who participated in the first Princeton-Prague Symposium and worked with me as I edited their papers for publication. I also wish to express my gratitude again to Bill Eerdmans and Sam Eerdmans for receiving and publishing the papers in an attractive format. I am also appreciative to them for distributing effectively the books I publish through William B. Eerdmans Publishing Company.

The Foundation on Judaism and Christian Origins, the Edith C. Blum Foundation, Princeton Theological Seminary, the Centre for Biblical Studies of the Academy of Sciences of the Czech Republic, and Charles University in Prague have offered funding so that scholars may attend the symposia and also have helped cover the costs of editing and publishing the proceedings. All of us are deeply grateful for this support. I would also

Appreciations

add how appreciative I am to Wilbur and Frances Friedman of the Edith C. Blum Foundation for decades of support and to all who make contributions to PTS and to the FJCO.

I am pleased to thank those who have helped me edit this volume, especially Jan Roskovec, Jonathan Soyars, and Brian Rhea.

JHC
Princeton
4 December 2007

Abbreviations

Modern Publications

AASF	Annales Academiae scientiarum fennicae
AB	Anchor Bible
ABD	*Anchor Bible Dictionary*, ed. D. N. Freedman, 6 vols. (New York, 1992)
ABRL	Anchor Bible Reference Library
AGJU	Arbeiten zur Geschichte des antiken Judentums und des Urchristentums
AJBI	*Annual of the Japanese Biblical Institute*
ANRW	*Aufstieg und Niedergang der römischen Welt: Geschichte und Kultur Roms im Spiegel der neueren Forschung*, ed. H. Temporini and W. Haase (Berlin, 1972–)
ANTJ	Arbeiten zum Neuen Testament und Judentum
ASOR	American Schools of Oriental Research
ASORDS	American Schools of Oriental Research Dissertation Series
ATANT	Abhandlungen zur Theologie des Alten und Neuen Testaments
BBET	Beiträge zur biblischen Exegese und Theologie
BECNT	Baker Exegetical Commentary on the New Testament
BETL	Bibliotheca ephemeridum theologicarum lovaniensium
BFCT	Beiträge zur Förderung christlicher Theologie
BG	Biblische Gestalten
BGBE	Beiträge zur Geschichte der biblischen Exegese
Bib	*Biblica*
BibInt Series	Biblical Interpretation Series
BJRL	*Bulletin of the John Rylands University Library of Manchester*
BJS	Brown Judaic Studies

Abbreviations

BK	*Bibel und Kirche*
BKAT	Biblischer Kommentar, Altes Testament, ed. M. Noth and H. W. Wolff
BTB	*Biblical Theology Bulletin*
BU	Biblische Untersuchungen
BZ	*Biblische Zeitschrift*
BZNW	Beihefte zur Zeitschrift für die neutestamentliche Wissenschaft
CahRB	Cahiers de la Revue biblique
CBQ	*Catholic Biblical Quarterly*
CIL	*Corpus inscriptionum latinarum*
CJA	Christianity and Judaism in Antiquity
CM	Christianity in the Making
ConBNT	Coniectanea neotestamentica or Coniectanea biblica: New Testament Series
CRINT	Compendia rerum iudaicarum ad Novum Testamentum
DJD	Discoveries in the Judaean Desert
DNP	*Der neue Pauly: Enzyklopädie der Antike,* ed. H. Cancik and H. Schneider (Stuttgart, 1996–)
DSD	*Dead Sea Discoveries*
EBib	*Etudes bibliques*
EKKNT	Evangelisch-katholischer Kommentar zum Neuen Testament
EncJud	*Encyclopaedia Judaica,* 16 vols. (Jerusalem, 1972)
EvT	*Evangelische Theologie*
ExpTim	*Expository Times*
FGH	*Die Fragmente der griechischen Historiker,* ed. F. Jacoby (Leiden, 1954–64)
FIOTL	Formation and Interpretation of Old Testament Literature
FRLANT	Forschungen zur Religion und Literatur des Alten und Neuen Testaments
FSC	Faith and Scholarship Colloquies
FzB	Forschung zur Bibel
GNS	*Good News Studies*
GTS	Gütersloher Taschenbücher Siebenstern
GW	Gesammelte Werke
HBS	Herders biblische Studien
HNT	Handbuch zum Neuen Testament
HTKNT.S	Herders Theologischer Kommentar zum Neuen Testament, Supplement
HTR	*Harvard Theological Review*
ICC	International Critical Commentary
Int	*Interpretation*

JBL	*Journal of Biblical Literature*
JETS	*Journal of the Evangelical Theological Society*
JJRS	*Japanese Journal of Religious Studies*
JJS	*Journal of Jewish Studies*
JPS	Jewish Publication Society
JR	*Journal of Religion*
JRA	*Journal of Roman Archaeology*
JRASS	*Journal of Roman Archaeology Supplementary Series*
JSHJ	*Journal for the Study of the Historical Jesus*
JSNT	*Journal for the Study of the New Testament*
JSNTSup	Journal for the Study of the New Testament: Supplement Series
JSOTSup	Journal for the Study of the Old Testament: Supplement Series
JTS	*Journal of Theological Studies*
KBANT	Kommentare und Beiträge zum Alten und Neuen Testament
LCL	Loeb Classical Library
LD	Lectio divina
LG	Land of Galilee
MThA	Münsteraner theologische Abhandlungen
NAC	New American Commentary
NAWG	*Nachrichten (von) der Akademie der Wissenschaften in Göttingen*
NEAEHL	*The New Encyclopedia of Archaeological Excavations in the Holy Land,* ed. E. Stern, 4 vols. (Jerusalem, 1993)
NovT	*Novum Testamentum*
NovTSup	Novum Testamentum Supplements
NRSV	New Revised Standard Version
NTAbh	Neutestamentliche Abhandlungen
NTD	Das Neue Testament Deutsch
NTOA	Novum Testamentum et Orbis Antiquus
NTS	*New Testament Studies*
NTTS	New Testament Tools and Studies
ÖBS	Österreichische biblische Studien
OEANE	*The Oxford Encyclopedia of Archaeology in the Near East,* ed. E. M. Meyers, 5 vols. (New York, 1997)
ÖTK	Ökumenischer Taschenbuch-Kommentar
OTL	Old Testament Library
OTP	*Old Testament Pseudepigrapha,* ed. J. H. Charlesworth, 2 vols. (New York, 1983)
PTSDSSP	Princeton Theological Seminary Dead Sea Scrolls Project
QD	Quaestiones disputatae
RB	*Revue biblique*

Abbreviations

RGG	*Religion in Geschichte und Gegenwart,* ed. K. Galling, 7 vols. (Tübingen, 1957–1965 [3rd ed.])
RS	Religionsvetenskapliga skrifter
RSV	Revised Standard Version
SBB	Stuttgarter biblische Beiträge
SBEC	Studies in the Bible and Early Christianity
SBLDS	Society of Biblical Literature Dissertation Series
SBS	Stuttgarter Bibelstudien
SESJ	Suomen Eksegeettisen Seuran julkaisuja, Publications of the Finnish Exegetical Society
SFSHJ	South Florida Studies in the History of Judaism
SG	Sammlung Göschen
SJLA	Studies in Judaism in Late Antiquity
SJOT	*Scandinavian Journal of the Old Testament*
SNT	Studien zum Neuen Testament
SNTSMS	Society for New Testament Studies Monograph Series
SNTSU	Studien zum Neuen Testament und seiner Umwelt
SPIB	Scripta Pontificii Instituti Biblici
StOR	Studies in Oriental Religions
SUNT	Studien zur Umwelt des Neuen Testaments
TANZ	Texte und Arbeiten zum neutestamentlichen Zeitalter
TBei	*Theologische Beiträge*
ThB	Theologische Bücherei
Them	*Themelios*
Theol	*Theology*
THKNT	Theologischer Handkommentar zum Neuen Testament
ThWAT	*Theologisches Wörterbuch zum Alten Testament,* ed. G. J. Botterweck and H. Ringgren (Stuttgart, 1970–)
TJR	*Tenri Journal of Religion*
TP	*Theologie und Philosophie*
TRE	*Theologische Realenzyklopädie,* ed. G. Krause and G. Müller (Berlin, 1977–)
TUGAL	Texte und Untersuchungen zur Geschichte der altchristlichen Literatur
TWNT	*Theologische Wörterbuch zum Neuen Testament,* ed. G. Kittel and G. Friedrich (Stuttgart, 1932–1979)
TynBul	*Tyndale Bulletin*
TZ	*Theologische Zeitschrift*
VF	*Verkündigung und Forschung*
VT	*Vetus Testamentum*
VTSup	Vetus Testamentum Supplements

WBC	Word Biblical Commentary
WD	*Wort und Dienst*
WMANT	Wissenschaftliche Monographien zum Alten und Neuen Testament
WUNT	Wissenschaftliche Untersuchungen zum Neuen Testament
ZNW	*Zeitschrift für die neutestamentliche Wissenschaft und die Kunde der älteren Kirche*
ZTK	*Zeitschrift für Theologie und Kirche*

Ancient Documents

Bible

Gen	Genesis
Exod	Exodus
Lev	Leviticus
Num	Numbers
Deut	Deuteronomy
Josh	Joshua
Judg	Judges
Ruth	Ruth
1–2 Sam	1–2 Samuel
1–2 Kgs	1–2 Kings
1–2 Chr	1–2 Chronicles
Ezra	Ezra
Neh	Nehemiah
Esth	Esther
Job	Job
Ps/Pss	Psalms
Prov	Proverbs
Eccl	Ecclesiastes
Song	Song of Songs
Isa	Isaiah
Jer	Jeremiah
Lam	Lamentations
Ezek	Ezekiel
Dan	Daniel
Hos	Hosea
Joel	Joel
Amos	Amos
Obad	Obadiah

Jonah	Jonah
Mic	Micah
Nah	Nahum
Hab	Habakkuk
Zeph	Zephaniah
Hag	Haggai
Zech	Zechariah
Mal	Malachi
Matt	Matthew
Mark	Mark
Luke	Luke
John	John
Acts	Acts
Rom	Romans
1–2 Cor	1–2 Corinthians
Gal	Galatians
Eph	Ephesians
Phil	Philippians
Col	Colossians
1–2 Thess	1–2 Thessalonians
1–2 Tim	1–2 Timothy
Tit	Titus
Phlm	Philemon
Heb	Hebrews
Jas	James
1–2 Pet	1–2 Peter
1–2–3 John	1–2–3 John
Jude	Jude
Rev	Revelation
QLk	Q as found in Luke

Apocrypha and Pseudepigrapha

2 Bar.	*2 Baruch*
Bel	Bel and the Dragon
1 En.	*1 Enoch*
Gos. Thom.	*Gospel of Thomas* (Nag Hammadi II,2)
Inf. Gos. Thom.	*Infancy Gospel of Thomas*
Jdt	Judith
Jos. Asen.	*Joseph and Aseneth*
Jub.	*Jubilees*

1–2 Macc	1–2 Maccabees
Prot. Jas.	*Protevangelium of James*
Pss. Sol.	*Psalms of Solomon*
Sir	Sirach/Ecclesiasticus
T. Levi	*Testament of Levi*
T. Mos.	*Testament of Moses*
Tob	Tobit
Wis	Wisdom of Solomon

Mishnah, Talmud, and Related Literature

[*y.* and *b.* denote Jerusalem and Babylonian versions of the Talmud, respectively]

Ber.	*Berakhot*
Ketub.	*Ketubbot*
Meg.	*Megillah*
Meʿil.	*Meʿilah*
Parah	*Parah*
Pesiq. Rab Kah.	*Pesiqta of Rab Kahana*
Rab.	*Rabbah*
Sanh.	*Sanhedrin*
Sukkah	*Sukkah*
Zabim	*Zabim*

Targumic Texts

Tg. Esth. I, II	*First or Second Targum of Esther*
Tg. Onq.	*Targum Onqelos*
Tg. Ps.-J.	*Targum Pseudo-Jonathan*

Other Rabbinic Works

Mek.	*Mekilta*
Midr.	*Midrash*
Pirqe R. El.	*Pirqe Rabbi Eliezer*

Dead Sea Scrolls

1QapGen/1Q20	*Genesis Apocryphon*
1QH[a]	*Hodayot*[a] or *Thanksgiving Hymns*
1QM	*Milhamah* or *War Scroll*
1QpHab	*Pesher Habakkuk*
1QS	*Rule of the Community*
1QSa/1Q28a	*Rule of the Congregation* (Appendix a to 1QS)

Abbreviations

4Q196–199	Tobit (Aramaic)
4Q256	4QS^b (4Q frgs. of *Rule of the Community*)
4Q285	*Serekh ha-Milhamah*
4Q428	*Thanksgiving Hymns*^b
4Q500	*Benediction*
4QMMT/	*Some Works of the Torah*
4Q394–399	
11QT^a/11Q19	*Temple Scroll*^a
CD	*Damascus Document* (Cairo Genizah)

Greek and Latin Works

Ant.	Josephus, *Antiquities of the Jews*
Apion	Josephus, *Against Apion*
Carm.	Horace, *Carmina*
1 Clem.	*1 Clement*
Comm. Jo.	Origen, *Commentarii in evangelium Joannis*
Cyr.	Xenophon, *Cyropaedia*
Deipn.	Athenaeus, *Deipnosophistae*
Dial.	Justin, *Dialogus cum Tryphone*
Did.	*Didache*
Ench.	Epictetus, *Enchiridion*
Ep.	Seneca, *Epistulae morales*
Epict. diss.	Arrian, *Epicteti dissertationes*
Hist. eccl.	Eusebius, *Historia ecclesiastica*
Ios.	Philo, *De Iosepho*
Leg.	Philo, *Legum allegoriae*
Life	*Life of Josephus*
Nat.	Pliny the Elder, *Naturalis historia*
Plant.	Philo, *De plantatione*
Prob.	Philo, *Quod omnis probus liber sit*
Recogn.	Pseudo-Clement, *Recognitions*
Seneca, *Dial.*	Seneca, *Dialogi*
Tract. Ev. Jo.	Augustine, *In Evangelium Johannis tractatus*
Verg. Aen.	Servius, *Commentary on Vergil's Aeneid*
War	Josephus, *Jewish War*

Contributors

STANLEY E. PORTER is President, Dean, and Professor of New Testament at McMaster Divinity College, McMaster University, Hamilton, Ontario, Canada.

JENS SCHRÖTER is Professor of New Testament in the Faculty of Theology at the University of Leipzig, Germany.

JAMES H. CHARLESWORTH is George L. Collord Professor of New Testament Language and Literature and Director and Editor of the Dead Sea Scrolls Project at Princeton Theological Seminary, Princeton, New Jersey, U.S.A.

CARSTEN CLAUSSEN is Assistant Lecturer in the Department of New Testament Theology at the Ludwig-Maximilians-Universität, Munich, Germany.

GERD THEISSEN is Professor of New Testament Theology in the Faculty of Theology at the Ruprecht-Karls-Universität, Heidelberg, Germany.

MICHAEL WOLTER is University Professor of New Testament in the Faculty of Protestant Theology at the Rheinische Friedrich-Wilhelms-Universität, Bonn, Germany.

KLAUS HAACKER is Professor of New Testament at the School of Theology, Wuppertal, Germany.

RUDOLF HOPPE is Dean of the Faculty of Catholic Theology and Professor of New Testament at the Rheinische Friedrich-Wilhelms-Universität, Bonn, Germany.

Contributors

PETR POKORNÝ is Professor of New Testament Studies in the Protestant Theological Faculty at the Univerzita Karlova, Prague, Czech Republic.

CRAIG EVANS is Payzant Distinguished Professor of New Testament at Acadia Divinity College, Acadia University, Wolfville, Nova Scotia, Canada.

TOM HOLMÉN is Adjunct Professor of New Testament Exegetics in the Faculty of Theology at Åbo Akademi University, Turku, Finland and the University of Helsinki, Finland.

ULRICH LUZ is Professor Emeritus of New Testament in the Faculty of Catholic and Protestant Theology at the Universität Bern, Switzerland.

The Princeton-Prague Symposia:
Origins and Intention

In 1999 the Center for Biblical Studies here in Prague was established. This research institute is sponsored jointly by the Cabinet of Classical Studies at the Academy of Sciences of the Czech Republic and the Protestant Theological Faculty of Charles University. We created an institute for research into the Old Testament, the New Testament, and early Christian literature. We think that our geographical position, our multicultural past, and our traditions of critical exegesis, as well as our ecumenical orientation, enhance the success of the Center.

One of the first activities of the Center was a small Jesus symposium in 1999, which confronted the main theses of "the Third Quest" or Jesus Research and the advances within German critical research. Gradually, we extended our discussion, especially after I spent a period working in the Center of Theological Inquiry in Princeton in 2003-2004. Professor James H. Charlesworth, with his scholarly intuition and openness to reexamining even the pivotal axioms of biblical scholarship, visited our Center in Prague several times. In 2005, together with Charlesworth's Princeton Dead Sea Scrolls Project, we organized a full international symposium in Prague. This symposium was devoted predominantly to the methodology of Jesus Research and to discussions about its theological and hermeneutical dimensions. We realized that it is necessary to make a clear distinction between the history of Jesus and the ways in which his significance is expressed in Christian confessions of faith (including his post-Easter evaluation). At the same time it became obvious that it is not possible to separate these two dimensions from each other. On the one hand, the Christ of Christian confessions of faith inspires our critical research into Jesus. On the other hand, the adoration of Christ is linked with some ideas contained in his earthly teaching (such as apocalyptic messianic expectations) and the earthly Jesus is the point of reference or hermeneutic key for all later Christology. This is the general framework of our discussions. Jesus Research has to be aware of these complex relations. This, incidentally, is why we avoid the non-precise term "historical Jesus" and we speak mostly about Jesus Research.

The researchers that we invited to Prague represent, as you can see, a good cross-section of scholars currently involved in research in this field, and the results included in this volume undoubtedly signify a certain broadening of the area of research. It was a logical consequence of our discussions that we decided to devote the next conference to mapping the various branches of research that can be useful as our allies in Jesus Research, ranging from linguistics to psychology, numismatics, hermeneutics, and archaeology. We decided to meet in 2007 in Princeton. In this way we launched the tradition of the Princeton-Prague Biennales, each one concentrating on a specific dimension or set of problems of our research.

We are aware of the fact that Jesus Research is taking place along various lines. Our project intends at regular intervals to review and evaluate the main results of research, to provide further inspiration in the form of new stimuli, and to support small groups or individuals cooperating with us. Please accept this volume as the starting-point for this scholarly journey.

PETR POKORNÝ
Director of the Center
for Biblical Studies
Prague, 4 December 2007

INTRODUCTION:
Why Evaluate Twenty-Five Years of Jesus Research?

James H. Charlesworth

With the cooperation of leading experts in Jesus Research from numerous areas of our globe and the inestimable help of my long-time colleague Petr Pokorný, Director of the Centre for Biblical Studies in Prague, I was able to help launch the Princeton-Prague Symposium on the Historical Jesus. This volume contains the proceedings of the first symposium, which was held in Prague. The purpose of the first symposium was to evaluate where we are in the study of the historical Jesus and what makes it possible to move forward in a better re-presentation and comprehension of Jesus who descended from Nazareth and into the consciousness of the West.

Why evaluate Jesus Research? It is important to evaluate the present state of research since what had been perceived to be a developing consensus in the 1980s has collapsed into a chaos of opinions. Jesus cannot be a marginal Jew (Meier) and a Cynic (Crossan). Jesus cannot be closely linked with the Essenes (Venturini, Graetz, and Kohler)[1] and a Jew significantly influenced by Pharisaism (Flusser). Jesus cannot be deeply influenced by apocalyptic eschatology (Sanders) and also announce a message that is fundamentally non-eschatological (Borg). Such conclusions are not compatible. How can such divergent views be possible when all scholars employ a disinterested scientific methodology?

Why evaluate and assess Jesus Research over the past 25 years? That point will become clear as we proceed; suffice it now to adumbrate such

---

1. See J. H. Charlesworth, *Jesus and the Dead Sea Scrolls* (New York, London: Doubleday, 1992, 1995), p. 73 n. 333. I am grateful to Professor Walt Weaver for helping me improve this introduction.

reflections by indicating that if academic debates produce more heat than light something needs to be assessed and corrected.

In the following introduction to this collection, I will both highlight the insights presented in the chapters and add to the discussion my own reflections. Five sections highlight the new dimensions of Jesus Research: First, the Quest for the historical Jesus has been enriched, and sometimes replaced by, Jesus Research. Second, the new research is improved by the inclusion of all relevant methodologies. Third, perceptions have been clarified and errors are more obvious, and often corrected. Fourth, Jesus Research is enriched by fresh sources. Fifth, scholars are beginning to recognize the fundamental importance of topography and archaeology.

1. Quests and Jesus Research

Many phases in the appreciation and study of the historical Jesus can be discerned. For almost 1800 years the Gospels were deemed biographical representations of Jesus of Nazareth; it was assumed that they were composed by apostles or eyewitnesses of Jesus' life and teaching. Beginning with the European Enlightenment, critics eventually demonstrated that the Gospels were compositions by the second generation of Jesus' followers. The apostle Matthew and the apostle John did not compose respectively the First and Fourth Gospels. If Mark was the scribe of Peter, then he had not known the Jesus of history. If Luke had been the companion of Paul, he needed eyewitnesses, as he admits in the opening verses of the Third Gospel.

Old Quest (Reimarus in 1774 to Schweitzer in 1906)

Most likely the first attempt to compose a life of Jesus was Reimarus (1694-1768), but only portions of his work were published posthumously by G. H. Lessing in 1774 and 1778. Reimarus stressed an absolute distinction between Jesus' teaching and that of the apostles. Jesus' message was the eschatological and apocalyptic future coming of the Kingdom of Heaven which "must" be understood in light of Jesus' thought. Jesus was not a founder of a new religion. In 1835, David F. Strauss published a life of Jesus that cast a shadow on the nineteenth century. Subsequently, many attempted to write a biography of Jesus. In 1906, Albert Schweitzer (1875-1965) proved that these various attempts were conditioned by the presuppositions and wishes of the authors. As George Tyrrell (1861-1909) imagined, these allegedly scientific experts on antiquity were looking for Jesus' face, but what they saw was usually their own face refracted in the bottom of a deep well.

The So-called Moratorium (1906 to c. 1953)

Too many New Testament scholars speak about a moratorium on the study of the historical Jesus from 1906 until 1953. Such a moratorium never existed, as Walter P. Weaver shows in his magisterial *The Historical Jesus in the Twentieth Century, 1900-1950*.[2] From 1906 until 1953 some books on the historical Jesus appeared, especially in Great Britain. This period was preoccupied with a theological return to the more normative portrayal of Jesus (Dialectical Theology). In many Christian academic circles a pronounced focus on the Christ of faith (such as in Tillich and Barth) obliterated an interest in the historical Jesus. Most New Testament experts, especially those influenced by Bultmann, were more interested in separating Jesus from the Christ and concentrating on the reigning Lord of the Easter Faith.

New Quest (c. 1953 to c. 1980)

Beginning in 1953, perhaps, a New Quest of Jesus appeared. According to many critics, the New Quest was too closely aligned with Existentialism which tended to minimize historiography and archaeology, focusing on Jesus' message and its salvific promise. That is, the New Quest was deeply influenced by the philosophy of Martin Heidegger who in his later work emphasized the significance of language in the disclosure of Being-Itself. This focus on Being and language was transferred by Christian theologians to Jesus as the Word-Event. The result was a mimimizing of purely historical research and archaeology. The most influential and attractive publication

2. W. P. Weaver, *The Historical Jesus in the Twentieth Century, 1900-1950* (Harrisburg, Pa.: Trinity, 1999), p. 367.

seems to have been Bornkamm's *Jesus of Nazareth* (1959 [German], 1960, 1975, 1995).

Jesus Research (c. 1985 to the Present)

In 1985 something new began to appear. The renewed study of the historical Jesus indicates something different than the previous "quests." I have labeled it "Jesus Research." Now Jews, like David Flusser and Geza Vermes, become intimately involved in trying to examine the life and mind of Jesus, using the best historical methods; and they are certainly not interested in finding a Savior who would be worthy to follow. Ed Sanders joined the research, and his monumental studies should not be categorized as a theological "search" for the historical Jesus. Sanders rightly shifts the focus from Jesus' words to Jesus' actions and words. These experts who are intent on grounding a study of a man of history in scientific historiography and primary sources are now joined by some modern experts who are not disinterested historians but are searching for a Galilean who could be admired and followed.

The Princeton-Prague Symposia were founded to gather distinguished scholars who could collegially help find a core or consensus in the best research focused on Jesus. The unstated but guiding question may be: Is there a hidden consensus in Jesus Research? Related questions follow: Is it true that oral tradition is unreliable and that none of the Evangelists had access to reliable eyewitness accounts? The latter questions become more noticeable in the second symposium, and can be foreshadowed only now.

As we assess the new developments, we may borrow Walter P. Weaver's judgment of the appearance of the New Quest against the tide of Barthianism: "newer forces were making their way more widely into the western world and still crossing swords with the old guard."[3]

2. Improved and Increased Methodologies

In the present collection, Stanley Porter attempts to improve the methods employed in Jesus Research. He focuses on the methods for discerning au-

---

3. Weaver, *The Historical Jesus*, p. 367.

thentic Jesus tradition among all the traditions attributed to Jesus. Porter rightly points out that the criteria for authenticity have been a topic of renewed discussion. He emphasizes that Schweitzer's influence on the development and utilization of criteria for authenticity has not been adequately appreciated. He corrects that oversight by offering a useful evaluation of the nature and purpose of these criteria in relation to Schweitzer's work.

The best experts now devoted to Jesus Reseach utilize the insights and observations developed within sociology and anthropology. In the present collection, Gerd Theissen indicates the importance of sociology for comprehending the Palestinian Jesus Movement. It describes the complex social environment in which Jesus lived. Sociologists offer an indirect understanding of Jesus' identity by considering how his contemporaries perceived him. Everyone is faced with the expectations attached to certain roles. Given such expectations, Theissen focuses on Jesus' role as an itinerant teacher and prophet. What expectations were associated with these titles, as understood in pre-70 Palestinian society? How was Jesus similar to and different from other itinerant teachers? Jesus had to deal with more than the expectations accompanying the roles of teacher, prophet, and miracle worker. Some Jews expected still more from him; they expected him to be the Messiah. No one should now doubt that during his lifetime some Jews imagined that Jesus was the long-awaited Messiah.

Continuing the need to improve methodologies, Michael Wolter makes use of categories for the analysis of a narrative text that have been proposed by Claude Bremond. While Wilhelm Egger insightfully employed Bremond's model in interpreting the synoptic narrative tradition, Wolter shows how this method is much more helpful for the interpretation of Jesus' parables.

Ulrich Luz indicates the importance of comparing early "Christianity" with other nascent religions. Luz explores the possible ways different historical, social, and cultural situations impact the birth of religions. He ponders what features are generally present as *a new religion* appears and develops. For Christians who tend to view Christianity as something unique, such comparison offers important correctives. Comparing Jesus with founding figures in the new religions in Japan helps clarify Jesus' commonality with other leading figures and helps us better perceive what may be meant by thinking of Jesus as unique and a founder of a new religion.

Craig Evans demonstrates how the scholars of the Jesus Seminar tend to disregard the presence of Old Testament Scripture in the dominical tradition, assuming that its presence is due to apologetic interests of the early community. While the Palestinian Jesus Movement embellished the scriptural witness, especially as seen in their attempts to prove that Jesus is the long-awaited Messiah (i.e., proof-texting), Evans demonstrates that Jesus himself was devoted to biblical interpretation. The very essence of Jesus' proclamation sprang from the good news that God's reign had begun. This reign was promised by the eighth-century prophet Isaiah. Evans also points out how scholars have rightly compared Jesus' method of biblical interpretation to scriptural interpretation in Rabbinics.

Evans explores one stunning aspect of Jesus' creative use of Scripture. Jesus appears deliberately to present a subversive interpretation of Scripture. Such interpretation may be seen in Jesus' remarkable subversions of passages and themes from Daniel and Zechariah, as well as in cases involving legal materials. This subversive interpretation of Scripture was not a tendency among Jesus' followers. Their proof-texting emphasized correspondence and agreement, not dissonance. Thus, subversive interpretation of Scripture may be an aspect of authentic Jesus tradition and represent his own mission.

What distinguishes the novice from the scholar is methodology. All the scholars in this volume help us see ways to improve and increase the methodologies for discerning and re-presenting the historical Jesus.

3. Refined Perspectives

Petr Pokorný helps us refine our perspectives. He rightly argues that the ecclesiastical image of John the Baptist may include some historical truth, even though the whole is a post-Easter construct, illustrating not only the power of Easter experience but also the role of the Baptist in "Christian" tradition and piety. Pokorný is not so much interested in the Baptist as in his relation to Jesus. Pokorný asks us to ponder two main questions: Why did Jesus cause a division among John the Baptist's students? Did Jesus cause this division, or was there something about Jesus that caused others to leave the Baptist? These questions lead to a far-reaching question: What is the difference in the teaching of the Baptist and of Jesus?

Tom Holmén focuses on the situations in which Jesus is expressly said to have cleansed people from impurity. There are reasons to trust the basic historicity of Jesus' behavior and thought regarding ritural purity. In Matt

11:5, Jesus refers to his own work by mentioning, *inter alia,* the cleansing of lepers. Actual instances of such cleansing are mentioned in Mark 1:40-45 and Luke 17:11-19. These three traditions in Matthew, Mark, and Luke thus indicate that Jesus saw his activity as resulting in the purification of uncleanness. The criterion of multiple attestation indicates the authenticity of this common idea.

Klaus Haacker argues that all the verbs used in connection with "kingdom" or with "life" can be traced back to one and the same root, and thus to one specific tradition. They all occur repeatedly in Israel's history with God. They appear in the story of God's promise and gift of the land of Canaan to Abraham, Isaac, Jacob, and their descendants. Along with the work of Evans, Haacker thus provides a new focus on the Jewishness of Jesus, emphasizing the connection between Jesus' message and Israel's Scriptures.

Rudolf Hoppe asks us to contemplate how Jesus himself "understood" his death. What attitude did Jesus take to a perceived failure of his message? In expecting his violent death, did Jesus reassess the viability of the message he had formulated during his public ministry? That means what is important is not how Jesus understood *himself,* but what image, persona, or message he presented *to the outside world.*

Hoppe concentrates on one aspect of this problem, without any pretensions to completeness. A probable consensus may be reached that the eschatological prospect in Mark 14:25 ("I tell you the truth, I will not drink again of the fruit of the vine until that day when I drink it anew in the kingdom of God") was decisive for Jesus' expectation of, and interpretation of, his death with a view to the coming Rule of God. Mark 14:25, together with the fundamental statement in Mark 1:15, most likely forms a framework for the proclamation of Jesus' message.

The proclamation in Mark 1:15 is echoed in the parables in Mark 4:3-9, 4:26-29, and 4:30-32. In the Second Gospel, these parables connect proclamation and eschatological prospect. With the transmission of the parables, therefore, it is possible to relate Jesus' message about the dawning Rule of God, on the one hand, and Jesus' attitude about his impending death, on the other hand.

Gerd Theissen interprets the ethical radicalism of Jesus as an "itinerant radicalism." The historical Jesus seems to have had no fixed home, was distant from his family, renounced property, and offers little defense for his actions. All these elements are more easily upheld by people with nonconforming lifestyles than by those who are integrated into a settled way of life.

Theissen argues that these refined perspectives do not imply that Jesus was a "marginal Jew." His message about the Rule of God fits within the heart of Second Temple Judaism. Jesus espoused a radical monotheism that was central in Second Temple Judaism. Jesus held convictions that were central to Judaism.

4. Fresh Sources

In 1957, J. Daniélou rightly pointed out that manuscript discoveries from Jesus' time and nation help resolve numerous problems that biblical exegesis alone could not solve.[4] The importance of such early Jewish writings for Jesus Research is reflected in many of the following chapters. Indeed, one of the most important dimensions of Jesus Research is the use of fresh sources for imagining or describing Jesus' life and message within pre-70 Palestinian society.

Tom Holmén, for example, indicates how to use such fresh sources. He turns our attention to 2 Sam 5:8b: "The blind and the lame shall not come into the house" (NRSV). Jewish authorities judged that the blind and the lame should not enter the Temple because they would directly or indirectly profane the Temple. Holmén rightly includes a fresh source: the *Temple Scroll*. This scroll (11QT[a] 45.12-14) elaborates on 2 Sam 5:8. According to this scroll, the blind are to be excluded so that they "shall not defile the city in the center of which I dwell." In other words, the blind are regarded as defilers. Further, the *Rule of the Congregation* (1QSa 2.9b-10) establishes that people with physical blemishes, especially the lame and the blind, should be regarded as contaminated.

I can imagine one more reason for excluding the impaired, this time the blind and the deaf, from the Temple. Jewish leaders probably excluded the blind and the deaf from the Temple because they would each inadvertently break a law or commandment and defile the Temple. The blind could not read Torah and thus perhaps might not fully understand it. The deaf could not hear Torah read aloud in synagogues and in the Temple;

---

4. Jean Daniélou, *Les manuscrits de la Mer Morte et les origines du Christianisme* (Paris: Editions du Seuil, 1957); see esp. p. 123.

thus, they might not know the rulings in the Torah and the interpretations of it. The source of these decisions are my reflections on both well-known texts (Deut 23:2-5 and *Kiddushin 4*) as well as fresh data, especially *Some Works of the Torah* lines 39-42 and *Florilegium* 4Q174 Frgs. 1-2 and 21 1.3-4. But, I readily admit that the evidence is not clear and obvious. Again, historical reconstruction is impossible without imagination.

For those who shared the view represented by these diverse texts, Jesus' cures of disabilities would have carried important purity connotations. The restoration of sight, movement, and hearing would have included a visible restoration of purity.

Jesus' healings thus not only restore health, they also restore purity. This dual restoration is expressly suggested by the cleansing of the lepers; it is also clear in the exorcisms of the unclean spirits.

Alterations of old traditions and the appearances of new viewpoints made Early Judaism creatively alive. In particular, purity issues aroused varying interpretations. Debates concerning purity contributed to Jewish sectarianism. Even within this diversity, Jesus' view of purity implied by his healing of the unclean must be characterized as exceptional and radical.

Thus, it becomes clear that fresh sources, especially the Dead Sea Scrolls, have helped to transform our understanding of purity issues and related sectarianism in Early Judaism. More will be reported in the final section devoted to topography and archaeology.

The use of fresh sources for comprehending the historical Jesus is also evident in Evans's work. He draws attention to the *Thanksgiving Hymns* which were composed at Qumran and defined that Community. Several times an author says: "I give thanks to you, O Lord," for wisdom, understanding, insight, and truth (cf. 1QH^a 4:21; 6:19, 38; 15:29 [= 4Q428 frg. 9 line 1]). As will Jesus a few generations later, an author of passages in the *Thanksgiving Hymn* extols God for revealing God's truth. Unlike Jesus, however, the author of the *Thanksgiving Hymns* thanks God for revealing his truth to those well versed in Scripture.

These fresh sources help us situate Jesus among his contemporaries. They also help us hear his message as many early Jews might have heard it. Such reflections help us better comprehend how Jesus' mind is similar to others within Early Judaism, and also how his thoughts were probably radically different from fellow Jewish teachers.

5. The Inclusion of Topography and Archaeology

Jesus Research is enriched by reflections on how Jesus' message and life were shaped by topography and archaeology.[5] Jens Schröter's chapter deals with the topography and archaeology of Galilee. Most importantly, he adds his voice to the chorus of those who have shown that Galilee developed differently from Samaria. In 1983, during the archaeological explorations in Galilee, Zvi Gal found no signs of Assyrian settlement in the seventh and sixth centuries BCE.[6] Quite surprisingly, these sites cumulatively exhibit a 200-year gap in occupation after the eighth century BCE. In light of some Old Testament historians, one would have expected Galilee to have been settled by the Assyrians, but unlike Samaria and the coastal region, virtually no Assyrian pottery or imitations of it were found in Galilee.

Archaeological discoveries seem to indicate that unlike Samaria, where a foreign population was settled following the deportation, Galilee was largely uninhabited until Persian times. This means that Albrecht Alt's hypothesis of a continuous population in Galilee from the ancient Israelite period through the Maccabean era into Roman times should be abandoned.

Scholars should comprehend that a partial resettlement of Galilee took place during Persian and Hellenistic times. Even then, however, we should not postulate a mixed population of Jews and Gentiles in Lower Galilee. The new city-states founded by the Ptolemies and the Seleucids were not established inside Jewish territory. These cities were located only on the coast or in areas that were not part of the Jewish heartland.

The crucial turning-point in the history of Galilee occurred in the Hasmonean period.[7] As part of the continuous conquest of Palestine and contiguous regions by the Maccabees, the first Hasmonean king Aristobulus succeeded around 103 BCE in reshaping Galilee in line with Judean Judaism. The result included a change in the structure of the population. The archaeological evidence unearthed during the Meiron Excavation Project

5. For further reflections, see my "The Jesus of History and the Topography of the Holy Land," *Handbook on the Historical Jesus,* in press. Also, see my "Jesus Research and Archaeology: A New Perspective," in *Jesus and Archaeology* (Grand Rapids: Eerdmans, 2006), pp. 11-63.

6. I did not know this discovery when I published *Jesus within Judaism: New Light from Exciting Archaeological Discoveries* (ABRL 1; New York, London: Doubleday, 1988).

7. For further discussion, see Charlesworth and M. Aviam, "Reflections on Reconstructing First Century Galilee," in a German book edited by C. Claussen, in press.

in 1976 shows that Gentile settlements were abandoned. Why? Perhaps, the Gentiles fled to avoid forced circumcision.

Archaeologists found evidence not only of abandonment by Gentiles, but also of an increase in Jewish inhabitants. Consequently, the Galilean population did not consist, as has sometimes been supposed, of Gentiles forcibly circumcised during the Maccabean conquest and thus integrated into a putative Jewish population.

We should now imagine Jews migrating from Judea to Lower Galilee, since pots and coins and other *realia* found in Lower Galilee prove a close connection between Judea and Galilee. Thus, we should abandon Renan's assumptions that Galilee greatly contrasted with Judea, since it had a mixed population of Jews and Gentiles.

Those working in Jesus Research should imagine the culture of Galilee differently than it was understood in previous periods of the study of the historical Jesus. Jesus grew up and worked in Lower Galilee. Its culture was shaped by Judean norms that began to appear sometime after 103 BCE. His "hometown," Capernaum, for example, appeared in the first century BCE.

The new insight regarding the topography and culture of Lower Galilee in Jesus' time is summarized in a book that appeared when this introduction was nearly completed. Note Jonathan Reed's conclusion: "Galilee changed when Herod Antipas took over after his father's death in 4 BCE. It had been a marginal part of Herod's kingdom, inhabited by Jews who themselves or their parents or grandparents had come from Judea."[8] Thus, exegesis is deepened as we contemplate that the scribes and Pharisees who questioned Jesus were sent out from Judea and Jerusalem (cf. Mark 3:22; cf. John 8:3), and that Jesus, as a Galilean Jew, wished to worship in Jerusalem especially during the required pilgrimages to the Holy City.

As one might expect from the previous publications by Gerd Theissen, his portrayal of Jesus includes topography. The Evangelists depict Jesus located in places near the Sea of Galilee. The center of his activity is Capernaum, where a "house" is mentioned (Matt 9:10; 17:25). The following questions thus appear: Was Jesus' home based in Capernaum to which he could return in the evening from many different places in Galilee? Was Jesus a teacher with a small area in which to range or a large area to cover?

An argument against the restriction to a small area is provided by Je-

8. J. L. Reed, *The HarperCollins Visual Guide to the New Testament* (New York: Harper-Collins, 2007), p. 66.

sus' wanderings in the rural areas surrounding the neighboring towns. Jesus is reputed to have travelled northwest to the areas of Tyre and Sidon (Mark 7:24, 31), north to the villages of Caesarea Philippi (Mark 8:27), and southeast in the Decapolis (Mark 5:1, 20; 7:31). Since Jews lived in the territories of these Hellenistic cities, the wanderings are historically credible. These reports meet with only an indirect echo in the Sayings Source: a saying of Jesus cites the people of Tyre and Sidon as potential examples (QLk 10:14). If these wanderings have a core of historical truth, then Jesus cannot normally have returned to Capernaum each evening.

The Synoptic Gospels' depiction of Jesus as an itinerant teacher is surely correct. It is easier to explain the phenomenon of itinerant charismatic figures in early "Christianity" as a consequence of the model of Jesus than it is to see the image of Jesus as itinerant teacher as being a projection backward of this post-Easter itinerant charismatic phenomenon.

Carsten Claussen correctly shows how archaeological findings support the Fourth Evangelist's knowledge of Palestine and Jerusalem.[9] Alone among the Evangelists, the Fourth Evangelist knows about the Pools of Siloam (John 9) and Bethesda (or Bethzatha; John 5:2-9), stone vessels (cf. John 2:6), and the outdoor paving stones which may have been part of the Roman Praetorium in Jerusalem (John 19:13).[10] The Fourth Evangelist intimately knows the topography and architecture of Jerusalem;[11] perhaps the first edition of the Fourth Gospel took place within Jerusalem.[12]

The Fourth Evangelist's itinerary and chronology of Jesus' ministry and death are taken by some interpreters now to be more reliable than those of the Synoptics. The Fourth Evangelist's report of the debates and trials during Jesus' passion provides a better representation of what happened than do the Synoptics. Thus, the Fourth Evangelist intermittently provides reliable historical information regarding the historical Jesus.

Claussen also clarifies how the archaeological excavations at Khirbet

---

9. Also see the contributions in Charlesworth, ed., *Jesus and Archaeology.*

10. I disagree with Claussen that these massive stones were near the Antonia Fortress; they better fit Herod's Palace in the Upper City.

11. See esp. L. Ritmeyer, *The Quest: Revealing the Temple Mount in Jerusalem* (Jerusalem: Carta, 2006).

12. I argue in favor of this hypothesis in "The Priority of John? Reflections on the Essenes and the First Edition of John," in *Für und wider die Priorität des Johannesevangeliums: Symposium in Salzburg am 10. März 2000,* ed. P. L. Hofrichter (Theologische Texte und Studien 9; Hildesheim, Zürich, New York: Georg Olms Verlag, 2002), pp. 73-114.

Qana have enlarged our knowledge of Galilee as Jesus' geographical setting, a prominent feature of recent Jesus Research.[13] The presence of observant Jews representing a range of status levels concurs with the use of
large and expensive stone vessels for ritual purity (John 2:6). When the
wedding wine was depleted, Jesus orders six *stone jars* to be filled with water. The Fourth Evangelist states, correctly, that such vessels were required
by Jewish purity regulations. Since stones did not transmit uncleanness,
they protected religious Jews from contamination.

Archaeologists have found stone jars at many Jewish sites in Judea,
Lower Galilee, and the Golan. They appear during the reign of Herod the
Great and quickly disappear after 70 CE. While they are present in Palestine, they are virtually absent in the Diaspora. Recently, a few small vessels
have also been found at Khirbet Qana. The jars mentioned in John 2:6-7
can be identified with large vessels, which were turned on a lathe. They
could contain about 100 liters each. Due to the expensive production technique, they were luxury items. The informed reader is impressed by a luxurious wedding feast, crowned by an incredible 600 liters of wine, of excellent quality, in rather expensive stone vessels.

It seems wise to conclude this introduction by citing Petr Pokorný.
While Jesus Research is a scientific study of Jesus from Nazareth, it is also
imperative for the thoughtful Christian. He rightly perceives that since the
oldest texts from the Palestinian Jesus Movement

> (a) proclaim him [Jesus] to be a representative of God himself and
> (b) still identify him with Jesus of Nazareth, we have to gather as much
> historical evidence about his life and teaching as possible. Even in New
> Testament times, Christians realized that the statements of their faith
> and their proclamation could and should be tested as to whether they
> are in accordance with the earthly Jesus, or at least that they do not op-
> pose him: "This is how you can recognize the Spirit of God; every spirit
> which confesses that Jesus Christ has come in the flesh is from God."
> (1 John 4:2; cf. 2 John 7).[14]

---

13. See esp. P. Richardson, "Khirbet Qana (and Other Villages) as a Context for Jesus,"
in *Jesus and Archaeology*, pp. 120-44.

14. P. Pokorný, *Jesus in the Eyes of His Followers* (Dead Sea Scrolls and Christian Origins
Library 4; North Richland Hills, Tex.: BIBAL Press, 1998), pp. 21-22.

James H. Charlesworth

Conclusion

Retrospect

The scholars in this collection know that historians can only approximate probabilities. Historical research does not lead to certainties; it provides probabilities that depend on the changing source material and are thus constantly open to modification. Yet, the scholars involved in the Princeton-Prague Symposia tend to concur that a sketch of Jesus is beginning to appear that is both increasingly reliable, historically, and helpful, theologically.

Historical portrayals of Jesus are also partially hypothetical. We need to be aware that perceptions of Jesus within Early Judaism, like portrayals of all past individuals, are conditioned by present needs and perspectives. The historians in this volume do not imagine that they can find the "real" Jesus behind the perceptions and theologies of the Evangelists.

Jesus Research helps clarify which interpretations of Jesus can be reconciled with the primary source material and which ones cannot. Imagination and reflections on topography, archaeological discoveries and *realia* help produce a more reliable depiction of Jesus. In the process, the contributors would agree that a historian should consult all relevant data and employ all pertinent methods. Moreover, all attempts can be improved, especially through dialogues among world-renowned experts in Jesus Research and in New Testament exegesis and hermeneutics.

Those who composed the following chapters contribute to a challenging international dialogue. All of them concur, with differing degrees of emphasis, that Jesus' message should be studied within the creative and sometimes diverse world of Second Temple Judaism, that the Evangelists did use sources and altered them in light of their own theology, that attempts to portray the historical Jesus were often distorted by Confessionalism and Anti-Semitism, and — most importantly — that *it is possible to pursue Jesus Research*. The life and mind of Jesus from Nazareth is no longer lost in the fog of theological pronouncements.

Prospect

In the second Princeton Prague Symposium, Jesus Research will be grounded with additional insights. Geza Vermes will reflect on methodologies in Jesus Research. Lee McDonald will examine Jesus Research in light of canonical criticism. Kathy Ehrensperger will explore how Paul is important for understanding the historical Jesus. Gerd Theissen will continue his forays into sociological methodologies and Jesus Research. Richard Bauckham will argue that we should recognize eyewitness testimonies in the Gospels. Werner Kelber will clarify the importance of orality in the transmission of authentic Jesus traditions. Gerbern S. Oegema will increase our understandings of Jesus' use and interpretation of Scripture. Jan Roskovec will investigate the historicity of Jesus' miracles. Peter Flint will illustrate how and why the Dead Sea Scrolls are fundamentally important in Jesus Research. Petr Pokorný will discuss possible historical reconstructions of Jesus' crucifixion. Henry Rietz will discuss the importance of time in Judaism and Jesus' teachings. Dale Allison will focus on ways to improve our understanding Jesus' eschatology. Robert Webb will explain how John the Baptist may have influenced Jesus. David Hendin will illustrate how numismatics is important in recovering aspects of Jesus' life and thought. Many other experts will also contribute to a significant international dialogue among those focused on Jesus Research.

A Dead End or a New Beginning?
Examining the Criteria for Authenticity
in Light of Albert Schweitzer

Stanley E. Porter

Introduction

The criteria for authenticity have been a topic of renewed discussion for the last twenty years or so, especially in English-speaking circles.[1] Elsewhere, I have chronicled the major criteria that have been used within the last century, and I have made an attempt to examine them in the light of the development of form and redaction criticisms.[2] There is much more that could be done in these areas, including examining in more detail the presuppositions, contributions and limitations of each of these criteria. What I wish to do here, however, is to revisit the issue of the criteria in terms of their place within the development of historical Jesus research, especially as it has a relationship to the fundamental work of Albert Schweitzer. Schweitzer's influence upon studies of the historical Jesus has long been recognized — although his relationship to the development and utilization of criteria for authenticity has perhaps not been readily acknowledged or fully appreciated.[3] I wish to

---

1. This study builds upon material found in S. E. Porter, *The Criteria for Authenticity in Historical-Jesus Research: Previous Discussion and New Proposals* (JSNTSup 191; Sheffield: Sheffield Academic Press, 2000) and updated in places in S. E. Porter, "Reading the Gospels and the Quest for the Historical Jesus," in S. E. Porter, ed., *Reading the Gospels Today* (McMaster New Testament Studies; Grand Rapids: Eerdmans, 2004), pp. 27-55; and especially S. E. Porter, "Luke 17.11-19 and the Criteria for Authenticity Revisited," *JSHJ* 1 (2003): 201-24. I will not cite the evidence given in these sources unless context demands, but will occasionally add other sources.

2. Porter, *Criteria for Authenticity*, pp. 63-123.

3. Schweitzer published his *Von Reimarus zu Wrede: Eine Geschichte der Leben-Jesu-*

correct that oversight in this paper. In the first section, I will briefly introduce my perspective on the quest for the historical Jesus in relation to Albert Schweitzer; I will then examine certain criteria for authenticity in relation to Schweitzer's programmatic statements regarding researching the historical Jesus. On this basis, I will offer a useful evaluation of the nature and purpose of the criteria in relation to Schweitzer's work.

Albert Schweitzer and the Quest for the Historical Jesus

The typical scenario of the development of historical Jesus research is as follows: After writers presented innumerable post-Enlightenment depictions of Jesus in the eighteenth and nineteenth centuries, in 1906 Schweitzer, along with a few others such as Kähler and Bultmann,[4] brought this old or first quest to a halt. These scholars brought the widespread recognition that it was in fact impossible to write a life of Jesus; the evidence was too sparse, and traditional Christian dogma impeded the kind of objective depiction that was sought. As a result, so the story continues, for a period of over forty years the quest for the historical Jesus was supposedly held in abeyance. Then one of Bultmann's pupils, Ernst Käsemann, ventured in a 1953 lecture to suggest that in fact more could be known about Jesus than had heretofore been realized.[5] The new or second quest was thus born. This re-awakening finally blossomed in the 1980s into what has come to be called the third

---

Forschung (Tübingen: Mohr Siebeck, 1906), which appeared in a second edition simply as *Geschichte der Leben-Jesu-Forschung* (Tübingen: Mohr Siebeck, 1913 [2nd ed.], 1951 [6th ed.]), and in English translation of the first edition as *The Quest of the Historical Jesus: A Critical Study of Its Progress from Reimarus to Wrede* (trans. W. Montgomery; London: A. & C. Black, 1910). A new English edition has recently appeared (London: SCM Press, 2000; Minneapolis: Fortress, 2001), but I use the earlier English translation and the 1913 German edition (repr. as the 6th edition with a new preface) as the ones that have figured most significantly in historical Jesus research to this point (see below).

4. M. Kähler, *Der sogenannte historische Jesus und der geschichtliche, biblische Christus* (Leipzig: Deichert, 1892); ET: *The So-Called Historical Jesus and the Historic, Biblical Christ* (trans. C. E. Braaten; Philadelphia: Fortress, 1964). On Bultmann, see below.

5. E. Käsemann, "Das Problem des historischen Jesus," *ZTK* 51 (1954): 125-53; ET: "The Problem of the Historical Jesus," in his *Essays on New Testament Themes* (trans. W. J. Montague; London: SCM Press, 1964), pp. 15-47. The story is filled with high intrigue because Käsemann, a pupil of Bultmann, delivered this lecture to a gathering of those who had studied with Bultmann at Marburg.

quest for the historical Jesus, distinguished by the further recognition that we now know more about the time when Jesus lived, especially his Jewish background, than we had thought, and that we can come to some firm understandings of a number of key events in Jesus' life around which we can construct with levels of certainty other key events and understandings.[6] The significant problem with such a scenario, especially in its sometimes more rigidly presented form, is that it is a fabrication of later scholarship with little connection to the actual development of research into the historical Jesus.[7]

This intriguing yet fictitious narrative does not account for a variety of factors. These factors include: (1) questing after Jesus began soon after his death, as the early Church disputes clearly reflect; (2) a number of original or first questers (many not German) were able to use critical methods and not separate the Jesus of history from the Christ of faith as has often been contended; (3) the writing of lives of Jesus did not halt with the supposed clarion call of Schweitzer, since others had anticipated his critique and even figured into his analysis (e.g., Weiss and Wrede);[8] (4) developments in form and redaction criticisms promoted the development of criteria for determining authenticity which cut across such temporal categories; (5) in the eyes of many Jesus scholars, the third quest has not sufficiently distinguished itself, in terms of its emphasis upon either the Jewish background

6. See Porter, *Criteria for Authenticity*, pp. 28-59. See also D. S. Du Toit, "Redefining Jesus: Current Trends in Jesus Research," in M. Labahn and A. Schmidt, eds., *Jesus, Mark and Q: The Teaching of Jesus and Its Earliest Records* (JSNTSup 214; Sheffield: Sheffield Academic Press, 2001), pp. 82-124, esp. pp. 98-99 n. 74; D. Hagner, "An Analysis of Recent 'Historical Jesus' Studies," in D. Cohn-Sherbok and J. M. Court, eds., *Religious Diversity in the Graeco-Roman World: A Survey of Recent Scholarship* (Sheffield: Sheffield Academic Press, 2001), pp. 81-106, esp. pp. 82-95 (but who on p. 85 considers the "no-quest" period a "misnomer"); and with some modifications to the basic framework, J. D. G. Dunn, *Jesus Remembered* (CM 1; Grand Rapids: Eerdmans, 2003), pp. 17-97.

7. Porter, *Criteria for Authenticity*, esp. p. 56.

8. It must also be remembered that Schweitzer's *Quest of the Historical Jesus* addressed about 250 scholars who were virtually all German, one of the exceptions being Ernst Renan. (The second edition included a few more non-Germans, such as John M. Robertson, William B. Smith and Thomas Whittaker, in *Geschichte*, ch. 22, pp. 444-97.) See S. Neill and T. Wright, *The Interpretation of the New Testament 1861-1986* (Oxford: Oxford University Press, 1988), p. 206; S. J. Gathercole, "The Critical and Dogmatic Agenda of Albert Schweitzer's *The Quest of the Historical Jesus*," *TynBul* 51 (2000): 261-83, esp. p. 264 and n. 11. In fact, Schweitzer analyzes himself along with Wrede (*Quest of the Historical Jesus*, pp. 328-95).

of Jesus or other factors, to merit distinction as a new quest; and (6) other scholars have begun to recognize the continuity of the quest, from its earliest days (whether one looks to the early Church, the Renaissance or the eighteenth century) to the present, even during the twentieth century. The standard narrative does not even adequately explain German biblical scholarship of the time, since numerous Germans continued to write lives of Jesus in the first half of the twentieth century.[9] In fact, what such a scenario might explain is merely the attitude (but not even the practice) of a few form-critical German scholars for a few years. The facts of the case are that lives of Jesus continued to be written, not only in the USA, Great Britain, France, Scandinavia and elsewhere, but even in Germany.[10] Rather than discontinuity in historical Jesus studies, as the scenario promotes, there is greater continuity on a number of fronts. These include the continued investigation of the life of Jesus by both historical skeptics and historical advocates, the development of form criticism as a major tool in historical Jesus research, the development of various criteria for determining the plausibility of the occurrence of events in Jesus' life, and the gaining of increased knowledge of the socio-cultural and religious background of first-century Palestine and its environs,[11] among others.

Schweitzer has also been misrepresented in this caricature of the development of the quest for the historical Jesus. As noted above, Schweitzer is often depicted as having, with one singular devastating critique, reined in the previous work of the first or old quest and called the entire enterprise to a halt. Perhaps a better way to read the evidence is to recognize that Schweitzer, though highly critical of what had gone on before, had no intention of calling the quest to a halt per se, not least because he himself

---

9. See W. P. Weaver, *The Historical Jesus in the Twentieth Century, 1900-1950* (Harrisburg, Pa.: Trinity, 1999), who chronicles such work in detail. Weaver's work arrived too late for my consideration in *Criteria for Authenticity* (p. 36 n. 22), but he substantiates in even greater detail what I was arguing there.

10. See Porter, "Reading the Gospels," pp. 32-37; "Luke 17.11-19," pp. 204-9. Cf. G. Theissen and D. Winter, *The Quest for the Plausible Jesus: The Question of Criteria* (trans. M. E. Boring; Louisville: Westminster John Knox, 2002), p. 2.

11. The discovery and publication of the Dead Sea Scrolls have no doubt helped in this area, but earlier interpreters' ignorance of the Scrolls does not mean they were unconcerned with religious, and especially Jewish, practice and belief. To the contrary, a number of interpreters were very interested in such topics. The so-called third quest has also been very much interested in relating Jesus to popular Mediterranean philosophy, such as Cynicism, as evidenced by the work of the Jesus Seminar — again work anticipated by other, earlier scholars.

had been involved in the earlier quest for the historical Jesus. His first published book had put forth his thoroughgoing eschatological view of Jesus, but it was widely ignored. Schweitzer then further elucidated and developed this position in his *Quest*, which itself "made little impact" in Germany or elsewhere. Only *Quest*'s English translation (and then German second edition) garnered more attention, and that attention was more focused upon Schweitzer's critique of previous work rather than upon his positive proposal regarding Jesus.[12] Schweitzer depicted an eschatological Jesus who died as a failed man who had tried to move the hand of God.[13]

There is clearly a second reason indicating Schweitzer was not attempting to call discussion of Jesus to a halt. Reading the introduction to his *Quest*, one realizes that he was struggling to set an agenda for future life of Jesus research.[14] One comes away with a very different impression,

12. This response is described in the introduction to the English translation by Walter Lowrie of A. Schweitzer, *Das Abendmahl im Zusammenhang mit dem Leben Jesu und der Geschichte des Urchristentums, Zweites heft: Das Messianitäts- und Leidensgeheimnis: Eine Skizze des Lebens Jesu* (Tübingen: Mohr Siebeck, 1901); ET: *The Mystery of the Kingdom of God: The Secret of Jesus' Messiahship and Passion* (London: A. & C. Black, 1914), pp. 17-58, esp. pp. 17-23; cf. T. F. Glasson, "Schweitzer's Influence: Blessing or Bane?," *JTS* 28 (1977): 289-302 (repr. in B. Chilton, ed., *The Kingdom of God* [London: SPCK, 1984], pp. 107-20), here p. 107 for quotation above.

13. Schweitzer, *Mystery of the Kingdom of God*, passim, but pp. 253-73; *Quest for the Historical Jesus*, pp. 328-95, and pp. 368-69 for the graphic description of Jesus' being crushed by the wheel of the world; *Geschichte der Leben-Jesu-Forschung*, pp. 399-443. Dunn (*Jesus Remembered*, p. 47 n. 101) notes that the passage about Jesus being crushed (though he cites it) is not in subsequent editions of Schweitzer's work. He finds it "regrettable that English readers of the 1910 translation remained unaware of Schweitzer's second thoughts regarding the passage," but he includes it because of its influence on the English-speaking world. I am not convinced that it is regrettable, since Schweitzer's passage presents a graphic and memorable metaphor that is in many ways descriptive of his position, even if he chose to rephrase it at greater length in subsequent editions. As Dunn notes, it is the one passage that has influenced much English scholarship despite his reconsideration. Glasson contends that the evidence indicates Schweitzer held his eschatological views of Jesus until the end of his life ("Schweitzer's Influence," p. 111). Neill rightly points out that what Schweitzer calls eschatology is usually referred to today as apocalyptic (Neill and Wright, *Interpretation of the New Testament*, p. 210).

14. That Schweitzer expected the quest to continue is indicated in the following statement: "To put it briefly: Does the difficulty of explaining the historical personality of Jesus lie in the history itself, or only in the way in which it is represented in the sources?" He answers: "This alternative will be discussed in all the critical studies of the next few years" (*Quest of the Historical Jesus*, p. 11).

namely that Schweitzer was calling for more than simply a stop to what was going on. To the contrary, he set the agenda for much subsequent theological work and its development, including (I contend) providing a primary impetus for development of the criteria of authenticity.[15] One of Schweitzer's major concerns was that dogma had become too closely allied with study of Jesus; he wished to separate the two, to enable studying Jesus without the later developments of Greek and Hellenistic theological categories. So, he writes, "The history of the critical study of the life of Jesus is of higher intrinsic value than the history of the study of ancient dogma or of the attempts to create a new one."[16] Unfortunately, Schweitzer believes, previous interpreters had tended to see too much of themselves in their Jesus: "But it was not only each epoch that found its reflection in Jesus; each individual created Him in accordance with his own character. There is no historical task which so reveals a man's true self as the writing of a Life of Jesus."[17] It is not because the materials for such study are lacking, however. Even though we lack adequate information fully to know Jewish thought

15. See Glasson, "Schweitzer's Influence," p. 113, saying Schweitzer's "so-called apocalyptic view seemed to carry everything before it. According to Bultmann it is universally held on the Continent." I am arguing that not only did Schweitzer influence theological conception of Jesus, but his theological views had an impact on the development of the method for describing these theological views of Jesus, i.e., the criteria.

16. Schweitzer, *Quest of the Historical Jesus*, p. 2. It is with some surprise, therefore, that one finds the first chapter introduced with the following words: "When, at some future day, our period of civilisation shall lie, closed and completed, before the eyes of later generations, German theology will stand out as a great, a unique phenomenon in the mental and spiritual life of our time. For nowhere save in the German temperament can there be found in the same perfection the living complex of conditions and factors — of philosophic thought, critical acumen, historical insight, and religious feeling — without which no deep theology is possible" (p. 1). This statement appears in the 1951 printing of the sixth edition as well (*Geschichte*, p. 1). Neill simply, and ironically, dismisses this as "some characteristically modest statements" (*Interpretation of the New Testament*, p. 207). I believe that it is reflective of something far more important. It reflects German historicism, which has been influential in Germanic countries since the eighteenth century. The central notion of historicism is "that all cultures are moulded by history . . . the customs and beliefs of any group are the products of the group's historical experience. Nothing can be understood in isolation from its past" (D. Bebbington, *Patterns in History: A Christian View* [Downers Grove, Ill.: InterVarsity, 1979], p. 92; cf. pp. 92-116). Bebbington admits that such a view of history has been subject to abuses, including a failure to define human nature (pp. 113-14), extreme nationalism (pp. 114-15), and a lack of foundation for determining right and wrong (pp. 115-16). For a trenchant critique, see K. J. Popper, *The Poverty of Historicism* (London: Routledge, 1957).

17. Schweitzer, *Quest of the Historical Jesus*, p. 4.

of the time and the developments of early Christianity,[18] according to Schweitzer:

> The cause of this lies in the nature of the sources of the life of Jesus, and in the character of our knowledge of the contemporary religious world of thought. It is not that the sources are in themselves bad. When we have once made up our minds that we have not the materials for a complete Life of Jesus, but only for a picture of his public ministry, it must be admitted that there are few characters of antiquity about whom we possess so much indubitably historical information, of whom we have so many authentic discourses. The position is much more favorable, for instance, than in the case of Socrates; for he is pictured to us by literary men who exercised their creative ability upon the portrait. Jesus stands much more immediately before us, because He was depicted by simple Christians without literary gift.[19]

One need not get hung up on the last phrase to recognize that Schweitzer acknowledges both limitations and provisions in the sources. Although the materials for a nineteenth-century type of complete life may not be available, Schweitzer still accepts there is plenty of material to work with. He deems it possible to study Jesus at least as well as most other historical figures of the ancient world — and in fact in the way that ancient biographies themselves depicted their protagonists, emphasizing their public lives and accomplishments.[20]

What is crucial for Schweitzer is the proper method for study. One might think that the Jesus studies of the eighteenth and nineteenth centuries that had had theology at their core — and many of them did, even if they were rebelling against that theology in the wake of the Enlightenment — would have moved Schweitzer to promote a purely historical method. That is not the case. Schweitzer highlights at least two major factors which lead to his endorsed method. The first is that "[t]he personal character of the study is not only due, however, to the fact that a personality can only be awakened to life by the touch of a personality."[21] Schweitzer seems to want to recognize something unique or at least distinctive about the nature of

---

18. Schweitzer, *Quest of the Historical Jesus*, p. 8.

19. Schweitzer, *Quest of the Historical Jesus*, p. 6.

20. See R. Burridge, *What Is a Gospel? A Comparison with Graeco-Roman Biography* (Grand Rapids: Eerdmans, 2004 [2nd ed.]), who corrects some of these misconceptions.

21. Schweitzer, *Quest of the Historical Jesus*, p. 6.

human personality and the nature of the person or personhood, such that purely historical methods are inappropriate tools for such consideration. One needs a subjective method, or at least one that fully involves the human being.[22] He apparently did not find that in current historical methods. The second major factor is that the historical method is based to a large extent upon the notion of analogy. One understands a given event on the basis of analogies with other, hopefully better understood, events, so that facts are described and explanations can be offered.[23] Schweitzer states:

> For the problem of the life of Jesus has no analogue in the field of history. No historical school has ever laid down canons for the investigation of this problem, no professional historian has ever lent his aid to theology in dealing with it. Every ordinary method of historical investigation proves inadequate to the complexity of the conditions. The standards of ordinary historical science are here inadequate, its methods not immediately applicable. The historical study of the life of Jesus has had to create its own methods for itself.[24]

This statement leads to several observations. Firstly, according to Schweitzer, the nature of the quest is beyond the methods of contemporary historical investigation, and its current tools are inadequate. Whether this was true or not I am not prepared to say, but his statements certainly appear to lay down a challenge for those who would attempt to continue to write lives of Jesus. What transpired after Schweitzer shows that as a discipline New Testament studies has generally acted as if it was true. Secondly, and more important for this paper, the discipline of biblical studies did go on to develop new methods and tools for the study of Jesus, including what are conveniently labeled as the criteria for authenticity.[25]

---

22. In this sense, Schweitzer reflects one of the common discussions in historical method, namely the issue of subjectivity. See W. H. Dray, *Philosophy of History* (Englewood Cliffs, N.J.: Prentice-Hall, 1964), pp. 21-40.

23. See D. H. Fischer, *Historians' Fallacies: Toward a Logic of Historical Thought* (New York: Harper, 1970), p. xv n. 1, for this formulation of the relation between event, fact and explanation. There are other conceptions of this relationship: Dunn adopts the distinction between event, data and fact (*Jesus Remembered*, p. 102 and n. 3) from R. G. Collingwood, *The Idea of History* (Oxford: Oxford University Press, 1946), pp. 133, 176-77, 251-52.

24. Schweitzer, *Quest of the Historical Jesus*, p. 6.

25. Other methods and tools were developed as well, including form and redaction criticisms, among others.

In essence, Schweitzer claims that prior to writing his thoroughgoing critique of German scholarship there were inadequate methods to undertake the writing of a historical account of Jesus. His treatment is primarily historical and retrospective, but he points to literary and theological issues to be considered in the future. As he says, the data seem to indicate both historical and literary solutions. The question is how "to explain the contradiction between the Messianic consciousness of Jesus and His non-Messianic discourses and actions."[26] In other words, Schweitzer sees the issue as boiling down to distinguishing, if adequate tools might be developed, how historically Jesus saw himself in theological terms (which Schweitzer defines in terms of eschatology) and how literarily Jesus is depicted in the Gospels by the early Church.[27] Schweitzer does not despair of critical scholarship examining Jesus, even if he fails to recognize that the emerging portrait of Jesus is historically confined and not readily applicable to the contemporary theological context.[28] As Schweitzer says, "Whatever the ultimate solution may be, the historical Jesus of whom the criticism of the future, taking as its starting-point the problems which have been recognized and admitted, will draw the portrait, can never render modern theology the services which it claimed from its own half-historical, half-modern, Jesus."[29]

So, rather than bringing the quest to a halt — as many have posited —

26. Schweitzer, *Quest of the Historical Jesus*, p. 11.

27. We might even speculate that Schweitzer, based upon his Germanic historicistic view of history, wished such discussion to remain with German scholars (and it is to be noted that German scholars were hugely instrumental in subsequent developments). I believe that the standard scenario regarding development of historical Jesus research, disputed above, reflects a similar kind of German historicism. At most, this model was confined to a small group of German scholars, mostly those identified with form criticism and the use of the standard criteria, such as double dissimilarity (see below).

28. This is not surprising in the light of his definition of Jesus' eschatological consciousness and mission that ends with him dying alone on the cross, having failed to compel God to usher in the kingdom. There is nothing very hopeful for contemporary theology in such a conception, which no doubt forces Schweitzer to take the mystical view of Jesus' present existence that he does: "He comes to us as One unknown, without a name, as of old, by the lake-side, He came to those men who knew him not. . . . And to those who obey Him, whether they be wise or simple, He will reveal Himself in the toils, the conflicts, the sufferings which they shall pass through in His fellowship, and as an ineffable mystery, they shall learn in their own experience Who He is" (*Quest of the Historical Jesus*, p. 401; cf. *Geschichte*, p. 642).

29. Schweitzer, *Quest of the Historical Jesus*, p. 396.

24

or secularizing it by ripping it apart from other areas of biblical study and placing it firmly within a non-dogmatic environment — as many think the result of Schweitzer's work was — or promoting a method to make the historical Jesus the Jesus of the present theological context — as others had previously attempted and are still attempting — Schweitzer's theological and literary endeavor to describe more adequately this historical figure of Jesus led to the emerging criteria of authenticity. In fact, Schweitzer laid down a significant challenge that was directly addressed by the development of a number of the criteria. The result is that the criteria were developed both as historical and literary tools and as theological tools to take research into the historical Jesus beyond the confines of previous historical analysis. In a sense (paraphrasing a well-known phrase), development of at least some of the criteria for authenticity was a series of footnotes to the historical (or literary) and theological program laid out by Albert Schweitzer.

The Criteria Examined in the Light of Schweitzer

An examination of the major criteria reflects the kind of theologically and historically or literarily induced response that Schweitzer had called for. Even though some had anticipated these criteria used in historical Jesus studies, the major formulations took place after the work of Schweitzer — and, I contend, at least in part in direct or indirect response to his challenge toward further developments in historical Jesus research. Briefly recounting their development makes clear that their major formulations followed in response to Schweitzer's work and took up the formulation that he had proposed for further consideration.

The earliest and no doubt most significant criterion is that now called the criterion of double dissimilarity. This criterion is a direct response to Schweitzer's challenge for historical method. His definition of the dilemma in studying the historical Jesus points the direction to the development of the criterion. In defining the dilemma between the literary and theological conceptions of Jesus, Schweitzer asks whether they will be solved

> by means of a conception of His Messianic consciousness which will make it appear that He could not have acted otherwise than as the Evangelists describe; or must we endeavour to explain the contradiction by

taking the non-Messianic discourses and actions as our fixed point, denying the reality of His Messianic self-consciousness and regarding it as a later interpolation of the beliefs of the Christian community into the life of Jesus? In the latter case the Evangelists are supposed to have attributed these Messianic claims to Jesus because the early Church held Him to be the Messiah, but to have contradicted themselves by describing his life as it actually was, viz., as the life of a prophet, not of one who held Himself to be the Messiah.[30]

In nuce, Schweitzer poses his question in terms of the criterion of double dissimilarity, drawing distinctions between contemporary Jewish messianic expectations and the way the early Church wished to depict Jesus.[31] Although scholars such as Schmiedel and Heitmüller anticipated this criterion's more precise formulation,[32] the first significant figure to do so was apparently Bultmann, writing soon after Schweitzer. He formulated this criterion in terms resembling Schweitzer, stating (in a discussion of issues surrounding the synoptic tradition): "We can only count on possessing a genuine similitude of Jesus where, on the one hand, expression is given to the contrast between Jewish morality and piety and the distinctive eschatological temper which characterized the preaching of Jesus; and where, on the other hand, we find no specifically Christian features."[33] This distinction was put more succinctly by Käsemann, who formulated the distinctiveness in terms of one criterion that he thought was generally secure:

30. Schweitzer, *Quest of the Historical Jesus*, p. 11.

31. Perhaps it should not surprise us too much that Schweitzer formulates the issues in this way, since there is a lengthy depiction of this dichotomy in relation to the development of the criterion of double dissimilarity that dates from Luther to the present. See Theissen and Winter, *Quest for the Plausible Jesus*, pp. 261-316, although they do not cite Schweitzer.

32. P. Schmiedel, "Gospels," in T. K. Cheyne and J. S. Black, eds., *Encyclopaedia Biblica* (4 vols.; London: A. & C. Black, 1899-1907), vol. 2, cols. 1761-1898, esp. cols. 1847, 1881-3; W. Heitmüller, "Jesus Christus I," *RGG* (Tübingen: Mohr Siebeck, 1912), vol. 3, cols. 343-62, esp. col. 361 (*Jesus* [Tübingen: Mohr Siebeck, 1913], pp. 34-35).

33. R. Bultmann, *History of the Synoptic Tradition* (trans. J. Marsh; Oxford: Blackwell, 1963 [1921]), p. 205; see also his "The New Approach to the Synoptic Problem," *JR* 6 (1926): 337-62 (repr. in S. Ogden, ed., *Existence and Faith: Shorter Writings of Rudolf Bultmann* [New York: Meridian, 1960], pp. 35-54, esp. p. 43). We must remember that it is often Bultmann who is cited along with Schweitzer as one of those who brought the notion of questing after Jesus to a halt (although often his later *New Testament Theology* is cited [trans. K. Grobel; 2 vols.; New York: Scribners, 1951, 1955 (1948)], vol. 1, p. 3, rather than his earlier *History of the Synoptic Tradition* [1921]), so it is not surprising that he is one of the first to pick up on the challenge.

"when there are no grounds either for deriving a tradition from Judaism or for ascribing it to primitive Christianity."[34] The classic formulation by Perrin states in explicit terms that authenticity attaches to sayings that are "dissimilar to characteristic emphases both of ancient Judaism and of the early Church."[35] In his recent assessment of the criteria, Dunn places his treatment of this criterion within his discussion of the "second quest."[36] This is somewhat misleading, since the criterion's basis was clearly laid much earlier and developed in the form-critical work of Bultmann and others, even if it was further refined and codified later.

This criterion has been soundly and repeatedly criticized, especially recently: It cannot delimit or define the authentic Jesus material, only dispute proposed material and arrive at a minimalist Jesus. It equivocates over the meaning of "dissimilar" and ends up disputing the degree of difference, rather than difference in kind, when it is most effective. It addresses only content, not actual wording, of Jesus' speech. It requires exhaustive knowledge of Judaism and early Christianity to ensure accuracy, knowledge that we may never possess despite continual advances (and thereby reducing the authentic material of Jesus?). And this criterion may work better emphasizing either Judaism or Christianity, as there are proponents for either side.[37] Moreover, some have contested whether this criterion holds any relevance to authenticity at all, since it may only define difference and distinction, not authenticity itself.[38] It is noteworthy that

34. Käsemann, "Problem of the Historical Jesus," p. 37.

35. N. Perrin, *Rediscovering the Teaching of Jesus* (London: SCM Press, 1967), p. 39; cf. his *What Is Redaction Criticism?* (Philadelphia: Fortress, 1970), p. 71.

36. Dunn, *Jesus Remembered*, pp. 81-82.

37. Some have wanted to see it as a single criterion, such as Bultmann, who used it especially in terms of Jesus' teaching and Jewish wisdom (*Synoptic Tradition*, pp. 101-8).

38. The notion of authenticity as it is used in historical Jesus research is a contentious one. See Porter, *Criteria for Authenticity*, p. 56 n. 66. There has been an effort to define method more closely in historical Jesus research and to utilize the notion of critical realism. See, e.g., B. F. Meyer, *Critical Realism and the New Testament* (Allison Park, Pa.: Pickwick Publications, 1989); N. T. Wright, *The New Testament and the People of God* (London: SPCK, 1992), pp. 31-46; and most recently Dunn, *Jesus Remembered*, pp. 110-11 (although I am not convinced that Dunn has sorted out all of the methodological issues that he outlines in his chapter on history, hermeneutics and faith, esp. pp. 99-125). Surprisingly, none of these three refers to Karl Popper's *Conjectures and Refutations: The Growth of Scientific Knowledge* (London: Routledge and Kegan Paul, 1963), whose view of method is consonant with theirs (see, e.g., Wright, p. 37).

there is little attention in this criterion to how Jesus would have related to the Roman world, or to how his depiction would have related to non-Jewish figures of the time. As a result of such criticism,[39] Du Toit speaks of the "demise" of this criterion.[40] However, despite criticisms of it, this criterion continues to be used by historical Jesus scholars — even if begrudgingly.[41] The criterion most noticeably focuses on the agenda of distinguishing Jesus from Judaism and early Christianity, the two major points of comparison that Schweitzer had mentioned in his programmatic statements regarding future developments in Jesus research.

Related to this criterion are two others needing mention. One is that of embarrassment, itself a form of the criterion of dissimilarity.[42] Käsemann, as part of his formulation of the criterion of double dissimilarity, adds to his definition of dissimilarity, "especially when Jewish Christianity has mitigated or modified the received tradition, as having found it too bold for its taste."[43] This notion of embarrassment has been framed in terms of elements going against the redactional tendency (see below), but more convincingly in terms of material distinct from what might have been created by the early Church. Meier says that that tradition, creating some difficulty for the early Church, but left even at the possible cost of embarrassment, is probably authentic.[44] In formulation and history of development (as an appendix to Käsemann's definition of dissimilarity), this criterion very much resembles such forms of the criterion of dissimilarity emphasizing only one area of difference. In this regard, many of the same criticisms apply. For the purpose of this paper, what is most relevant is that

39. Major recent criticism of this criterion is found in Theissen and Winter, *Quest for the Plausible Jesus,* pp. 1-171; and T. Holmén, "Doubts about Double Dissimilarity: Restructuring the Main Criterion of Jesus-of-History Research," in B. Chilton and C. A. Evans, eds., *Authenticating the Words of Jesus* (Leiden: Brill, 1998), pp. 47-80.

40. Du Toit, "Redefining Jesus," pp. 104-7, who emphasizes the diversity in Judaism as a major factor against the criterion.

41. For example, D. Allison (*Jesus of Nazareth: Millenarian Prophet* [Minneapolis: Fortress, 1998], pp. 4-5) offers a critique of this criterion (as well as others), but he admits that he has no other tools to use (pp. 6-7). I suggest in my review of Theissen and Winter's *Quest for the Plausible Jesus* that the criterion of dissimilarity may still be "dictating the agenda for at least some historical Jesus research," including theirs (*JETS* 47 [2004]: 507-10, esp. p. 510).

42. See Porter, *Criteria for Authenticity,* pp. 106-7.

43. Käsemann, "Problem of the Historical Jesus," p. 37.

44. J. P. Meier, *A Marginal Jew: Rethinking the Historical Jesus* (3 vols.; New York: Doubleday, 1991), vol. 1, p. 169.

the embarrassment is seen against developments in the early Church, as opposed to Judaism, which is often emphasized in the single versions of dissimilarity.

The second related criterion is in effect a turning on its head of the criterion of double dissimilarity by Wright. In direct response to what he sees as the counter-productive tendencies of the criterion of double dissimilarity and its largely negative results, he argues for a criterion of what he calls "double similarity": "when something can be seen to be credible (though perhaps deeply subversive) within first-century Judaism, *and* credible as the implied starting point (though not the exact replica) of something in later Christianity."[45] He defines this criterion in terms of responding to five "questions": (1) "Jesus fits believably into first-century Judaism"; (2) his purpose is that of "regrouping Israel"; (3) he will draw "hostility" for his actions "from the Temple authorities," but if "the Romans hear of a major renewal movement among the Jews, they too will want to stamp it out"; (4) Jesus' vindication indicated the arrival of the kingdom; and (5) the story is told in "theologically consistent" terms.[46] One might well argue that, both in its formulation and in its application, this is simply a toned-down or modified version of the criterion of double dissimilarity. In his definition, Wright wants to ensure the possibilities of both Jesus' potential subversiveness to first-century Judaism and his not simply replicating later Christianity. This formulation seems to make this criterion an issue of what it means to be dissimilar, and to what degree. Wright is still arguing for dissimilarity, even if it is not as dissimilar as some others desire. Wright's examples are consonant with this, since Jesus' fitting believably into Judaism of his time may still imply distinctiveness. In any case, this criterion emphasizes Jesus' relationship to Judaism and the early Church, the two factors that Schweitzer saw as crucial.

The criterion of least distinctiveness is even more closely tied to form-critical (and hence what are sometimes equated with "no quest") developments.[47] Form-critical proponents such as Dibelius, Bultmann and Taylor

---

45. N. T. Wright, *Jesus and the Victory of God* (Minneapolis: Fortress, 1996), pp. 131-33, here p. 132. A generally positive review of my *Criteria for Authenticity* indicated that I had not "discussed" this criterion by Wright (C. Blomberg in *Themelios* 26.2 [2001]: 83-84, here p. 84 — I note that Blomberg calls me Paul on that page as well; I am truly flattered). See, however, p. 57, where I may not "discuss" Wright but I certainly mention him and his criterion in my conclusion.

46. Wright, *Jesus,* p. 132.

47. Dunn does not offer criticism of this criterion, since he ends up using it as the basis

sought to define the laws of transmission for a particular literary form. They based their proposals upon work previously done in Old Testament studies and in related Hellenistic literature, especially folklore.[48] Generally speaking, traditions gain distinctive features through the process of transmission. One can then use the changes as an indication of the difference between the original form and the secondary tradition. As Bultmann states, "Whenever narratives pass from mouth to mouth the central point of the narrative and general structure are well preserved; but in the incidental details changes take place, for imagination paints such details with increasing distinctiveness."[49] One can readily see this criterion's utility for determining the relation between Jesus' messianic consciousness and the degree to which this is authentic to the Gospel depictions.

This criterion has been called into question on two fronts, however. One is based in internal examination of the Gospels themselves. As Sanders says, "there are no hard and fast laws of the development of the Synoptic tradition. . . . For this reason, *dogmatic statements that a certain characteristic proves a certain passage to be earlier than another are never justified.*"[50] It is also called to account by systematic study of non-Jewish literature, such as that of Homer and other epic tellers of tales, and not just folklorists.[51] The work of the form critics, despite their references to extrabiblical literature (whether Jewish or Hellenistic), tends to refer to rules of transmission, but it does not do so within a context of extended and systematic quantification of these presuppositions. One senses, instead, a high level of anecdotal evidence brought to bear on the discussion, with examples cited in unsystematic ways throughout the work for the purpose of comparison. In any event, there are no systematic studies of what consti-

---

of his criterion of characteristics and distinctives of the Jesus tradition (*Jesus Remembered*, p. 333).

48. See M. Dibelius, *From Tradition to Gospel* (trans. B. Woolf; London: Ivor Nicholson & Watson, 1934 [1919]), pp. 6-7; Bultmann, *Synoptic Tradition*, p. 6; V. Taylor, *The Formation of the Gospel Tradition* (London: Macmillan, 1933), pp. 26-27. The emphasis upon folklore, rather than literature per se, stems from the belief that the New Testament literature was *Kleinliteratur*, rather than *Hochliteratur*. See H. Gunkel, *The Legends of Genesis: The Biblical Saga and History* (trans. W. H. Carruth; New York: Schocken, 1964 [1901]).

49. Bultmann, "New Approach," pp. 41-42.

50. E. P. Sanders, *The Tendencies of the Synoptic Tradition* (SNTSMS 9; Cambridge: Cambridge University Press, 1969), p. 272 (italics his).

51. E.g., G. S. Kirk, *The Songs of Homer* (Cambridge: Cambridge University Press, 1962), pp. 55-101.

tutes change and development and how that would be measured in any meaningful way. Schweitzer's concern was to see how, from a literary standpoint, the messianic or eschatological features were depicted in relation to Jesus' consciousness. The method of distinctiveness appears unable to address this important issue for establishing the relation of the literary to the theological source.

The last criterion to consider here is that of the criterion of Semitic language and environment. I consider it here because of Schweitzer's concern for literary traditions in Judaism, as well as his devotion of an entire chapter in his *Quest* to the study of Aramaic.[52] In that chapter he critiques the various authors in terms of how their study of Aramaic bore relationship to fundamental Jewish notions such as Son of Man. The criterion of Semitic environment relates to features of Palestine, and states that those features showing acquaintance with the environment would presume to be authentic. This part of this criterion is less important, and far less widely emphasized, than that of Semitic language. Although discussion of the Aramaic features of Jesus' language goes back to at least the seventeenth century, one can see interesting development in this criterion in the nineteenth and twentieth centuries, especially in comparison with Schweitzer's work. Several of the major proponents of the Semitic language criterion — that one can retrovert to Jesus' original Aramaic statements through exploiting translational difficulties in the Greek of the Gospels — wrote their major works before Schweitzer (who critiqued them in his survey).[53] These early proponents, such as Dalman, often considered Aramaic within the context of the surrounding Greek linguistic milieu, and often in conjunction with the more widespread discussion of whether Jesus possibly spoke Greek.[54] After Schweitzer, this consideration of the larger linguistic context — whether that meant Palestinian

52. Schweitzer, *Quest of the Historical Jesus*, pp. 269-85 (incidentally, on pp. 273-75, Schweitzer discusses multilingualism in Palestine); *Geschichte*, pp. 260-76.

53. G. Dalman, *Grammatik des jüdisch-palästinischen Aramäisch* (Leipzig: Hinrichs, 1894); idem, *The Words of Jesus Considered in the Light of Post-Biblical Jewish Writings and the Aramaic Language* (trans. D. M. Kay; Edinburgh: T&T Clark, 1909 [1898]); idem, *Jesus-Jeshua: Studies in the Gospels* (trans. P. P. Levertoff; London: SPCK, 1929 [1922]); A. Meyer, *Jesu Muttersprache: Das galiläische Aramäisch in seiner Bedeutung für die Erklärung der Reden Jesu und der Evangelien überhaupt* (Freiburg: Mohr Siebeck, 1896).

54. Whether Jesus spoke Greek never developed as a criterion in historical Jesus research (apparently until my *Criteria for Authenticity*, part II).

multilingualism, or Mediterranean linguistic usage, bilingualism, language interference, or issues such as prestige languages — was severely minimized in many circles of discussion.[55] Such scholars as Burney, Torrey, Jeremias, M. Black, Dunn, Chilton and now Casey,[56] among others, are often almost monolingual in their emphases, if not in fact.[57] The emphasis has clearly been upon Jesus as an Aramaic language user — to the virtual exclusion of even recognizing the possibility that Jesus spoke Greek, or at least that he communicated within a Hellenistic milieu in which Greek and Hellenistic culture were highly influential. From the start, all that this criterion does is place a tradition in Palestine and possibly within the Aramaic-speaking church, but nothing more specific.[58] The question is whether that emphasis upon Aramaic has helped us to arrive at a clearer understanding of crucial terminology that Jesus used, especially as it may have related to his self-consciousness. The Son of Man

55. Another factor, which I noted in my *Criteria for Authenticity,* pp. 129-30, was the death of Albert Thumb in 1915, James Hope Moulton in 1917, and Adolf Deissmann in 1937. See M. Reiser, *Syntax und Stil des Markusevangeliums im Licht der hellenistischen Volksliteratur* (WUNT 2.11; Tübingen: Mohr Siebeck, 1984), p. 2.

56. See, e.g., C. F. Burney, *The Poetry of Our Lord* (Oxford: Clarendon Press, 1925); C. C. Torrey, "The Translations Made from the Original Aramaic Gospels," in D. G. Lyon and G. F. Moore, eds., *Studies in the History of Religions* (FS C. H. Toy; New York: Macmillan, 1912), pp. 269-317; idem, *Our Translated Gospels: Some of the Evidence* (Cambridge, Mass.: Harvard University Press, 1916); J. Jeremias, *The Parables of Jesus* (trans. S. H. Hooke; London: SCM Press, 1972 [3rd ed.] [1947]); idem, *The Eucharistic Words of Jesus* (trans. A. Ehrhardt; Oxford: Blackwell, 1955 [1935]); idem, "Characteristics of the *Ipsissima Vox Jesu,*" in his *The Prayers of Jesus* (trans. J. Bowden, C. Burchard and J. Reumann; London: SCM Press, 1967), pp. 108-15; idem, *The Proclamation of Jesus* (trans. J. Bowden; London: SCM Press, 1971); M. Black, *An Aramaic Approach to the Gospels and Acts* (Oxford: Clarendon Press, 1946; 1967 [3rd ed.]); J. D. G. Dunn, *The Evidence for Jesus: The Impact of Scholarship on Our Understanding of How Christianity Began* (London: SCM Press, 1985), p. 3; idem, *Jesus Remembered,* p. 315 and nn. 288-89; B. Chilton, *A Galilean Rabbi and His Bible: Jesus' Use of the Interpreted Scripture of His Time* (Wilmington, Del.: Michael Glazier, 1984), pp. 57-147; M. Casey, *Aramaic Sources of Mark's Gospel* (SNTSMS 102; Cambridge: Cambridge University Press, 1998); idem, "An Aramaic Approach to the Synoptic Gospels," *ExpTim* 110.7 (1999): 175-78. An exception was J. Wellhausen, *Einleitung in die drei erste Evangelien* (Berlin: Reimer 1905; 1911 [2nd ed.]), which shows greater appreciation for Greek in the second edition (pp. 7-32) than in the first (pp. 7-43).

57. An exception is J. A. Fitzmyer, "The Languages of Palestine in the First Century AD," *CBQ* 32 (1970): 501-31 (reprinted many times).

58. Meier, *Marginal Jew,* vol. 1, pp. 179-80. The tendency has been to downplay the significance of this criterion in recent research. See Porter, *Criteria for Authenticity,* pp. 98-99.

is a good case in point, but it is not the only one. There has been much discussion, but there is still a fair amount of disagreement.[59] This criterion has clearly failed to deliver on its early expectations.

I will not treat here several other criteria, because of their derivative nature. Coherence and some of its related, more circumscribed forms, such as the criterion of rejection, must rely upon other criteria to establish that with which something is coherent, such as dissimilarity or the like. This criterion thus assumes its conclusions. Multiple attestation was not so much a product of German scholarship but of English-language scholarship and is limited in its application to distinguishing between different sources that, in this case, stem from an admittedly common event. The recently developed criterion of historical plausibility,[60] which amounts essentially to an amalgam of the criteria of resistance to the redactional tendency (embarrassment — see above),[61] coherence, conformity to context (least distinctiveness — see above) and contextual individuality (dissimilarity — see above), is subject to the same criticisms as above, where I suggested that this criterion, proposed by Theissen and Winter, may well indicate that the criterion of double dissimilarity is still functioning.

Conclusions

A paper such as this can only sketch briefly the broad outlines of what I am proposing. Nevertheless, the true significance of Schweitzer's important book on the so-called old quest for the historical Jesus — in reality those works of the eighteenth and nineteenth centuries that preceded his writing — has probably not been fully appreciated. It is often seen as the publication that effectively shut down research into the historical Jesus. We have seen that this conclusion is simply not true — even within more restricted German scholarly circles, to say nothing of the non-German world, where

59. See, e.g., D. Burkett, *The Son of Man Debate: A History and Evaluation* (SNTSMS 107; Cambridge: Cambridge University Press, 1999).

60. See Theissen and Winter, *Quest for the Plausible Jesus*, pp. 172-225; critiqued in Porter, *Criteria for Authenticity*, pp. 113-22.

61. However, in resistance to the redactional tendency, there is a greater emphasis upon the literary text (and subject to many of the same strictures as were noted above regarding distinctiveness; see Porter, *Criteria for Authenticity*, p. 108) than there is with the criterion of embarrassment, which deals with the nature of the events depicted.

writing about Jesus as a historical figure continued. Part of the reason for this, I believe, is that this is not what Schweitzer ever intended.

If Schweitzer's work did not have this effect, what effect did it have? The impact of his eschatological proposal regarding Jesus was not significant at the time he first published it, and even when it was republished in his later work it was not the major feature of that volume — even though his eschatological views became widespread and significant especially in German scholarship. Instead, I propose that Schweitzer had a far more constructive impact than most have realized. In this paper, I have tried to show that the major criteria for authenticity in historical Jesus research are to a large extent (either directly or indirectly) a positive reaction to and extension of the programmatic agenda set by Albert Schweitzer in his fundamental work, *Quest of the Historical Jesus*. Rather than calling work to a halt, Schweitzer laid out what he thought needed to be done to redeem historical Jesus study. His critique had shown that certain approaches were subject to criticism. But, Schweitzer thought, efforts that weighed carefully in historical terms the relation of the personality of Jesus to features of Judaism and of the early Church would have the best chance of succeeding. As a result, we see the development of a variety of criteria that attempt to address these issues raised by Schweitzer. To be sure, not all of the criteria emerged in direct response to Schweitzer's programmatic agenda. Some were already being developed, and for others the direct lines of influence are hard to find. However, there are a number of criteria that do seem to have been developed, or at least more actively refined and promoted, in the light of Schweitzer's work. We examined first the related criteria of double dissimilarity, embarrassment, and double similarity and discovered that these are all concerned to distinguish the traditions regarding Jesus from what is found in Judaism and early Christianity — although in varying ways and certainly in varying degrees. Nevertheless, they try to establish distinctiveness in terms of various theological, literary and historical elements. The criterion of least distinctiveness addresses the issue of textual transmission and development, the literary dimension that Schweitzer was concerned to balance against theology. The last criterion was that of Semitic language features. Schweitzer himself introduced this element into his study and saw its importance, even if it did not live up to that potential.

What can we say about the effectiveness of Schweitzer's program? In a sense it was a success because it in many ways prolonged and sustained at least a certain type of historical Jesus research up to the present time.

Much of twentieth-century research utilized the several criteria in various ways. However, there have also been a number of criticisms raised; this is especially true of the fundamental criterion of double dissimilarity and its related forms, to the point where this criterion is no longer considered to be as robust as it once was. This criterion is the one most directly related to Schweitzer's research program. In that sense, Schweitzer's agenda, though it was extended because of this criterion, has come to the effective end of its useful life, and its productivity has been curtailed. Nevertheless, the ongoing quest for the historical Jesus continues as it has for centuries, if not with Schweitzer's inspired criteria, then with others developed for new and differing purposes and agendas.

Jesus of Galilee: The Role of Location in Understanding Jesus

Jens Schröter

The Importance of Galilee in Jesus Research

One of the most important developments in Jesus Research has been the preoccupation with Galilee as the place of Jesus' origin and center of activity. Investigating Jesus' cultural and social context through contemporary Jewish writings and archaeological evidence, as well as considering extra-canonical Jesus traditions and re-examining historical hermeneutic issues, have grounded Jesus Research (or the "Third Quest") more firmly than earlier so-called Quests. In more recent portrayals of Jesus, the concrete conditions in which Jesus' ministry took place clearly play a substantially greater role than in any previous phase.[1]

Methodologically, however, this expansion of the source basis does not thereby entail overcoming the provisional and changing nature of historical reconstruction, leading to a supposedly more definite knowledge of the facts. Neither the preoccupation with the cultural and social milieu nor the involvement of archaeological sources necessarily leads to a more objective, neutral picture of Jesus' times and ministry.[2] As has been fre-

---

1. Cf. for example the portrayals by E. P. Sanders, *Sohn Gottes: Eine historische Biographie Jesu* (Stuttgart: Klett-Cotta, 1996) [Sanders, *The Historical Figure of Jesus* (London, New York: Penguin, 1993)]; J. D. G. Dunn, *Jesus Remembered* (CM 1; Grand Rapids: Eerdmans, 2003); M. Ebner, *Jesus von Nazaret in seiner Zeit: Sozialgeschichtliche Zugänge* (SBS 196; Stuttgart: Kath. Bibelwerk, 2003); S. Freyne, *Jesus, a Jewish Galilean: A New Reading of the Jesus-Story* (London and New York: T&T Clark, 2004). [Also see, Charlesworth, ed., *Jesus and Archaeology*. Ed.]

2. Cf. S. Freyne, "The Geography, Politics, and Economics of Galilee and the Quest for

quently stressed right from the beginning of the modern academic study of history, because the study of the past always takes place from the perspective of the present and leads to a better understanding of the present, it is something that always changes. This fact can also be observed in Jesus Research.[3] The way the historical Jesus is portrayed at any particular time varies in relation to the source material available at that time and the position from which that portrayal is made. Thus, for example, the earlier depiction of Judaism during the Hellenistic-Roman period, prior to the recent discovery and editing of many Jewish texts, differs considerably from most current portrayals. In addition, the current sensitivity to the Jewish roots of Christianity, much greater than in earlier stages of Jesus Research, is due not least to the theological reflection that occurred in the wake of the *Shoa*. Both elements have contributed to the current situation in Jesus Research, in which Judaism is no longer depicted as a negative background from which Jesus' ministry stands out. Early Judaism is certainly the historical context within which Jesus' ministry can be understood.

This realization, that study of the past never occurs independently of the particular present in which that study takes place, leads to a more precise definition of the expression "the historical Jesus." The term refers to a perspective based on current historical knowledge, filtered through the methods of historical criticism and the viewpoint of the specific researcher to arrive at an outline of the person of Jesus. Such an outline can never be identical with the actual person who lived in Palestine some 2000 years ago. For this reason, recent Jesus Research has drawn a distinction between the *historical* and the *earthly* Jesus, expressing the necessity to distinguish between the results of historical research and the actual events occurring in the past.[4] When referring to the Gospels, therefore, one should not talk about the *historical* Jesus, because this is a product of modern historical criticism; this is not, of course, the approach the Gospel writers would have taken.

Historical research thus does not lead to unchanging certainties, but to probabilities that are oriented towards the source material and open to

---

the Historical Jesus," in B. Chilton and C. A. Evans, eds., *Studying the Historical Jesus: Evaluations of the State of Current Research* (NTTS 19; Leiden: Brill, 1994), pp. 75-121, esp. pp. 75-76.

3. Cf. Dunn, *Jesus Remembered*, pp. 99-136.

4. J. P. Meier, *A Marginal Jew: Rethinking the Historical Jesus*. Volume One: *The Roots of the Problem and the Person* (ABRL; New York: Doubleday, 1991), pp. 21-40.

modification. Historical portrayals of Jesus, therefore, are also hypotheses about how things *could have been*. This insight makes us aware that portrayals of Jesus, like other historical portrayals, are based on a link between the present and the past, and it is precisely here that they contribute to an understanding of the present as something that has taken shape. It is therefore not a question of trying to find the "real" Jesus *behind* the evidence from early Christian times. Rather, historical criticism makes clear which interpretations can be reconciled with the source material and which ones cannot. The sources have a corrective function or, as Reinhart Koselleck expressed it, a "right of veto." They prohibit certain interpretations and can protect us from making mistakes, but they do not tell us what a story sketched out on a critical basis should look like.[5] To achieve this we also need the power of "historical imagination." As a historical discipline, Jesus Research is therefore committed to subjecting the statements it makes to a continuous process of inspection. Having made these preliminary methodological remarks, I will now proceed to examine the importance of Galilee for a picture of the historical Jesus, first reviewing the development of this field of scholarship.

Galilee, as the setting for Jesus' ministry, had already played a role in Jesus Research in the nineteenth century, although admittedly in a different way. The description by Ernest Renan, who painted a romantic picture of Galilee as the setting for Jesus' ministry, has become famous.[6] According to Renan, this "earthly paradise" brought forth a "hardworking, upright, cheerful population" and contrasted with the inhospitable nature of Judea and Jerusalem and the form of Judaism found there, influenced by the priests and Pharisees.[7] Renan then took this contrast between Galilee and Jerusalem and applied it to the difference between Christianity and Judaism: Galilee was the homeland of Christianity, Jerusalem the stronghold of hostile Judaism. The shortcomings of making such a connection between the character of a landscape and the mentality of its inhabitants are obvious. Nevertheless, Renan's view that the examination of Jesus' cultural milieu was important for an understanding of his ministry is still worth noting. Of course, this connection needs to be described in a different way.

---

5. R. Koselleck, *Vergangene Zukunft: Zur Semantik geschichtlicher Zeiten* (Frankfurt: Suhrkamp, 1979).

6. E. Renan, *Das Leben Jesu* (Leipzig: Reclam, 1929).

7. Renan, *Das Leben Jesu*, p. 129; see also pp. 165-68.

The criticism of the nineteenth-century lives of Jesus, triggered largely by Albert Schweitzer, was accompanied by an increasing lack of interest in Jesus' historical context. Schweitzer, and after him Rudolf Bultmann, recognized the mistaken trust in the temporary nature of historical knowledge, which they contrasted with the "will" of Jesus as being "original" and timeless.[8] Bultmann explicitly limited his portrayal to the teaching or proclamation of Jesus and was firmly opposed to describing Jesus' life or personality. In so doing he moved away from the historical writing of the nineteenth century, which was oriented towards the historical impact made by prominent people.[9]

The disruption caused by the collapse of liberal Jesus research was far-reaching. Subsequently, scholars dared to embark on portrayals of the historical Jesus only if they had first given an assurance that it was not in fact possible to write a life of Jesus. In the forefront of such descriptions was the "message" proclaimed by Jesus, dealing briefly with the specific context of the proclamation by simply surveying Jewish history from the Exile to John the Baptist.[10] This concentration on the teaching of Jesus has its continuation in parts of more recent Q research, in which the supposed oldest layer of Q is identified with the message proclaimed by Jesus. Sayings and parables, without any context, are considered to be the core of Jesus' teaching; they are regarded as being capable of interpretation independent from their contexts of origin. It is no coincidence that this research approach attaches considerable importance to the *Gospel of Thomas*. This source's collection of sayings and parables, without any context, fits in well with the approach that views Jesus' teaching as the decisive feature in his ministry, containing no statements about his divine nature or the imminent end of the world.[11]

---

8. A. Schweitzer, *Geschichte der Leben-Jesu-Forschung* (Tübingen: Mohr Siebeck, 1913 [9th ed., 1984]), p. 623; R. Bultmann, *Jesus* (Berlin: Deutsche Bibliothek, 1926; Tübingen: Mohr Siebeck, 1983), pp. 10-11.

9. It should be remembered that Bultmann's book on Jesus originally appeared as the first volume of a series entitled "Die Unsterblichen: Die geistigen Heroen der Menschheit in ihrem Leben und Wirken" [The Immortals: The Spiritual Heroes of the Human Race in Their Lives and Work]. Bultmann's foreword reads as a clear rejection of any such concept.

10. See for example G. Bornkamm, *Jesus von Nazareth* (Stuttgart: Kohlhammer, 1956 [15th ed., 1995]).

11. Cf. the criticism by P. Jenkins, *Hidden Gospels: How the Search for Jesus Lost Its Way* (Oxford: Oxford University Press, 2001), pp. 54-81.

The concentration on the "message" or teaching of Jesus represents a reduction of scope that is problematical. In view of the historical hermeneutical premises mentioned earlier, it must remain one of the tasks of historical Jesus Research to paint as accurate a picture as possible of the world in which Jesus lived and worked. More recent portrayals of Jesus have therefore once again devoted greater attention to describing this context. There can be no doubt that the New Testament Gospels are the crucial sources for this — not because they were later included in the canon, but because they are the oldest sources that place Jesus' ministry in a geographical and cultural milieu.[12] The setting in which Jesus lived and worked is here not a secondary "framework" that can be ignored, but part of the "historicizing tendency" of the first stories told by Jesus.[13] We need not emphasize that from today's perspective they should be read critically in terms of the distinction between historical information and post-Easter interpretation. Regardless of this, these narratives enable us to place Jesus in his historical context.

Galilee in the Time of Jesus

Galilee was not just the part of Palestine in which Jesus was born and grew up. It was above all the region in which his public activities began. As we will see, this is of considerable importance for an understanding of his ministry. First of all, however, we will take a look at the factors shaping the milieu of Galilee in the time of Jesus.

Firstly, the historical background is important. As part of the Northern Kingdom, Galilee was conquered by the Assyrians in 733/732 BCE. According to 2 Kgs 15:29, Tiglath-pileser led off large sections of the population as prisoners to Assyria, a report confirmed by Assyrian sources. In the period following, Galilee apparently developed differently from Samaria. In 1983, during the archaeological investigations of Galilean excavation sites, Zvi Gal found no signs of an Assyrian settlement in the seventh and

---

12. Here I will not enter into the debate on the historical value of the extra-canonical Jesus traditions, but I refer the reader to J. Schröter, "Jesus im frühen Christentum: Zur neueren Diskussion über kanonisch und apokryph gewordene Jesusüberlieferungen," *VF* 51 (2006): 25-41.

13. Cf. S. Freyne, *Galilee, Jesus, and the Gospels: Literary Approaches and Historical Investigations* (Philadelphia: Fortress, 1988).

sixth centuries BCE.[14] Instead, most of these sites exhibit a 200-year gap in archaeological findings after the eighth century BCE. Unlike in Samaria and the coastal region, virtually no Assyrian pottery or imitations of it were found in Galilee, although one would certainly have expected such if Galilee had been settled by the Assyrians.[15] The archaeological findings thus seem to indicate that after the indigenous inhabitants left Galilee there was no new settlement by their conquerors.[16] Unlike Samaria, where a foreign population was settled following the deportation, Galilee was largely uninhabited until Persian times.[17] This means that Albrecht Alt's hypothesis of a continuous population,[18] from the ancient Israelite period through the Maccabean era right down to Roman times, must be abandoned.[19] Instead, we should assume that a resettlement of the region — albeit only a sparse one — took place in Persian and Hellenistic times. Even then, however, a mixed population of Jews and Gentiles was not formed. The new city-states founded by the Ptolemies and the Seleucids were not established inside Jewish territory, but on the coast or in areas that were not part of the Jewish heartland.[20]

The crucial turning-point in the history of Galilee as regards Jesus' ministry took place in the Maccabean period. As part of the gradual conquest of the Palestinian region by the Maccabees, the first Hasmonean king Aristobulus succeeded in integrating Galilee into the territory under Jewish rule at the end of the second century BCE (104/103). The result was a change in the structure of the population. The archaeological evidence unearthed during the Meiron Excavation Project in 1976 shows that Gentile settlements were abandoned, possibly to avoid enforced cir-

---

14. Z. Gal, *Lower Galilee During the Iron Age* (ASORDS 8; Winona Lake, Ind.: Eisenbrauns, 1992).

15. Gal, *Lower Galilee*, p. 82.

16. M. Chancey, *The Myth of a Gentile Galilee* (SNTSMS 118; Cambridge: Cambridge University Press, 2002), p. 33.

17. Z. Gal, "Galilee: Chalcolithic to Persian Periods," *NEAEHL* 2 (1993): 450-53: see esp. p. 451; Z. Gal, "Galilee in the Bronze and Iron Ages," *OEANE* 2 (1997): 369-70; see esp. p. 370.

18. More recently, this view is held by R. Horsley, *Galilee: History, Politics, People* (Valley Forge, Pa.: Trinity, 1995), pp. 25-61. Cf. also R. Hoppe, "Galiläa — Geschichte, Kultur Religion," in L. Schenke et al., *Jesus von Nazaret — Spuren und Konturen* (Stuttgart: Kohlhammer, 2004), pp. 42-58; see esp. pp. 45, 58.

19. Cf. J. L. Reed, *Archaeology and the Galilean Jesus: A Re-Examination of the Evidence* (Harrisburg, Pa.: Trinity, 2000), pp. 28-34.

20. Chancey, *Myth*, pp. 34-36.

cumcision.[21] Corresponding to this, a substantial increase in Jewish settlement was discovered.[22] Consequently, the Galilean population did not
consist, as has sometimes been supposed, of Gentiles forcibly circumcised during the Maccabean conquest and thus integrated into the Jewish
population, but rather of Jews originating from Judea.[23] All of this points
to Galilee having a predominantly Jewish milieu, rather than the long-
supposed significant Gentile influence. In addition, these findings suggest a close connection between Judea and Galilee, and call into question
the assumptions of Renan (and subsequent researchers) that Galilee
greatly contrasted with Judea, having had a mixed population of Jews
and Gentiles.[24]

Jesus would therefore have known a Galilee decisively impacted by
cultural and religious influences stemming from the first century BCE.[25]
These influences continued after the region was taken over by the Romans.
Pompey and Caesar took measures to reorganize the region, reducing the
territory conquered by the Maccabees. The Gentile regions — the Phoenician coastal towns and those areas merged into the Decapolis — were separated from Samaria, while the Jewish territory remained under
Maccabean administration. The idea of re-establishing Israel within the
former boundaries of the twelve tribes, despite a fillip during the
Maccabean period, fell victim to the prevailing conditions of political
power; it henceforth existed only as a vision. At the same time, however,
during the Roman division of the region, Galilee was still regarded as part
of the Jewish heartland and was dealt with accordingly.[26]

This Roman division between Jewish and non-Jewish territories is also
apparent under Herod the Great. Herod transgressed the laws by constructing pagan temples, but Josephus specifically mentions Herod did so

21. Cf. the events described by Josephus in Iturea under Aristobulus: *Ant.* 13.318-19.

22. Cf. Reed, *Archaeology,* pp. 39-43.

23. Cf. S. Freyne, "Archaeology and the Historical Jesus," in S. Freyne, *Galilee and Gospel: Collected Essays* (WUNT 125; Tübingen: Mohr Siebeck, 2000), pp. 160-82; see esp. pp.
177-79; S. Freyne, "Galilee," *OEANE* 2 (1997): 370-76; see esp. pp. 372-73.

24. Cf. S. Freyne, "The Geography of Restoration: Galilee–Jerusalem Relations in Early
Jewish and Christian Experience," *NTS* 47 (2001): 289-311.

25. Among more recent portrayals of Jesus these findings are taken into account by
Dunn, *Jesus,* pp. 293-302, and Ebner, *Jesus von Nazaret,* pp. 30-49.

26. Cf. S. Freyne, *Galilee from Alexander the Great to Hadrian, 323 BCE to 135 CE: A
Study of Second Temple Judaism* (Wilmington, Del., and Notre Dame: Michael Glazier, 1980),
pp. 57-63.

not in the Jewish territories, only in other areas and cities. And Herod's building activity did not extend to Galilee.[27]

Herod's son Antipas was also clearly aware of ruling over a Jewish territory; he ruled over Galilee, together with the geographically unconnected district of Perea on the east bank of the Jordan, during the time of Jesus' public ministry. Antipas went against convention by not having coins minted bearing his image or that of the Emperor. As late as the time of the Jewish War (66-70 or 74), coins without the Emperor's image (although admittedly bearing his name) were minted in Sepphoris, praising the peaceful nature of the town as ΕΙΡΕΝΟΠΟΛΙΣ because it had not taken part in the Jewish uprising against Rome in the year 66.[28]

Whether out of political shrewdness or genuine tolerance, Antipas thus showed consideration for the Jewish population. Gentile settlements were not forced on them, no pagan temples were built, and Hellenistic influences were kept within manageable limits and mostly restricted to Sepphoris and Tiberias. In this Antipas' policy differed from that of his half-brother Philip, whose subjects were mostly Gentiles; Philip had coins minted bearing the Emperor's image and also renamed Paneas Caesarea. In so doing he continued the policy of his father, who had had a temple built there in honor of Augustus.[29]

In Sepphoris and Tiberias Antipas embarked on a busy building program that transformed Galilee's social and economic conditions. He rebuilt Sepphoris, which had been destroyed by the Roman general Varus immediately before Antipas took office; Antipas made Sepphoris into what Josephus described as the "adornment of all Galilee" and named the city Αὐτοκρατόρις.[30] Some 20 years later he founded a new city by Lake Gennesareth, naming it Tiberias after the Roman Emperor, and moved his

27. *Ant.* 15.328-30. Cf. E. Netzer, "Herod's Building Program," *ABD* 3 (1992): 169-72; M. Vogel, *Herodes: König der Juden, Freund der Römer* (BG 5; Leipzig: EVA, 2002), pp. 180-206; Chancey, *Myth*, pp. 50-51.

28. A coin minted in Sepphoris in the year 68/69 bore the inscription ΕΠΙ ΟΥΕΣΠΑΣΙΑΝΟΥ ΕΙΡΗΝΟΠΟΛΙΣ ΝΕΡΩΝΙΑ ΣΕΠΦΩ ("Under Vespasian the town of peace Neronias Sepphoris").

29. D. C. Braund, "Philip," *ABD* 5 (1992): 310-11. One coin, for example, had a picture of Tiberius on the obverse and on the reverse a picture of the temple to Augustus that Herod had had built in Paneas.

30. *Ant.* 18.27: καὶ Ἡρῴδης Σέπφωριν τειχίσας πρόσχημα τοῦ Γαλιλαίου παντὸς ἡγόρευεν αὐτὴν Αὐτοκρατορίδα.

residence there. With the construction or reconstruction of the cities, elements of Hellenistic and Roman art appeared in Galilee. The layout of Sepphoris was designed following the Roman model to include a *cardo* and *decumanus,* a marketplace in both the upper and lower towns, and a basilica. Tiberias had the administration of a Hellenistic πόλις with a βουλή of 600 members headed by ἄρχοντες, a stadium and a marketplace. Antipas also had a palace based on the Hellenistic model built in Tiberias.[31] The population clearly considered the city a foreign body, as Antipas had to carry out forced settlements there. Such measures were necessary not least because in constructing the city he had had to remove graves, thus making it an unclean area for the Jews.[32]

At the same time it must not be overlooked that these two cities differed considerably from the Hellenistic coastal cities or the πόλεις that made up the Decapolis.[33] The size of their population (ca. 8,000-12,000) was only half as big as the cities in the surrounding regions. Coin findings indicate the influence of Hellenistic-Roman culture and religion was far smaller than in the non-Galilean cities. As mentioned, they bore neither the image of Antipas nor the Emperor, but often carried Jewish symbols such as reeds or palm branches. (This changed during the reign of Agrippa I, who had coins minted with pictures of the family of Caligula and Nike figures.)[34] Sepphoris, in particular, had a strong Jewish influence. When residential houses were excavated as part of the Joint Sepphoris Project and the Sepphoris Regional Project in the 1980s and 1990s, finds of earthenware vessels and *mikvaot* were made, but no pig bones, indicating that a substantial proportion of the city's population was Jewish.[35]

Jewish graves have been found outside Sepphoris, dating from the Second Temple era. Temples to pagan gods, on the other hand, have so far not been discovered. The theatre, too, is thought by most current experts to date from the end of the first century, perhaps even from the second century, and was thus probably not yet built under Antipas.

Some of the inscriptions found give interesting insights into the cultural milieu. A pottery shard from the second century BCE bears the He-

---

31. Cf. J. F. Strange, "Tiberias," *ABD* 6 (1992): 547-49; Josephus, *War* 2.615, 2.618, 2.641; *Life* 64, 169, 279, 284.

32. *Ant.* 18.37-38.

33. Cf. Reed, *Archaeology,* pp. 62-99.

34. Cf. Chancey, *Myth,* pp. 91-92; Reed, *Archaeology,* p. 123.

35. Cf. Chancey, *Myth,* pp. 79-80; Reed, *Archaeology,* p. 49.

brew inscription אפמלסל, possibly a transliteration of the Greek ἐπιμελετής. This may indicate that even before the Hasmonean conquest there were Jews not only living in Sepphoris but even holding administrative functions.[36] Moreover, a weight from the first century BCE bears on one side the Latin measure for half a liter given in Greek lettering, surrounded by a depiction of the Agora; on the back it carries the names Simeon and Justus. It is therefore a Roman unit of measurement in Greek writing, together with at least one Jewish name for a market supervisor.[37]

In Tiberias two lead weights were found that mention market supervisors (ἀγορανόμοι), one of whom has a Latin name (Gaius Julius) and the other a Jewish one (Iaesaias). The first probably comes from the time of Antipas and indicates either a non-Jewish market supervisor or else the adoption of a Roman name by a member of the Herodian family. If the latter, then it may refer to Antipas' brother-in-law, the later king Agrippa I. The second weight probably dates from the time of Agrippa II.[38]

The policy initiated by Antipas led to a boom in the region's economy and trade.[39] An extensive network of trade links with cities both inside and outside Galilee is indicated by finds in Upper and Lower Galilee of coins minted in Tyre, as well as finds of pottery from the Galilean villages of Kefar Hanania (on the border between Upper and Lower Galilee) and Shikhin (near Sepphoris) in various parts of Galilee, in Golan, in Akko, and in Caesarea Philippi.[40] Among other Galilean exports, some of the most important were fish from Lake Gennesareth and olive oil; imports included parchment, paper, jewelry and marble. Although Galilee differed from the

36. Cf. E. M. Meyers, "Sepphoris on the Eve of the Great Revolt (67-68 CE): Archaeology and Josephus," in E. M. Meyers, ed., *Galilee Through the Centuries* (Winona Lake, Ind.: Eisenbrauns, 1999), pp. 109-22; see esp. pp. 112-13; M. Chancey, "The Cultural Milieu of Ancient Sepphoris," *NTS* 47 (2001): 127-45; see esp. p. 129. As Meyers shows, on the basis of references in Josephus, ἐπιμελετής can denote a higher function than "market supervisor" and may have been used here as an equivalent of *procurator* or στρατηγός.

37. Cf. Reed, *Archaeology*, pp. 121-22; Chancey, *Myth*, pp. 77-78.

38. J. D. Crossan and J. L. Reed, *Jesus ausgraben: Zwischen den Steinen — hinter den Texten* (Düsseldorf: Patmos, 2003), p. 85; Chancey, *Myth*, pp. 90-91.

39. Cf. H. W. Hoehner, *Herod Antipas* (SNTSMS 17; Cambridge: Cambridge University Press, 1972), pp. 65-79; D. E. Edwards, "The Socio-Economic and Cultural Ethos of the Lower Galilee in the First Century: Implications for the Nascent Jesus Movement," in L. I. Levine, ed., *The Galilee in Late Antiquity* (New York and Jerusalem: The Jewish Theological Seminary of America, 1992), pp. 53-73; see esp. p. 63.

40. Cf. S. Freyne, "Archaeology and the Historical Jesus," pp. 167-70.

surrounding territories because of its Jewish character, it was hardly an isolated region. On the contrary, Galilee was integrated into a network of trade links facilitated by a well-constructed road system. At Ptolemais a road branched off eastwards from the *Via maris,* one of the main Roman communication arteries, and connected Alexandria with the Phoenician coast and Syria. This eastward branch road divided north of Sepphoris into two further roads leading south and east, which then joined up again near Scythopolis. The road continued further to Gerasa, via Pella in the region east of the Jordan. This meant that both Sepphoris and Tiberias were integrated into the inter-regional road system. Two further branch roads off the *Via maris,* running from west to east and linking the *Via maris* with the Royal Road in the east, passed by Galilee to the south and north. While the purpose of these main roads was to facilitate international trade and transport — and not least to enable the Roman troops to be moved quickly — this meant the Galilean villages were linked by roads enabling easier trade links between them.

The Jesus movement thus originated in a Jewish area that had flourishing exchanges with the surrounding non-Jewish regions. The Gospel descriptions of Jesus meeting Gentiles only outside Galilee, in the Syrian-Phoenician coastal region or in the Decapolis, correspond to this profile of the region ascertained from literary and archaeological sources. The question of why Jesus visited these areas, while in striking contrast the closer Galilean cities of Sepphoris and Tiberias are never mentioned in the Gospels, is something we will return to later.

Not all sections of the population profited equally from the economic boom. The building activity in Sepphoris and Tiberias led to a developing gap between these cities and the rural areas. The cities controlled the region and also purchased the agricultural goods produced by the surrounding villages. Major urban building projects also offered opportunities for village craftsmen to work — such as, hypothetically, the construction craftsman Joseph from Nazareth. On the one hand, therefore, the relationship between city and countryside can be described as symbiotic: the cities gave rise to a prosperous economic area, created jobs and served as markets for agricultural produce. On the other hand, conditions of forced labor and contractual debt were created, and the gap between the well-to-do and the dependent increased.[41] The contrast between poor and rich in the

41. Cf. Reed, *Archaeology,* pp. 77-89; Freyne, "Jesus and the Urban Culture of Galilee," in Freyne, *Galilee and Gospel,* pp. 183-207; see esp. 190-96.

Jesus tradition should be seen against this background: the poor, the hungry, and those who weep are called blessed; we hear of the rich in soft garments living in palaces; we hear of contractual debt and of laborers hired by the day. There can be no doubt that this reflects the real situation of life in Galilee under Antipas.

We would fail to grasp the full extent of Jesus' ministry, however, if we considered the social tensions and economic discrimination as the central features underlying his message.[42] Not only do the observations on the political and economic situation oppose such an analysis, the Jesus tradition itself points in another direction. In Mark 10:28-31 the consequences of following Jesus are described as abandoning not only family, but also house and land. The house in Capernaum of Peter and his family was apparently large enough to accommodate the great crowds of people that gathered when Jesus was there. James and John, the sons of Zebedee, came from a family which had a business owning several boats and hiring laborers (Mark 1:19-20). The boat dating from the first century CE — discovered in Lake Gennesareth in 1986 and now exhibited in the Ginnosar kibbutz — in view of its considerable size, may also indicate that fishing in the lake was a productive line of business.[43]

Galilean fishermen, the closest followers of Jesus, were certainly not part of the well-to-do sector of the population, but neither did they belong to the lower end of the social spectrum.[44] The Jesus movement was no movement of the rural poor, and its program was no social "revolution from below." In the Gospels it is never Antipas or the Romans who are mentioned as the opponents of the kingdom of God, but Satan and the demons.

Finally we should look at the political situation under Antipas. The period of his rule in Galilee seems to have been marked by political stability

42. Cf. also the fundamental critique of this theory by K.-H. Ostmeyer, "Armenhaus und Räuberhöhle? Galiläa zur Zeit Jesu," *ZNW* 96 (2005): 147-70.

43. Cf. R. Riesner, "Das Boot vom See Gennesaret," *BK* 41 (1986): 135-38; R. Riesner, "Neues vom See Gennesaret," *BK* 42 (1987): 171-73; S. Wachsmann, "Galilee Boat," *OEANE* 2 (1997): 377-79; O. Cohen, ". . . ein Schiff wird kommen. . . . Die Bergung und Restaurierung eines 2000 Jahre alten Bootes am See Gennesaret," in G. Fassbeck et al., *Leben am See Gennesaret: Kulturgeschichtliche Entdeckungen in einer biblischen Region* (Mainz am Rhein: Zabern, 2003), pp. 147-52. It is also possible, however, that the boat was rebuilt during the Jewish-Roman war, only then acquiring its size. This possibility is mentioned on the descriptive panels in the exhibition hall.

44. Freyne, *Jesus, a Jewish Galilean*, p. 52.

and economic upturn. This can be seen from the unusually long period of 43 years during which Antipas ruled without Rome seeing any reason for intervening — unlike his brother Archelaus, who was removed from office after only ten years because of complaints about his cruelty. There is no evidence of insurrections in Galilee during the time of Antipas. It is true that Josephus presents the impression of an escalating situation, starting from the Galilean unrest connected with the "Robber War" after Herod the Great's death, and continuing through the opposition of Judas the Galilean in Judea against Quirinus' census and the uprising by the two sons of Judas, Simon and James, in 44 CE, up to the Jewish-Roman war in the years 66-70 CE. However, this construction is clearly influenced by the attempt to show all the Jewish resistance struggles against Roman rule in a negative light. When we look at Galilee under Antipas, on the other hand, the uprising by Judas in Sepphoris after the death of Herod the Great and the city's subsequent destruction are the last uprising and the last Roman intervention for a long time. The other examples of unrest either occurred in Judea and Samaria, and were thus aimed directly against the Roman prefecture, or else happened after the time of Antipas and Jesus. In this connection it should be noted that until ca. 120 Rome apparently did not station any troops in Galilee.[45] Galilee was thus not occupied by the Romans in the time of Jesus, but was a client kingdom under Roman supervision. It was therefore not a region offering fertile ground for a political or social revolution.[46]

The findings can be summarized as follows: While the Maccabean conquest under Aristobulus I was the decisive historical turning-point for the subsequent history of Galilee, it was under Antipas that the region acquired the character forming the background to Jesus' ministry. This period should be distinguished from the preceding one due to the developments after the death of Herod the Great, and from the following one because of the brief phase of the reign of Agrippa I and the subsequent direct subordination to Roman rule. Its essential characteristics are the development of a distinctive Jewish identity (even including a Galilean dialect),[47] the consequent orientation towards Jerusalem, the contrast

45. E. P. Sanders, "Jesus' Galilee," in I. Dunderberg, C. Tuckett, and K. Syreeni, eds., *Fair Play: Diversity and Conflicts in Early Christianity. Essays in Honour of Heikki Räisänen* (Leiden: Brill, 2002), pp. 3-41; see esp. pp. 9-13.

46. Cf. U. Rappaport, "How Anti-Roman Was the Galilee?," in Levine, *Galilee*, pp. 95-102.

47. Cf. Matt 26:73.

between the cities and the Galilean villages resulting from the urban construction, and the integration of Galilee into the economic and trading networks of the surrounding regions.

Jesus in Galilee

In what ways do this picture of Galilee we have sketched relate to the ministry of Jesus? One point immediately striking us is that the Gospels provide little specific information about the setting in which Jesus lived. There are no descriptions of the geographical situation of Galilee or the district round Lake Gennesareth comparable to what can be found in Josephus.[48] Similarly, political circumstances such as the rule of Antipas or the relations to the neighboring regions are only referred to implicitly and are never the subject of any discussion. Even with the description of the death of John the Baptist, probably the most radical intervention by Antipas from the viewpoint of early Christianity, it is the religious motive that takes center stage: John, as an upright and holy man, criticizes the levirate of Antipas and thus exposes the intrigue of Herodias (Mark 6:17-29). By contrast, there is no reference (as in Josephus) to the political motive for removing John, his influence with the people.[49] Indeed, Antipas appears only in passing, as when he hears about the activities of Jesus (Mark 6:14) or when Jesus is warned against him (Luke 13:31). But he is not presented as an opponent with whom Jesus should take issue. This way of portraying Antipas can hardly be attributed to the Gospel authors' ignorance of the real circumstances. It more likely displays a facet of Jesus' ministry that we will return to shortly.

In spite of this economy of description, the Gospels still enable us to recognize the geographical and cultural context in which Jesus' ministry took place, even if it is described from a later viewpoint. This includes the mention of Galilean place names such as Capernaum, Chorazin, Bethsaida, Nazareth, Cana and Nain, together with Lake Gennesareth, which is called a "Sea" (θάλασσα) in Mark, Matthew and John, and also synagogues throughout Galilee, especially in Capernaum and Nazareth.[50]

---

48. *War* 3.35-38, 506-21.

49. *Ant.* 18.116-19.

50. Here we will not go into the question of whether these mentions of synagogues refer to actual buildings or to assemblies of the Jews. (The only clear-cut case of the former is in

As mentioned, a characteristic feature in this connection is the lack of any reference to Sepphoris or Tiberias. The more aware we become of these cities' importance for Galilee under Antipas, the more eloquent becomes the fact that they are completely ignored in the Gospels. Many conjectures have posited reasons for this. The most plausible explanation appears to be that Jesus saw the addressees of his message as being the villages of Galilee rather than the cities, in which rich people and palaces were to be found. Jesus' cultural milieu seems to have been that of the villages of Galilee, not that of the cities. The cultural divide, which is also mentioned by Josephus, may well have played a role here too. The only city playing a major role is Jerusalem. This expresses an important characteristic of Jesus' ministry: rather than a matter of social or political conflict, Jesus' ministry is directed towards Jerusalem as the *religious* center of Israel.

The content of Jesus' message and the character of the controversies arising out of it are in keeping with the setting of the villages and synagogues of Galilee. The mention of Pharisees and Sadducees probably does indicate the groups with which Jesus actually came into conflict.[51] The controversies over Jewish purity laws and the observance of the Sabbath describe a milieu shaped by Jewish life in the Galilean villages and thus certainly differ from the time of the Gospels' composition, when the Jesus movement had already expanded into an urban context.

Further details help flesh out the environment in which Jesus lived. The names and professions of his followers are given. When the villages belonging to Caesarea Philippi are mentioned in Mark 8:27 (κῶμαι Καισαρείας τῆς Φιλίππου), this presupposes the connection between the city and its catchment area. Incidentally, here too Jesus does not go into the city itself, but only into the surrounding villages. The disciples being sent into towns (πόλεις) to preach (QLk 10:10), and the mentions of marketplaces (ἀγοραί: QLk 7:32; 11:43), streets (πλατεῖαι: Matt 6:5; Luke 10:10; 13:26; 14:21), bank

---

Luke 7:5, where the *construction* of a synagogue is mentioned.) It is well known that there is no archaeological evidence of Galilean synagogues in the period before 70 CE. Only in Gamla, in the area ruled over by Philip, and in Judea, have buildings, or, with the Theodotos inscription, epigraphic evidence for synagogues before 70 CE been found. Cf. C. Claussen, *Versammlung, Gemeinde, Synagoge: Das hellenistisch-jüdische Umfeld der frühchristlichen Gemeinden* (SUNT 27; Göttingen: Vandenhoeck & Ruprecht, 2002).

51. Although Matthew, in naming the two groups together and having the Sadducees appear in Galilee, shows that the specific characteristics of the two groups are no longer something he has first-hand knowledge of.

transactions and contractual debts (QLk 19:23; Matt 6:12; 18:23-34; Luke 16:3-7), merchants (Matt 13:45), and courts and prisons (QLk 12:57-59; Matt 18:30) all indicate knowledge of the social environment.

Finally, we can discern in the Gospels an awareness of ethnic and political circumstances. For instance, Jesus expands his ministry into the Decapolis and the coastal region without any complications; this is quite plausible for the 20s of the first century, but scarcely conceivable during the period when the Gospels were written, around or after the time of the Jewish-Roman war in 66-70.[52] In this area, Jesus meets a Gentile (the Syro-Phoenician woman), and encounters a herd of swine in the Decapolis, demonstrating the difference between the Jewish and Gentile regions. If we further consider that Greek-speaking Jews also lived outside the Jewish areas — for example in Scythopolis, which was part of the Decapolis — then the supposition that Jesus carried out his ministry in these regions becomes increasingly plausible.[53]

The Gospels thus place the ministry of Jesus in a particular social and political milieu and take into account the circumstances to have been expected at that time. At the same time it is clear that the writers integrated this atmosphere into their own narrative perspective, drawn up from hindsight. A crucial modification here is the depiction of Jesus' ministry as the beginning of the mission to the Gentiles. For Mark, Jesus' journeys in the Decapolis and the coastal regions reflect a turning towards the Gentiles; Matthew makes use of a quotation from Isaiah in order to represent even Jesus' coming to Galilee as a turning towards the Gentiles;[54] in Luke the initial sermon in Nazareth signifies the importance of Jesus' message as pointing beyond Galilee and Judea towards the Gentiles. In spite of modifications like this, the "historicizing tendency"[55] of the Gospels remains an important feature of their narratives. In preserving the memory of the places, people, and social and religious background connected with Jesus' ministry, they represent it as being set in a particular time and place. It is not detached from these specifics and offered as a timeless teaching, as in the *Gospel of Thomas*. This geographical and cultural milieu outlined by

---

52. Cf. S. Freyne, "Jesus and the Urban Culture," p. 187.

53. In a cemetery north of Scythopolis, 30 Jewish ossuaries with Greek inscriptions have been found. Four bilingual (Greek and Aramaic) ossuary inscriptions from Scythopolis have also been found near Jerusalem. Cf. D. Edwards, "Ethos," p. 70.

54. Isa 9:1-2 in Matt 4:15-16.

55. Cf. Freyne, *Jesus*, p. 5.

the Gospels is an important basis for grasping the significance of Jesus' ministry.

When Jesus comes to Galilee after his time in the desert with John the Baptist, it is not simply a return home.[56] As with John, so too with Jesus: proclamation and location are connected. John made a conscious choice of the desert for his sphere of activity. The desert is a place of withdrawal and the place of God's encounter with Israel, the place where God had once protected Israel and where, according to prophecies, God wants to again meet with them to renew their covenantal relationship. The desert thus points towards the fundamental restoration of Israel's relationship towards God that John is calling for.

Jesus' transition from being a disciple of John in the desert to proclaiming the rule of God in and around Galilee is thus an important facet of the content of his ministry. This is however not simply in contrast to John. When some descriptions, including very recent ones, imply a fundamental re-orientation in Jesus' separation from John, they are creating an impression that is incorrect. In spite of its own particular emphasis, Jesus' ministry by no means departs from the conceptual framework it shares with that of John. This is characterized by the conviction that God's judgment is imminent; simply belonging to Israel is not sufficient to pass muster before it. In this respect John and Jesus have their place in a broader context of Jewish renewal movements including, each in their own way, the Qumran Community, the Pharisees, and the prophetic or messianic figures mentioned by Josephus. The specific characteristic of the options presented by John and Jesus lies in this conviction of the imminence of God's judgment over Israel. Faced with this, John and Jesus each offer an exclusive possibility of avoiding this judgment: John announces the repentance and confession of sins symbolically sealed by the immersion in the Jordan, and Jesus offers the involvement in the establishment of the rule of God bound up with his mission. The ministry of Jesus thus takes place in close connection with that of the Baptist. They differ not, as some think, through one proclaiming judgment and the other salvation,[57] but through differing concepts of the restoration of Israel.

56. Cf. S. Freyne, *Jesus, a Jewish Galilean*, pp. 40-44.
57. Cf. M. Wolter, "'Gericht' und 'Heil' bei Jesus von Nazareth und Johannes dem Täufer," in J. Schröter and R. Brucker, eds., *Der historische Jesus: Tendenzen und Perspektiven der gegenwärtigen Forschung* (BZNW 114; Berlin and New York: de Gruyter, 2002), pp. 355-92.

Jesus' coming to Galilee must be seen in this context. It was no accident that he chose this region for his public ministry. Regardless of what historical value should be attached to the story of his rejection in Nazareth, it is clear that Jesus' hometown no longer plays a central role in his ministry. Rather than simply returning to Nazareth, Jesus comes into Galilee as a whole (Mark 1:14), and thus directs his message of the imminent kingdom of God to the whole of the region. Against this background the idea of a "centre of Jesus' ministry" in Capernaum needs to be qualified. It is true that we often find Capernaum mentioned in the Gospels as the place where Jesus was staying.[58] However, his ministry is characterized by an itinerant existence without any fixed abode. The same applies to Matthew's report of a move by Jesus: according to 4:13 Jesus leaves Nazareth in order to live in Capernaum, which in 9:1 is even described as "his town." Matthew explains this in terms of the history of salvation: Jesus is said to have settled in Capernaum so as to fulfill the words of the scripture in Isaiah 9:1-2, whereby the land of Zebulun and the land of Naphtali would see a great light (Matt 4:12-16). Matthew presents things as though Jesus, by changing places like this, was coming into the territory of the Israelite tribes of Zebulun and Naphtali and thus into the "Galilee of the Gentiles." In fact, however, Nazareth lay in the territory of Zebulun, Capernaum in that of Naphtali, and of course both of them in Galilee. Matthew's scriptural attempt to bolster the idea of Jesus coming to the Gentiles as well as to the Jews cannot therefore be evaluated as central to the real circumstances of Jesus' ministry. This also applies analogically to the programmatic episode in Luke 4:16-30, in which Nazareth symbolizes Jerusalem and the whole of Israel. On the contrary, when we consider that words of judgment are addressed not only to Capernaum but also to Chorazin and Bethsaida, and that according to John's Gospel Jesus' public ministry began in Cana, then Capernaum's supposed special role must be qualified still further. Perhaps this role is due primarily to certain episodes becoming attached to the place where Peter lived, episodes that took on an important position in the synoptic tradition.

Other passages have more to tell us about the actual historical situa-

---

58. It is certainly possible that on the occasions when he was in Capernaum he stayed in Peter's house, or probably more accurately, the house of Peter's wife's family. Whether the dwelling-space known as "Peter's house" that has been discovered during excavations was already used for gatherings of the Christian community in the first century remains uncertain, however.

tion. For example, the phrase in QLk 9:58, "The foxes have holes, the birds of the air have nests, but the Son of Man has nowhere to lay his head," probably part of the oldest body of the Jesus tradition, describes Jesus as someone with no home, something even animals have. This sheds light on the lifestyle associated with Jesus' message: his ministry is not tied to one place, but is characterized by the establishment of the rule of God in various settings. The phrase is of course not a proverb formulating a general insight, whereby "Son of Man" might be understood as "human beings in general." Against such an interpretation is the fact that this saying's addressees did indeed have homes. Rather, the saying makes a statement about Jesus: it is *he,* as a result of his specific existence as the one in whose ministry the rule of God becomes a reality, who has no fixed home. "The Son of Man" is thus here an expression that Jesus uses to characterize his ministry and the way he sees himself.[59]

It is also necessary to bear in mind the pragmatic aspect of the saying. In its context in Matthew and Luke it deals with the conditions associated with following Jesus. It thus makes clear that belonging to the close circle surrounding Jesus involves giving up a fixed abode. This means that the message of the rule of God proclaimed by Jesus, in contrast to that of John or the Qumran Community, is not connected with a particular place — a fact influencing the shape taken by the community that Jesus founded.

Jesus' detachment from any particular place reinforces the impression he directed his ministry to the whole of the regions where he proclaimed his message. As early as Mark 1:39 "the whole of Galilee" is described as the scene of his ministry. In Mark 3:7-8 the entire territory of the twelve tribes of Israel comes into view: the people who came to hear Jesus arrive from Galilee and Judea, Jerusalem, Idumea, and the regions beyond the Jordan and around Tyre and Sidon. This indicates that the scope of Jesus' mission embraced the whole of Israel, a truth reinforced by the institution of the symbolic group of twelve apostles and the explicit instruction sending his disciples to Israel found in Matthew and Luke. The ministry in Galilee and the neighboring territories is part of this broader context, best explained in light of Israel's hope for the re-establishment of the people and the re-attainment of the Promised Land. But Jesus does not take up the militant option of the Maccabees or the idea of the anointed one from the *Psalms of*

---

59. Cf. H. Moxnes, *Putting Jesus in His Place: A Radical Vision of Household and Kingdom* (Louisville: Westminster John Knox, 2003), pp. 49-51.

Solomon. His concept of the rule of God is characterized by God's work of salvation in the land promised to Israel, a work that is bound up with his own ministry.

It is therefore no coincidence that, as the early testimonies unanimously show, Jesus only came into indirect contact with Antipas and his policies. Jesus' ministry had its origins in John the Baptist and his call to repentance and obedience to God's will. If Jesus' message took on concrete shape in the social, political, and religious conditions in and around Galilee, then this was because Galilee was part of the territory making up Israel as a whole. Antipas, as a ruler dependent on Rome, naturally adopted an attitude towards Galilee contrary to the claim Jesus made regarding this region. Jesus did not oppose him, however, with a socio-political or economic program, but with a different value system.[60] Consequently, Jesus saw his actual rivals as the Pharisees, who were also concerned with putting God's law into practice in everyday life. Antipas and the πρῶτοι τῆς Γαλιλαίας (Mark 6:21) were only incidental figures in this regard. When told about Antipas' intention to kill him, Jesus countered with a reference to the real confrontations of his ministry: "I drive out demons and heal people and my journey will reach its end in Jerusalem" (Luke 13:32). The hostile rule against which Jesus set the rule of God was the rule of Satan, not that of an unimportant "fox."[61] His ministry in Galilee (and its extensions to the neighboring territories and even Jerusalem) was therefore a symbolic activity, complementing the establishment of the group of twelve apostles, whereby he marked out the territory in which the rule of God would take shape. That this mission's political implications could be understood differently is perhaps most explicit in the use of the expression "the anointed one," conceivably expressing hope for a social and political liberation as precondition to the establishment of the rule of God. But the really provocative aspect of Jesus' ministry lies in the claim whereby he saw his own activity as the establishment of the rule of God. It is thus only against this background that the significance of his coming to Galilee at the beginning of his independent public ministry starts to become apparent.

60. S. Freyne, "Herodian Economics in Galilee," in S. Freyne, *Galilee and Gospel,* pp. 86-113.

61. The metaphor of the fox can signify a person's cunning (usually in the negative sense of slyness), but also one's obsequiousness and lack of importance. In this passage it is more likely the latter meaning: Jesus considers Antipas to be an unimportant figure, who cannot seriously stand in the way of his healings and driving out of demons.

From Old to New:
Paradigm Shifts concerning Judaism,
the Gospel of John, Jesus, and the
Advent of "Christianity"

James H. Charlesworth

The twenty-first century begins with a worldwide recognition of massive paradigm shifts. Unfortunately, too many students and scholars tend to use commentaries and scholarly monographs without noting their date of publication. In the process, their own work and insight suffer from failing to perceive that more advances have been achieved in biblical research over the past twenty-five years than in the preceding 250 years. One cannot use scholarly works published from the nineteenth century to the present assuming naively that scholars are examining the same texts with similar methodology, sophistication, and perception.

At least five significant factors distinguish recent work from previous publications. First, we are much more sensitive to the distortions caused by the intrusion of inappropriate philosophy. In the nineteenth century, D. F. Strauss shaped his studies by following Hegelianism. In the twentieth century, R. Bultmann, his School, and even the "New Quest for the Historical Jesus" were marred by viewing ancient texts through the presuppositions of Existentialism. These two examples are focused and limited to Germany. What we learn from these masters is that we must be aware of our presuppositions and methodologies and be more accurate historians of Judaism and cultures influential in shaping ancient Palestinian thought and life.

Second, we have observed that prejudices blind us to what we seek to see. Consider, for instance, how Confessionalism and Anti-Semitism (along with supersessionism) have distorted the re-creations of first-century phenomena, and especially the presentation of the historical Jesus. Too many interpreters are unperceptive of how they have been influenced, for example, by Kant and Spinoza, both of whom imagined Second Temple Judaism as corrupt.

We bring numerous unexamined assumptions to the text. Too many readers miss the fact that, according to Mark 9:1, Jesus, at least at times, thought the eschaton and the dynamic eruption of God's Rule (the Kingdom of God) would occur in his own lifetime or, at least, the lifetime of those who heard him. Likewise, a perception of the meaning of Genesis 3 and John 3 is often distorted, because of a hatred of snakes and a refusal to explore the meaning of ophidian symbology. The first blindness has been pointed out by G. Theissen and D. Winter in their *Quest for the Plausible Jesus.*[1] The second myopia is demonstrated in my *The Good & Evil Serpent.*[2]

Third, slowly we have grown to realize the tendencies *(Tendenzen)* and anachronisms of what were once our main literary sources: the intracanonical gospels, as well as Philo, Josephus, and early rabbinic and targumic texts. Those who labored on re-creating Second Temple Judaism and Jesus' environment before 1945 were consigned to work on documents and books that were biased and provided a *post facto* mirror of pre-70 Judaism.

Fourth, today, we have hundreds of ancient Jewish documents that are not edited by Christian scribes; and many of them were unknown before the forties. Indeed, recent research has been enriched by the exploration and comprehension of a flood of new and often previously ignored sources: the 65 Old Testament Pseudepigrapha, the Old Testament Apocrypha, the Jewish magical papyri, the Nag Hammadi Codices, and the more than 950 Qumran Scrolls.

Fifth, the explosion of archaeological data that is Jewish and clearly pre-70 has changed the landscape of historical Jesus studies. Henceforth, archaeology will be not only significant but fundamental in re-creating both the cultural and sociological setting of Jesus and also his own life and message.

These few comments indicate that works published after 1980 are often paradigmatically different from those issued in the preceding 1900 years. Too many scholars mislead too many students by using scholarly

---

1. Gerd Theissen and Dagmar Winter, *The Quest for the Plausible Jesus: The Question of Criteria* (trans. M. E. Boring; Louisville: Westminster John Knox, 2002).

2. James H. Charlesworth, *The Good & Evil Serpent* (ABRL; New York: Doubleday, in press).

works published over the past century, as if the early ones are not seriously dated by old perceptions and the paucity of sources. Works published before 1980, the emergence of Jesus Research, must not be confused with more recent informed research; a synchronic malaise obscures not only the development of research but the re-creation of first-century Palestine.

To demonstrate the fundamental nature of this transformation in Jesus Research, we shall examine several specific paradigm shifts in selected areas. It should now be clear that a new and more informed approach to historical questions regarding Jesus from Nazareth is operative in many recent publications.

Judaism

Old Paradigm

For centuries scholars assumed that Second Temple Judaism was orthodox, monolithic, cut off from other cultures (especially the Greeks and Romans), and defined by four sects: Pharisees, Sadducees, Essenes, and Zealots.

New Paradigm

Now scholars are more critical of inherited assumptions. It is certain that Josephus was wrong to divide Jewish thought into four sects. Most likely, the most important and influential Jewish groups were the conservative Sadducees, the more liberal and politically influential Pharisees,[3] the diverse and learned Essenes, and the pugnacious Zealots, who may have appeared only at the beginning of the First Revolt (66-70/74). But one can now perceive over twenty groups, subgroups, and sects. Obviously, the Samaritans were also Jews, with a Pentateuch almost identical to that preserved in the Tanak. One must also include the Baptist groups, the Enoch groups, and many others, including the Palestinian Jesus Movement.

Some scholars have tended to think about Jewish thought before 70 CE

---

3. The Pharisees were astoundingly latitudinarious with Hillel, usually disagreeing with Shammai.

as being chaotic; but chaos broke out in 66 CE. Likewise some scholars see disunity and talk about "Judaisms." Other scholars are still too influenced by post-second-century Rabbinic texts and imagine a unified Judaism or "Covenantal Nomism." Such a term is not found in pre-70 Jewish texts, and one might wonder if it is a modern construct that miscasts the world of Second Temple Judaism. Moreover, "covenant" and "Nomism" (which is not clear to me and may represent Torah) were like the Temple cult, often signaling not only unity but also disunity among pre-70 Jews. Most likely, there was a powerful and influential ruling party within Jerusalem; but it was mixed, composed of Pharisees, Sadducees, and most likely other types of Jews (the Boethusians were intermittently powerful). The Shema and the Psalter, in my opinion, helped to check the centripetal forces that eventually produced the ill-conceived Revolt; after all, the Jews revolted against the Roman Imperium without an army and in the midst of what might be labeled a civil war.

This picture of Second Temple Judaism derives from studying sources unknown or unexamined by our grandparents. They examined Philo, the New Testament, Josephus, and especially Rabbinics. These are now exposed as sources needing to be used with caution in light of their *Tendenzen* to distort historical and social realities. The primary sources are clearly pre-70 Jewish documents only recently unearthed, and therefore unedited by later Christian scribes. These documents are the Qumran Scrolls; and the corpus is now voluminous. If 66 books define the Christian Bible, more than 900 documents are now known to be preserved, usually in fragmentary form, within the Qumran corpus. Secondly, in light of these clearly Jewish works, we can examine with new sensitivity the 65 documents in the Old Testament Pseudepigrapha. The Septuagint is now perceived to preserve ancient text types, as well as translation additions and revisions. Studying all of these sources helps place pieces together in the massive attempt to re-create a historical jigsaw puzzle.

The Gospel of John

Old Paradigm

For hundreds of years, experts approached the Gospel According to John with the presupposition that this gospel was a supplement to the Synoptics

(Matt, Mark, Luke), and since it was not a Jewish composition it should be studied in light of non-Jewish cultures and religion. Before 216, when he died, Clement of Alexandria, according to Eusebius (*Hist. Eccl.* 6.14.7), claimed that "John, perceiving that the external facts had been explained in the (Synoptic) Gospels, . . . being carried along by God in the Spirit . . . composed a spiritual gospel." St. Augustine found the Fourth Gospel attractive; the Evangelist portrayed Jesus weeping (John 11:35), suggesting to Augustine the truth "the Word assumed soul and flesh" (*Tract. Ev. Jo.* 49.18-19). While Luther highlighted the Fourth Gospel, because of the elevated discourses, and while Schleiermacher preferred this gospel over the Synoptics, because it best revealed Jesus' utter dependence on God, the tide was turning against the Fourth Gospel.

In 1835[4] and the following years, in his influential tomes on Jesus' life, D. F. Strauss not only denied the apostolic authorship of the Fourth Gospel, but set up a false paradigm still plaguing some publications; that is, Strauss postulated an orthodox Judaism in Jesus' time and clearly separated "Christianity" from Judaism. In 1853, Strauss's teacher, F. C. Baur, interpreted the Christology of John in a way requiring a "complete disengagement" from any forms of Judaism.[5] Subsequently, in 1913 in *Kyrios Christos*,[6] W. Bousset led the way in seeking the origin and understanding of the Fourth Gospel within Greek and Roman religions. The stage had been set for R. Bultmann to claim, in numerous influential publications, the existence of a non-Jewish source, the *Offenbarungsreden (Revelatory Source)* which represented Oriental Gnosticism and which definitively shaped the Christology of the Fourth Gospel.[7] In fact, Bultmann thought the Gnostic source behind the Fourth Gospel was anti-Jewish.

4. David Friedrich Strauss, *Das Leben Jesu* (Tübingen: C. F. Osiander, 1835-6); ET: *The Life of Jesus Critically Examined* (trans. M. Evans; New York: Calvin Blanchard, 1860).

5. Ferdinand Christian Baur, *Das Christenthum und die christliche Kirche der drei ersten Jahrhunderte* (Tübingen: L. F. Fues, 1853); ET: *The Church History of the First Three Centuries* (2 vols.; trans. Allan Menzies; London: Williams and Norgate, 1878-79 [3rd ed.]), pp. 153-83.

6. Wilhelm Bousset, *Kyrios Christos: Geschichte des Christusglaubens von den Anfängen des Christentums bis Irenaeus* (Göttingen: Vandenhoeck & Ruprecht, 1913); ET: *Kyrios Christos: A History of the Belief in Christ from the Beginnings of Christianity to Irenaeus* (trans. John E. Steely; Nashville: Abingdon, 1970).

7. This claim first appeared in Bultmann's *Das Evangelium des Johannes* (Göttingen: Vandenhoeck & Ruprecht, 1941); ET: *The Gospel of John: A Commentary* (ed. Rupert W. N. Hoare and John K. Riches; trans. George R. Beasley-Murray; Philadelphia: Westminster, 1971).

Bultmann's student, E. Käsemann, who characteristically distinguished himself from his teacher, continued the overwhelming tendency of contextualizing the Fourth Gospel in non-Jewish sources and settings. In his 1966 work *Jesu letzer Wille nach Johannes 17,* Käsemann chose a historical approach to the Fourth Gospel, but the context was perceived to be a Christian intra-church conflict.[8]

New Paradigm

Against this contextualizing of the Fourth Gospel in anything but a Jewish setting, a new position is rapidly becoming a near consensus. Scholars around the world are now perceiving that John is a very Jewish work. They claim that this gospel should be studied within Judaism.[9]

To this new paradigm, I now choose to emphasize one point: The Fourth Evangelist is exceptional among the four evangelists for his knowledge of pre-70 Jewish religious customs and especially of the topography and architecture of Jerusalem. Such elements in his narrative pop up intermittently without relevance for the narrative or rhetoric of persuasion.

In the past these details were either overlooked or explained away as theological reflections that were not grounded in historical observation. Space precludes exhaustive treatment; thus, I have chosen to focus only on Jerusalem and limit my comments to five seemingly irrelevant architectural or topographical details. These cumulatively disclose that the Fourth Evangelist is not ignorant of Jerusalem, as many commentators have assumed; he is amazingly cognizant of Jerusalem in 30 CE which ceased to exist after the city's destruction in September of 70 CE.

The first example of the Fourth Evangelist's knowledge of Jerusalem concerns the Pool of Bethzatha (or Bethesda) with its "five porticoes" (John 5:2). Interpreters focused only on Johannine theology have pointed out that Josephus and others acquainted with Jerusalem never mention such a major pool. These thinkers, who often have their eyes focused on dogmatics, report that in antiquity no architect constructed a pentagon

---

8. Ernst Käsemann, *Jesu letzer Wille nach Johannes 17* (Tübingen: Mohr Siebeck, 1966); ET: *The Testament of Jesus: A Study of the Gospel of John in the Light of Chapter 17* (trans. Gerhard Krodel; Philadelphia: Fortress, 1968).

9. See the chapter in this collection by C. Claussen.

which could have five porticoes; hence, they conclude that John could not have known Jerusalem. What then is the meaning of John 5:1-9? It must mean that the five porticoes in which the sick man wished to be healed denote the Pentateuch. Jesus thus provides what was lacking. The man is healed, takes up "his pallet and walked."

This is problematic and reveals a lack of attention to Johannine theology. There is no tension between Moses and Jesus in this gospel. The history of salvation is "grace upon grace"; the Fourth Evangelist emphasizes that the Law was "given through Moses" and "grace and truth came through Jesus Christ" (1:16-17). While some theologians imperceptively imagine an adversative connective between the protasis and apodosis, the two parts of the sentence in 1:17 are an example of asyndetic contiguity, whereby the connection is immediate and not separated by an otiose conjunctive: "The Law through Moses was given; grace and truth through Jesus Christ came." As the appositional genitive denotes identity — as in *Bath Zion* denoting "Daughter Zion" — so asyndetic contiguity (the lack of any connective) usually denotes similarity; thus, God has revealed through Moses God's will (the Torah) and through Jesus God's grace and truth. The Fourth Evangelist presents no antithesis between Moses (or the Pentateuch) and Jesus (or the Good News about the incarnation of God's Son). Hence, the five porticoes cannot be a metaphorical reference to the Pentateuch.

In fact, the pool of Bethzatha does exist, although only the Fourth Evangelist mentions it. Archaeologists have unearthed this pool. It is situated precisely where the Evangelist states: north of the Temple Mount and inside the Sheep Gate (5:2). It has five porticoes, because there are two pools, arranged from the north to south so as to catch the rain water that runs from the hills to the northwest. Porticoes are on the north, east, south, and west . . . and also through the area that separates the two pools. These two pools even seem to be noted in the *Copper Scroll* found in Qumran Cave III. We begin to perceive that saluting the Fourth Evangelist as a brilliant theologian does not mean he is a misinformed historian.

The second example of the Fourth Evangelist's exceptional knowledge of Jerusalem concerns the Pool of Siloam and *mikvaot*[10] (John 9:1-12). New Testament scholars, dogmaticians, and theologians have rightly pointed out that the Pool of Siloam honored by the Byzantines as the place where

---

10. A *mikveh* (plural, *mikvaot*) was a Jewish pool for ritual cleansing. A number of *mikvaot* have been discovered, including at Qumran, at Masada, and on the Temple Mount.

Jesus healed a man born blind is not Herodian. It does not date from Jesus' time and is rightly to be dated to Hezekiah's building projects in the eighth century BCE. Having discredited this false "Pool of Siloam," they then pointed out the deep theological profundities of John 9. The man has been in darkness since his birth; but Jesus proclaims that he is "the light of the world" (9:5). Jesus then spat on the ground, made clay from the spittle, and anointed the man's eyes with the clay. Surely, here is an allusion to Jesus being the Anointed One. There is more: Jesus tells the blind man with Jesus' spittle on his eyes, "Go, wash in the pool of Siloam" — and the Evangelist provides all the meaning one needs: "which means Sent" (9:7). *This* is the meaning of the pericope: since Jesus is one sent from God. Christology is perceived to define the Pool of Siloam, "which means Sent."

Such theological reflection may be insightful, but it presumes we are reading only a christological story. The Evangelist would not be pleased, since he has stressed the Incarnation (1:14) and depicts Jesus as very human. Jesus sits on a well, because he is exhausted. Jesus requests water from a woman, because he is thirsty. Jesus weeps, because Lazarus, whom he loved, has died. Is there no Pool of Siloam from Jesus' time? Are we left with theologoumena devoid of historical reality?

No. The Pool of Siloam from Jesus' time has recently been unearthed. An attempt to repair a large sewer pipe demanded the removal of soil. Beneath the soil was revealed a pool with long and numerous steps. The pool is south of the Temple Mount, where Jesus met the man born blind (John 9:1), and it is the largest *mikveh* discovered in ancient Palestine or anywhere. Ronnie Reich and Eli Shukrun showed me the pool and stressed that the construction is clearly Herodian, meets the requirements of a *mikveh,* and would have been used only when the Temple cult was active. Pilgrims stopped here to purify themselves so that they could enter the Temple to worship. The destruction of Jerusalem in 70 CE buried the ancient mikveh; the pool was not used and was unknown to those living nearby until a sewer pipe needed to be repaired.

A third example of the Fourth Evangelist's precise knowledge of Jerusalem concerns Herod's expanded Temple area and oxen within it. The following account is full of details found only in the Fourth Gospel: "In the Temple he (Jesus) found those who were selling oxen and sheep and pigeons, and the money-changers at their business. And making a whip of cords, he drove them all, with the sheep and oxen, out of the Temple" (John 2:14-15). This account may seem fanciful and legendary, until one

63

learns that Herod the Great expanded the Temple Mount to the west and to the south. The action depicted here occurred in the southern section of the Temple mount. The expanded area was part of the Temple Mount, but not part of the sacred space within it. If oxen had been moved within the southern extended area of the Temple Mount, and some think this occurred just before 30 CE, then the corridor leading from the so-called Solomon's Stable to the steps inside the Hulda Gate would be where Jesus saw these large animals (and their droppings) and could have fashioned a "whip" out of the "cords" used to tether the large animals.

A fourth example demonstrating the Fourth Evangelist's exceptional knowledge of Jerusalem pertains to the different locales in which Jesus is interrogated after his "arrest" in the Garden of Gethsemane. The author independently, but accurately, refers to Gethsemene as a garden "across the Kidron Valley" (John 18:1). The band of soldiers and the officers of the Judean authorities (= *Ioudaiōn*) take Jesus first to Annas (18:13). Apparently Annas, the father-in-law of the reigning high priest Caiaphas, was living in the house of the high priest. The description of "the court of the high priest" (18:15) is detailed, disclosing intimate knowledge of the area (18:15-18, 25-27). Annas subsequently sends Jesus to Caiaphas. The author assumes Caiaphas is nearby, perhaps elsewhere in the complex of buildings controlled by the high priestly families; but the oblique references are frankly obscure and give the impression the Evangelist may be working from his own memory of the topography and architecture of pre-70 Jerusalem.

Next, Jesus is led from "the house of Caiaphas" (18:28) to "the praetorium" (18:28). The author provides the irrelevant theological detail that "it was early" (18:28), without any aside to the Johannine light-darkness paradigm, and adds that the Judean leaders "did not enter the praetorium, so that they might not be defiled, but might eat the Passover" (18:28). Hence, Pilate was forced to go out to them. Pilate returns to the praetorium and calls for Jesus. A conversation is recorded between Pilate and Jesus (18:33-38). As most commentators have seen, it is difficult to ascertain the source of this dialogue, since no follower of Jesus is described as present. Then Pilate goes out again to the Judean authorities, informing them he can find no fault in Jesus. Finally, Pilate acquiesces to the Judean authorities (which for the Evangelist includes "the chief priests and the officers," 19:6), scourges Jesus, and the soldiers mock him.

How should the historian assess such remarkable details? The Fourth Evangelist seems to know how to get around Jerusalem, how Annas's house and Caiaphas's house and Pilate's praetorium are geographically related; and he intimates an eyewitness view of "the court of the high priest." Was the Evangelist an eyewitness of these events? Was he informed by an eyewitness (perhaps the Beloved Disciple)? We are not confronted with a narrative devoid of surprising architectural and topographical detail. However we may answer such questions, we should admit that the Fourth Evangelist knows Jerusalem intimately, and he assumes his readers can fill in what he has only outlined. Reading and re-reading chapters 18 and 19 provides the impression that the author assumes his readers share with him a rather intimate knowledge of Jerusalem. I often hear asides or assumptions; for example, when the author describes the "court of the high priest," he seems to mention "the maid," as if the reader already knew that she "kept the door" (18:16). Likewise, the irrelevant theological detail that the servants and officers had "made a charcoal fire" (18:18) suggests the reader might know, surmise, or remember that "it was cold" that evening (18:18).

How should a historian and a New Testament exegete evaluate and explain such details? I would think it forced to dismiss such irrelevant details as serving Johannine rhetoric. The Fourth Evangelist seeks to demonstrate that Jesus is from above *(anōthen)* and is returning to "the Father" who has sent him into the cosmos. Rather than created solely to serve rhetoric, the topographical and architectural details we have examined may indicate a keen memory and reliable knowledge of Jerusalem.

The Evangelist seems to assume his implied readers are familiar with a great amount of historical detail. To what extent are we confronted with oral tradition and eyewitness accounts? In any case, we now perceive that much of the detail can be verified archaeologically.

The fifth and final example I would highlight concerns Pilate's Judgment Seat. Alone among the Evangelists, the Fourth Evangelist refers to this public area as *Lithostrōton* in Greek and *Gabbatha* in Hebrew (John 19:13). The Greek designates a large paved area or "Pavement." The Hebrew is not a translation of the Greek; it means an elevated place. The Evangelist seems to have exceptional and precise knowledge of the place in which Jesus was brought before Pilate who had taken his authoritative chair or "the judgment seat" (John 19:13). Massive stones have been disclosed in and near the area of Herod's palace, Pilate's praetorium and Judgment Seat. Apparently, the Fourth Evangelist, or his sources, knew intimately this area of Jerusalem.

These five examples must now suffice for readers to obtain the point, although it is tempting to add others.[11] Archaeologists have repeatedly demonstrated that the Fourth Evangelist reflects an intimate knowledge of the Jerusalem of Jesus' day.[12] The evidence indicates that the Fourth Gospel must be understood within its Jewish context and that the Fourth Evangelist had personal knowledge of Jerusalem.

Jesus

As is well known, the scientific study of Jesus of Nazareth has gone through many phases. Over the past forty years scholars have generally come to comprehend that Jesus must not be understood over *against* Judaism, nor should we talk about "Jesus *and* Judaism"; Jesus is to be studied *within Judaism,* as I tried to show in a book by that title.

There is an exception that should be noted. The Jesus Seminar in the United States has consistently portrayed Jesus without the prerequisite sensitivity to his context within Second Temple Judaism. The members of the Seminar have argued for a Cynic Jesus, a Mediterranean peasant, and a man who was not eschatological. A critic might label such productions as remnants of Anti-Judaism. I would prefer to contend that the members of the Jesus Seminar have failed to immerse themselves within Jewish texts, like the Pseudepigrapha and the Qumran Scrolls, and thus miss the point of how fundamentally Jewish were Jesus and his followers.

Jesus was clearly a very devout Jew. The claim that Jesus broke the commandments and did not honor Shabbat is misinformed. Jesus knew

---

11. For instance, Bethany (which Jerome in his *Onomasticon* defines as *domus adflictionis* or "house of affliction") was a place for a sick person, especially a leper, which is precisely the area designated for lepers according to the traditions in the *Temple Scroll.* Perhaps Lazarus of Bethany (John 11:1) had suffered from leprosy. R. T. Fortna includes John 11:1 as an example of incidental data that may reflect memory. Fortna in *Jesus in Johannine Tradition,* edited by R. T. Fortna and T. Thatcher (Louisville: Westminster John Knox, 2001), p. 203. See J. P. Meier's impressive methodology for discerning tradition behind the Fourth Evangelist's superbly suspenseful narratives. Meier, "The Johannine Tradition: The Raising of Lazarus (John 11:1-45)," *A Marginal Jew: Rethinking the Historical Jesus* (New York, London: Doubleday, 1994), vol. 2, pp. 798-832. Clearly, Lazarus's illness is to reveal God's glory, but the historian will note that Lazarus is ill in Bethany (11:1), precisely where the *Temple Scroll* locates lepers and presumably other sick persons.

12. See Charlesworth, ed., *Jesus and Archaeology* (Grand Rapids: Eerdmans, 2006).

that according to Genesis 2:2, God continued creating on Shabbat, and then rested: "On the seventh day *God completed the work that He had been doing*, and He ceased (or rested) on the seventh day from all the work that He had done."[13] Perceiving the Torah's concept of God working on Shabbat informs Jesus' comment that he is working on Shabbat to heal the sick, just as the Father worked on Shabbat completing the creation. The meaning of John 5:16-18 takes on deeper meaning, and perhaps for the first time the context is theologically and sociologically clear:

> And this was why the Judean leaders persecuted Jesus, because he did this on Shabbat. But Jesus answered them, "My Father is working still, and I am working." This, therefore, was why the Judean leaders sought all the more to kill him, because he not only broke the Shabbat but also called God his own Father, making himself equal with God.

Jesus' deep Jewish devotion is also evident in his worship. During his last week alive, Jesus was in Jerusalem. Why? He had ascended to the Holy City to celebrate Passover, as required by Torah. During this week, Jesus taught in the Temple and declared it "my Father's House." His followers, James and John (Acts 3:1), and later Paul (cf. Acts 21:26; 22:17), continued to worship in the Temple.

Thus, Jesus should not be imagined as the first Christian. He was a very devout Jew. It is conceivable that the reference to the fringe of his garment (Mark 6:56; Luke 8:44; Matt 9:20; 14:36; cf. 23:5) may indicate that he wore the religious garment of a conservative Jew, the *ṣiṣit*.

Jesus' words sometimes make sense only when understood in light of newly discovered Jewish traditions. His comments make best sense within the hermeneutic of pre-70 Judaism and the vastly different interpretations of Torah of his day. Jesus affirmed Torah as the revelation of God's will that must be followed accurately and perceptively. Thus, Jesus differed from the interpretations of Shabbat that he knew were against God's will. For instance, Jesus' comment about leaving an animal in a pit on Shabbat (Matt 12:11) makes no sense to a religious person. But now Jesus' comment becomes clear, because the *Cairo Damascus Document* legislates that one must not help a struggling animal out of a pit on Shabbat. Likewise, Jesus' aside that the hairs of one's head are numbered (Matt 10:30; Luke 12:7)

---

13. JPS Tanakh, italics mine.

seems meaningless, even absurd. But its meaning now becomes clear, since the *Cairo Damascus Document*[14] contains instructions for one with a skin disease on the head to see a priest and have the hairs of your head counted. These two examples provide proof how sometimes Jesus' intended meaning, once unknown and confusing, obtains clarification and importance in light of archaeological discoveries. At other times, familiar terms — like the Son of Man, the Messiah, and God's Kingdom — now obtain fuller meaning. The obscure sometimes becomes known, and the known frequently becomes clarified.

Once scholars portrayed Jesus only within "emerging Christianity." Then, Jesus was imagined to be partially Jewish and comprehended with Judaism as a background. Now more and more experts acknowledge that Jesus was a very devout Jew who must be grasped *within Second Temple Judaism*.

The Advent of "Christianity"

False Presuppositions

For 200 years, New Testament experts have tended to assume that the great theological and Christological masterpieces in the New Testament corpus must be dated late; a late date presumably shows the development of thought and the guidance of the Holy Spirit. This penchant must be exposed as absurd.

Such reasoning would mean that Jesus, Paul, and the earliest thinkers in the Palestinian Jesus Movement were not advanced and that we need to wait decades for brilliance. Many scholars, including myself, have tried to demonstrate that Second Temple Judaism was the most advanced symbolic and theologically sophisticated culture in the ancient Mediterranean world. Jewish thought was not only indigenous to Palestine, developing in line with an improved interpretation of Torah, God's will; it was also enriched by Greek, Roman, Egyptian, Persian, and other cultures. Material borrowed from these other cultures was re-thought and re-minted in light

---

14. These fragments from Qumran are now published in James H. Charlesworth, et al., eds., *Damascus Document II, Some Works of the Torah, and Related Documents*. Vol. 3 of *The Dead Sea Scrolls: Hebrew, Aramaic and Greek Texts with English Translations*. Ed. James H. Charlesworth, et al. PTSDSSP 3. (Tübingen: Mohr Siebeck; Louisville: Westminster John Knox, 2006).

of Torah, as witnessed by the vast amount of parabiblical works and compositions that expanded or developed stories, concepts, and dreams imbedded within Tanak, or the Hebrew Bible (the Old Testament).

The five or more books composed, perhaps in Galilee from 300 to 4 BCE, under the name of Enoch, are so advanced theologically that with the advent of the Messiah, the Son of Man, no more development in theological vocabulary was requisite. It was necessary instead to explore how to transfer to Jesus of Nazareth the terms for the coming One developed within Second Temple Judaism, and to search for how and in what ways prophecy, canonized in Torah, proved Jesus was the Messiah. This task was performed before Paul and indeed by Paul and the Evangelists.

The Qumran *Pesharim* provide a paradigm for assisting scholars to discern the ways early Jews not in the Palestinian Jesus Movement understood scripture. Scripture had been composed not for the past; it was recorded (without insight or comprehension) for the present Community defined by the special revelation and knowledge given by God only to the Righteous Teacher (1QpHab 7). God's promises were trustworthy; indeed members of the Qumran Community could see in their own history how God has mysteriously proved trustworthy. Such interpretation was aided by the Holy Spirit from God and was comprehended and communicated in light of the conviction that the present was the Latter Days. These had been spoken about by the prophets, especially Isaiah and Habakkuk, even though God had not disclosed to the early prophets the meaning of the words they recorded. Hence, it was even possible to correct their records; that is, scripture could be corrected in the scriptorium. Thus exegesis of scripture at Qumran was pneumatic, eschatological, and an example of fulfillment hermeneutics.

This Jewish Community at Qumran, which antedates Jesus and his group by at least one hundred years, helps us comprehend the exegetical moves and hermeneutical norms of the earliest members of the Palestinian Jesus Movement. Two noted differences appear as we compare the *Pesharim* with the gospels and Paul's earliest letters. While messianism is found at Qumran, it does not shape the *Pesharim*. Only in the Palestinian Jesus Movement can one faithfully talk about messianic exegesis. The perspective that the Messiah has come and all promises are fulfilled in him distinguishes Jesus' group from all others. Secondly, all is explained in light of what is remembered about Jesus' life and thought.

The source of messianic speculation within the Palestinian Jesus

Movement was to a certain extent the ancient prophecies and the concepts of the Messiah found, for example, in the *Psalms of Solomon;* but the fundamental source of messianic understanding for Jesus' followers was their understanding of Jesus himself. Thus, while an exegesis of Isaiah's suffering servant passages is not present in Jewish messianic thought prior to Jesus and his group, such an interpretation defined his group, and the source of the reflection is primarily a focus on the man from Nazareth. Likewise, while the Messiah was not one who was to perform healing miracles, such undisputed aspects of Jesus' ministry defined messianism for Jesus' followers. In summation, the source of thought for Jesus' earliest followers was a vast store of written and oral traditions, all deemed revelatory and infallible; but the fundamental source of Christological thought within the Jesus Movement was the one who founded and defined the Movement: Jesus from Nazareth.

These widely recognized perceptions and articulations represent a new consensus emerging among historians and archaeologists devoted to re-creating first-century Palestinian social and religious phenomena; yet we have not encountered the term "Christian" or the concept "church," as we did so repeatedly when the Bultmannian School was regnant. These two nouns are clearly anachronistic within first-century phenomena. In order to re-present ancient social organizations without confusing them with modern concepts, we ought to transfer to our task of translating the New Testament Greek what we learned from translating papyri. That is, we usually translate *synagōgos* as "assembly" in pre-70 papyri; hence, we should translate *hē ekklēsia,* as "the assembly," as in Act 19:32 in the RSV (cf. 19:39 also).

It should now be clear that what was once called Earliest Christianity is now perceived to be a Jewish phenomenon. The group, probably a sect, was centered in Palestine.[15] It originated with Jesus of Nazareth. Unlike Qumran, disappearing under the flames ignited by Vespasian's troops in 68 CE, the group became a movement that survived 70. Hence, for terms like "church," we now should use the term "Palestinian Jesus Movement."

The term "Christianity" — which is too often understood as an antithesis to Judaism — is thus revealed as misleading in describing first-century religious phenomena. The disciples of Jesus were labeled by some at

15. Gk. *Palaistinē;* Lat. *Palestina,* from Heb. P*^eleshet.* This term antedates the first century, being Herodotus' term for the land of the Philistines. "Philistia" is the land of the Philistines, the coastal plain from Joppa to Gaza.

Antioch as "Christians" (Acts 11:26); but they would have been as pleased with that label as the early Methodists were with the surrogate "Bible moths." Paul prefers to refer to the followers of Jesus as a Jewish "sect" known as the "Way" (Acts 9:2; 22:4; 24:14 and 24:22; cf. 24:5), and that brings into focus a concept and term well known from the Qumran Scrolls; the Qumranites, under the influence of Isa 40:3, portrayed themselves as members of the Way. As we refine the terms by which we portray first-century social groups, we might do well to use terms and concepts they themselves coined, inherited, and used.

In the sixties I used the term "Johannine Christians" to describe those within the Johannine Circle (or School). Now, over forty years later, I prefer to refer to a struggle within Judaism between synagogal Jews and Johannine Jews. As is well known, the term *aposunagōgos* (only in John 9:22, 12:42 and 16:2), which denotes being cast out of the synagogue, discloses not only that some in the Johannine Circle were being thrown out of the synagogue but that they wanted to attend synagogal services.[16] These followers of Jesus are thus clearly Jews.

One may argue that this new perspective is anachronistic, because it reads back into the first century the definition that a Jew is one who has a Jewish mother. Such a claim misses my point.[17] This was not my method or intention. As far as I know, early Jews did not call others who were Jews "non-Jews." A case study is provided by the polemics in the *Pesharim.* Those ministering in the Temple were "Sons of Darkness," but the Qumranites did not claim that they were not Jews. Many early Jewish texts, like *Some Works of the Torah,* clarify that one who was a suspect Jew was a *mamzer;* but this charge usually comes from the top down. That is, it was a way of exerting pressure and authority. The real question among Jews was an interpretation of Lev 19:18: "Who is my neighbor?" That should not be confused with "Who is a Jew?"

My point now is simply to point out that to claim we can talk about "Jews" and "Christians" in the first century is anachronistic and distorts our attempts at reconstructing first-century Palestinian society.[18] The new emerging consensus, in my judgment, moves away from calling "Chris-

16. According to Acts 18:8, Crispus, who is the *archisunagōgos* of a synagogue, "believed in the Lord." I have profited from conversations on this text with C. Claussen.

17. This question was raised by a member of the symposium in Prague.

18. According to Phil 3:20, followers of Jesus perceived that their *politeuma* was in heaven.

tians" those who believed that Jesus had been raised by God. Those who made that claim in the first century continued to affirm that they were Jews (e.g., Paul and Peter [according to Acts]).

These brief reflections help clarify new perspectives of Judaism, the Gospel of John, Jesus, and the advent of "Christianity." Not only are the new methodologies and perspectives more attuned to Jesus and his Judaism, but both open avenues of communication with Jews who have been miscast, castigated, and even murdered because of poor biblical exegesis and hermeneutics. Perhaps with renewed honesty in biblical research and a living out of the command of love, as evidenced by the man from Nazareth, those who are abandoning the institution called "the church" for religious and spiritual reasons may hear the echo of *quo vadis*.

Turning Water to Wine:
Re-reading the Miracle at the Wedding in Cana

Carsten Claussen

Over the centuries the question of "what actually happened"[1] has led most critical interpreters of the Gospel of John, from David Friedrich Strauss and Ferdinand Christian Baur onwards, to radical skepticism. Already in the early third century CE Clement of Alexandria characterized its significance as "a spiritual Gospel."[2] Unlike the Gospels of Mark and Luke,[3] which the author of the Fourth Gospel probably knew, this later account may be regarded as "the Evangelist's meditations on significant words and deeds of Jesus,"[4] tempting one to affirm Martin Kähler's verdict against the

1. Leopold von Ranke, *Geschichten der romanischen und germanischen Völker von 1494 bis 1514* (*Sämtliche Werke* 33/34; Leipzig: Duncker und Humblot, 1874 [2nd ed.]), p. vii.

2. *Apud* Eusebius, *Hist. Eccl.* 6.14.7: "But John, last of all, perceiving that what had reference to the body in the gospel of our Savior, was sufficiently detailed, and being encouraged by his familiar friends, and urged by the spirit, he wrote a spiritual gospel." Translation follows: *Eusebius' Ecclesiastical History: Complete and Unabridged* (trans. C. F. Cruse; Peabody, Mass.: Hendrickson, 1998).

3. Jörg Frey, "Das Vierte Evangelium auf dem Hintergrund der älteren Evangelienliteratur: Zum Problem: Johannes und die Synoptiker," in *Johannesevangelium — Mitte oder Rand des Kanons? Neue Standortbestimmungen* (QD 203; ed. T. Söding; Freiburg: Herder, 2003), pp. 60-118; for an overview of the discussion concerning the relationship between John and the Synoptics, see: D. Moody Smith, *John Among the Gospels* (Columbia: University of South Carolina Press, 2001 [2nd ed.]).

4. James D. G. Dunn, *Jesus Remembered* (CM 1; Grand Rapids: Eerdmans, 2003), p. 167; Martin Hengel, "Das Johannesevangelium als Quelle für die Geschichte des antiken Juden-

I am grateful to Prof. Dr. A. J. M. Wedderburn and Prof. Dr. J. Frey, both from the University of Munich, for correcting my English and for helpful comments.

search for the "so-called historical Jesus."[5] Therefore, on one hand one may call John's Gospel the least historical of the four Gospels.

However, this seems to be only one side of the coin. For instance, it has been frequently observed that the author of John contributes a number of accurate details about the geography of first century CE Palestine, about Jewish customs, and about certain historical personalities.[6] Archaeological findings support John's knowledge of Palestine and Jerusalem, such as the Pools of Siloam[7] and of Bethesda (or Bethzatha; John 5:2-9),[8] stone vessels (cf. John 2:6),[9] and the outdoor paving stones near the Antonia Fortress which may have been part of the Roman Praetorium in Jerusalem (John 19:13).[10] His itinerary and chronology of Jesus' ministry and death are taken by some interpreters to be more reliable than those of the Synoptics.[11] The debates and trials on the way to

---

tums," in *Judaica, Hellenistica et Christiana: Kleine Schriften II* (WUNT 100; ed. *idem* in collaboration with J. Frey and D. Betz with contributions by H. Bloedhorn and M. Küchler; Tübingen: Mohr Siebeck, 1999), pp. 293-334, here p. 334: "Vielleicht könnte man bei seinem Werk von einem mit christologischer Leidenschaft erfüllten relativ frei ausgestalteten 'Jesus-Midrasch' sprechen."

5. Martin Kähler, *Der sogenannte historische Jesus und der geschichtliche, biblische Christus* (ed. E. Wolf; Munich: Chr. Kaiser Verlag, 1953); ET *The So-Called Historical Jesus and the Historic Biblical Christ* (ed. C. E. Braaten; Philadelphia: Fortress, 1964).

6. Hengel, "Johannesevangelium," pp. 297-334. However, there is a geographical mistake in the narrative between John 5:1 where Jesus is said to be in Jerusalem and 6:1 where he "went to the other side of the Sea of Galilee."

7. Etgar Lefkovits, "2nd Temple pool found," *Jerusalem Post*, June 10, 2004, p. 5, reports the find of the Pool of Siloam by Eli Shukrun of the Israel Antiquities Authority and Dr. Roni Reich of the University of Haifa.

8. Hengel, "Johannesevangelium," pp. 308-16.

9. See Roland Deines, *Jüdische Steingefässe und pharisäische Frömmigkeit: ein archäologisch-historischer Beitrag zum Verständnis von Joh 2,6 und der jüdischen Reinheitshalacha zur Zeit Jesu* (Tübingen: J. C. B. Mohr, 1993).

10. See J. H. Charlesworth, "Jesus Research and Near Eastern Archaeology: Reflections on Recent Developments," in *Neotestamentica et Philonica: Studies in Honor of Peder Borgen* (ed. D. E. Aune, T. Seland, and J. H. Ulrichsen; NovTSup 106; Leiden: Brill, 2003), pp. 37-70, esp. pp. 51-2; John F. Wilson, "Archaeology and the Origins of the Fourth Gospel: Gabbatha," in *Johannine Studies: Essays in Honor of Frank Pack* (ed. J. E. Priest; Malibu, Calif.: Pepperdine University, 1989), pp. 221-30.

11. For a balanced judgment see, e.g., Paula Fredriksen, *Jesus of Nazareth, King of the Jews: A Jewish Life and the Emergence of Christianity* (New York: Knopf, 1999), pp. 28-34, 197-214; she remarks (p. 290): "Given what we know about Jesus, the sort of itinerary that John presents makes much more sense than the one-year, one-way itinerary in Mark (followed by

Jesus' execution seem to provide a better representation of what happened. Thus, on the other hand, John's Gospel appears to provide historical data complementing our knowledge of the historical Jesus and even proving more accurate.[12]

Therefore, at the heart of the interpretation of the Fourth Gospel we end up with a largely paradoxical situation. In some respects John's Gospel seems the least historical of the four NT gospels, but nevertheless provides a number of historical details we cannot gain from any other sources.[13] As a consequence of this tension, authors like C. H. Dodd (1965)[14] and J. Louis Martyn (1968)[15] have made a strong case that one finds not only theology in John (which certainly no one should doubt) but also historical information (which is sometimes too easily overlooked). While the earlier "quests" for the historical Jesus largely neglected the Fourth Gospel, more recently a growing number of authors are taking John's evidence into account.[16] Of particular interest for such an examination are the texts unique to John, for here we may find information about the historical Jesus that is

---

Matthew and Luke) that itself so much obliges Mark's distinctive theology. I do not defend the historicity of particular words, phrases, or the exact details of John's itinerary per se. As all the conflicting erudition shows, the evidence is simply too problematic to yield any unarguable conclusions."

12. Gerd Theissen and Annette Merz, *Der historische Jesus: Ein Lehrbuch* (Göttingen: Vandenhoeck & Ruprecht, 2001 [3rd ed.]), p. 51.

13. R. Alan Culpepper, *The Gospel and the Letters of John* (Nashville: Abingdon, 1998), p. 15.

14. Charles Harold Dodd, *Historical Tradition in the Fourth Gospel* (Cambridge: Cambridge University Press, 1965).

15. J. Louis Martyn, *History and Theology in the Fourth Gospel* (Louisville: Westminster John Knox Press, 2003 [3rd ed.]).

16. Theissen and Merz, *Jesus*, p. 51; Hengel, "Johannesevangelium," pp. 293-334; Paula Fredriksen, *From Jesus to Christ: The Origins of the New Testament Images of Jesus* (New Haven and London: Yale University Press, 1988), pp. 19-26, 198-99; Fredriksen, *Jesus of Nazareth*; Derek M. H. Tovey, *Narrative Art and Act in the Fourth Gospel* (JSNTSup 52; Sheffield: Sheffield Academic Press, 1997); Paul N. Anderson, *The Christology of the Fourth Gospel: Its Unity and Disunity in the Light of John 6* (Valley Forge, Pa.: Trinity, 1996); Bart D. Ehrman, *Jesus: Apocalyptic Prophet of the New Millennium* (New York: Oxford University Press, 1999); Bruce Chilton, *Rabbi Jesus: An Intimate Biography* (New York: Doubleday, 2000); Francis J. Moloney, SDB, "The Fourth Gospel and the Jesus of History," *NTS* 46 (2000): 42-58; John P. Meier, *A Marginal Jew*, 3 vols. Vol 1: *The Roots of the Problem and the Person* (ABRL; New York: Doubleday, 1991), pp. 41-55; James H. Charlesworth, "Jesus Research," pp. 42-43.

otherwise unavailable. Among the seven miracles of Jesus reported in the Gospel of John, only two are completely without any parallel material in the other NT gospels. These are the gift miracle[17] of the replacement of the water with wine (2:1-11) and the raising of Lazarus (11:1-44). While there are other reports about raisings in the New Testament,[18] the miracle at a wedding in Cana has no analogue in the Synoptic tradition.[19] As Jesus' first public act (2:11) in John's Gospel, his appearance at a community celebration in Cana of Galilee is obviously important. The Fourth Gospel reminds its readers of this miracle again in 4:46 and mentions Cana two more times (4:46; 21:2), while it is never mentioned in the Synoptics. Why does John put so much emphasis on this Galilean miracle, which the other Evangelists either did not know or did not care to mention?

In addition to this question, one may wonder whether a wedding presided by a head steward (2:9) with huge amounts of wine (2:6) seems to be somehow out of place in a mostly unknown Galilean village. Many interpreters find this kind of production of enormous amounts of wine simply unnecessary. David Friedrich Strauss thus called it "a miracle in the service of luxury."[20] These are a few of the most puzzling questions that have vexed interpreters of this story over the centuries.[21] While there are numerous theological interpretations[22] of this miracle, any attempt to ask for the his-

17. Gerd Theissen, *Urchristliche Wundergeschichten: Ein Beitrag zur formgeschichtlichen Erforschung der synoptischen Evangelien* (Gütersloh: Chr. Kaiser Gütersloher Verlagshaus, 1998 [7th ed.]), pp. 112-13.

18. Mark 5:21-43/Matt 9:18-26/Luke 8:40-56; Luke 7:11-17; Matt 11:5/Luke 7:22; Acts 9:36-43; 20:9-12.

19. Cf. Robert T. Fortna, *The Fourth Gospel and Its Predecessor: From Narrative Source to Present Gospel* (Philadelphia: Polebridge, 1988), p. 52.

20. David Friedrich Strauss, *The Life of Jesus Critically Examined* (trans. M. Evans, from the 4th German ed.; New York: Calvin Blanchard, 1860), vol. 2, p. 585.

21. Birger Olsson, *Structure and Meaning in the Fourth Gospel: A Text-linguistic Analysis of John 2:1-11 and 4:1-42* (Lund: CWK Gleerup, 1974), p. 18: "one of the most mysterious texts in the NT"; Howard Clark Kee, *Miracle in the Early Christian World: A Study in Sociohistorical Method* (New Haven: Yale Univ. Press, 1983), p. 230, calls it an "enigmatic account." Karel Hanhart, "The Structure of John I 35–IV 54," in *Studies in John: Presented to Professor Dr. J. N. Sevenster on the Occasion of His Seventieth Birthday* (NovTSup 24; Leiden: Brill, 1970), pp. 22-46, here: "a most puzzling narrative. It reads like an act in a play." Hartwig Thyen, *Das Johannesevangelium* (HNT 6; Tübingen: Mohr Siebeck, 2005), p. 151: "höchst rätselhafte Erzählung."

22. For a number of different theological interpretations see Rudolf Schnackenburg, *Das erste Wunder Jesu (Joh. 2,1-11)* (Freiburg: Herder, 1951), pp. 11-30.

toricity of the features of the sign's setting is tormented by John's specific type of *anamnesis*.[23] Much current exegesis of this pericope seems occupied with the question of where the author may have received his *Vorlage* to write this story.

The still dominant view argues in favor of a Dionysiac background,[24] while others look for an Old Testament or an ancient Jewish origin.[25] Finally, some take the story as if the narrator invented it "word by word."[26] These basic interpretive directions need to be considered before we can begin setting John 2:1-11 into its historical framework.[27] We need to keep in mind that both Jesus' and John's different contexts must be taken into

23. Cf. Peter Stuhlmacher, "Spiritual Remembering: John 14.26," in *The Holy Spirit and Christian Origins: Essays in Honor of James D. G. Dunn* (ed. G. N. Stanton, B. W. Longenecker, and S. C. Barton; Grand Rapids: Eerdmans), pp. 55-68, esp. pp. 60-67.

24. Rudolf Bultmann, *The Gospel of John: A Commentary* (trans. George R. Beasley-Murray, Rupert W. N. Hoare, and John K Riches; Philadelphia: Westminster, 1971), pp. 118-19. Cf. similar views in Eta Linnemann, "Die Hochzeit zu Kana und Dionysos, *NTS* 20 (1974): 408-18; Walter Lütgehetmann, *Die Hochzeit von Kana (Joh 2,1-11): zu Ursprung und Deutung einer Wundererzählung im Rahmen johanneischer Redaktionsgeschichte* (BU 20; Regensburg: Friedrich Pustet, 1990), pp. 277-82; Ingo Broer, "Noch einmal: Zur religionsgeschichtlichen 'Ableitung' von Joh. 2,1-11," SNTSU.A 8 (1983): 103-23; idem, "Das Weinwunder zu Kana (Joh 2,1-11) und die Weinwunder der Antike," in *Das Urchristentum in seiner literarischen Geschichte: Festschrift für Jürgen Becker zum 65. Geburtstag* (BZNW 100; ed. U. Mell and U. B. Müller; Berlin and New York: Walter de Gruyter, 1999), pp. 291-308; Jürgen Becker, *Das Evangelium nach Johannes: Kapitel 1-10* (ÖTK 4/2; Gütersloh: Gütersloher Verlagshaus Gerd Mohn/Würzburg: Echter, 1991 [3rd ed.]), p. 132; Michael Labahn, *Jesus als Lebensspender: Untersuchungen zu einer Geschichte der johanneischen Tradition anhand ihrer Wundergeschichten* (BZNW 98; Berlin and New York: Walter de Gruyter, 1999), pp. 146-60; Peter Wick, "Jesus gegen Dionysos? Ein Beitrag zur Kontextualisierung des Johannesevangeliums," *Bib* 85 (2004): 179-98.

25. So, e.g., Heinz Noetzel, *Christus und Dionysos: Bemerkungen zum religionsgeschichtlichen Hintergrund von Johannes 2,1-11* (Stuttgart: Calwer Verlag, 1960), p. 39; Roger Aus, *Water into Wine and the Beheading of John the Baptist: Early Jewish-Christian Interpretation of Esther 1 in John 2:1-11 and Mark 6:17-29* (BJS 150; Atlanta: Scholars Press, 1988), pp. 1-37; Martin Hengel, "The Interpretation of the Wine Miracle at Cana: John 2:1-11," in *The Glory of Christ in the New Testament: Studies in Christology in Memory of George Bradford Caird* (ed. L. D. Hurst and N. T. Wright; Oxford: Clarendon, 1987), pp. 83-112; however, for Aus (cf. pp. 34-37) and Hengel (cf. pp. 111-12) there is no strict opposition between "here Dionysus, there old Israel and Judaism" (Hengel, p. 112), as motifs of Hellenistic wine gods had influenced Judaism since early antiquity.

26. Thyen, *Johannesevangelium*, p. 151.

27. Dunn, "John," pp. 311-14.

account. Neither is it sufficient to read the Fourth Gospel as a report of Jesus' life in the 20s and 30s of the first century CE,[28] nor to read this Gospel through the later spectacles of early church fathers,[29] Mandaism and later Gnostic systems,[30] or rabbinic literature.[31] Such attempts unduly separate questions of theology and interpretation from the recognition of historical tradition. One need also to recognize that an author at the end of the first century CE encountered tradition with what Gadamer calls a "fusion of horizons" *(Horizontverschmelzung)*.[32]

For the most part, John's Gospel does not allow for reliably recon-

---

28. This is the impression one sometimes gets in Craig L. Blomberg, *The Historical Reliability of John's Gospel: Issues & Commentary* (Downers Grove, Ill.: InterVarsity Press, 2001), pp. 17-22, 56-57.

29. See the excellent summary and discussion by Adolf Smitmans, *Das Weinwunder von Kana: Die Auslegung von Jo 2,1-11 bei den Vätern und heute* (BGBE 6; Tübingen: J. C. B. Mohr [Paul Siebeck], 1966).

30. See, e.g., Bultmann, *John*, pp. 7-9; James M. Robinson, "The Johannine Trajectory," in *Trajectories through Early Christianity* (ed. James M. Robinson and Helmut Koester; Philadelphia: Fortress, 1971), pp. 232-68; Luise Schottroff, *Der Glaubende und die feindliche Welt: Beobachtungen zum gnostischen Dualismus und seiner Bedeutung für Paulus und das Johannesevangelium* (WMANT 37; Neukirchen-Vluyn: Neukirchener Verlag, 1970); Siegfried Schulz, *Das Evangelium nach Johannes* (NTD 4; Göttingen: Vandenhoeck & Ruprecht, 1972 [12th ed.]), pp. 28, 211.

31. See, e.g., Klaus Wengst, *Das Johannesevangelium: 1. Teilband: Kapitel 1–10* (THKNT 4, 1; Stuttgart: Kohlhammer, 2000), pp. 19-28.

32. Hans-Georg Gadamer, *Wahrheit und Methode: Grundzüge einer philosophischen Hermeneutik* (Ges. Werke 1; Tübingen: Mohr Siebeck 1986), p. 311; Franz Mussner, *Die johanneische Sichtweise und die Frage nach dem historischen Jesus* (QD 28; Freiburg: Herder, 1965), pp. 14-17; Ferdinand Hahn, "Sehen und Glauben im Johannesevangelium," in *Neues Testament und Geschichte: historisches Geschehen und Deutung im Neuen Testament: Oscar Cullmann zum 70. Geburtstag* (Zürich: Theologischer Verlag/Tübingen: Mohr, 1972), pp. 125-41; here pp. 140-41. Cf. Takashi Onuki, "Zur literatursoziologischen Analyse des Johannesevangeliums — auf dem Wege zur Methodenintegration," *AJBI* 8 (1982): 162-216; here pp. 193-95; idem, *Gemeinde und Welt im Johannesevangelium: Ein Beitrag zur Frage nach der theologischen und pragmatischen Funktion des johanneischen "Dualismus"* (WMANT 56; Neukirchen-Vluyn: Neukirchener Verlag, 1984), p. 34 *et passim*; Christina Hoegen-Rohls, *Der nachösterliche Johannes: Die Abschiedsreden als hermeneutischer Schlüssel zum vierten Evangelium* (WUNT 2/84; Tübingen: Mohr Siebeck, 1996), pp. 27-28; Jörg Frey, *Die johanneische Eschatologie*, 3 vols. Vol. 1: *Ihre Probleme im Spiegel der Forschung seit Reimarus* (WUNT 96; Tübingen: Mohr Siebeck, 1997), pp. 339-40, 456-65, esp. 463-64; idem, Vol. 2: *Das johanneische Zeitverständnis* (WUNT 110; Tübingen: Mohr Siebeck, 1998), pp. 133, 249; idem, Vol. 3: *Die eschatologische Verkündigung in den johanneischen Texten* (WUNT 117; Tübingen: Mohr Siebeck, 2000), pp. 10, 115.

structing the historical events supposedly behind the text.[33] However, scholars have examined Gospel texts for inferences concerning ancient Judaism as Jesus' historical context. One of them, Paula Fredriksen, describes the situation as follows:

> Academic attention has refocused on the gospels, examined not for individually authentic or inauthentic statements but for such inferences as can be drawn from the light of relevant historical knowledge — of Judaism, of first century Palestine, of Roman legal procedure and colonial policy, and so on.[34]

Fredriksen is well aware of Martin Kähler's, Rudolf Bultmann's and their followers' objections against any attempt to reconstruct the historical Jesus, and she takes them seriously. She goes on:

> The intuition of earlier scholars was sound: 'what really happened' during Jesus' ministry is not recoverable from the evangelical descriptions of what happened. But by examining these descriptions in light of our knowledge of Jesus' historical context, we can establish with reasonable security what *possibly* happened, what *probably* happened, and what *could not possibly* have happened.[35]

Likewise, while absolute certainty must elude us, by considering material previously thought irrelevant we will seek new interpretive possibilities or even probabilities.

Thus, after discussing a possible background of John 2:1-11, this paper attempts two kinds of readings of this text. First, we shall look for potential historical data from the text. Second, we shall approach the text by reading it in light of John's theology. This will finally lead us to review our thesis of an inseparable fusion of history and theology in the Fourth Gospel.

33. Hengel, "Interpretation," p. 90, rightly concludes: "The time is past for attempts to 'reconstruct' the historical event."

34. Fredriksen, *Jesus,* pp. 96-97. Fredriksen calls this type of approach "The Second Reading" as opposed to "The First Reading," which is "distilling an outline of Jesus' story as given in the gospels and, necessarily to a lesser degree, in Paul, recalling *grosso modo* the evangelists' own interpretation of these events. Such an outline is extremely hypothetical, depending as it does ultimately on Mark, who freely constructed the narrative framework of his story for his own purposes" (p. 94).

35. Fredriksen, *Jesus,* p. 97 (ital. original).

Searching for the Background and the Context

The origin of this story of Jesus at Cana is shrouded in mystery. While for a long time most interpreters followed Rudolf Bultmann's contention for including the miracle in a supposed signs source,[36] others have argued in favor of a "Two-Signs-Hypothesis," containing John 2:1-11 and 4:46-54 (and maybe 21:1-14).[37] Today the signs source theory has lost most of its acceptance.[38]

Nevertheless, at present there are two main approaches seeking a *Vorlage* for the production of this particular miracle story. They can be divided into those who favor the story of the god Dionysus and those who favor an Old Testament background, such as the prophet Isaiah or the book of Esther with its early traces of the feast of Purim.

The Dionysus Tradition and the Wine Miracle

Much of the interpretation of the miracle at Cana is guided by the argument of Rudolf Bultmann that the story seemed to be influenced by pagan tradition. He writes:

> There can be no doubt that the story has been taken over from heathen legend and ascribed to Jesus. In fact the motif of the story, the changing of the water into wine, is a typical motif of the Dionysus legend.[39]

36. See the bibliographies in Jürgen Becker, "Wunder und Christologie: Zum literarkritischen und christologischen Problem der Wunder im Johannesevangelium," *NTS* 16 (1969/70): 130-48, here p. 132 n. 1; W. Nicol, *The Semeia in the Fourth Gospel* (NovTSup 32; Leiden: Brill, 1972), p. 12 n. 1; cf. the seminal study by Robert T. Fortna, *The Gospel of Signs: A Reconstruction of the Narrative Sources Underlying the Fourth Gospel* (SNTSMS 11; Cambridge: Cambridge University Press, 1970), pp. 1-109.

37. Sydney Temple, "The Two Signs in the Fourth Gospel," *JBL* 81 (1962): 169-74; Hans-Peter Heekerens, *Die Zeichen-Quelle der johanneischen Redaktion: Ein Beitrag zur Entstehungsgeschichte des vierten Evangeliums* (SBS 113; Stuttgart: Katholisches Bibelwerk, 1984), adds John 21:1-14 to such a source.

38. Gilbert van Belle, *The Signs Source in the Fourth Gospel: Historical Survey and Critical Evaluation of the Semeia Hypothesis* (BETL 116; Leuven: Leuven University Press, 1994), *passim*, has shown that meanwhile the critique of this hypothesis outweighs the acceptance. Cf. the literature in Udo Schnelle, *Das Evangelium nach Johannes* (THKNT 4; Leipzig: Evangelische Verlagsanstalt, 2000 [2nd ed.]), p. 14 n. 60.

39. Bultmann, *John*, pp. 118-19. Cf. n. 24 for the argument in favor of a Dionysiac background of John 2:1-11.

Jesus' wine miracle is thus merely characterized as a christianized Dionysiac tradition. Although Bultmann was not the first to publish this interpretation,[40] his commentary helped to support its broad acceptance.[41] Most commentators who follow this line of argumentation interpret John 2:1-11 as a missionary story, presenting Jesus as greater than Dionysus.[42]

There can be no doubt that the worship of Dionysus was familiar in the Ancient Near Eastern and in the wider Mediterranean cultures. Dionysus was not only associated with wine but also with fertility and vegetation in general. In the Greek world the cult became firmly established as early as the seventh century BCE. In Palestine the Seleucids tried to impose formal worship of Dionysus, together with Zeus, in the Hellenistic reform of 167 BCE, which failed due to the resistance of the Maccabees.[43] Nevertheless, this opposition to such formal worship of Dionysus does not exclude the possibility that Dionysiac motifs were adapted and (re-)integrated in Judaism from early antiquity onwards.[44] Such Hellenistic influence was

40. For a list of earlier representatives of this interpretation, see Carl Clemen, *Religionsgeschichtliche Erklärung des Neuen Testaments: die Abhängigkeit des ältesten Christentums von nichtjüdischen Religionen und philosophischen Systemen* (Giessen: Töpelmann, 1924 [4th ed.]).

41. See, among many others who read John 2:1-11 against a Dionysiac background: Morton Smith, *Jesus the Magician* (San Francisco: Harper & Row, 1978), pp. 25, 120; C. K. Barrett, *The Gospel According to St. John: An Introduction with Commentary and Notes on the Greek Text* (Philadelphia: Westminster, 1978 [2nd ed.]), pp. 211-12; Joachim Jeremias, *Neutestamentliche Theologie: Erster Teil: Die Verkündigung Jesu* (Gütersloh: Gütersloher Verlagshaus Gerd Mohn, 1988 [4th ed.]), p. 92; Lütgehetmann, *Hochzeit*, pp. 261-82; and more recently: Margaret Davies, *Rhetoric and Reference in the Fourth Gospel* (JSNTSup 69; Sheffield: Sheffield Academic Press, 1992), p. 88; Theissen and Merz, *Jesus*, p. 115; Dodd, *Tradition*, pp. 224-25, sees a possibility "that the transformation of water into wine may have been adapted to Christian use without any consciousness of its pagan associations" (p. 225); against any dependence on Dionysiac tradition argue: Noetzel, *Christus;* cf. also Schnelle, *Johannes*, p. 61; G. R. Beasley-Murray, *John* (WBC 36; Nashville: Thomas Nelson, 1999 [2nd ed.]), p. 35; John P. Meier, *A Marginal Jew,* vol. 2: *Mentor, Message, and Miracles* (ABRL; New York: Doubleday, 1994), pp. 1021-22, n. 255.

42. See, e.g., Lütgehetmann, *Hochzeit*, p. 282; Labahn, "Jesus," pp. 159-60. Wick, "Jesus," pp. 179-98, goes even further. He argues, "The gospel of John as a whole disputes in an implicit way the worship of Dionysos" (p. 198). However, this seems to be an over-interpretation of the evidence.

43. Cf. 2 Macc 6:7; 14:33.

44. Hengel, "Interpretation," pp. 108-11, esp. p. 111; Morton Smith, "On the Wine God in Palestine," in *Salo Wittmayer Baron Jubilee Volume* (ed. S. Lieberman; Jerusalem: American Academy for Jewish Research, 1975), pp. 815-29; Sean Freyne, "Jesus the Wine-Drinker: A

even more likely in the Diaspora of Asia Minor. In Ephesus, where John's Gospel may have been written, the Dionysus cult had a very strong presence. This definitely allows for a "Dionysus-reading" of John 2:1-11.[45]

The questions that arise, however, are how closely such supposed traditions parallel the wedding-at-Cana story and how early they may have been available to the author. A careful survey of the evidence[46] reveals that close parallels to the changing of water into wine are considerably rare and of these only three or four are from pre-Christian times.[47]

The earliest extant reference to the changing of water into wine appears in a fragment of Sophocles (497/6-406 BCE). It reads:

So Achelous runs with wine in our place (οἴνῳ πάρ' ἡμῖν Ἀχελῷος ἄρα νᾷ)[48]

The reference is to the river Achelous[49] in western Greece, which for some unknown reason is said to run with wine instead of water. The river god of the same name, known for having fathered the sirens, is not linked to wine. However, Achelous can also stand for freshwater.[50] Sophocles may be using some kind of euphemism, calling freshwater wine. To take this fragment as evidence for the concept of changing water into wine would be an overinterpretation.

A second supposed reference appears in Ovid's *Metamorphoses*:

Friend of Women," in *Galilee and Gospel: Collected Essays* (WUNT 125; ed. S. Freyne; Tübingen: Mohr Siebeck, 2000), pp. 274-79.

45. Sjef van Tilborg, *Reading John in Ephesus* (NovTSup 83; Leiden: E. J. Brill, 1996), pp. 95-98, esp. p. 98.

46. A large number of supposed Hellenistic parallels to John 2:1-11 can be found in Udo Schnelle, in collaboration with Michael Labahn and Manfred Lang, *Neuer Wettstein: Texte zum Neuen Testament aus Griechentum und Hellenismus: Band I/2: Texte zum Johannesevangelium* (Berlin: Walter de Gruyter, 2001), pp. 87-131; see also: Klaus Berger and Carsten Colpe, *Religionsgeschichtliches Textbuch zum Neuen Testament* (Texte zum Neuen Testament/NTD 1; Göttingen: Vandenhoeck & Ruprecht, 1987), pp. 151-52.

47. So, e.g., Broer, "Weinwunder," pp. 302-7. Broer rightly concludes that other examples from pre-Christian times and from the first century CE are even further remote from the motif in John 2:9. Cf. Diodorus Siculus (1st c. BCE) 3.66.2; Horace (65-8 BCE) *Carm.* 2.19.9-12; Silius Italicus (26/35 — ca. 100 CE) *Punica* 7.186-194.

48. Sophocles *Athamas* frg. 5 (Lloyd-Jones, LCL).

49. Today this river, which is by far the greatest river in Greece, is called Megdova and also includes the lower reaches of the Aspropotamos or Aspros.

50. Hans-Peter Isler, "Acheloos [2]," *DNP* 1 (1996): 72.

But to my daughters Liber gave other gifts, greater than they could pray or hope to gain. For at my daughters' touch all things were turned to corn and wine and the oil of grey-green Minerva, and there was rich profit in them.

Dedit altera Liber femineae stirpi voto maiora fideque munera: nam tactu natarum cuncta mearum in segetem laticemque meri canaeque Minervae transformabantur, divesque eart usus in illis.[51]

Liber Pater,[52] an ancient Roman god of nature, fertility, and wine, is to be identified with Dionysus/Bacchus. Ovid informs us that Liber bestowed on the daughters of Apollo's son, the Delian priestly king Anios, the gift to turn "all things" into corn, wine, and olive oil. These girls were well known in later Greek mythology as the *oinotrophoi,* the "winemakers." Their suggestive names Oino, Spermo, and Elais clearly confirm that they were responsible for more than producing wine. Although this is truly a concept of transformation, it does not indicate water is involved. On the contrary, the mythographic handbook Βιβλιοθήκα (attributed to Apollodorus, *180 BCE, but certainly later)[53] says: "Dionysus granted them the power of producing oil, corn, and wine from *earth.*"[54] This early interpretation of this special gift suggests a special blessing to produce a rich harvest. A more differentiated interpretation appears, however, in Servius' early fifth century CE commentary on Vergil's *Aeneid.* Here one finds the interpretation that the *oinotrophoi* were able to convert water into wine and everything else into grain and olive oil.[55] However, this understanding probably originated through the Dionysian tradition itself. Thus Ovid's reference cannot be taken as an early allusion to changing water into wine.

A third author who supposedly references this motif is Pliny the Elder in his *Natural History.* Listing a number of miraculous types of waters, he includes

---

51. Ovid *Metam.* 13.650-54 (F. J. Miller, LCL). However, Miller translates "Liber" as "Bacchus."

52. The earliest known occurrences are: *CIL* I 2.563 (4th c. BCE); I 2.381 (3rd/2nd c. BCE).

53. Cf. Franco Montanari, "Apollodorus 7, aus Athen," *DNP* 1 (1996): 857-60, esp. p. 859.

54. Apollodorus *Library Epitome* 3.10 (J. G. Frazer; LCL), italics mine; the text was attributed to Apollodorus.

55. Servius, *Verg. Aen.* 3.80.

> Water flowing from a spring in the temple of Father Liber on the island of Andros always has the flavour of wine on January 5; the day is called God's Gift Day.

> Andro in insula, templo Liberi patris, fontem nonis Ianuariis semper vini sapore fluere; . . . dies Θεοδοσία vocatur.[56]

Again, Liber Pater is linked to some kind of wine miracle. Even the date seemed to support the link to early Christian interpretation: Wilhelm Bousset pointed out that the Christian feast of Epiphany, celebrated on January 6, was meant to contrast the Epiphany of Christ with that of Dionysus.[57] However, the history of the Christian feast of Epiphany is extremely complicated.[58] A connection between the story of the miracle at Cana and this feast cannot be verified until the fourth century CE.[59] And even if some elements of the Dionysiac tradition should have been relevant for the later understanding of John 2:1-11, the differences between the miracle story at Cana and Pliny's account are significant. The type of liquid flowing from the spring is not even termed wine; it just tastes like wine *(vini sapor)*. It also remains unknown whether this spring usually runs with water or may be dry altogether. A parallel account is not much closer to a changing-of-water-into-wine miracle:[60]

> At Andros, from the spring of Father Liber, on fixed seven-day festivals of this god, flows wine, but if its water is carried out of sight of the temple the taste turns to that of water.

> Andre e fonte Liberi patris statis diebus septenis eius dei vinum fluere, si auferatur e conspectu templi, sapore in aquam transeunte.

Although much in this passage remains mysterious, there is a connection of water and wine, even if the reported change is the other way around. We should note, however, that again it is the taste that turns from water into

---

56. Pliny the Elder *Nat.* 2.231 (H. Rackham, LCL).

57. Wilhelm Bousset, *Kyrios Christos: Geschichte des Christusglaubens von den Anfängen des Christentums bis Irenaeus* (Göttingen: Vandenhoeck & Ruprecht, 1921 [2nd ed.]), pp. 62, 270-74.

58. Smitmans, *Weinwunder,* pp. 165-86.

59. Noetzel, *Christus,* pp. 29-38, esp. p. 38.

60. Pliny the Elder *Nat.* 31.13 (W. H. S. Jones, LCL).

wine. Does this suggest that this special liquid coming from the spring during a special time is not wine, but rather water that tastes like wine?

A fourth example actually mentions the miraculous activity of Dionysus, whereas the above texts simply imply such divine activity. The Greek historian Memnon of Heraclea, probably first century CE,[61] wrote a history of Heraclea Pontica. Here one finds notice of the following tradition:[62]

> He [i.e. Dionsysus] filled the spring from which Nicaea used to drink when she was exhausted from hunting, with wine instead of water.

> πληροῖ τοίνυν τὴν κρήνην, ἀφ' ἧς εἴωθεν Νίκαια πίνειν, ἐπειδὰν ἀπὸ τῆς θήρης κοπωθείη, ἀντὶ τοῦ ὕδατος οἴνου.

The story concerns Dionysus being rejected by the water nymph Nicaea. However, after she drinks from the spring, whose water had been replaced by the god with wine, she gets drunk and falls asleep. Dionysus then takes advantage of her, thereby fathering Satyrus and other sons. While this may be the closest earlier parallel to the changing of water into wine in John 2:9, there are still significant differences between both miracles. First, while the six stone water jars are filled (γεμίζω) with water (John 2:7) which then miraculously turns into wine (John 2:9), here Dionysus fills (πληρόω) a spring with wine instead of water. Thus Dionysus does not change water into wine but rather replaces one with the other. Second, the special quality of the wine is noted in John 2:10, as is the special taste in some of the texts discussed above. The wine consumed by Nicaea, probably in large amounts given the reason and result, seems to taste no different from the ordinary fresh water usually running from this spring. Otherwise, Nicaea would have noticed the difference and the whole plot would not have worked. The similarities between both stories are not very close.[63]

In summary, none of the scant supposed parallels from Hellenistic sources displays a changing of water into wine. The parallels are not close

---

61. A dating until the second century CE is possible. Cf. Klaus Meister, "M(emnon) aus Herkleia," *DNP* 7 (1999), pp. 1205-6.

62. Only a compressed account of books 9-16 has survived in Photius' *Bibliotheca*. See *Bibliotheca* 224; Memnon of Heraclea quoted after *FGH* 434 frg. 1. Translation mine.

63. A bit closer is the much later parallel account in Nonnos (5th c. CE) *Dionysica* 16.252-54, where the yellow color of the water (!) and the sweetness of the stream turned into wine are mentioned.

enough to explain the origin of the tradition behind John 2:1-11. This does not, however, exclude the possibility that later hearers, readers and interpreters have noted a connection between the Dionysus tradition and the changing of water into wine at Cana. At a time much later than the composition of the Fourth Gospel, at the end of the second century CE, Pausanias in his *Description of Greece* tells the following story:

> Three pots are brought into the building by the priests and set down empty in the presence of the citizens and of any strangers who may chance to be in the country. The doors of the building are sealed by the priests themselves and by any others who may be so inclined. On the morrow they are allowed to examine the seals, and on going into the building they find the pots filled with wine. . . . The Andrians too assert that every other year at their feast of Dionysus wine flows of its own accord from the sanctuary.[64]

Although at first glance this later story looks like a much closer parallel to the Cana miracle, even here the pots are empty; again, one cannot speak of a changing of water into wine.

It is simply unjustified to regard the Dionysus tradition as a generic source for John 2:1-11. This has been demonstrated looking carefully at all relevant pre-Christian and first century CE sources. Craig Koester is right to conclude that the legends of Dionysus "probably tell us little about how the story of the first Cana miracle originated, but they do help us understand how the story could *communicate* the significance of Jesus to Greeks as well as Jews."[65]

---

64. Pausanias, *Description of Greece* 6.26.1-2 (W. H. Jones, LCL); cf. the parallel traditions in Ps-Aristotle, *Mirabilia* 123; Athenaeus, *Deipn.* 15.34a.

65. Craig R. Koester, *Symbolism in the Fourth Gospel: Meaning, Mystery, Community* (Minneapolis: Fortress, 1995), p. 81; cf. Willis Hedley Salier, *The Rhetorical Impact of the Semeia in the Gospel of John* (WUNT 2/186; Tübingen: Mohr Siebeck, 2004), pp. 64-70, here p. 69, who considers the impact "that the account in John 2 might have made on readers familiar with the Dionysian stories." Glen W. Bowersock, *Hellenism in Late Antiquity: Thomas Spencer Jerome Lectures* (Ann Arbor, Mich.: University of Michigan Press, 1990), shows the prominence of the Dionysus tradition in post-Constantine times.

The Wine Miracle and Old Testament and Jewish Traditions

While the Dionysiac tradition does not provide a *Vorlage* for the wine miracle at Cana, we are still left to consider a supposed Old Testament or Jewish background for the story.

Heinz Noetzel, a strong critic of Dionysiac influence on John 2:1-11, argues that abundance of wine is a marker of the messianic time of salvation.[66] He highlights this passage in the *Apocalypse of Baruch:*

> The earth will also yield fruits ten thousandfold. And on one vine will be a thousand branches, and one branch will produce a thousand clusters, and one cluster will produce a thousand grapes, and one grape will produce a cor of wine.[67]

In addition, rabbinic interpretations of Gen 49:11-12 express hope for high quality wine in the messianic age.[68] However, Noetzel concedes that the motif of the changing of water into wine does not have any parallels in ancient Jewish literature.[69]

Rogers Aus draws our attention to a number of parallels between John 2:1-11 and the book of Esther.[70] He argues "that the author [of the Fourth

66. Noetzel, *Christus*, p. 45. He mainly refers to the rabbinic exegesis of Gen 49:11-12: "Binding his foal to the vine and his donkey's colt to the choice vine, he washes his garments in wine and his robe in the blood of grapes; his eyes are darker than wine, and his teeth whiter than milk." Cf. also Joel 3:18; Zech 14:8; Isa 30:25. Cf. already Joachim Jeremias, *Jesus als Weltvollender* (BFCT 33/4; Gütersloh: Bertelsmann, 1930), pp. 28-29, who relates the expectation of wealth of wine in the messianic age to Gen 9:20; 49:11-12; Num 13:23-24; Mark 14:25; John 2:1-11; 15:1-8.

67. 2 *Bar.* 29:5; cf. *1 En.* 10:19. According to Josephus one "cor" is about 400 liters (*Ant.* 15.314); cf. Luke 16:7.

68. Noetzel, *Christus*, p. 46; cf. Amos 9:13; Jer 31:12.

69. Edmund Little, *Echoes of the Old Testament in The Wine of Cana in Galilee (John 2:1-11) and The Multiplication of the Loaves and Fish (John 6:1-15): Towards an Appreciation* (CahRB 41; Paris: J. Gabalda, 1998), pp. 8-35, presents a helpful investigation on "Wine in Scripture" (pp. 17-35), but cannot provide any ancient Jewish evidence for the changing of water into wine either. Unlike Noetzel, he does not exclude Dionysian influence in John (pp. 54-59); reference to the "Sinai Screen" by Olsson, *Structure*, pp. 102-9, appears mainly in the frame ("third day" in 2:1; δόξα in 2:11); Charles Harold Dodd, *The Interpretation of the Fourth Gospel* (Cambridge: Cambridge University Press, 1958), pp. 298-99 referred to Philo *Leg.* 3.82 ("Melchizedek shall bring forward wine instead of water"). But this does not refer to a changing of water into wine.

70. Aus, *Water*, pp. 1-37; see also idem, "The Release of Barabbas (Mark 15:6-15 par.;

Gospel] has very creatively adapted for his own purposes Judaic haggadic traditions on the feast(s) of Ahasuerus in Esther 1:1-8." The book of Esther may go back to the late fourth or early third century BCE and its final form emerged by the second century.[71] It concerns the deliverance of the Jews from threatened genocide during the Persian Empire. The story's historicity, however, is rather doubtful. As the book now stands, it serves as an etiology for the festival of Purim (Esth 9). Josephus mentions the festival at the end of the first century.[72] Thus, Palestinian Jews certainly already observed Purim in the first century.

If one looks for miracles as signs (cf. John 2:11), it is striking that more than any other biblical book, Esther could be described with the term sign (Hebrew: נֵס; Aramaic: נִיסָא).[73] Parallel to the mentioning of the third day (John 2:1), Esther approaches the king on the third day after three days of fasting (Esth 4:16; 5:1). The link between weddings and the Esther story is also quite obvious as the LXX interprets the feast in Esth 1:3-5 as a wedding: "When the days of the wedding (αἱ ἡμέραι τοῦ γάμου) were completed."[74] Wine in large quantities and of excellent quality is also a motif that appears in both John 2:9-10 and Esth 5:6; 7:2. Although these are striking parallels, the book of Esther does not provide any reference to a changing of water into wine, which is central to John 2:1-11 and, of course, the rabbinic interpretations are much later than John's Gospel.[75]

To sum up: neither the pagan nor the Jewish sources provide any evidence for the motif of changing water into wine.[76] There is no indication

---

John 18:39-40), and Judaic Traditions on the Book of Esther," in idem, *Barabbas and Esther and Other Studies in the Judaic Illumination of Earliest Christianity* (SFSHJ 54; Atlanta: Scholars Press, 1992), pp. 1-27.

71. Carey A. Moore, *Esther: Introduction, Translation and Notes* (AB 7B; Garden City, N.Y.: Doubleday, 1971), pp. lvii-lx.

72. *Ant.* 11.295. Cf. "Mordecai's day" in 2 Macc 15:36.

73. Cf. Aus, *Water,* p. 3; *b. Meg.* 13b; 14a; 15b; *Tg. Esth.* I 9.26, 29; *Tg. Esth. II* 2.6, 11; 4.13; 6.11; 7.10; 9.26, 29.

74. Cf. Esth 2:18.

75. Aus, *Water,* pp. 20-23, refers to a changing of drinking cups (Esth 1:7) and "becoming like lead" in rabbinic interpretations of Esth 1:7. cf., e.g., *b. Meg.* 11b (Soncino Talmud pp. 65-66); 12a on Esth 1:7 (Soncino Talmud p. 70); *Pirqe R. El.* 49. But these interpretations report a different kind of transformation and it is totally unknown whether the author of the Fourth Gospel knew the book of Esther, considering, e.g., it is the only OT text not present in any Qumran document.

76. Noetzel, *Christus,* p. 47.

the author of the Fourth Gospel took a story from another context and transformed it into a story about Jesus.[77] Some commentators[78] ignore the question of possible sources or traditions behind the story. However, such abstinence does not seem to be warranted. After a careful investigation into the religious background of the text we are left with a number of details that locate the story in a certain geographical, religious and cultural setting in history. These details, which we shall now turn to, suggest this miracle story goes back to a local tradition during the time and life of Jesus.[79]

Searching for "Historical Data"

By a number of issues this story is rooted in history. It takes place in Cana in Galilee "on the third day" (2:1). By referring to Jesus' mother (2:1, 3-5, 12), brothers (2:12) and disciples (2:2, 12) the story is connected to earlier references to his home in Nazareth (1:45-46), the calling of the first disciples, and implicitly also his father Joseph (1:45). The description of the wedding may allow a comparison to Jewish wedding customs of that time. Finally, the stone jars may be similar to those found at a number of sites by modern day archaeologists.[80] In contrast to the high Christology of the prologue (1:1-18), for example, we are here presented with the geographical and social context of the historical Jesus. All of these features prompt a historical investigation.

77. So, e.g., Olsson, *Structure*, p. 98: "There is no indication in the text that he [the Evangelist] himself does not regard it as historically accurate. It is presented as an occurrence in Jesus' historical situation which is a sign of something else."

78. Thyen, *Johannesevangelium*, p. 151.

79. Cf. Hengel, "Interpretation," p. 108: "There is no doubt that the narrative has a Jewish-Palestinian background and this is clear on the basis of its location and circumstances."

80. Deines, *Steingefässe;* Jonathan L. Reed, "Stone Vessels and Gospel Texts: Purity and Socio-Economics in John 2," in *Zeichen aus Text und Stein: Studien auf dem Weg zu einer Archäologie des Neuen Testaments* (TANZ 42; Tübingen: Francke Verlag, 2003), pp. 381-401.

Carsten Claussen

Cana in Galilee

Jesus' first miracle is located at a Jewish wedding in Cana.[81] The Fourth
Evangelist locates the historical Jesus and the people around him at a
number of places. John the Baptist and his ministry are situated in
"Bethany across the Jordan" (1:28) and Aenon near Salim (3:23). The disciple Philip stems from Bethsaida (1:44) and Nathanael from Cana (21:2).
Jesus travels three times to Jerusalem for Passover (2:13, 23; 6:4; 11:55). He
goes into the Judean countryside (3:22), from Judea back to Galilee
through Samaria (4:3-4), enters the city of Sychar (4:5), performs another
miracle at Cana in Galilee (4:46) and one beside a pool "in Jerusalem by
the Sheep Gate" (5:2), and later heads "to the other side of Galilee" (6:1; cf.
7:1). Jesus twice visits Mary, Martha and their brother Lazarus at Bethany
(11:1; 12:1). He comes to a garden "across the Kidron valley" (18:1), finally
carries his cross to Golgotha (19:17) and is entombed in a nearby garden
(19:41). These localizations may reflect concrete examples of native tradition. Stories were remembered in connection with certain geographical
data. In any case such geographical details are employed to support the
Evangelist's credibility.

The mention of Cana frames the pericope in John 2:1 and 11 and also
Jesus' early ministry in Galilee.[82] Archaeologists have searched for Cana,
also referenced by Josephus (*Life* 86), at several places in Galilee and
southern Lebanon,[83] but most scholars now identify it with Khirbet
Qana.[84] This site is situated on a hill on the northern side of the Beth
Netofa Valley at Wadi Yodefat, about 13 km south of Nazareth Illit. It was
occupied from the Neolithic to the Ottoman periods. By the sixth century

81. For an overview of the site, see James F. Strange, "Cana of Galilee," *ABD* 1 (1992): 827.
82. Cf. Cana again in 4:46; cf. Luke 4:14-16 who, unlike the other Synoptics, also reports
Jesus' early ministry in the Galilean hill country in the area of Nazareth.
83. See Richardson, "Cana," p. 100; Charlesworth, "Jesus Research," pp. 55-56.
84. See Charlesworth, "Jesus Research," p. 56; Douglas R. Edwards, "Khirbet Qana:
From Jewish Village to Christian Pilgrim Site," in *The Roman and Byzantine Near East* (ed.
J. H. Humphrey; *JRASS* 49; Portsmouth, R.I.: JRA, 2002): vol. 3, pp. 101-32; Peter Richardson,
"Khirbet Qana (and Other Villages) as a Context for Jesus," in *Building Jewish in the Roman
East* (ed. idem; Waco, Tex.: Baylor University Press, 2004), pp. 55-71; idem, "What Has Cana
to Do with Capernaum?", in idem, *Building Jewish,* pp. 91-107. [Also see, P. Richardson,
"Khirbet Cana (and Other Villages) as a Context for Jesus," in *Jesus and Archaeology,* edited
by Charlesworth (Grand Rapids: Eerdmans, 2006), pp. 120-44. This note was added by the
Editor.]

CE, it had become a popular pilgrimage destination.[85] Comparing it with Capernaum, Peter Richardson, involved in excavating the site, describes Khirbet Qana as follows:

> Capernaum was fishing based and Cana was agriculturally based, but in other respects they were similar, with similar developments from the early Roman through early Byzantine periods. Both were small peasant villages, each within sight of a capital of Galilee; both were associated with Jesus and with events of the First Revolt. Both may have had early Jewish-Christian communities, though evidence for this is slender and later. The character of the housing is similar, though Khirbet Qana's seems more varied. The presence of a synagogue is similar; though Khirbet Qana's is still uncertain. The evidence of social and religious life is somewhat similar, though there is more evidence of observant Judaism at Khirbet Qana than at Capernaum (*mikvaoth*, stoneware, Hasmonean coinage, *columbaria*).[86]

The archaeological excavations at Khirbet Qana have enlarged our knowledge of Galilee as Jesus' geographical setting, a prominent feature of recent Jesus Research.[87] The presence of somehow "observant Jewish inhabitants

---

85. Richardson, "Cana," pp. 100-101, summarizes the main references in pilgrim literature.

86. Richardson, "Cana," p. 106.

87. See among others: Séan Freyne, *Galilee, Jesus, and the Gospels: Literary Approaches and Historical Investigations* (Philadelphia, 1988); idem, *Galilee and Gospel: Collected Essays* (WUNT 125; Tübingen: Mohr Siebeck, 2000); idem, *Jesus, a Jewish Galilean: A New Reading of the Jesus-Story* (London: T&T Clark International, 2004); Richard A. Batey, *Jesus and the Forgotten City: New Light on the Urban World of Jesus* (Grand Rapids: Baker, 1991); Richard A. Horsley, *Galilee: History, Politics, People* (Valley Forge, Pa.: Trinity, 1995); idem, *Archaeology, History, and Society in Galilee: The Social Context of Jesus and the Rabbis* (Valley Forge, Pa.: Trinity, 1996); Douglas R. Edwards and C. Thomas McCullough, *Archaeology and the Galilee: Texts and Contexts in the Graeco-Roman and Byzantine Periods* (SFSHJ 143; Atlanta: Scholars Press, 1997); Eric M. Meyers, ed., *Galilee Through the Centuries: Confluence of Cultures* (Winona Lake, Ind.: Eisenbrauns, 1999); Jonathan L. Reed, *Archaeology and the Galilean Jesus: A Re-examination of the Evidence* (Harrisburg, Pa.: Trinity, 2000); Halvor Moxness, "The Construction of Galilee as a Place for the Historical Jesus — Part I," *BTB* 31 (2001): 26-37; Part II, *BTB* 31 (2001): 64-77; Mordechai Aviam, *Jews, Pagans and Christians in the Galilee: 25 Years of Archaeological Excavations and Surveys: Hellenistic to Byzantine Periods* (LG 1; Rochester, N.Y.: University of Rochester Press, 2004); Peter Richardson, *Building Jewish*. [Esp. see *Jesus and Archaeology*, edited by Charlesworth. Ed.]

across a range of status levels"[88] concurs with the use of large and expensive stone vessels for ritual purity (John 2:6).

The Third Day

The dating of the wedding "on the third day" (τῇ ἡμέρᾳ τῇ τρίτῃ) has discouraged many interpreters from looking for a historical meaning. An ancient Jewish wedding seemingly lasted seven days.[89] However, "the third day" clearly does not refer to a certain day of the wedding festivities. Rather, what is meant is the day when the celebration started. From later rabbinic sources we are informed that virgins were married on the fourth day of the week, while widows were married on the fifth day.[90] This practice may have been common already in first century Palestine. There is, however, no ancient evidence that "the third day" was a preferred day for weddings in early times.[91]

While other elaborate explanations, especially symbolic ones,[92] may seem more attractive, the simplest, most obvious meaning of "the third day" is a temporal connection with the gathering of Jesus' first disciples.[93] If we take ἡ ἡμέρα ἐκείνη in John 1:39 as the first day, ἐπαύριον in John 1:43 as referring to the second day, then τῇ ἡμέρᾳ τῇ τρίτῃ may simply mark the last link of a chain of events.[94] Thus, the Evangelist connects the wedding

88. Richardson, "Cana," p. 106.

89. Raymond E. Brown, *The Gospel According to John I–XII: A New Translation with Introduction and Commentary* (AB 29; New York: Doubleday, 1966), p. 98 cites Judg 14:12; Tob 11:19; Craig S. Keener, *The Gospel of John: A Commentary* (Peabody, Mass.: Hendrickson, 2003), vol. 1, p. 496 n. 37, also cites *Jos. Asen.* 21.8 (*OTP* 2:236)/21.6 (Greek); *Sipra Behuq. pq* 5.266.1.7; *b. Ketub.* 8b; *p. Meg.* 4.4, §3; *Ketub.* 1.1, §6; Judg 14:17; *Pesiq. Rab Kah.* 28.9; *Lam. Rab.* 1.7, §34.

90. *M. Ketub.* 1.1; *b. Ketub.* 2a; *p. Ketub.* 1.1, §1; *Pesiq. Rab Kah.* 26.2.

91. See, e.g., Pinchas Lapide, *Ist die Bibel richtig übersetzt?* (Gütersloh: Mohn, 1986), vol. 1, p. 89; Gerald L. Borchert, *John 1–11* (NAC 25A; Nashville: Broadman & Holman, 1996), p. 153, who both argue for an identification of the "third day" with the modern practice of Jewish weddings on Tuesdays.

92. For the various attempts cf. Dodd, *Interpretation*, p. 300; Smitmans, *Weinwunder*, pp. 64-153; Rudolf Schnackenburg, *Das Johannesevangelium 1–4* (HTKNT IV/1; Freiburg: Herder, 1979 [4th ed.]), pp. 341-44; Hengel, "Interpretation," pp. 83-112, here: pp. 86-90; Frey, *Eschatologie* 2, pp. 192-95.

93. So, e.g., Meier, *Marginal Jew,* vol. 2, p. 938.

94. For a similar chain of events cf. ἐπαύριον in Matt 27:62 and the "third day" as the day of the resurrection in Matt 27:63-64.

story "with the gathering of the first disciples in general and with Jesus' promise to Nathanael in particular.[95] This interpretation, however, does not preclude the attempt to regard "the third day" as referencing a literary scheme of six days in John 1:19–2:11,[96] or even seven days in John 1:1–2:11 suggesting a new creation week (cf. Gen 1:1–2:4a).[97] In any case the text does not provide us with a historical dating, as the *terminus a quo* is not clear.

Jesus, His Disciples, His Brothers and His Mother

Jesus is accompanied at the wedding by his disciples and by his mother (2:1, 3-5). From John 2:12 we learn that his brothers had also been present at the celebration.

We know surprisingly little about the mother of Jesus. Our earliest evidence comes from the apostle Paul, who identifies her as a Jewish woman (Gal 4:4) but does not even mention her name. According to Mark's Gospel, she had other children beside Jesus: four sons, named James, Joses, Judas and Simon, and also daughters whose names are not reported (Mark 3:32; 6:3). Jesus' family does not support his ministry; instead, believing him to be mad, they attempt to restrain him (Mark 3:21).[98] While Mark suggests a considerable distance between Jesus and his mother (3:21, 31-35), John portrays this relationship quite differently. The Fourth Evangelist never uses her name, calling her instead "the

95. So, e.g., Meier, *Marginal Jew*, vol. 2, p. 938. Bultmann, *John*, p. 114, n. 3, sees the dating as "perhaps only intended to bring out the sequences, as in 1:29, 35, 43."

96. See already Origen, *Comm. Jo.* 6.258-59; cf. Olsson, *Structure*, pp. 21-25, 102-4; Barrett, *John*, p. 190.

97. Heinrich Lausberg, "Der Johannes-Prolog: Rhetorische Befunde zu Form und Sinn des Textes, *NAWG* 5 (Göttingen: Vandenhoeck & Ruprecht, 1984), pp. 189-279; idem, "Der Vers J 1,27," *NAWG* 6 (Göttingen: Vandenhoeck & Ruprecht, 1984), pp. 281-96, here p. 284; idem, "Der Vers J 1,19 (im Rahmen des 'redaktionellen Kapitels' J 1,19-2,11: Rhetorische Befunde zu Form und Sinn des Textes," *NAWG* 2 (Göttingen: Vandenhoeck & Ruprecht, 1987), pp. 9-19, here p. 11; idem, "Die Verse J 2,10-11 des Johannes-Evangeliums. Rhetorische Befunde zu Form und Sinn des Textes," *NAWG* 3 (Göttingen: Vandenhoeck & Ruprecht, 1986), pp. 113-25, here pp. 122-25.

98. For an excellent survey and discussion of the entire material see Beverly Roberts Gaventa, *Mary: Glimpses of the Mother of Jesus* (Minneapolis: Fortress, 1999), pp. 3-5 *et passim*.

mother of Jesus" (John 2:1, 3) and "his mother" (2:5, 12; 19:25-26) or "woman" (2:4; 19:26; cf. 20:13, 15), but this is not a sign of disrespect.[99] While in Matthew and Luke Mary figures primarily in the birth and infancy stories of Jesus,[100] in the Fourth Gospel her two appearances span his whole ministry, from his first miracle in Cana (2:1-11) to the cross (19:25-27).[101] Mary is thus depicted as showing special faith in her son (2:5) from the beginning of his ministry onwards, and still present when he receives a final drop of wine (19:29-30).

A Jewish Wedding

The Synoptic Gospels never show Jesus attending a wedding feast.[102] However, Jesus uses wedding imagery in some of his parables, such as the "Wedding of the King's Son" (Matt 22:1-14), the "Ten Virgins" (Matt 25:1-13), and the "Waiting Servants" (Luke 12:35-36).[103] The wedding ceremony in John 2:1-11 is sparsely characterized by a (probably large) number of guests (John 2:1-2), the consumption of large amounts of wine (2:3, 6-10), and by the presence of the bridegroom (2:9), a number of servants (2:5, 9) and even a chief steward (ἀρχιτρίκλινος; 2:8-9). The reader is left wondering why Jesus, his friends, and family were invited, and about the identification of the bridegroom and the bride, who are not even mentioned.

Wedding celebrations usually lasted seven days.[104] Many friends and family of the couple may have stayed for the whole celebration, and perhaps most of the village joined in. It comes as no surprise, then, that a shortage of wine occurred, although employing a chief steward should have prevented such an embarrassment. In any case the presence of a num-

---

99. Cf. Josephus, *Ant.* 17.74: Pheroras, who has great affection for his wife, nevertheless addresses her as "Woman."

100. Matt 1:16, 18, 20; 2:11; Luke 1–2; cf. 11:27-28.

101. Cf. Mary with the apostles in Jerusalem following the crucifixion (Acts 1:14).

102. For the ritual of an ancient Jewish wedding cf. Ruben Zimmermann, *Geschlechtermetaphorik und Gottesverhältnis: Traditionsgeschichte und Theologie eines Bildfeldes in Urchristentum und antiker Umwelt* (WUNT 2/122; Tübingen: Mohr Siebeck, 2001), pp. 230-48; Keener, *John*, vol. 1, pp. 498-501.

103. This is not sufficient reason to suggest, as Dodd, that "the traditional nucleus of this *pericopé* may have been a parable" (*Tradition*, p. 227).

104. See, e.g., Judg 14:12; Tob 11:19; *t. Ber.* 2.10; 4Q545 line 6; Brown, *John*, vol. 1, pp. 97-98; Keener, *John*, vol. 1, p. 499.

ber of servants and even an ἀρχιτρίκλινος[105] reveals considerable wealth.[106] The reader may be puzzled by this wedding's apparent luxury in a small peasant village like Cana.

Six Stone Vessels

When the wine is lacking at the wedding, Jesus orders six stone jars to be filled with water. Such vessels were required by Jewish purity regulations. The water they contained was used for ritual cleansing of the hands.[107] Since stone did not contract uncleanness, stone vessels seemed most appropriate. Archaeologists have found such jars at many Jewish sites in Palestine, Judea, Galilee, and the Golan. They appear during the reign of Herod the Great and quickly disappear after 70 CE. While they are widespread in Palestine, they are almost absent in the Diaspora.[108] Recently, a few small vessels have also been found at Khirbet Cana.[109] The jars mentioned in John 2:6-7 can be identified with large vessels, which were turned on a lathe. They could contain about 100 liters each. The Mishnah calls them *kallal*.[110] Jonathan L. Reed rightly stresses that, due to their sophisticated production technique, they were "luxury items." Such luxurious jars are virtually absent in peasant villages like Capernaum, but rather frequent in rich urban sites like Sepphoris.[111] The reader is again impressed by this rather luxurious wedding feast, crowned by an incredible 600 liters of wine, of excellent quality, in rather expensive stone vessels.

Historical Data and Theological Tendencies

The historical details in this story, such as the peasant village of Cana in Galilee, the relationship of Jesus with his mother, the sparse description of

105. Apart from this passage, this term appears elsewhere in Jewish and Greek literature only in a work by Heliodorus (3rd c. CE).

106. Ps-Demosthenes, *Erotici* 7.27.

107. Cf. Mark 7:3-4.

108. Reed, "Stone Vessels," p. 384.

109. See the reference to the finds by Douglas Edwards in Reed, "Stone Vessels," p. 391 n. 32.

110. *m. Parah* 3.3.

111. Reed, "Stone Vessels," p. 395.

the wedding feast, and the six stone vessels, comport with what we know about the wider ancient Jewish context. Our "second reading" of John 2:1-11 has suggested a number of details plausible within the life of the historical Jesus and unknown from the Synoptic Gospels.

However, these historical details are not just bits and pieces of a historical biography of Jesus; we have not yet reached an appropriate interpretation of the text. More than the other Evangelists, the author of the Fourth Gospel makes us suspect he uses such details to serve his theological purposes.[112] Such an agenda is obvious in mentioning "the third day" (John 2:1), which is not a historical date but a literary device; it potentially alludes to the biblical tradition of God coming on Sinai on the third day (Exod 19:11, 16) and of the resurrection on the third day (John 2:4, 19-20). Likewise, Cana is not simply a geographical reference. In John's Gospel, Cana serves as Jesus' base, perhaps as a counterpart to Peter's Capernaum which is far more prominent in the Synoptics. Jesus is not present at an ordinary wedding, but at what seems to be a luxurious event. In line with Johannine tendency, this attempts to present Jesus at home in wealthier circles of society.[113] Theologically, the wedding imagery has eschatological overtones, becoming most obvious in John 3:29, when Jesus is identified as the (true) bridegroom.[114] Finally, the stone vessels are not only indications of a wealthy household, but refer to Jewish ritual purity. Does the changing of water into wine suggest Jesus fulfills the old ritual order, replacing the ritual means of the old covenant with wine, as an indication of the new life he is going to bring about (cf. John 15:1a)?

A careful look at the historical details in John 2:1-11 reveals the fusion of horizons of historicity and theology in John. In its final form John 2:1-11 is firmly integrated into the broader context of Johannine eschatology. The reader is informed that Jesus' "hour has not yet come" (2:4c). But then, puzzlingly, a miracle nevertheless follows at once, revealing Jesus' δόξα and even resulting in faith in the disciples (2:11). An informed "re-reader" may have already guessed that the context of this miracle is actually the hour of the resurrection, i.e. the third day (cf. 2:1 and 2:19). Charles H.

---

112. For a more extensive interpretation of the Johannine theological background of John 2:1-11, which is beyond the scope of this article, cf., e.g., Schnackenburg, *Johannesevangelium*, pp. 342-44.

113. Cf. John 3:1-21 in conversation with the Jewish leader Nicodemus; 4:43-54 meeting a royal official; 18:15: a disciple of Jesus with personal contacts to the high priest.

114. See John 2:16; cf. Mark 2:19 par.; Matt 22:2; Rev 19:7-9.

Giblin has shown that John 2:1-11 follows a narrative pattern of "suggestion" (2:3), "negative response" (2:4b), and "positive action" (2:7-8); this pattern is not only typical for miracle stories (John 4:46-54; 11:1-44), but also the story about Jesus at the feast of Tabernacles.[115] As this pattern is thus not limited to one specific form, we should attribute it to the Gospel's author and not to any sources. This pattern underlines the paradoxical narratological situation of John 2:1-11: On the "historical" side of the story Jesus' hour is not yet present (2:4c). However, as the author looks back from a time after the resurrection, already the miracle reveals the beginning of Jesus' δόξα. Therefore *in nuce* John 2:1-11 is another example of the typical Johannine tension between "the hour is coming" and "is now here" (John 4:21, 23; 5:25, 28).[116] John 2:1-11 illustrates the Johannine "fusion of horizons" of the "perspective of the time of Jesus" on the one hand and of the "perspective of the Johannine addressees" on the other.[117]

Conclusion

In sum, our historical investigation has demonstrated a number of details from John 2:1-11 fit well into the context of first century CE Galilee. They reveal possible and even probable details of the life of the historical Jesus. However, none of these features seem to be included merely to present historical information to the reader. As always, the historical details in John's Gospel carry theological significance when read in the context of John's theology. The "fusion of horizons" of historical context and Johannine theology does not allow for separating the two aspects. We cannot simply determine that these historical data appear, on the one hand, because they were part of some source, or on the other hand, because the final author included them for theological purposes. This may leave us only with possibilities and probabilities of what "really" happened (Fredriksen), but rather appropriately represents what, in the eyes of the author, "actually" (Ranke) happened.

115. Charles H. Giblin, "Suggestion, Negative Response, and Positive Action in St John's Portrayal of Jesus (John 2:1-11; 4:46-54; 7:2-14; 11:1-44)," *NTS* 26 (1980): 197-211, here pp. 202-4.

116. Cf. Frey, *Eschatologie*, vol. 3, pp. 2-4 *et passim*; idem, *Eschatologie*, vol. 1, p. 418. Frey rightly suggests "the σημεῖον-stories . . . need to be taken into account as texts of fulfilled expectation" (trans. mine); cf. idem, *Eschatologie*, vol. 2, pp. 224-26.

117. Frey, *Eschatologie*, vol. 3, p. 282.

Jesus as an Itinerant Teacher: Reflections from Social History on Jesus' Roles

Gerd Theissen

Social history is concerned with early Christian groups and society in antiquity, not with individuals. Its contribution to research into Jesus' life is only an indirect one, in that it describes the environment in which Jesus lived. In doing so, it examines structures and general developments, not individual events. We thus should not expect to find direct insights into Jesus' life and ministry in social history.[1] Nevertheless, it can throw light on many aspects of Jesus' ministry. Everyone becomes part of a society with predetermined patterns of behavior. Everyone is faced with role expectations that are attached to certain positions and which cannot be avoided. It was the same for Jesus. Being perceived in the role of teacher and prophet, he had to deal with the accompanying role expectations. Some people expected still more from him: he was supposed to be the Messiah.

Role expectations of Jesus as teacher can be demonstrated from the fact that he was addressed as teacher.[2] He taught in a different way from

1. Abbreviations are given following Standard Bibliographical Abbreviations, supplemented by *RGG* [4th ed.]. Apart from the basic exposition by Werner Stenger ("Sozialgeschichtliche Wende und historischer Jesus," *Kairos* 28 [1986]: 11-22), two further overall presentations of Jesus from the perspective of social history should be particularly mentioned: Christoph Burchard, "Jesus von Nazareth," in *Die Anfänge des Christentums: Alte Welt und neue Hoffnung* (ed. J. Becker; Stuttgart et al.: Kohlhammer, 1987), pp. 12-58; Martin Ebner, *Jesus von Nazaret in seiner Zeit: Sozialgeschichtliche Zugänge* (SBS 196; Stuttgart: Katholisches Bibelwerk, 2003). A section is also devoted to the historical Jesus in the revised edition of Gerd Theissen, *Soziologie der Jesusbewegung* (Theologische Existenz heute 194; Munich: Kaiser, 1977), published as: *Die Jesusbewegung: Sozialgeschichte einer Revolution der Werte* (Gütersloh: Gütersloher Verlagshaus, 2004), pp. 37-54.

2. Mark 4:38; 9:17, 38; 10:17, 35 and elsewhere; Matt 19:16; 22:16; Luke 7:40; 11:45 and else-

the teachers of the law, with authority, with ἐξουσία (Mark 1:22). We might say: he taught with charisma. That, too, is a sociological concept (or has become a sociological concept today, having been a theological concept in the New Testament). Charisma is not an individual ability attached to a person, such as intelligence or hair color. Rather, charisma — the gift of effortlessly exercising authority and influence — consists in an interaction between the charismatic person and the social environment. Charisma is evident in the way role expectations are handled.[3]

Closely linked to the role of teacher is that of prophet. While we do not find Jesus being addressed as a prophet, we do find him being described as a prophet in reactions to his ministry. People think he may be John the Baptist, Elijah, or one of the prophets (Mark 6:14, 15; 8:28). In some of his sayings Jesus speaks about the role of prophets in general, and he includes himself among them. He stresses that prophets are rejected: they are despised in their hometown (Mark 6:4) and are killed in Jerusalem (Luke 13:33-34). They are rejected by this generation (Luke 11:49-51). Rejection is part of the role of a prophet. This, too, can be expressed using a sociological concept: charisma and stigma belong together. People who are charismatic are rejected.[4]

In my view, three further categories of sociological role analysis can be successfully applied to the statements in the Gospels about Jesus as teacher and prophet: (1) the individual interpretation of roles, (2) conflicts with other roles (known as "inter-role conflicts") and (3) conflicts within a single role ("intra-role conflicts"). When applying these categories to the Jesus tradition, we can ignore for now the question of how far we are directly capturing the historical Jesus: role interpretations, inter-role conflicts and intra-role conflicts can be found in the texts, regardless of whether the historical Jesus lies behind them or not.

---

where. Other people speak of Jesus as "the teacher" (Mark 5:35) or "your teacher" (Matt 9:11; 17:24). Matthew's Gospel constitutes a special case. In it, apart from Judas, only people from outside the circle of disciples address Jesus as "teacher" or "rabbi." The other disciples use the title "Kyrios," in which the sovereignty of the post-Easter Jesus shows through. But in Matthew's Gospel, too, Jesus is the teacher per se, and the disciples should not have any other teacher beside him (Matt 23:8).

3. Cf. Theissen, *Die Jesusbewegung*, pp. 33-36.

4. Michael N. Ebertz, *Das Charisma des Gekreuzigten: Zur Soziologie der Jesusbewegung* (WUNT 45; Tübingen: Mohr, 1987); Helmut Mödritzer, *Stigma und Charisma im Neuen Testament und seiner Umwelt: Zur Soziologie des Urchristentums* (NTOA 28; Freiburg, Switz.: Universitätsverlag/Göttingen: Vandenhoeck, 1994).

Jesus shows that he has the freedom for an *individual role interpretation* by giving his role as a teacher its own emphases: he is an itinerant teacher and a miracle worker, he teaches women as well as men, and he visits areas outside the traditional Jewish territories. These emphases are by no means a matter of course. Like everyone else, Jesus interprets traditional role expectations of a teacher by adapting them. One of the most remarkable features of his charisma is his ability to modify and redefine role expectations.

The Jesus tradition also points to an *inter-role conflict*. As teacher, Jesus comes into conflict with his role as member of his family.[5] His family thought he was mad (Mark 3:21), but Jesus set up against them his "family of God" — all those whom he taught, all those who do God's will (Mark 3:31-35). At another point, the people from his region, after hearing him teaching in the synagogue, ask: "Where does he get this wisdom from? Isn't he the carpenter's son?" (Mark 6:1-6). His social status as a carpenter's son from a small village did not square with the expectations of a teacher. This can be shown from Sirach 38:25-34, where true wisdom is denied to craftsmen and farmers. It is interesting that Jesus interprets this role conflict as teacher by falling back on another role. He says that a prophet is despised in his hometown, among his relatives, and in his house (Mark 6:4) — in other words, in the three concentric social groups in which life in traditional societies takes place. As teacher, Jesus was successful; as prophet, he met with the typical fate of prophets: rejection.

And here we come to a third aspect of Jesus' ministry, to an *intra-role conflict,* which also appears in the dual role of Jesus as teacher and prophet. As an itinerant teacher Jesus was dependent on the support of patrons. Without the backing of circles of sympathizers he and his disciples could not have existed. But the power of his charisma presupposed independence from his milieu. It was an advantage when, as manual construction worker and woodworker, he could maintain a distance from the social world of his followers, in spite of his closeness to the world they lived in. "Charismatic distance" brings influence and independence.[6] Teachers are

5. Cf. in particular Halvor Moxnes, *Putting Jesus in His Place: A Radical Vision of Household and Kingdom* (Louisville: Westminster John Knox, 2003), pp. 49-53. Taeseong Roh, *Die "familia dei" in den synoptischen Evangelien* (NTOA 37; Freiburg, Switz.: Universitätsverlag/Göttingen: Vandenhoeck, 2000).

6. David A. Fiensy, "Leaders of Mass Movements and the Leader of the Jesus Movement," *JSNT* 74 (1999): 3-27.

dependent on the agreement of their listeners, but must endure rejection and dismissal for the sake of the cause. They will then become prophets. Betrayal is part of the structural risk for them. Agreement can turn into enmity.

This brings us to the connection between charisma and stigma. Charismatic people often deliberately assume roles in which they have little chance of being generally accepted. Through self-stigmatization they provoke outsiders, but also strengthen their influence over their followers. Those who survive rejection and condemnation by society are stronger than society. They have the power to call into question currently accepted standards and values. Charisma and stigma are therefore a power for value transformation. As teacher Jesus exerted an irrational attraction; as prophet he risked contempt and rejection.

Sociological role analyses were of course developed for modern societies. But applying them to the Jesus tradition is not anachronistic. Antiquity was familiar with the metaphor of *theatrum mundi,* the concept of life as a play in which everyone has a role assigned to them.[7] This legitimizes role analyses for the societies of antiquity as well. However, the metaphor also highlights the difference from the modern age. We live in the consciousness that we assume our roles on the basis of what we achieve. Prior to the modern age, on the other hand, the conviction prevailed that nobody could give themselves their own role. Everyone found their role already assigned to them. The only choice they had was whether to play the role well or badly. Antiquity had a consciousness of *status and role allocation.* Status was received, roles were assigned. Certainly, this was not set in stone: many wanted to be teachers (Jas 3:1). But it was essentially a charisma. And one could be a prophet only if one was called to be so. The role and status of prophet were assigned.

In this article we want to explore an element of Jesus' role which is usually not discussed: Jesus as itinerant preacher. To begin, we will look for arguments supporting the fact that the historical Jesus was indeed an itinerant preacher. We will then examine factors and models explaining why he was an itinerant preacher. Finally, we will consider the significance of his existence as a wandering preacher for the whole of his ministry.

---

7. Seneca, *Dial.* 1.2.8-9; *Ep.* 95.33; Epictetus, *Diatr.* 2.19.25; 3.22.59; *Ench.* 51.2 (here the Olympic games are used as a metaphor); *1 En.* 62:12; Heb 10:32-33.

Gerd Theissen

Arguments for the Historical Basis of Jesus' Itinerant Existence

With some exaggeration, we might almost say that quite a few people doubt whether Jesus really existed, but nobody has any doubt that he was an itinerant teacher. What is the reason for this certainty? There is a high degree of plausibility of impact favoring Jesus' itinerant existence: a broad attestation in potentially independent traditions, together with a limited opposition against prevalent tendencies in these traditions.

Jesus' itinerant existence is attested in the Logia Source (QLk 9:58), in Mark's Gospel (1:38 and in many other places), in Luke's special material (9:52-56; 13:31-33), in John's Gospel and in the *Gospel of Thomas* (John 4:3, 43; *Gos. Thom.* 86), but not in Matthew's special material.[8] Narrative and sayings traditions are here in agreement. In both forms we come across partly summary descriptions, partly programmatic assertions of the itinerant existence of Jesus.

A saying of a programmatic type in the Logia Source is that of the homeless Son of Man who has nowhere to lay his head (QLk 9:58; cf. *Gos. Thom.* 86). Here Jesus' wandering existence appears as a burden. In Mark's Gospel, on the other hand, it is seen as a positive calling, when Jesus says, "Let us go somewhere else — to the nearby villages — so that I can preach there also. That is why I have come" (1:38).

To such programmatic statements by Jesus can be added narrative summaries. In the first summary in Mark's Gospel the crowd flocked to Jesus, who was in a house in Capernaum (1:32-34). Jesus was forced to leave Capernaum and, against his will, became an itinerant teacher. Summaries in Mark's Gospel describe him right from the start as a wandering miracle-worker whom people flock to see (1:45; 3:7-11; 6:53-56). But there is also a summary in the Acts of the Apostles which says that Jesus "went around" doing good and healing people (Acts 10:38). Summaries are editorial constructions, but historically they are not implausible. For example, they report only exorcisms and healings, that is, the two forms of miracle that cannot be denied the historical Jesus; they do not mention natural miracles. When they attribute an itinerant existence to Jesus, they are historically correct.

---

8. Although Jesus could have been presupposed as itinerant teacher in the beatitude of the weary and burdened (Matt 11:28-30). In another passage we find a clear reference to the disciples as itinerant preachers (Matt 10:23).

The few place names mentioned show a certain agreement in the narrative and sayings traditions. Jesus is located in places near the Sea of Galilee. The center of his activity is Capernaum, where a "house" is mentioned (Matt 9:10; 17:25). The question has therefore justifiably been raised:[9] did Jesus perhaps lead a life with relatively large *stabilitas loci,* in other words with a home base in Capernaum, to which he could return in the evening from many different places in Galilee? Was he more of a short-range preacher than a long-range one?

An argument against the restriction to a small area is provided by Jesus' wanderings in the rural areas surrounding the neighboring towns: he travelled northwest to the areas of Tyre and Sidon (Mark 7:24, 31), north to the villages of Caesarea Philippi (Mark 8:27), and southeast in the Decapolis (Mark 5:1, 20; 7:31). Since Jews lived in the territories of these Hellenistic cities, these wanderings are historically credible. They meet with only an indirect echo in the sayings tradition: a saying of Jesus cites the people of Tyre and Sidon as potential examples (QLk 10:14). If these wanderings have a core of historical truth, then Jesus cannot normally have returned to Capernaum in the evening.

This also applies to his last journey, which lasted three days. At the end of his life Jesus travelled to Jerusalem for the Passover feast, although he would be unable to celebrate this Passover. According to the chronology in John (which in my view is more reliable), he was executed before the Passover feast. The motive for his journey to Jerusalem is not entirely clear. If we consider the entry into Jerusalem to be historical, then it took place as a Messianic demonstration — as a counter-demonstration to the entry of the Prefect followed by his cohort. It may have been the expectation of an ultimate intervention by God that determined this journey to Jerusalem; in Luke's Gospel we find the remark: "because he was near Jerusalem and the people thought that the kingdom of God was going to appear at once" (19:11).

Part of the plausibility of impact of a tradition are elements of opposition against prevalent tendencies in Early Christian traditions. With our theme these are only partially to be found. The post-Easter phenomenon of wandering charismatics continued the itinerant life pattern of Jesus. It is

---

9. John S. Kloppenborg Verbin, *Excavating Q: The History and Setting of the Saying Gospel* (Edinburgh: T&T Clark, 2000), p. 211, assumes simply daily excursions for the representative group in Q.

therefore possible that the memory of Jesus was brought into line with the lifestyle of the early Christian itinerant charismatics. However, their wandering existence differed in some respects from the pre-Easter itinerant existence of Jesus; some of the early Christian wandering charismatics carried out missions among the Gentiles, were active beyond Palestine, in some cases earned money for their travels through their own work, like Paul and Barnabas (1 Cor 9:6), or came with letters of recommendation for the Christian communities (2 Cor 3:1). Nevertheless, all this applies to itinerant charismatics outside Palestine. In Syria-Palestine itself the continuity between Jesus' lifestyle (the τρόποι κυρίου, as it is called in *Did.* 11:8) and that of his followers appears to have been greater.[10]

Irrespective of this, the congruence between the itinerant teacher Jesus and the early Christian wandering charismatics — both inside and outside Palestine — was restricted by the growing importance of the local communities, where the rootless life of Jesus gave rise to embarrassment.[11] At least, we can detect an apologetic tendency in the Gospels when Jesus' itinerant life is described.

Mark's Gospel interprets Jesus' itinerant existence as a consequence of the enormous success he encountered. Already on the first day of his ministry in Capernaum so many people flocked to see Jesus that he had to leave the town. By the end, the situation is summed up, "Jesus could no longer enter a town openly but stayed outside in lonely places. Yet the people still came to him from everywhere" (Mark 1:45). The author endeavors to make it clear that Jesus was no homeless vagabond who was not tolerated anywhere. On the contrary, it was his great success that drove him to the next town.

In *Matthew's Gospel* Jesus moves from Nazareth to Capernaum in order to settle there: κατῴκησεν (Matt 4:13). He has a house there (Matt 9:10; 17:24-27).[12] However, on his first appearance in Capernaum he does not enter this house, but that of Peter (Matt 8:14). It is in his homeland, of all places, that he complains of his homelessness as Son of Man (Matt 8:20).

---

10. Cf. the description by Markus Tiwald, *Wanderradikalismus: Jesu erste Jünger — ein Anfang und was davon bleibt* (ÖBS 20; Frankfurt: Lang, 2002).

11. Celsus also criticizes the itinerant life style of Jesus (Origen, *Cels.* 1.65).

12. Cf. Georg Strecker, *Der Weg der Gerechtigkeit: Untersuchung zur Theologie des Matthäus* (FRLANT 82; Göttingen: Vandenhoeck, 1962), pp. 94-96. Strecker believes that in Matt 8:14; 9:10, 28; 13:1, 36; 17:25 the reference in each case is to the same house in Capernaum, his "own town."

Jesus' domicile in Capernaum is intended to improve his image as a homeless itinerant preacher to some extent, but the overall picture of a wandering life remains in Matthew's Gospel too.

Luke's Gospel extends Jesus' wanderings into a long travel story.[13] It frequently stresses that Jesus is on a journey; the verb πορεύεσθαι recurs constantly.[14] The fact that Jerusalem is the goal of this journey is emphasized at its beginning (9:51-53) and its end (19:28), and also in statements made during its course (13:33-34; 17:11). In this way Jesus' itinerant existence becomes part of a pilgrimage to Jerusalem, in other words part of the "normal" life of a Jew in Palestine. But Luke also describes Jesus as a wanderer before this (cf. πορεύεσθαι in 4:30, 42; 7:6-11).

In all three synoptic gospels, in spite of apologetic motifs like this, Jesus is depicted as an itinerant teacher. There can be no doubt that this is what he was. It is easier to explain the phenomenon of itinerant charismatic figures in early Christianity as a consequence of the model of Jesus than it is to see the image of Jesus as itinerant teacher as being a projection of this post-Easter itinerant charismatic phenomenon. For there were only a few models for itinerant preachers in Judaism. This was something new that was beginning. And it is easier to explain it through the historical Jesus than through his disciples.

And here we come to the contextual plausibility of the itinerant existence of Jesus. Wisdom teachers and teachers of the law were a well-known

13. Luke has composed this travel story deliberately. His reasons for doing so cannot be reduced to a single motive. In Christological terms, the road to the cross and resurrection is emphasized (Peter v.d. Osten-Sacken, "Zur Christologie des lukanischen Reiseberichts," *EvT* 33 [1973]: 476-96), while ecclesiologically it is the road to the Gentiles that is presented (Eduard Lohse, "Missionarisches Handeln Jesu nach dem Evangelium des Lukas," *TZ* 10 [1954]: 1-13), and paraenetically teachings and debate with opponents are arranged together (Bo Reicke, "Instruction and Discussion in the Travel Narrative," in *StudEv I = TUGAL* 73 (1959): 206-14. The interpretation of Jesus' itinerant existence on the basis of a familiar pattern as behavior is only one motif among others. His itinerant existence is "transfigured" through a theological interpretation. Cf. Gerhard Schneider, *Das Evangelium nach Lukas Kap. 1-10* (ÖTB NT 3/1; GTS 500; Gütersloh/Würzburg: Gütersloher Verlagshaus/Echter, 1977), pp. 226-28: "Jesus is therefore not presented simply as a wanderer who calls in on people, nor just as an itinerant preacher, but as one who in accordance with God's purpose (Luke 22:22) consistently moves towards the goal of *Jerusalem* (i.e. his 'taking up') (9:51; 13:22, 31-33; 17:11; 19:28)." A survey of the various interpretations is given by Wolfgang Wiefel, *Das Evangelium nach Lukas* (THKNT 3; Berlin: Ev. Verlagsanstalt, 1988), pp. 186-89.

14. Luke 9:51, 53, 56, 57; 10:38; 13:31, 33; 17:11; 19:28.

phenomenon in the Palestine of that time. Jesus combined features of both. As a wisdom teacher he was part of a long Jewish tradition. In his conversation with a teacher of the law he referred to the Torah, which he summarized in the double commandment of love. At the same time Jesus differed from other teachers, most conspicuously in his itinerant existence. A contextually linked unusual feature like this is in my view a good indication of historicity. With the establishment of this fact, however, our task is not finished. We have to explain how it was historically possible for Jesus to have lent this individual note to his role as teacher. And so in our second section we will ask: Which models inspired Jesus to be active as an itinerant teacher? Which experiences could have prompted him to do so?

Models for Jesus' Itinerant Existence

Was Jesus the only one to lead a wandering existence? Did he come up with this idea himself? The new is usually a combination of the old. Jesus could have been prompted to live his life as an itinerant preacher by various factors and models: firstly by his *professional role* in society as a carpenter, a role associated with a greater mobility than that of a farmer; secondly by itinerant *prophets* like Elijah and Jonah, whom Jesus would have found as literary models in his cultural tradition; and thirdly by *wandering teachers* in his own day. Here I can only offer a hypothesis, as direct proof is lacking. Perhaps Jesus also felt that his itinerant existence was backed up, fourthly, by a *mythical model:* by wisdom, that sought a home on earth — if that is not an interpretation of his ministry made from a later standpoint.

The Professional Role of Jesus as a Model for His Itinerant Existence?

Farmers are tied to their land, whereas fishers with their boats have a far greater local range; four of Jesus' first followers were fishermen (Mark 1:16-20). Jesus himself, however, was a craftsman, a carpenter. Craftsmen in rural areas needed many different areas of competence in order to support themselves.[15] Jesus probably earned his living through different forms of

---

15. Cf. Xenophon, *Cyr.* 8.2.5: "For in small towns the same craftsmen make a bed, a door, a plough, and a table, and often the same man also builds a house and is glad when he

woodwork. According to Justin he manufactured ploughs and yokes.[16] In a small village like Nazareth or Capernaum there would not have been much need for a carpenter or woodworker like this. It is therefore possible that Jesus had already travelled round Galilee a lot because of his profession, before his public ministry as itinerant teacher. For this reason he probably had a larger local radius than many of his followers.[17] For example, the suggestion has often been made that he worked with his father on the reconstruction of Sepphoris (after 4 CE) and the construction of Tiberias (around 20 CE).[18] This cannot be proved, but it is not impossible. The silence of the Jesus tradition about the two main cities of Galilee is ambiguous. It could be related to the assessment that his message had no chance of being accepted there, or that he was in danger in these cities. Both interpretations presuppose a certain degree of knowledge of these cities. But for our purposes the professional role of Jesus does not explain a great deal. It was not every carpenter who appeared in public as a teacher. After the reaction to his public appearance in his hometown it was improbable. There must have been a further factor involved.

---

can acquire enough customers in this way, in order to be able to earn his living." In the big cities, on the other hand, it was possible to specialize to a much greater extent.

16. *Dial.* 88; *Inf. Gos. Thom.* 13. On Jesus' profession cf. Douglas E. Oakman, *Jesus and the Economic Question of His Day* (SBEC 8; Lewiston/Queenston: Edwin Mellen, 1986), pp. 175-82.

17. Oakman, *Jesus and the Economic Question,* pp. 182-204: "Jesus' occupation as a carpenter took him not only to other villages and perhaps to the large estates in the Esdraelon Plain, . . . but in all probability to major urban centers of Palestine. Itineracy gave him opportunities for broad social contacts, taking him far beyond the confines of his village cultural horizon" (pp. 197-98). The mobility of carpenters and construction craftsmen is taken for granted in the Old Testament: King Hiram sent carpenters to Solomon (2 Sam 5:11). In the *Protogospel of James,* Joseph returns from his building work (*Prot. Jas.* 13:1), from a journey (*Prot. Jas.* 15:1), and finds Mary to be pregnant. This is not, of course, a historical source for the life of Jesus, but we can learn from it what an author in antiquity imagined the life of a carpenter to be like.

18. Shirley Jackson Case, *Jesus: A New Biography* (Chicago: University of Chicago, 1927), pp. 20-21. Richard A. Batey, *Jesus and the Forgotten City: New Light on Sepphoris and the Urban World of Jesus* (Grand Rapids: Baker, 1991), pp. 65-82.

Traditional Historical Models in the Religious Tradition?
Jonah and Elijah

Can the concept of an itinerant prophet be derived from the tradition of Israel? It is notable that the Jesus tradition relates only two prophets from the history of Israel closely to Jesus: Jonah and Elijah. Both of them were wandering prophets. Jonah had to travel from Palestine as far as Nineveh in order to prophesy the destruction of the city (Jon 1:2; 3:2). His preaching to the Ninevites is taken up again in the Jesus tradition (Luke 11:30). Elijah and Elisha are presented as wandering prophets — and in some cases surrounded by a crowd of disciples. On a number of occasions Elijah was instructed to go to another place. In 1 Kings 17:2-3 we read, "The word of the Lord came to Elijah: 'Leave here and turn eastward!'" The word of the Lord commanded him: "Go at once to Zarephath of Sidon and stay there. I have commanded a widow in that place to supply you with food. So he went to Zarephath . . ." (1 Kgs 17:9-10). We come across such instructions to travel on two further occasions in the Elijah tradition.[19] But the wanderings of Elijah are also a flight; he is threatened. We read: "Elijah was afraid and ran for his life" (1 Kgs 19:3). The call of Elisha occurred when Elijah was passing by (1 Kgs 19:19-21). The synoptic stories of the calling of the disciples are stylized following this model. In them, Jesus takes on the role of Elijah and his disciples that of Elisha. It is true that in the synoptic gospels it is mostly John the Baptist who is considered to be Elijah redivivus. But according to Mark 8:28 some of the people also think that Jesus is Elijah or one of the prophets (Mark 6:14-15)! Now, the belief that Jesus was the Baptist redivivus presupposes that Jesus was not yet well-known, for those knowing Jesus came from Nazareth and was a disciple of the Baptist could not possibly think that he was the Baptist who had returned. Mark 6:14-15 and 8:28 therefore give a reaction to the appearance of Jesus that must go back to the lifetime of Jesus, when he was still unknown to the public. Shortly after his first appearance, the people around him had the impression he was like the Baptist[20] and Elijah redivivus. His wandering existence

---

19. Cf. 1 Kgs 18:1: ". . . the word of the Lord came to Elijah: 'Go and present yourself to Ahab'" and 1 Kgs 21:18: "Go down to meet Ahab king of Israel." When Elijah met the God-fearing Obadiah, the latter said, "I don't know where the Spirit of the Lord may carry you when I leave you. If I go and tell Ahab and he doesn't find you, he will kill me" (18:12). Here, too, Elijah is presented as an itinerant prophet.

20. John the Baptist lived in the desert. If people flocked to the desert to see him, this

may have been one of the reasons for this. But after all these reflections the only probability we can establish is that this itinerant existence was interpreted by others as following the model of Elijah. This has little to say about how Jesus saw himself or whether he consciously followed the model of these prophets. We therefore need to ask whether there were other models for itinerant teachers who were alive at that time.

Living Models in the Time of Jesus: Judas Galilaeus

Here I can only present one candidate: Judas Galilaeus![21] Josephus calls him a "Sophist" (*War* 2.118; 2.433). Michel and Bauernfeind translate this on one occasion as "itinerant speaker" (*War* 2.118). This is possible, but must not necessarily be so, for Josephus also applies the term Sophist (σοφιστής) to Jewish teachers who were not wandering teachers (*War* 1.648; 1.650; cf. *Ant.* 17.152). Nevertheless, we can infer a certain mobility on the part of Judas. He originally came from the Gaulanitis, from the town of Gamala.[22] It is likely that he taught for a while in Galilee and at this time he was probably called "the Gaulanite," since Josephus uses this name when he first mentions him in *Ant.* 18.4. It was only after 6 CE, in other words af-

---

presupposes a certain *stabilitas loci*. In John 3:23 he is located in Aenon and Salim — slightly further north than the area where the desert extended right to the River Jordan. It is possible that the Baptist shifted the centers from which he operated. But he was not really an itinerant preacher. However, his ascetic way of life was a precondition for a wandering existence full of deprivation.

21. Cf. Martin Hengel, *Die Zeloten: Untersuchungen zur jüdischen Freiheitsbewegung in der Zeit von Herodes I. bis 70 n. Chr.* (AGJU 1; Leiden: Brill, 1976), pp. 79-150.

22. It may be that he is identical with Judas the son of Hezekiah. This Judas led the uprising in Galilee that broke out throughout the land after the death of Herod in 4 BCE. Was he active in Judea once more after the deposition of Archelaus ten years later? If the two were identical, then it is certain that Judas operated first in Galilee and then in Judea. However, the question of whether they are identical is disputed. Martin Hengel (*Zeloten*, pp. 337ff.) is in favor of this hypothesis, while David M. Rhoads (*Israel in Revolution, 6-74 CE: A Political History Based on the Writings of Josephus* [Philadelphia: Fortress, 1976], pp. 50-51) argues against it. The first Judas is called "son of Hezekiah," and the second "the Gaulanite" (*Ant.* 18.4), because he came from the town of Gamala in that region, or "the Galilean" (*Ant.* 18.23; 20.102; *War* 2.118, 433; Acts 5:37). Is it possible that it is the same person in Josephus? As Josephus probably changed his source between *Ant.* 17 and 18 — he could only have based himself on Nicholas of Damascus for the story of Herod I — it is possible that the two "Judases" were the same person, even if Josephus did not think that they were identical.

ter Judea had passed under direct Roman administration, when Judas began to agitate in Judea against the taxation assessment, that he came to be called "the Galilean" there. This is the name that Josephus nearly always uses for him subsequently (*Ant.* 18.23; 20.102; *War* 2.433; an exception is *War* 7.253). We find the same name in the New Testament (Acts 5:37). These two names derived from geographical locations allow us to suppose that Judas changed his "place of residence" twice. Did he do this by changing the house he taught from? Or did he also operate as an itinerant preacher and teacher? An argument in favor of the second possibility is the general consideration that if Judas Galilaeus wanted to appeal to the entire people to refuse to pay taxes, then he could not wait in a teacher's house like other teachers until disciples came to him. He had to reach the people in the villages and bring his message to them. It therefore seems likely that Judas and his associate, the Pharisee Sadduk, operated as itinerant teachers during the period of their campaign. An analogy between their campaign against paying taxes and a later campaign in favor of paying them makes this plausible. Shortly before the outbreak of the Jewish war, the Judean aristocracy made a last effort to preserve peace: "The leaders of the people and council members spread out in the villages and collected the taxes" (*War* 2.405). Would not the opponents of paying the tax have to have spread out in the villages in the same way? How else could they have influenced the whole of the people?

Jesus, too, wanted to reach the whole of the people with his message. In an oral culture this is only possible through sending messengers. In my view, the sending out of the disciples is historical, although it is frequently disputed. When they are sent out, the disciples are not given any task that would have been conceivable only after Easter: they do not preach the *parousia* of the returning *kyrios,* but, like John the Baptist, the repentance of human beings (Mark 6:12) and, like Jesus, the coming of the rule of God (QLk 10:9). They do not want to baptize, but to preach and to heal. They do not call for any belief. It can be noted that in the speech Jesus makes when sending them out, he appears to make a distinction between himself and other groups in two ways.

Firstly, he strictly enjoins the disciples to enter houses with the greeting of peace. This is more than a conventional greeting; this peace is supposed to be granted to the house with a magical power of dissemination and to be withdrawn again if it is rejected. In Luke's version of the speech of sending out, the peace is dependent on the disciples finding a "son of peace" in the house (Luke 10:6). This does not mean that the greeting of peace makes each of them a "son of peace," but that it serves as a test to ascertain if there is a "son of peace" in the house who deserves the peace blessing. Only this interpretation fits in with Matthew's version of the speech of sending out. According to this version, the disciples should first find out who is worthy of them entering his house. If the house is worthy, then they should enter it with their peace (Matt 10:13). It is therefore not necessary to date such messengers of peace to the time of the Jewish war, in which Christian missionaries had to make a distinction between themselves and the war party.[23] It is more likely that the speech of sending out is intended to make a distinction between the mission of Jesus' disciples and the campaign of Judas Galilaeus. His refusal to pay taxes had been a declaration of war. Jesus' messengers were supposed to make clear right from the beginning that their appearance was not a revival of this campaign — firstly by demonstratively keeping their distance from the rebellious families (from those who were not "sons of peace"), and secondly by demonstratively affirming their desire for peace. Since the discussion about paying taxes (Mark 12:13-17) shows that Jesus did indeed have to make a distinction between himself and the campaign of Judas Galilaeus, a corresponding distinction in the speech of sending out is historically quite likely.

There is a further feature of the speech of sending out that contains a distinction. The instructions on how the disciples should equip themselves include a critical reference to the external identifying characteristics of the Cynic itinerant philosophers. Unlike the Cynics, Jesus' messengers were not supposed to take any bag or staff with them on their journey.[24] This would have made sense only if wandering preachers in the Cynic style were known to the disciples. And in fact there is good evidence for Cynic traditions in the neighborhood of Galilee. They (and other philosophical traditions) can be traced over a number of centuries in Gadara.[25] It is therefore historically

---

23. Paul Hoffmann, *Studien zur Theologie der Logienquelle* (NTAbh N.F. 8; Münster: Aschendorf, 1972, 1982), pp. 296-302, 310-11.

24. A number of commentators have suspected a distinction from the Cynics, e.g. Hoffmann, *Logienquelle,* p. 318; Risto Uro, *Sheep Among The Wolves: A Study of the Mission Instructions of Q* (AASF 47; Helsinki: Suomalainen Tiedeakatemia, 1987), pp. 122-23.

25. The Cynic and satirist Menippus of Gadara lived in the third century BCE. The epigrammatist Meleager of Gadara (ca. 130-70 BCE) considered himself to be a follower of Menippus. The Epicurean Philodemus came from Gadara (ca. 110-40 BCE). The rhetorician

possible that the external identifying characteristics of the Cynic itinerant philosophers were known in Galilee.

Both these distinctions need to be evaluated separately. They do not necessarily relate to the same group. But it may well be that they are connected. Could it be that Judas Galilaeus (and some of his followers) adopted the style of Cynic wandering philosophers? Josephus describes him as the founder of a fourth philosophy among the Jews (*Ant.* 18.23). He compares him with a philosopher. Indeed, his party is the only one of the four religious tendencies for which Josephus names a leader of the school, although this was something that we would normally (by analogy with other cases) have expected of philosophical schools in ancient times. The comparison of the four Jewish groups with philosophical schools may therefore have been inspired by the public mission of Judas Galilaeus. It is generally agreed that Josephus is trying to impress his non-Jewish readers with this comparison. He therefore compares the Essenes with the Pythagoreans (*Ant.* 15.371), the Pharisees with the Stoics (*Life* 12), and suggests a relationship between the Sadducees and the Epicureans, although he avoids a direct parallel.[26] Among the remaining possibilities for his fourth philosophy were the Cynics. Was Josephus thinking of them when he described Judas Galilaeus as the founder of the fourth philosophy in Judaism?[27]

The following argument would seem to support this theory. Josephus emphasizes that Judas Galilaeus with his fourth philosophy followed the Pharisees in all respects — except for an unbridled love of freedom. This is not just a vague classification. For in Josephus' account a Pharisee named Sadduk appears alongside Judas Galilaeus (*Ant.* 18.4). As Josephus sees it,

---

Theodorus, who came from Gadara, taught the future emperor Tiberius rhetoric in Rome around 33/32 BCE. During the reign of Hadrian, in the second century CE, the Cynic tradition was revived in the person of Oenomaus of Gadara. In the third century CE there is evidence of a rhetorician Apsines of Gadara. There must therefore have been at least a continuity in the education tradition in Gadara. Since Gamala, the hometown of Judas Galilaeus, was not far from Gadara, it is possible that Cynic philosophers were known about (more or less superficially) in the Gaulanitis. It is true that the deep valley of the Jarmuk lay between Gadara and Gamala. There was no road joining the "neighboring" towns.

26. Cf. his remarks on the Epicureans in *Ant.* 10.277; 19.32. In *Apion* 2.180, however, he inveighs against the Epicurean denial of Providence and assures his readers that all Jews are united in the rejection of such teachings. This is probably one of the reasons why Josephus does not develop further the comparison between the Sadducees and the Epicureans which he hints at.

27. The same conjecture is to be found in Hengel, *Zeloten*, p. 83 n. 1.

Judas Galilaeus' philosophy is a radical splinter group that has broken away from the Pharisaic philosophy. In *Life* 12 he had compared this Pharisaic philosophy with the Stoa. He must therefore have led educated contemporary readers to suppose that Judas Galilaeus should be seen as a kind of Cynic, for Cynicism was a radicalized Stoicism. We can make this plausible by posing the further question: Were there features in the way this "fourth philosophy" of Judas Galilaeus presented itself that might remind us of the Cynics?

Josephus describes Judas Galilaeus with words that would be appropriate for Cynics: he is described as someone who "reviles" the Jews (κακίζων *War* 2.118 and ὀνειδίσας *War* 2.433). This indicates a morally insistent appeal. Josephus also speaks of him "admonishing" (παρακαλεῖν *Ant.* 18.4). This can hardly be the chiding words of a prophet.[28] Josephus never implies any claim on the part of Judas Galilaeus to be a prophet, as he does with Theudas (*Ant.* 20.97). For him Judas was a Sophist. He must presumably have operated as a teacher. Perhaps, like a number of Cynic philosophers, he "reviled" those he was speaking to in order to encourage them to lead a good life.[29]

Josephus also emphasizes the fact that Judas Galilaeus taught that God alone should be recognised as Lord and no human lord should be recognised beside him. It would be a sin "if they accepted any mortal master apart from God" (*War* 2.118). He criticized the fact "that they wanted to be subject not only to God but also to the Romans" (*War* 2.433). His followers had "a love of freedom that was difficult to overcome," consisting in the fact that they "accepted God alone as their leader and Lord" (*Ant.* 18.23).[30] The

28. Hengel, *Zeloten*, p. 94.

29. Josephus characterizes Nabal as a representative of the "Cynic way of life" (ἐκ κυνικῆς ἀσκήσεως) (*Ant.* 6.296). This characterization as a Cynic is probably due to the offensive words about David with which he refuses to pay him a "tribute" from his herds: "So conceited a view do those have of themselves who (sc. like David) have fled from their masters and now behave in an improper and insolent way" (*Ant.* 6.298). Both Nabal and Judas Galilaeus refuse to pay a tribute — Nabal to the guerrilla fighter David, Judas Galilaeus to the Emperor. Josephus' judgement on Nabal is quite clearly a negative one; he calls him a "harsh and wicked" man.

30. Philo mentions the Cynics twice. In his treatise on freedom he presents the Cynic Diogenes as an example of the paradoxical freedom of the wise man who demonstrated his freedom even when in captivity (*Prob.* 121-24). This characterization fits in well with the followers of Judas Galilaeus and their unbridled love of freedom. Philo also names Aristippus and Diogenes in *Plant.* 151 as representatives of the Cynic school of thought.

later figure of Eleazar, in his great speech in Masada, stressed that the insurgents had resolved "to be subject neither to the Romans nor to anyone else, but to God alone, for he alone is the true and legitimate Lord of human beings" (*War* 7.323). This sharp contrast between God and human beings may have reminded some people of the contrast made by the Cynics between nature and convention, which was differently motivated.[31] It is therefore possible that Judas Galilaeus adopted an external style for his "philosophy" like that of a variant of Cynicism, and in the process he took on the attributes of an itinerant Cynic philosopher — not least in order to camouflage his message behind a role that was widespread in antiquity. A Cynic influence is historically possible. Judas Galilaeus came from Gamala, a Jewish town on the Golan Heights,[32] that was not too far away from Gadara. And in Gadara philosophical and Cynic traditions can be shown to have existed over a period of several centuries. But the Cynic exterior was most probably only superficial. The use of the forms of the Hellenistic culture often served only to show the local issues to better advantage. It was quite possible to wander around with a beard, a bag and a staff, without being a real Cynic. It was enough to propagate a similarly unconventional message.

In my view, it is historically fairly certain that Jesus had to distance himself from the teachings of Judas Galilaeus. This is shown by the discussion about the payment of taxes (Mark 12:13-17), for only Judas Galilaeus had raised this issue to this extent prior to Jesus. If Jesus had to defend himself in an open debate against being placed in the same category as Judas Galilaeus, then it is not inconceivable that he dissociated himself from Judas indirectly in other instances. The message Jesus was proclaiming had a basic feature in common with that of Judas Galilaeus: the radical theocratic message of the rule of God. This must have been understood as

31. The fact that the contrast between nature and convention could be interpreted by the Jews as a contrast between God's will and human tradition is shown in Philo's treatise on freedom, in the section on the Essenes (*Prob.* 75-91).

32. Josephus described the town, and its siege and destruction during the Jewish War, in detail (*War* 4.1-83; *Life* 46ff.; 114ff.; 179ff.). Excavations showed that it was a Jewish town through and through. Evidence was found of a synagogue and several *mikveh* baths. A find of rebel coins with the legend "For the deliverance of the holy city of Jerusalem" fits in well with Josephus' description of the stubborn resistance of the town. Cf. Shmaryahu Gutman, "Gamala," in *The New Encyclopedia of Archaeological Excavations in the Holy Land*, vol. 2 (ed. E. Stern; Jerusalem/New York: The Israel Exploratory Society, 1993), pp. 459-63; Steven Fine, "Gamala," in *The Oxford Encyclopedia of Archaeology in the Near East*, vol. 2 (ed. Eric M. Meyers; New York/Oxford: Oxford University Press, 1997), p. 382.

a revival of Judas Galilaeus' teaching that God alone should rule. If Jesus was sending his disciples out into the villages of Galilee and Judea with the message of the imminent kingdom of God, then it was a good idea to give them instructions for their mission that kept them from being confused with representatives of the last major campaign. Thus the emphasis on the message of peace and the dissociation from the Cynic "outfit."[33]

It must be stressed once again that this is only a hypothesis. In its favor we can point to the convergence of conclusions drawn from two independent sources, the synoptic Gospels and Josephus. This hypothesis could include the element of truth in the disputed "Cynic thesis."[34] However, unlike the latter it does not reckon with any direct Cynic influence, only with an indirect influence through dissociation from the Cynic school. Nor does it suppose that Judas Galilaeus was a genuine Cynic. He was no more a Cynic than the Pharisees were Stoics or the Essenes were Pythagoreans. All that it assumes is an external similarity to the Cynics. In this sense, Jesus' wandering existence could have had its origin indirectly in the Cynic influence. This would fit in with the radical call for renunciation of property, for which there are no analogies in Judaism (Mark 10:21), or the provocative violation of norms of piety, when a follower is not allowed to bury

---

33. The parallel drawn between the Jesus movement and the movements led by Theudas and Judas Galilaeus in the advice given by Gamaliel (in Acts 5:36-37) may indicate that the three movements took on a comparable form. We know for certain that Theudas led his followers away from their personal ties and wanted to cross the Jordan with them: "Now it came to pass, while Fadus was procurator of Judea, that a certain magician, whose name was Theudas, persuaded a great part of the people to take their effects with them, and follow him to the river Jordan; for he told them he was a prophet, and that he would, by his own command, divide the river, and afford them an easy passage over it; and many were deluded by his words" (*Ant.* 20.97-98). Here, too, a certain mobility is assumed. However, it is conditional on the expectation of a particular miracle, and so we cannot necessarily infer that Theudas had led an itinerant existence previously.

34. The Cynic thesis has been developed by F. G. Downing, "Cynics and Christians," *NTS* 30 (1984): 584-93; F. G. Downing, *Christ and the Cynics* (JSOTSup 4; Sheffield: Sheffield Academic Press, 1988); F. G. Downing, *Cynics and Christian Origins* (Edinburgh: T&T Clark, 1992); F. G. Downing, "The Jewish Cynic Jesus," in *Jesus, Mark and Q: The Teaching of Jesus and Its Earliest Records* (ed. M. Labahn and A. Schmidt; JSNTSup 214; Sheffield: Sheffield Academic Press, 2001), pp. 184-214. Independently of Downing, it has also been supported by Burton L. Mack, *A Myth of Innocence: Mark and Christian Origins* (Philadelphia: Fortress, 1988), pp. 53-77, 69; Leif E. Vaage, *Galilean Upstarts: Jesus' First Followers According to Q* (Valley Forge, Pa.: Trinity, 1994), pp. 102-6; J. Dominic Crossan, *The Historical Jesus: The Life of a Mediterranean Jewish Peasant* (San Francisco: Harper, 1991).

his dead father (Matt 8:21-22). But neither Judas Galilaeus nor Jesus of Nazareth followed the wisdom of the Greeks; they followed the wisdom of the Jews. They were deeply rooted in the Jewish people's own traditions. This leads us to our last point in the search for analogies.

A Mythical Model: The Sophia?

In the Jesus tradition, Jesus is interpreted as messenger of the Sophia.[35] However, it is disputed whether or not this motif can be traced back to the historical Jesus.[36] It is often closely linked with the motif of the rejected prophet, and may therefore be historical, for there is no evidence before Jesus of the connection between Wisdom and the killing of her messengers in the tradition. But even if Jesus' mission was interpreted in this way only after the event, his existence as an itinerant teacher could have helped support such an interpretation.

Mythological statements about the Sophia contain the motif of the wandering Sophia, who has no home on earth until she finds a dwelling with some of her followers. In Sirach the pre-existent Wisdom is represented as a restless being who wanders throughout the entire cosmos: "Alone I encircled the vault of the sky, and I walked on the bottom of the deeps. Over the waves of the sea and over the whole earth, and over every people and nation I have held sway" (24:5-6). This Wisdom set out to find a home on earth as well — among one of the many peoples there: "Among all these I searched for rest, and looked to see in whose territory I might pitch camp" (24:7). But God commanded her to settle down in Israel, where she found a fixed place in the Temple.

35. On the Sophia cf. Felix Christ, *Jesus Sophia. Die Sophia-Christologie bei den Synoptikern* (ATANT 57; Zürich: Zwingli Verlag, 1970). Martin Hengel, "Jesus als messianischer Lehrer der Weisheit und die Anfänge der Christologie," in *Sagesse et Religion* (ed. Edmond Jacob; Paris: Presses Univ. de France, 1979), pp. 147-90 = revised in: Martin Hengel and Anna Maria Schwemer, *Der messianische Anspruch Jesu und die Anfänge der Christologie* (WUNT 138; Tübingen: Mohr, 2001), pp. 81-131. Petra von Gemünden, "'Draw near to me, you unlearned' (Sir 51:23): Concepts of Wisdom in Biblical Times," *AJBI* 31 (2005): 63-106.

36. The idea of Jesus as messenger of the Sophia is only found in the Logia Source (QLk 7:31-35; 11:29-32; 11:49-51; 13:34-35), not in Mark. The connection between Jesus and the Sophia can therefore be seen as a specific interpretation of the Logia Source. Nevertheless, the spread of Wisdom motifs in post-Easter Christology can be explained very well historically if the historical Jesus had seen himself as a messenger of Wisdom.

In the time period we are considering, this certainty had been disturbed by a great agitation. Some Jews were questioning whether Wisdom had found her dwelling place on earth. In the Parables of the Ethiopian Enoch, Wisdom leaves the earth in order to return to heaven. We read there: "Wisdom found no place where she might dwell; then a dwelling-place was assigned her in the heavens. Wisdom went forth to make her dwelling among the children of men, and found no dwelling-place: Wisdom returned to her place, and took her seat among the angels" (*1 En.* 42:1-2).

The synoptic tradition speaks of a Wisdom with no fixed home, who sends her prophets and messengers to Israel in vain. Her messengers are killed (QLk 11:49-51). She has still not found a place of rest — and certainly not in Jerusalem. For as a hen gathers her children around her, so had she tried in vain again and again to win the support of Jerusalem. But she was rejected (QLk 13:34-35). As early as in the Logia Source, the homelessness of Jesus was interpreted as the homelessness of Wisdom. If the Sophia motif is traced back to Jesus himself, then consequently this interpretation of his wandering existence is also to be traced back to the historical Jesus. In the same way as the Wisdom of the Greeks motivated some people to travel around as her messengers, so too did the Wisdom of the one and only God. But we can leave the question open as to whether the motif of the Sophia and her homeless messengers can be traced back to Jesus. In any case, even if it was a subsequent interpretation, it is a material part of Jesus' itinerant existence and should therefore be mentioned.

The Function of the Itinerant Existence of Jesus

We might now ask what difference it makes whether a teaching is spread from a teacher's house or by a wandering teacher. Is this not simply a triviality? By no means! The itinerant existence of Jesus correlates with several features of his teaching. If things correlate it does not mean they are dependent on each other. The correlations simply indicate that it is no coincidence that an itinerant teacher upholds these particular teachings and not other ones. Among such teachings that should be mentioned are the radical ethical teaching of the Jesus tradition, its openness towards women, the role played by foreigners within it, and its effect as an oral message.

Gerd Theissen

The Ethos of the Jesus Tradition as an Itinerant Radicalism

The ethical radicalism of Jesus is in my view an "itinerant radicalism." Having no fixed home, being far from one's family, and renouncing property, and likewise a demonstrative defencelessness, are elements that can more easily be upheld by people with deviant lifestyles than by those who are integrated into a settled way of life. But this does not mean that Jesus was a "marginal Jew." His message about the kingdom of God finds a place in the heart of Judaism. It is radical monotheism. But his wandering existence was a way of life for outsiders. As an outsider he upheld convictions that were central to Judaism. The key to resolving this paradox is to be found in the analogy of the Cynics. It also helps us even if we do not see in Jesus a Jewish Cynic. Due to their lifestyle, Cynics were outsiders in the pagan world of antiquity. There were itinerant Cynics and settled Cynics with varying degrees of closeness to everyday life. Both represented an outsider existence, in which they lived out what people in the center of this society also strove after: a life of trust in the power of reason, a self-sufficiency in human life through consistently distinguishing between natural needs and conventions from which it was possible to liberate oneself. The Cynics are only marginal so far as their lifestyle is concerned, not in terms of their convictions. On the contrary: their marginal way of life enabled them to be more consistent in practicing the axioms of the ethics of antiquity than would have been possible within the framework of a normal life with its compromises. Applying this to Jesus, we can say that he, too, was on the margins of Judaism in terms of his lifestyle, but because of this he was able to uphold the fundamental convictions of Judaism more clearly and in a more "extreme" way than he would have been able to do in normal life.

Women as Addressees of His Teaching

Those whom Jesus addressed in his teaching included *women*. In the pericope of Jesus and the *Familia Dei* they are mentioned directly as his listeners. They appear as the sisters and mothers of Jesus (Mark 3:31-35). In the story of Martha and Mary his teaching is directed only at women. The direct witnesses also include the women who are mentioned as being in the group surrounding Jesus. According to Mark 15:40-41, women followed him like the other disciples. In other words they were not just adherents in the broader sense but part of the inner circle of disciples who accompanied him on his wanderings. Luke 8:1-3, on the other hand, only mentions women who had been cured and were serving the group. The stories of healing mostly end with the people who had been healed returning to their normal life and being given back to their families. We therefore cannot necessarily assume that the mention of women who had been cured refers to wandering followers of Jesus. But Mary Magdalene, who is mentioned in this passage, was without doubt a follower in the full sense of the word. Her surname, "the woman from Magdala," was given to her outside her native town. There may well be a connection between the itinerant existence of Jesus and his openness towards women. In a teacher's house it is possible to keep a check on those who listen to the teacher. In the open air, anyone — including women — can mingle with the crowd of listeners. When a wandering preacher wants to find food and shelter, he is particularly dependent on women. They were in charge in the home. We must not conclude from this that Jesus' openness towards women was just an accidental consequence of his itinerant existence. Jesus had women in mind as listeners to his message.

This can be inferred from the gender-symmetric formation of pairs in his sayings, when he placed images and examples from the male and from the female world next to one another.[37] There is no analogy for this in the Jewish wisdom writings. The sayings of Solomon and Jesus ben Sirach are always directed only at young men; nowhere in their examples do we find images relating to men symmetrically alongside images relating to women. In the Logia Source alone, however, there is evidence of four such pairs being formed. In QLk 11:31-32 the men of Nineveh repent and the Queen of the South comes to Solomon. In QLk 12:22-32 the ravens neither sow nor reap, and the lilies neither spin nor weave. Sowing and reaping is intended to describe the work outside the house, and spinning and weaving the work of women inside it. The parable of the mustard seed and the yeast (QLk 13:18-19/20-21) also relates to both areas. A man sows the mustard seed (outside), and a woman mixes the yeast into the dough (inside). The relationship between the working worlds can be the other way round: according to QLk 17:34-35 women are grinding outside at the mill, while the

---

37. Gerd Theissen, "Frauen im Umkreis Jesu" (1993), in Gerd Theissen, *Jesus als historische Gestalt* (FRLANT 202; Göttingen: Vandenhoeck, 2003), pp. 91-110.

Gerd Theissen

men lie inside on a bed — either sleeping or eating. In Luke the formation of three more pairs is to be found. Next to the shepherd who searches for the lost sheep appears the woman with her lost coin (Luke 15:3-10). In Jesus' first public speech in Nazareth, the widow from Zarephath and the Syrian Naaman are named as examples alongside each other (Luke 4:25-27). This cannot be a tendency that is particular to Luke. Otherwise Luke would have placed the related parables of the importunate friend and the importunate widow next to one another. But the first is now in the eleventh chapter and the second in the eighteenth (Luke 11:5-8; 18:1-8). The formation of such pairs clearly already existed in the Logia Source. In Mark there is no certain formation of pairs in the text that has come down to us. The picture word of the new patch on the old garment and the new wine in old wineskins cannot be definitely interpreted as being gender-related (Mark 2:21-22). To make up for this, Mark gives women a more prominent role in his narratives.[38] There are numerous examples, such as Peter's mother-in-law (Mark 1:29-31), the little daughter of Jairus and the woman with the hemorrhage (Mark 5:21-43), the Syro-Phoenician woman (Mark 7:24-30), the anointing in Bethany (Mark 14:3-9), and the women who were witnesses of his crucifixion, his burial, and the message of the resurrection at the empty tomb (Mark 15:40-41, 47; 16:1-8).

Jesus and the Neighbors of the Jews

Jesus visited areas outside the Jewish heartlands: the regions of Tyre and Sidon in the northwest, the villages around Caesarea Philippi in the north, and the land of the Decapolis in the southeast. In every case, he always travelled in the area surrounding the Gentile towns, not the towns themselves. He probably found in these rural areas Jews who were living in a precarious situation as scattered members of Jewish minorities. They may well have been particularly receptive to the preaching of a message that could have given them a new Jewish identity.[39] It is noticeable that some of the sayings of Jesus refer to the Gentile neighbors in a strikingly positive

38. Monika Fander, *Die Stellung der Frau im Markusevangelium* (MThA 8; Münster: Telos-Verlag, 1989).

39. Thomas Schmeller, "Jesus im Umland Galiläas: Zu den markinischen Berichten vom Aufenthalt Jesu in den Gebieten von Tyros, Cäsarea Philippi und der Dekapolis," *BZ* 38 (1994): 44-66.

way. For example, he said that the inhabitants of Tyre and Sidon in the northwest would have repented if they had seen his miracles (QLk 10:13). The Ninevites to the north of Palestine would have listened to him as they once listened to Jonah. The Queen of the South would have marvelled at him as she once marvelled at Solomon (QLk 11:31-32). Someone who has such a positive opinion of his neighbors (in practically every direction) will have fewer inhibitions about setting out towards them than someone with ethnocentric views. It is no wonder that Jesus saw people streaming into the kingdom of God from all points of the compass (QLk 13:29). Admittedly, the possibility cannot be excluded that Jesus' journeys outside the borders of Galilee were motivated by his desire to escape from the jurisdiction of Herod Antipas. Pharisees once warned him about Herod Antipas and advised him to leave the country (Luke 13:31-33). Through his frequently mentioned voyages by boat across the Sea of Galilee, Jesus was able to travel to other territories at any time, for this sea was the point where the territories of Antipas, Philip, and the Decapolis met. The wanderings of Jesus (and his voyages over the sea — including some at night) may also have served to help him escape from dangerous situations.

The Organization of the Oral Message

The most important thing for a teacher is his message. Jesus' itinerant existence primarily served to spread this message more effectively. In this he differed from his teacher John the Baptist. The Baptist taught in the desert, and people flocked to him there. Both the Gospels and Josephus are in agreement on this. We can only make out vague traces of any mobility on the part of the Baptist. According to John's Gospel, he was active at Aenon and Salim (John 3:23), according to the synoptic Gospels more in the south of the Jordan valley, where it turns into a desert (Mark 1:2ff. par.). Jesus differed from him considerably: he went out to meet people in the world they were living in and brought his message to them. The most important medium in his society was the spoken word. There were hardly any other "mass media." Coins could transport a message that reached the hands of everybody. Inscriptions could be drawn up that everybody could read, provided they were capable of reading. But these two "hard" media were a privilege of the powerful. The people could only be reached by oral messages; and it could only become active through oral communication. Jesus organized this medium in an effective way, by operating with his disciples as an itinerant teacher.

The familiarity of the disciples with Jesus' message was virtually an automatic consequence of his wandering existence. When Jesus travelled with them from place to place, they heard the basic elements of his message over and over again. There was no pressure on Jesus to say something different in every village. We can therefore assume that he repeated his words over and over again (with the variations that are typical of oral traditions). In this way the disciples learned them without any conscious learning, simply through the repetition that inevitably accompanied the existence of a wandering teacher. There is therefore no need to posit any well-ordered school system to locate the beginning of the transmission of Jesus' words during the pre-Easter life of Jesus.[40] The "disorderly" existence of an itinerant teacher naturally created many opportunities for repetition!

When, in addition, Jesus sent his disciples out on an itinerant mission, they must have had to repeat the same message in its basic features in a number of different places! Nothing reinforces the memory so much as active repetition. The disciples must therefore soon have had a stock of oral texts that they could reproduce by heart and vary as needed. Their content must have sunk in without any effort through active repetition! Three or four villages would have been enough! And since Jesus sent out his disciples in pairs, there was even an informal "social control" on conformity with his message. And so, through his organization of the oral communication medium, Jesus not only ensured that his message would reach all villages and other places in as short a time as possible; without intending it, he also created the basis for passing on his message after his death.

---

40. Birger Gerhardsson, *Memory and Manuscript: Oral Tradition and Written Transmission in Rabbinic Judaism and Early Christianity* (Lund: Gleerup, 1961, 1998). On the overall discussion, cf. the overview in James D. G. Dunn, *Jesus Remembered* (CM 1; Grand Rapids: Eerdmans, 2003), pp. 192-210.

Jesus as a Teller of Parables:
On Jesus' Self-Interpretation in His Parables

Michael Wolter

Parables and Their Context

1. When we include Jesus' parables within the search for the historical Jesus, we face the same methodological objection raised against Joachim Jeremias' "historicising" interpretation of the parables:[1] the uncertainty, if not impossibility, of reconstructing the historical context in which the parables were told. Jeremias himself understood this context to be "a particular historical place in Jesus' life."[2] He defined it more precisely as "the unique situation on each occasion during Jesus' ministry."[3] And here it was "generally, indeed in most cases" a case of "situations of struggle,"[4] so that for Jeremias the parables of Jesus were "not exclusively, but to a large extent, weapons to be used in a dispute."[5]

The approach used by Joachim Jeremias is in principle correct. The stories which we call "parables" were indeed told by Jesus as parables, or — considered in terms of the hermeneutics of reception — the stories Jesus told were genuinely intended to be understood as parables by their first real hearers. This means that these stories were told and understood as narratives pointing to something beyond what was narrated. The imagined scenes are invitations to enter into the world in which the narrator

---

1. J. Jeremias, *Die Gleichnisse Jesu* (Göttingen: Vandenhoeck & Ruprecht, 1977 [9th ed.] [1947]).
2. Jeremias, *Gleichnisse,* p. 18.
3. Jeremias, *Gleichnisse,* p. 19.
4. Jeremias, *Gleichnisse,* pp. 17-18.
5. Jeremias, *Gleichnisse,* p. 18.

and the listener live. The fact that this context can only ever be reconstructed hypothetically can therefore never be a *relevant argument* against the correctness in principle of the historicizing interpretation of the parables, but only at most an incentive to intensify efforts to achieve a methodically reliable reconstruction of this context.

2. In what follows I will now try to make further progress in this direction. In so doing I will only partly follow the aforementioned signposts left by Joachim Jeremias. I will ignore them wherever he applies the terms "concrete," "unique situation," "particular historical place," or "particular time."[6] On the contrary, I will restrict myself to the search for *typical* contexts in which Jesus appears. The reasons for this restriction are above all practical ones, for it is far easier to reach a consensus on the reconstruction of such typical contexts than on the reconstruction of *individual situations*. In the search for the historical Jesus, "typical contexts" in this sense can include, for example, Jesus' ministry as a charismatic healer and exorcist, or the fact that the "sovereign Rule of God" played an important role in what he preached, or the fact that he cultivated relations with people who were described by the double designation of "tax-collectors and sinners." The criterion for identifying a particular element as "typical" is quite simply "variety of testimony": Jesus' healing and exorcizing activities, the "sovereign Rule of God," and Jesus' friendship with "tax-collectors and sinners" all figure in Jesus' ministry in Mark, in Q, and in Luke's and Matthew's special material. In this way we can of course also identify Jesus' speaking in parables as something "typical" for him. (In order to avoid any misunderstanding, I should also stress that one cannot turn this argument around and make the lack of variety of testimony into a criterion for exclusion.)

These "typical" elements in Jesus' ministry can be further reinforced (and are in such cases particularly interesting) when they coincide. In relation to Jesus' parables this applies where they coincide with the feature of the "sovereign Rule of God,"[7] but also to the element of Jesus' friendship with "tax-collectors and sinners"; on a number of occasions Jesus responds to criticism on this count by speaking metaphorically:

- with a word-picture as in Mark 2:17 ("It is not the healthy who need a doctor, but the sick")

---

6. All quotes are from Jeremias, *Gleichnisse,* pp. 17-19.

7. Those termed "*Basileia* parables" are found in Mark, Q, and Matthew's special material.

- with the parable of the two debtors in Luke 7:41-43
- with the three parables of something that is lost in Luke 15

It is of course clear that we cannot generalise about just one particular "typical" context. That is the mistake that Joachim Jeremias made when he explained nearly all the parables as resulting from conflicts between Jesus and his critics.[8] On the other hand — and here Jeremias is correct[9] — all the parables are essentially related to one single context, namely the mission of Jesus as such. In this respect there is indeed something that may be termed the *one* typical context or the *one* typical narration situation which the stories that Jesus tells as parables point towards. And here it is not simply a question of the human relationship to God, but of a communicative structure which forms a kind of dramatic triangle involving the interaction between God, Jesus, and the listeners. All three factors are present in every parable.

Within the limits of this paper it is impossible to demonstrate in detail how this dramatic triangle works for every parable. In what follows I would therefore like to do two things. First, I will sketch out a general paradigm which opens the way to an interpretation of the parables within this dramatic triangle. Second, I will demonstrate how this kind of interpretation might work, taking the example of a particular type of parable. The actual thesis is to be found in the heading (which I will formulate in contradistinction to a phrase with which Gerd Theissen and Annette Merz summarized the issue of the parables in their book on Jesus):[10] "The original basic theme of the parables" is not "the whole of human life before God," but the self-interpretation of Jesus as the revelation of God's eschatological plan of salvation for the human race.

The Listener as Hermeneutic Key to Interpreting the Parables

If, then, it is the case that stories become parables when they point to something that goes beyond themselves and enter into a relationship with

---

8. Only a few of the parables were subsumed by Jeremias under the heading "Living Out Discipleship" (Chap. 3.7): Matt 13:44, 45-46; Luke 10:30-37; Matt 18:23-35.

9. Cf. the summary: "All of Jesus' parables force the listener to adopt a position with regard to his person and to his mission" (p. 227).

10. G. Theissen and A. Merz, *Der historische Jesus* (Göttingen: Vandenhoeck & Ruprecht, 1996), p. 297.

the context of the story-telling, then we must begin with those recipients of the story who carry out this transfer. We can distinguish three different listeners; in fact there are many more, but for the interpretation of the parables we only need these three: The real listeners, the historical listeners, and the intended listeners.

Three Different Types of Listener

THE REAL LISTENERS

A story can really *become* a parable only when there are real listeners. They make the story a parable by placing the events that are narrated into the world in which they live. In principle, they can do this with any story, including stories that were never intended by the narrator to be parables.

So when we search for the meaning of a parable, we need to search for the real listeners, for it is they who are the first to provide a meaning for the story. In the context of this paper I would like to restrict this to the real *original listeners* to the parables, i.e., the listeners who heard the parable directly from Jesus' lips. Apart from them, of course, the group of real listeners includes everyone else to whom the parable was told later on. The problem is, however, that the real listeners are an absolutely inaccessible quantity, for as soon as we reconstruct them, they change into the second type of listener:

THE HISTORICAL LISTENERS

Here we are dealing with a construct, the result of historiographical enquiry, cut from the same cloth as the "historical Jesus." Between the historical listeners and the real listeners there exists the same ontological difference as between the historical Jesus and Jesus of Nazareth. Apart from these two types of listener, we need to distinguish yet a third type:

THE INTENDED LISTENERS

Here we are talking about those listeners who exist in the consciousness of the narrator. These listeners are the image that the narrator has of them when he tells the parable. They are the listeners for whom the parable is told. They are an integral part of the intention of the narrator, who, with the help of the parables, wants to provoke them or stabilize them, alter them or console them. Naturally, this type of listener always has a part to play in the parables. Within the plot that is related in the parable, they take on certain roles.

(a) To help explain what I mean, I would like to examine the parable of the lost sheep (Luke 15:4-7 par. Matt 18:12-14), which Jesus tells in different rhetorical situations in the two gospels:

- In Luke 15 he tells the parable to the *Pharisees and teachers of the law,* who were protesting against his fellowship with the "tax-collectors and sinners."
- In Matthew 18 he tells it to the *disciples,* so that they might see to it that "not one of these little ones" should be lost.

Depending which listeners we assume to have been the historical ones, they have a different part to play in the parable:

- In Luke 15 the narrator assigns them the role of the friends and neighbours who are invited to share in the rejoicing (v. 6).
- In Matthew 18 the intended listeners are expected to identify with the shepherd who goes out looking for the lost sheep (v. 12).

The intended listeners to the parables can therefore be reconstructed by means of the text that is told, and it is characteristic for them that they appear not only *in different roles,*[11] but also *at different stages of the plot.* We will return to this point later.

(b) So far as the relationship between the real and intended listeners is concerned, there are several possible constellations:

- The real listeners recognize themselves in the intended listeners. This is the ideal case of a successful communication.
- The real listeners fail to recognize themselves in the intended listeners and reject the proposed transfer from the narrated world into the

---

11. See also G. Eichholz, *Gleichnisse der Evangelien* (Neukirchen-Vluyn: Neukirchener, 1971), p. 35: "One of the figures in the parable can be so tailor-made to fit him (i.e. the listener), that he encounters himself in it."

world that is being addressed. In this case the story is told as a parable, but not heard as one, and the communication is a failure.

- Another possible alternative is that the real listeners identify with completely different figures in the story from those the narrator intended. We can observe this taking place, for example, in the process of handing down the parable of the lost sheep, regardless of which figure in the story Jesus originally offered the intended listeners for them to identify with.

All Listeners Consist of Knowledge

However, we should not exaggerate the distinction between the different types of listener, for the intended listener and the real original listeners have more in common than what separates them. The reason for this is that the material from which listeners are formed consists of nothing other than *cultural knowledge* that they have acquired during the course of their socialisation. In this regard Umberto Eco has spoken of an "encyclopedic competence,"[12] equivalent to what the sociology of knowledge has called a "social stock of knowledge,"[13] which is constituted through language. From this we have good reasons for reaching the following conclusion: inasmuch as Jesus, the initial narrator of the parables, and their first real listeners were socialized in one and the same cultural context, then the image that Jesus had of his listeners (the intended listeners) and the listeners themselves (the real listeners) were connected with one another on the very elementary level of a basic common cultural knowledge.

So far as most of the parables are concerned, we are faced today with just the opposite situation: because of our socialization within a Christian culture, the parables have themselves become an integral part of our cultural encyclopedia. They are thus no longer "text," but have become part of the "context." By contrast, the context that *Jesus and his first listeners* had in common and with which they were familiar has become strange for *us* today, so that if we want to understand the intention of the parables we first

---

12. U. Eco, *Lector in fibula: Die Mitarbeit der Interpretation in erzählenden Texten* (Munich: dtv, 1998 [3rd ed.]), pp. 94ff.

13. P. L. Berger and T. Luckmann, *The Social Construction of Reality: A Treatise in the Sociology of Knowledge* (Garden City, N.Y.: Doubleday, 1966), pp. 41-46.

have to laboriously reconstruct that context using history-of-tradition methods.

Cultural and Historical Context

The first narrator of and first listeners to Jesus' parables shared a common cultural encyclopedia. Relating this idea to the aforementioned historical location of the parables, it follows that we should locate Jesus' parables at the point where two contexts meet:

- the *cultural* context of the common encyclopedia of Jesus and his first listeners;
- the *historical* context of Jesus' ministry.

The parables of Jesus have no other purpose than to elucidate the relationship between these two contexts. We will now leave the question of the context for a while and focus on the text.

The Narrative Structure of the Parables: Parables with Nodal Points

Claude Bremond's Model

We saw earlier that not only do the listeners enter into the dramatic action of a parable alongside certain figures in the story, but that it is also possible to identify the point in the chronological course of the story at which they make their appearance. The fact that this identification can turn out to be quite different for the intended and the real listeners does not alter the facts of the case as such. This open point, at which text and context enter into a relationship with each other, can be described more precisely by examining the narrative structure of the text.

In doing this, I would like to make use of categories for the analysis of a narrative text that have been proposed by Claude Bremond.[14] Wilhelm Egger has already used Bremond's model to good effect for the interpreta-

14. Cf. C. Bremond, *Logique du récit* (Paris: Ed. du Seuil, 1973).

tion of the synoptic narrative tradition,[15] but in fact it is much more helpful for the interpretation of the parables.

The central feature of this model is what Bremond refers to as "nodal points." His thesis is that every narrative sooner or later comes to a point at which there are various options for the future direction the narrative will take. It is at these points that the future course of the story is decided. We may graphically represent this progression of narratives as follows:

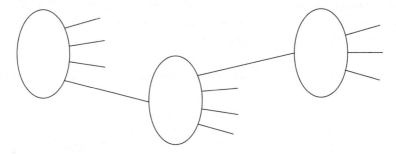

It is of crucial significance that on the one hand there are *a number* of potential continuations, and on the other hand that in each case only *one* of these continuations can ever actually become reality. However, the listeners are aware — on the basis of their cultural encyclopedia — which other continuations might have been possible.

When the narrative actually continues, there are basically two possibilities:

- the option that is in fact chosen diverges from the expectation of the listeners
- the option that is in fact chosen coincides with the expectation of the listeners

Between these two idealized extremes there are a number of intermediate positions.

I believe this model enables considerable progress in the discussion

---

15. W. Egger, *Nachfolge als Weg zum Lebe: Chancen neuerer exegetischer Methoden dargelegt an Mk 10,17-31* (ÖBS 1; Klosterneuburg: Österreichisches Katholisches Bibelwerk, 1979), pp. 28-34; W. Egger, *Methodenlehre zum Neuen Testament* (Freiburg/Basel/Vienna: Herder, 1987), pp. 123-24.

about typologically dividing the parable material into various categories ("parables," "similitudes," "picture-words," "exemplary stories," etc.). I would therefore like to illustrate Bremond's model with the help of four examples. In the process I will concentrate on the technical level and avoid any interpretation of the content.

Examples

One of the best examples of a nodal point occurs in the *parable of the shrewd steward* (Luke 16:1-8a). There, the inner monologue in vv. 3-4 is the point deciding how the story will continue.[16] The narrator even does the listeners a favor by having the steward go through the various options available for the continuation of the story; the listeners do not have to add them themselves from their cultural encyclopedia: "What am I to do? (τί ποιήσω;) . . . I'm not strong enough to dig, and I'm ashamed to beg. I know what I'll do." In fact this is not so much an "inner monologue" as a dialogue between the steward and the listeners in order to consider the various possibilities for the story's progression arising out of the basic cultural stock of knowledge:

> *Steward:* "What am I to do?"
> *Listeners:* "Dig!"
> *Steward:* "I'm not strong enough!"
> *Listeners:* "Beg!"
> *Steward:* "I'm ashamed!"

The option that the narrator then uses in the story lies outside what the listeners might expect, given their understanding of reality.

As the story unfolds, another nodal point presents itself. Here, too, the option chosen is not one confirming the expectations of the listeners, but calling those expectations into question: the reaction of the *kyrios* in v. 8a, when he praises the steward's actions as "shrewd."

When we interpret the parables on the basis of narrative nodal points,

---

16. Cf. B. Heininger, *Metaphorik, Erzählstruktur und szenisch-dramatische Gestaltung in den Sondergutgleichnissen bei Lukas* (Münster: Aschendorff, 1991), p. 80, noting inner monologues as "interfaces of communication . . . with the readers."

some instructive relations and connections emerge. For example, the parable of the shrewd steward has a counterpart in the *parable of the rich farmer* (Luke 12:16-20). Here, too, the first nodal point is marked by the question "What am I to do?" (τί ποιήσω;) in v. 17. In contrast to the story of the steward, the various different options are not expressed on the level of the text; these are left to the listeners. Moreover, the option that is in fact chosen remains within the bounds of what might be expected. From the list of possibilities available to him, the farmer chooses one that ethically lies in the middle (indicating the parable is intended to remain neutral on the ethical level): he neither distributes his newly-acquired wealth among the poor, nor uses it to become richer still. Rather, he simply wants to enjoy himself and take it easy (v. 19). The wisdom literature parallel to this verse[17] clearly shows this plot option lies well within the framework of what might be expected, including especially the rich man's assumption he will enjoy his wealth "for many years." This, says traditional wisdom, is precisely what rich people expect; they do not reckon that they might die at any moment — but, in this case, death comes immediately. The connection with the parable of the shrewd steward is primarily evident in the evaluations of the actions of the two protagonists: ἄφρων in this case (12:20) and φρόνιμος in the other (16:8a). The two terms are lexical antonyms; in both cases the judgment is spoken by God or Jesus, and in both stories there is a narrative gap between the action that is described and the concluding judgment. The interaction between the plot option chosen in each case and the concluding judgment of God brings the two parables very close together.

The third example, that of the *parable of the labourers in the vineyard* (Matt 20:1-15), shows that at these nodal points the narrator can even put himself in the place of the listeners and read their thoughts. In the exposition phase developing the story, the listeners are being conditioned without being aware of it. This happens in v. 4, where the "landowner" (οἰκοδεσπότης), as he is still referred to at this stage, promises the labourers who were hired at the third hour that he will pay them "what is right" (v. 4). The listeners are thus referred back to the wage agreement made in v. 2 with those labourers hired for the whole day, and so "the expectation of a proportionally graded payment at the end"[18] is created in them. When the narrative reaches the

---

17. Cf. Sir 11:16-17 (LXX: 18-19); 31:3; Eccl 2:24; 3:12-13; 5:18; 8:15.

18. K. Erlemann, *Gleichnisauslegung: Ein Lehr- und Arbeitsbuch* (Tübingen/Basel: Francke, 1999), p. 95.

point where this expectation should be fulfilled (after v. 9), it changes from the external level of the plot to "reporting thoughts"[19] that cannot be recognized externally: "So when those came who were hired first, they expected to receive more" (v. 10). It is here that the decisive nodal point is reached, and those whose narrative expectations are here formulated are of course none other than the listeners. Since they know the landowner pays "what is right" (v. 4), they expect that proportionally "more" will now be paid. And because the narrator knows the listeners are counting on this, he is able to place this expectation in the head of one of the figures in the story. It is therefore precisely at this point that the story makes the leap into the world of the listeners, and it is certainly no coincidence that the "landowner" (οἰκοδεσπότης) has now become the "owner of the vineyard" (ὁ κύριος τοῦ ἀμπελῶνος) (v. 8). And here an option for the continuation of the story is chosen that disappoints the narrative expectation of the listeners, finding themselves on the side of the labourers who have worked all day, just as it disappoints their expectations of God's justice.

In addition, it is interesting that the question at the end of v. 15 leads the story into a further narrative nodal point, but the narrative does not progress out of it again.[20] In the narrative world the story has ended, but in the spoken world it continues as the story of the listener; it is now up to them to choose the option appropriate for the newly-acquired insight into God's justice.

I will only touch briefly on the fourth example, that of the *parable of the lost son* (Luke 15:11-32). Here we find nodal points at three places during the course of the narrative, at which the further course of the story is decided:

- V. 17: "he came to his senses and said. . . ." Here the listeners ask themselves which decision the son will make to get out of his desperate situation.
- Vv. 20-21: "while he was still a long way off, his father saw him. . . ." Here the listeners ask themselves whether the father will really fulfill the wish of his son and make him one of his hired labourers (cf. v. 19b), or whether instead, for example, he will set his dogs on him.
- After v. 27, i.e., after the elder brother hears what has happened.

19. J. Vogt, *Aspekte erzählender Prosa* (Opladen: Westdeutscher Verlag, 1990), p. 157.
20. This incidentally links the end of this parable with the end of the book of Jonah (cf. Jonah 4:9-11).

At all three points the listeners have the opportunity to transfer the story into their own story. But all three nodal points also mark genuine alternatives, for it is not possible to imagine a listener who would play all three roles at the same time.

The Implicit Christological Substructure of the Parables

Going beyond this technical description, interpreting the content of the parables necessitates remembering that they were told as an integral part of the self-interpretation of Jesus. If we interpret the parables as an integral part of the search for the historical Jesus, then they cannot be seen independently of their narrator and his intention. This applies in two ways:

First, the situations in which plot options arise for the figures in the stories have, for the listeners to the context, an implicit Christological substructure. The dismissal of the steward in Luke 16 is intended as a metaphorical description of the situation in which people find themselves as a result of the coming of Jesus, just as are the equal pay for all the labourers in Matthew 20 and the cancellation of the debt in Matthew 18. They are not intended to communicate general truths about God, but they speak about God as explained through Jesus. Thus at the same time they speak about the situation in which the listeners find themselves as a result of their encounter with *Jesus*.

Second, in the same way, the parables can never be convincing as autonomous aesthetic objects able to be detached from their narrator. They work properly only when the listener accepts the hermeneutic assumption of the narrator. He is not simply telling stories about eccentric vineyard owners or sentimental fathers; he is talking about *God*. And that is the clever thing about these parables; every real listener who accepts that the parables have something to say about *God* encounters the intended listener, and in him none other than the narrator himself.

The Narrative Structure of the Parables:
Parables without Nodal Points

The model I have presented of Claude Bremond's narrative text analysis can be used not only in an analytical way, but also in a critical one. When we start to consider the synoptic parables from the viewpoint of this model, we very soon realise that there is a whole series of parables in whose narrative arrangement there are no nodal points in which the plot could have taken a different course. There is no single stage at which the question arises of how the story will continue. There is no doorway through which the listeners can enter into the narrative as potential actors, and also no opportunity for them to say anything about its course. Instead, they participate in the narrative action only as detached onlookers.

This is the situation we find in the parables of the seed growing by itself (Mark 4:26-29),[21] of the four different kinds of soil (Mark 4:3-8), of the mustard seed (Mark 4:30-32 par.), and of the yeast (Luke 13:20-21 par. Matt 13:33).[22] And naturally this also applies to what are known as the picture words. Of course there are narrative nodal points in these parables as well, but they are related in such a way that they do not offer the listeners any plot options, any opportunity to ask themselves how the story will continue. The listeners do not need to ask any questions at all, because on the basis of their cultural competence they always know how the story will continue.

The difference between the parables with plot options and those without them corresponds more or less to the line that classical parable research has drawn between "similitudes" and "parables." This relative distinction is a perfectly valid one, and my own proposal only aims at promoting a differentiated perception of the synoptic parable tradition. The difference from previous attempts is to be found primarily on two levels:

- The search for nodal points provides clear criteria. This dispenses with a serious problem involved in the previous distinction between "similitudes" and "parables." In many cases it was unclear whether narratives portrayed "a recurring, typical event" or related "an unusual single case."[23]
- This criterion raises the question of the listeners' involvement in the narrative and thus depends on its reception-hermeneutical context, the principal feature turning a narrative into a parable.

---

21. There is good reason to consider the word "automatic" in v. 28 as forming the center of the parable.

22. Cf. the contribution of Rudolf Hoppe in this volume.

23. Theissen and Merz, *Der historische Jesus*, p. 295.

But let us go back to our texts. The question we need to ask at this point is obvious: Why are stories like this, which simply reiterate the knowledge and experiences of the listeners without inviting them to take part, even told at all? Why are stories like this told, when the listeners know right from the start how they will finish?

I would like to link the answer to this question to a content-related thesis: They are told because it is precisely in *these* stories that Jesus' self-interpretation takes place; it is precisely *these* stories that presuppose the ministry of Jesus as a hermeneutic key, in a far more direct and immediate way than in the "major" parables.

Jesus and the Rule of God as Theme of the Parables

The answer to the question why such stories are told, when they reiterate something already well-known, is a very simple one. Such stories — and here I am practicing exactly what I am trying to explain — are told whenever something unknown, disconcerting, or new needs to be explained. The function of such stories is to integrate experiences of something different into the existing basic stock of cultural knowledge; the familiar packaging reduces the strangeness of the new content. Their intention is not to alienate what is familiar, but to make familiar what is alien. In this process, the text of the narrated world and the context of the world being addressed relate to each other in such a way that the alien element finds itself on the side of the context of the world that is addressed, and the text has the task of transforming this dissonance into harmony. The narrator offers a model whose purpose is to render comprehensible what was perceived as contradictory or difficult to understand.

The Cultural Context: The Expectation of the Rule of God

When we now ask of what this dissonance consisted, which these parables attempted to remove, the answer is not difficult to find. It is none other than the core of Jesus' message: the sovereign Rule of God (βασιλεία τοῦ θεοῦ). In this connection the dissonance arises because there is a marked difference between the semantic profile of this concept, as it was present in the cultural encyclopedia of Jesus' listeners, and the way in which *Jesus himself* speaks about the Rule of God.

When we examine the historical tradition to try to discover the image of the Rule of God that was prevalent in Judaism in Jesus' time, and what was expected from its eschatological realization, the results are amazingly coherent. Here I will simply mention the elements important for the questions dealt with in this paper:[24]

- The earthly establishment of the Rule of God is accompanied by a *theophany*. In other words, the expectation of the Rule of God is linked with the expectation of the direct presence of God in person. Correspondingly, nowhere is the early Jewish expectation of the *basileia* linked with the expectation of a messianic figure.[25] The earthly establishment of the Rule of God is seen rather as the very own work of God.
- The earthly establishment of the Rule of God occurs on a *universal* scale: it affects the entire world and results in Israel being liberated from pagan foreign rule. This is accompanied by a final judgment of wrath against the pagans and their rulers, ending either in their destruction, in their subjection to the rule of Israel, or in their turning towards the God of Israel. The Rule of God thus has a *universal* dimension, but Israel is central to it.
- The final theophany of God will naturally occur nowhere else than in Zion-Jerusalem, more specifically in the Temple. From here God will exercise sovereign rule over the whole world.

The Historical Context: Jesus' Own Ministry

It is easy enough to recognize the point at which Jesus' specific understanding of the Rule of God diverges from this concept. The essential dif-

---

24. For other elements, cf. M. Wolter, "Was heisset nu Gottes reich?" *ZNW* 86 (1995): 5-19; M. Welker and M. Wolter, "Die Unscheinbarkeit des Reiches Gottes," in *Marburger Jahrbuch Theologie: 11: Reich Gottes* (ed. W. Härle and R. Preul; Marburg: Elwert & Meurer, 1999), pp. 103-16, here pp. 104ff.

25. Cf. P. Vielhauer, "Gottesreich und Menschensohn in der Verkündigung Jesu" (1957), in P. Vielhauer, *Aufsätze zum Neuen Testament* (Munich: Chr. Kaiser, 1965), pp. 55-91, here p. 80.

ference is that the term "Rule of God" acquires a very specific denotation, namely Jesus' own ministry. This is evident in such texts as Q 11:20; 16:16; Luke 17:21. The theological profile of these texts does not consist in the fact that they claim the future to be present in the here and now, but in that Jesus defines his own ministry in Israel as the reality of the Rule of God that can be experienced here on earth. We should therefore not speak of the Rule of God as being "present" in the sense of time, but in the sense of place. The corresponding semantic dissonance consists in the fact that Jesus claims for himself something that in the basic eschatological stock of knowledge of his milieu was reserved exclusively for God. In addition, of course, there is also the fact that, when compared with the traditional expectation of the eschatological coming of the Rule of God as a theophanic event of universal dimensions, Jesus' concept of God's Rule, whereby this coming occurred through a few healings and exorcisms carried out by an itinerant Galilean preacher,[26] must have seemed trivial.

However, this difference does not mean Jesus had thereby abandoned the traditional expectation of the final theophany in Zion-Jerusalem and the universal establishment of the Rule of God. Such an interpretation is contradicted by the statements about the advent of the Rule of God that was still to come, and this expectation also provides a plausible explanation for Jesus' entry into Jerusalem and for his driving the money-changers out of the Temple. Both can exist together without problem: Jesus' claim that the reality of salvation of the Rule of God was present as a *local phenomenon* wherever he was at work, and the expectation that its *universal* establishment was still to come.

The Intention of the Parables without Nodal Points

This dissonance between Jesus' self-interpretation and the basic eschatological stock of knowledge of his Jewish environment form the context from which the parables without nodal points acquire their meaning. We are dealing with a dissonance between two contexts: the *individual historical context,* determined by the ministry and self-interpretation of Jesus, and the *collective cultural context,* determined by the basic eschatological stock of knowledge of his listeners. In this hermeneutic situation, the para-

26. Cf. the contribution of Gerd Theissen in this volume.

bles should explain the most difficult element in Jesus' self-interpretation; they clarify how the inconspicuous nature of his own ministry can be understood as an integral part of God's universal eschatological work of salvation. It is these parables, with their rather unexciting content, that are therefore of crucial importance for Jesus' self-interpretation, for they formulate an extremely distinctive implicit Christology. The various courses of events described in them are intended to make clear that every end must also have a beginning, that beginning and end are inextricably connected, and that this connection also includes the contrast between small and large. Accordingly these parables fulfill the purpose of drawing the attention of the listeners to everyday experience, so as to explain the inconspicuous ministry of Jesus as an integral part of the eschatological establishment of the universal Rule of God.

"What Must I Do to Inherit Eternal Life?" Implicit Christology in Jesus' Sayings about Life and the Kingdom

Klaus Haacker

Preliminary Remarks

For several decades the methodology of historical Jesus study was dominated by the criterion of dissimilarity. In German-speaking scholarship it had attained an almost canonical character because it had been proclaimed by two very influential scholars, Rudolf Bultmann and Ernst Käsemann. But towards the end of my studies at the University of Heidelberg, I began to doubt the validity of this criterion. I remember discussing it with Karl Georg Kuhn of the University of Heidelberg during my examination in May 1967. I could concede that the transmission of Jesus traditions included the possibility of erroneous attribution of sayings which had originated elsewhere — either in Jewish traditions or in early Christian convictions. Therefore, the criterion of dissimilarity is useful when applied to single sayings in order to achieve a higher degree of certainty about their authenticity. On the other hand I had come to the conclusion that a balanced overall picture of Jesus and his teaching cannot be built on the narrow basis of only those traditions which "pass the exam" of dissimilarity. After all, Jesus had grown up as a Jew and the early Church developed out of the Jesus movement.[1]

Meanwhile a growing number of scholars have "discovered" or acknowledged the risks involved in the traditional overestimation of this cri-

---

1. Cf. my introduction to the study of the New Testament, *Neutestamentliche Wissenschaft: Eine Einführung in Fragestellungen und Methoden* (Wuppertal: Brockhaus 1981 [1985, 2nd ed.]), pp. 73-78.

terion.[2] Especially the systematic downgrading of the Jewish roots of Jesus' teaching has been denounced as an unconscious or even conscious contribution to a theological anti-Judaism. In Germany this scholarly tradition had weakened the resistance of Christians against the secular ideology of anti-semitism. No doubt the shift of emphasis in recent Jesus Research owes at least part of its plausibility to a growing awareness of the consequences of this approach.[3]

On the other hand it can hardly be denied that the dramatic crisis of the crucifixion of Jesus and his appearances as the risen Lord created new convictions about his person and the essence of his mission. Insights revealed to his disciples in this process may have been erroneously traced back to his pre-Easter teaching, at least to instructions given to his disciples if not proclaimed in public. In our study of the Gospels, reflection along this line is of higher importance than the observation of continuity with Jewish tradition; the New Testament itself indicates the Jesus movement had to learn lessons which the disciples had not yet learned from their master while he was preaching in Galilee and Judea. Some of these lessons may have concerned the truth or relevance of Jesus' sayings which had escaped the attention or the understanding of his followers. But no doubt later discoveries did also color, enrich and specify the wording of the extant Jesus traditions. Especially explicit christological or soteriological statements which appear as anticipations of the gospel of the Early Church cannot escape the shadows of doubt as for their dating back to Jesus himself. That is why soteriological *implications* of Jesus' teaching which cannot be explained as an echo of the early Christian *kerygma* deserve special attention.

My contribution in this paper is located on this level. It is a study of the sayings about a person's share in the kingdom of God or (eternal) life. Formally, these sayings are either teachings on the conditions of such participation or promises of participation to individuals or specific groups. Some of these sayings may have been formulated by later tradition, but only in imitation of a bulk of original sayings of Jesus.[4] Therefore their

---

2. Cf. Gerd Theissen and Annette Merz, *Der historische Jesus: Ein Lehrbuch* (Göttingen: Vandenhoeck & Ruprecht, 1996), pp. 116-20; Gerd Theissen and Dagmar Winter, *Die Kriterienfrage in der Jesusforschung: Vom Differenzkriterium zum Plausibilitätskriterium* (Freiburg, Switz.: Universitätsverlag/Göttingen: Vandenhoeck & Ruprecht, 1997).

3. Cf. my study "Die moderne historische Jesus-Forschung als hermeneutisches Problem," *TBei* 31 (2000): 60-74; see pp. 65-69.

4. Cf. Friedrich W. Horn, "Die synoptischen Einlasssprüche," *ZNW* 87 (1996): 187-203.

mode of speech can be studied irrespective of the uncertainty about their authenticity in several cases.

A Survey of the Sayings in Question

Sayings about Entering the Kingdom or (Eternal) Life

Sayings formulated with "getting in" may be the best-known portion of the field of my study, especially because of the examples from the Sermon on the Mount (Matt 5:20; 7:21) and the final comment on the story of the "rich young ruler" (Matt 19:23-24).

Formulated with "Kingdom"

Matt 5:20: "For I tell you that unless your righteousness surpasses that of the Pharisees and the teachers of the law, you will certainly not enter the kingdom of heaven."

Matt 7:21: "Not everyone who says to me, 'Lord, Lord,' will enter the kingdom of heaven, but only he who does the will of my Father who is in heaven."

Mark 9:47: "It is better for you to enter the kingdom of God with one eye than to have two eyes and be thrown into hell."

Matt 18:3: "I tell you the truth, unless you change and become like little children, you will never enter the kingdom of heaven" (cf. Mark 10:15; Luke 18:17).

Matt 19:23-24: "It is hard for a rich man to enter the kingdom of heaven. . . . It is easier for a camel to go through the eye of a needle than for a rich man to enter the kingdom of God" (cf. Mark 10:23-24; Luke 18:24-25).

Matt 21:31: "I tell you the truth, the tax collectors and the prostitutes are entering the kingdom of God ahead of you."

John 3:5: "I tell you the truth, no one can enter the kingdom of God unless he is born of water and the Spirit."

Formulated with "Life"

Mark 9:43, 45: "It is better for you to enter life maimed than with two hands to go into hell. . . . It is better for you to enter life crippled than to have two feet and be thrown into hell . . ." (cf. Matt 18:8)

Matt 18:9: "It is better for you to enter life with one eye . . ." (cf. above Mark 9:47).

Matt 19:17: "If you want to enter life, obey the commandments" (cf. above Matt 19:23-24).

Outside of the gospels there is but one saying about entering the kingdom, found in a summary of what Paul and Barnabas taught to strengthen and encourage the disciples in congregations they had recently founded: "We must go through many hardships to enter the kingdom of God" (Acts 14:22). Given the lack of parallels in the rest of the New Testament, we may conclude that this way of speaking of eschatological hopes for individuals was in fact a peculiarity of Jesus.

The examples from Mark 9:43-47 and Matt 19:17, 23-24 show that in this context the terms "kingdom of God" and "life" were considered as equivalent.[5]

Sayings with Various Expressions for Receiving the Kingdom or Life

While "entering" suggests the notion of salvation as a place or space offering security and blessing, there are other expressions which seem to view it as a desirable object to be given or denied.

Sayings with "Kingdom"

Luke 12:32: "Do not be afraid, little flock, for your father has been pleased to give you the kingdom."

Matt 19:14 par. Mark 10:14 and Luke 18:16: "Let the children come to me, and do not hinder them, for the kingdom of heaven belongs to such as these."

Mark 10:15 par. Luke 18:17: "Anyone who will not receive the kingdom of God as a little child will never enter it."[6]

Matt 21:43: "The kingdom of God . . . will be given to a people who will produce its fruit."

---

5. The conversation with the rich young ruler in Matt 19:25 and parallels shows that entering the kingdom means to be saved. So, all these sayings are contributions to the soteriology of Jesus.

6. Obviously "receiving" and "entering" are tantamount!

Luke 22:29: "And I confer on you a kingdom, just as my father conferred one on me."[7]

Sayings with "Life"

In Mark 10:30 and Luke 18:30 Jesus promises to those who have left their homes or families for his sake and for the sake of the gospel that they will "receive a hundred times as much in this present age . . . and in the age to come eternal life."

In Matt 19:16 the question of the rich young ruler — "Teacher, what good thing must I do to get eternal life?" — presupposes that this is a topic of Jesus' teaching.

In John's Gospel we find no less than a dozen cases where eternal life appears as a gift to be obtained or denied (3:15, 16, 36; 5:24, 39, 40; 6:40, 47, 53, 54; 10:10; 20:31). Of these the last one is most important because it speaks of eternal life as the gift offered through the witness of this book to Jesus Christ.

Sayings about "Inheriting" the Kingdom or Life

The general notion of "giving" is transformed in a more specific metaphor when Jesus speaks of "inheriting" the kingdom or life. Obviously this mode of speech is used in a broader sense which does not presuppose the death of the testator (God)!

Sayings with "Kingdom"

Matt 25:34: "Come you who are blessed by my Father; take your inheritance, the kingdom prepared for you since the creation of the world."

---

7. This saying seems to be an exception in that it is addressed to a limited group of people — the disciples assembled at the last supper. Its topic is not soteriology but a special dignity promised to this inner circle, as the following verse reveals: "so that you may eat and drink at my table in my kingdom and sit on thrones, judging the twelve tribes of Israel" (cf. Matt 12:28).

Sayings with "Life"

Matt 19:29: "And everyone who has left houses or brothers or sisters or father or mother or children or fields for my sake will receive a hundred times as much and will inherit eternal life." While Matthew's version of this saying has "inherit," the parallels Mark 10:30 and Luke 18:30 speak of "receiving" the life. But at the beginning of this story it is Matthew who (in 19:16) prefers "receive" while Mark (10:17) and Luke (18:18) use "inherit." Obviously the variability of wording is not due to a predilection of one or another evangelist for one of these verbs but points to the fact that these verbs were deemed interchangeable.

In Luke 10:25, Luke 18:18 and Mark 10:17 the conditions of "inheriting" eternal life are a topic of questions addressed to Jesus — implying that this concern is part of his message.[8]

Paul, too, does occasionally speak of "inheriting" the kingdom (cf. 1 Cor 6:9-10; 15:50; Gal 5:21). One of his reasons for doing so may be that the imagery of being someone's "heir" plays an important role in his reception of the promises made to Abraham (cf. Rom 4:13, 14; Gal 3:18, 29; 4:30) and in his concept of being God's children (Rom 8:17; Gal 4:1, 7). As far as I can see these contexts are absent from the pertinent sayings of Jesus.

Sayings about "Seeing" the Kingdom or the Life

Sayings with "Kingdom"

In the Synoptic Gospels there is one example of this mode of speech in Mark 9:1 and its parallel Luke 9:27. The word is addressed to the listeners of Jesus at a certain occasion and promises that "some who are standing here will not taste death before they see the kingdom of God having arrived with power."[9]

The Johannine example with "seeing the kingdom" (John 3:3) does not speak of "staying alive" until the kingdom is realized but proclaims a new birth (or: birth from above) as the condition of this seeing.

8. See above on Matt 19:16.

9. The phrase "with power" is lacking in Luke. It may have been added in the canonical version of Mark while Luke used an earlier one or may have been left out by Luke for whatever reason.

Klaus Haacker

A Saying with "Life"

An instance with this variation is found in the same chapter in John 3:36: "Whoever believes in the Son has eternal life, but whoever rejects the Son will not see life, for God's wrath remains on him."

A comparison between the evidence in the Synoptics and that in the Fourth Gospel yields an interesting result: While in the Synoptics the kingdom of God is the central topic of Jesus' teaching in general and also in the group of sayings listed above, we notice a shift of emphasis towards the term (eternal) life in John's Gospel. However on both sides the two concepts occur alongside one another as interchangeable terms for an eschatological salvation. The predilection of John for "life" may be due to what C. F. D. Moule has called the "individualism of the Fourth Gospel."[10] The notion of "kingdom" as a metaphor borrowed from the political sphere implies the idea of a people or society living under the reign of God as their king. Therefore the message of God's kingdom to be revealed or realized soon is nearer to Israel's hope as a nation,[11] while the expectation of eternal life is more open to a version of the gospel addressing individuals irrespective of their nationality.

The Common Root of the Variable Verbs Used in Connection with the Kingdom and Eternal Life

The variability of expression in Jesus' sayings about one's share in the kingdom or in eternal life should not astonish us. After all, speaking of an *eschatological* salvation surpasses past and present experience and must make use of metaphors. Metaphors visualize certain aspects — always limited ones — and must be supplemented by others. So what is unusual or unexpected in the survey given so far? It is the fact that all these verbs used in connection with kingdom or with life can be traced back to one and the same root, to one specific tradition. They all occur repeatedly in one of the "great stories" of Israel's history with God: in the story of God's promise and gift of the land of Canaan to Abraham, Isaac and Jacob and their descendants, his chosen people. The evidence for this fact is so widespread

10. See C. F. D. Moule, "The Individualism of the Fourth Gospel," *NTS* 5 (1962): 171-90.
11. See for example Acts 1:4, 6.

146

that I must limit my quotations to a selection of the most significant examples. Let me begin with those texts which contain three of the pertinent verbs in close combination:

Deut 1:8: "See, I have *given* you this land. *Go in* and *take possession of* the land."

Deut 1:39: "Your children . . . will *enter* the land. I will *give* it to them and they will *take possession of* it."

Deut 9:5-6: "It is not because of your righteousness or your integrity that you are *going in* to *take possession of* their land. . . . It is not because of your righteousness that the Lord your God is *giving* you this good land to *possess*."

Then there are combinations of two of these verbs in the following texts:

WITH "ENTERING" AND "GIVING"

Deut 2:29: ". . . until we cross the Jordan into the land the Lord our God is giving us."

Josh 1:11: "You will cross the Jordan here to go in and take possession of the land the Lord your God is giving you for your own."

Neh 9:15: "You (God) told them to go in and take possession of the land you had sworn with uplifted hand to give them."

WITH "ENTERING" AND "INHERITING"

Deut 6:1: "These are the commands, decrees and laws the Lord your God directed me to teach you to observe in the land that you are entering to inherit."

Deut 6:18: "Do what is right and good in the Lord's sight, so that it may go well with you and you may go in and take over (or 'inherit') the good land that the Lord promised on oath to your forefathers."

Similarly in Deut 8:1; 9:5-6; 10:11; 12:29; 16:20; 31:13.

WITH "GIVING" AND "INHERITING"

Deut 5:31: ". . . all the commands, decrees and laws that you are to teach them to follow in the land I am giving them to possess (or 'inherit')" (cf. Deut 9:23; Josh 18:3).

WITH "SEEING" AND "GIVING"

Josh 5:6: ". . . For the Lord had sworn to them that they would not see the land that he had solemnly promised their fathers to give us. . . ."

As for instances with just one of these verbs I content myself with naming the warrants:

- phrases with "entering" the land: Num 14:24, 30; 20:24; Deut 4:5.
- phrases with "giving" or "receiving" the land: Gen 12:7; 13:15; 15:7, 18; 24:7; 26:3; 28:4, 13; 35:12; 48:4; Exod 32:13; Lev 20:24; Num 27:12; 33:53; Deut 1:21, 36; 19:8; 26:15; 27:2; 31:20; Josh 2:9, 14, 24; 24:13; Judg 6:9; 1 Kgs 8:34, 40 par. 2 Chr 6:25, 31; Neh 9:8, 35.
- phrases with "inheriting" the land: Num 14:31; Deut 3:20; 4:22; Josh 23:5.
- phrases with "seeing" the land: Num 14:23; 32:11; Deut 1:35; 3:25.[12]

The large number of parallels from the Old Testament make it certain that the verbs used by Jesus in his sayings about participation in the kingdom or (eternal) life have been borrowed from the tradition concerning the land promised to the descendants of Abraham, Isaac, and Jacob and given to the people of Israel. At the same time there can be no doubt that this tradition has been transposed on a different level and is used metaphorically; the kingdom of God is not territory but an age to come,[13] just as life eternal is not land but a perspective of future existence.

We need not further discuss the content of these two eschatological terms in our present study. What seems important to me is the situation of the addressees of these sayings as it is reflected in the use of this tradition. Obviously they are portrayed in a similar situation as the Israelites on their journey through the wilderness: a situation in which a whole generation, with but a few exceptions, failed to keep their trust in God with which they

---

12. The latter examples are noteworthy as anticipations of the New Testament sayings with "seeing" which also speak of a limited number of persons who will "see" (Mark 9:1 par. Luke 9:27: Only "some" will see the kingdom; John 3:3: Only those who have been born again will see the kingdom).

13. Cf. Mark 1:15 par.; 9:1 par.; Matt 6:10 par. According to Josephus, *Ant.* 9.243 and 17.66 the "coming" of a *basileia* means that someone becomes king or begins to rule. Therefore, to wait and hope for God's kingdom implies the conviction that as yet the earth is dominated by other powers — which is all too true to this present day.

had started on the journey (see Num 14:27; Deut 1:35; 32:5, 20; Pss 78:8; 95:10).

These memories also provide the background of critical words of Jesus about "this generation," part of which contain a prediction of judgment (cf. Matt 12:39 par. Luke 11:29; Matt 16:4 par. Mark 8:12; Matt 12:41, 42, 45 par. Luke 11:30-32; Matt 17:17 par. Mark 9:19 and Luke 9:41; Mark 8:38).[14] Thus, the use of this tradition is not confined to the eschatological sayings discussed above but seems to be a basic pattern of the mission of Jesus. There are, of course, two other examples of a typological reception of this tradition in the New Testament: 1 Cor 10:1-13 and the letter to the Hebrews with its leading metaphor of the "rest" (*katapausis;* cf. Heb 3-4). But both of these differ so much from the comparable Jesus traditions that the latter cannot be explained as early Christian teaching dated back into pre-Easter times. That calls for further investigation concerning the character of the mission of Jesus as he himself practiced and understood it.

Jesus as Eschatological Leader and Preacher of Promise

Since Jesus styled his audience after the model of Israel wandering through the wilderness, it is legitimate to consider his own role as an eschatological counterpart of Moses. Some of the sayings we have studied can be grouped together — under formal aspects — with utterances of Moses. This is true of unconditioned promises of the land in the case of Moses (cf. Deut 1:8, 21; 9:5-6; Num 33:53 etc.) as compared with equally unconditioned promises of Jesus as Luke 12:32 ("Fear not, little flock . . .") or Mark 10:14 ("The kingdom belongs to these [children]").[15] Likewise, the word on the nearness of the kingdom in Mark 9:1 (par. Luke 9:27) is an unconditioned promise; the limitation of its validity to "some" may be compared with words concerning Caleb and Joshua in Num 14:24; 32:11-12; Deut 1:35-38. The saying about children in Mark 10:14 par. can remind us of Deut 1:39: "The little ones that you said would be taken captive, your children who do not yet

---

14. Cf. E. Schnabel, *"geneá,"* in *Theologisches Begriffslexikon zum Neuen Testament* (ed. Lothar Coenen and Klaus Haacker; Wuppertal: Brockhaus/Neukirchen-Vluyn: Neukirchener, 1997), vol. 1, pp. 647-51, here pp. 648-49.

15. Matt 25:34 ("Take the kingdom as your inheritance . . .") is addressed to a limited group, but the scene of this picture is no longer a situation of promise but of final verdicts.

Klaus Haacker

know good from bad — they will enter the land. I will give it to them and they will take possession of it."[16]

However, the majority of the pertinent sayings of Jesus are not unconditioned promises; instead, they proclaim conditions to be fulfilled in order to have a share in the kingdom or (eternal) life. Models for such messages can be found in texts speaking of those people to whom entrance into the promised land will be *denied*. These texts have one topic in common: the emphasis on *faith*. The spiritual failure which excluded the majority of the generation of the exodus from entering the land is no less than three times defined as lack of trust in God; see Num 14:11 ("The Lord said to Moses: How long will these people . . . refuse to believe in me, in spite of all the miraculous signs I have performed among them?"); Deut 1:32 ("In spite of this, you did not trust in the Lord, your God"); 9:23 ("But you rebelled against the command of the Lord your God. You did not trust him or obey him"). In one text, the same reproach is also voiced against Moses and Aaron and mentioned as the reason why they, too, were not allowed to enter the land; cf. Num 20:12: "Because you did not trust in me enough to honor me as holy in the sight of the Israelites, you will not bring this community into the land I give them." These examples of unbelief or lack of confidence are recalled in Ps 78:7-8, 21-22, 32-33 and Ps 106:24, evidencing the abiding relevance attributed these traditions for all generations of Israel.[17]

Jesus' sayings about participation in the kingdom or (eternal) life do not speak of faith explicitly. However, there is another link between these traditions and the Jesus tradition: The positive attitude distinguishing Caleb and Joshua from the unbelief of the rest of the people is several times identified as "following behind" the Lord; cf. Num 14:24; 32:11-12; Deut 1:35-36. This connection between faith and following has been retained in rabbinical expositions of the wilderness story.[18]

In the Midrash on the Song of Songs, this necessity of faith and following is specified as the right attitude to the Messiah when he will be revealed:

16. If that should be the background of Mark 10:14 par. then its meaning is as "chronological" as Mark 9:1 par. and Mark 13:30 par.

17. Cf. Heb 3:12, 18-19 and 4:2-3.

18. Cf. Martin Hengel, *Nachfolge und Charisma: Eine exegetisch-religionsgeschichtliche Studie zu Mt 8,21f. und Jesu Ruf in die Nachfolge* (BZNW 34; Berlin: de Gruyter, 1968), p. 24, who references the Midrash on Exodus, the Mekilta of Rabbi Ishamel: *Mek.* 14.15 ed. in Lauterbach, vol. 1, p. 222, lines 82ff. par. *Mek.* 12.39, in Lauterbach, vol. 1, p. 110, lines 48ff. and *Mek.* 15.22 in Lauterbach, vol. 2, p. 84.

Then the Messiah will be revealed; he will lead Israel into the desert and will be hidden again. Whoever believes in him and follows him and patiently endures will have life.[19]

According to the eschatological discourse of Jesus in Matt 24:23-26, this messianic reception of the wilderness traditions existed already in the century of the New Testament:

At that time if anyone says to you: "Look, here is the Christ!" or, "There he is!" do not believe it. For false Christs and false prophets will appear and perform great signs and miracles to deceive even the elect — if that were possible. . . . So if anyone tells you, "There he is, out in the *desert,*" do not go out; or, "Here he is, in the inner rooms," do not believe.

According to Josephus theses warnings had a realistic background or came literally true in the decades before the Jewish rebellion against the Romans:

Deceivers and impostors, under the pretence of divine inspiration fostered revolutionary changes, they persuaded the multitude to act like madmen, and led them out into the *desert* under the belief that God would there give them tokens of deliverance. (*War* 2.259)

A still worse blow was dealt at the Jews by the Egyptian false prophet.[20] A charlatan who had gained for himself the reputation of a prophet, this man appeared in the country, collected a following of about thirty thousand dupes, and led them by a circuitous route from the *desert* to the Mount of Olives. From there he proposed to force an entrance into Jerusalem and, after overpowering the Roman garrison, to set himself up as a tyrant of the people. (*War* 2.261-62)

Impostors and deceivers called upon the mob to follow them into the *desert*. For they said that they would show them unmistakable marvels and signs that would be wrought in harmony with God's design. (*Ant.* 20.167-68)

19. Cf. Hengel, *Nachfolge*, p. 25.

20. Cf. Acts 21:38: The Roman officer asks Paul after his being arrested in the temple of Jerusalem: "Aren't you the Egyptian who started a revolt and led four thousand terrorists out into the *desert* some time ago?"

The Judean desert was also the scene where John the Baptist preached and baptized those who responded to his preaching, and it was John who anticipated Jesus' message of a nearness of the kingdom of God (cf. Matt 3:2 with 4:17).[21] In the case of John, it is not only the desert but also the banks of the river Jordan which he has in common with the type of prophet which Josephus describes as forerunners of the religious leaders of the uprising against the Romans:

> During the period when Fadus was procurator of Judaea, a certain impostor named Theudas persuaded the majority of the masses to take up their possessions and to follow him to the *Jordan* River. He stated that he was a prophet and that at his command the river would be parted and would provide an easy passage. (*Ant.* 20.97)

This miracle was certainly not meant as helping the people to leave the Holy Land permanently, but as a prelude to and token of a new conquest of the land with God's help (cf. Josh 3).

In summation, the first half of the first century CE witnessed a growing awareness of the fundamental relevance of Israel's wilderness traditions. One version of this development was the attempt to re-enact the events leading to the conquest of Canaan — as a liberation of the land from pagan dominance. In the case of John the Baptist and of Jesus a political interpretation of their respective message and movement was assumed or constructed by their enemies.[22] That this was a misunderstanding or intentional distortion is acknowledged by the vast majority of unprejudiced studies.[23] However, the *metaphorical* application of the desert traditions could easily have been mistaken as a prelude to a political development.[24] The rabbinical writings mentioned above together with Matt 24:23-26 illustrate that the term "Messiah" — though not rooted in the Mosaic layers

---

21. Although this anticipation is attested only by Matthew it should be taken as historical; the tendency of the Christian tradition was not to exaggerate but rather to downgrade the continuity between the Baptist and Jesus.

22. Cf. Josephus, *Ant.* 18.118-19 for John the Baptist and Mark 15:2-5 par. and 15:26 par. for Jesus.

23. A notable exception is the book of George W. Buchanan, *The Consequences of the Covenant* (Leiden: Brill, 1970).

24. In the eyes of autocratic rulers, a strong popular movement was in itself a political fact and a threat to the status quo; cf. Ellis Rivkin, *What Crucified Jesus?* (Nashville: Abingdon, 1984).

of Israel's memories — could be connected with the remembrance of Israel's first great leader. The roles of preacher and leader were not so far from each other as they are in our modern civilization (cf. John 6:14-15).[25] There may have been an ambiguity in the public performance of Jesus which ended only with his crucifixion.[26] Jesus had to die in order to make clear beyond doubt that his message was about an eschatological salvation, a universal victory of God over injustice and evil — including death; and Jesus had to be raised from the dead in order to bring that message home to the hearts of people.

25. In Peter's sermon in Acts 3 we find both the model of "a prophet like Moses" from Deut 18:15, 18 and the term "leader" applied to Jesus (cf. vv. 15 and 22). Deut 18:15 is also quoted in Acts 7:37. The reception of this promise has been described by H. M. Teeple, *The Mosaic Eschatological Prophet* (Philadelphia: Society of Biblical Literature, 1957). In the long run, mainstream Christology preferred the imagery of a ruler (Messiah and Lord) and — originally derived from it — the term "son of God."

26. Cf. Luke 24:21: "But we had hoped that he was the one who was going to redeem Israel."

How Did Jesus Understand His Death? The Parables in Eschatological Prospect

Rudolf Hoppe

Introduction: A Survey of the Discussion

The question of the relationship between Jesus' claims for his mission and his possible interpretation of his death as a sacrificial atonement necessary for salvation was first raised by Anton Vögtle in 1964.[1] The subsequent discussion on Jesus' understanding of his death, in the context of the search for the historical Jesus, was carried on with some force, primarily by Vögtle himself and his colleague in Erfurt, Heinz Schürmann, without any consensus being reached. Vögtle's pupils Peter Wolf, Peter Fiedler and Lorenz Oberlinner then took up Vögtle's ideas and carried them further.[2] The central element remained the controversy between Vögtle and Schürmann.[3] The main point of disagreement lay in

---

1. A. Vögtle, "Exegetische Erwägungen über das Wissen und Selbstbewusstsein Jesu," in A. Vögtle, *Das Evangelium und die Evangelien* (KBANT; Düsseldorf: Patmos, 1971), pp. 296-344, esp. 309-14; original version in J. B. Metz et al., *Gott in Welt I* (FS Karl Rahner; Freiburg et al.: Herder, 1964), pp. 224-53.

2. P. Wolf, "Liegt in den Logien von der 'Todestaufe' (Mk 10.38f; Lk 12.49f) eine Spur des Todesverständnisses Jesu vor?" (Dissertation, Freiburg, 1973); P. Fiedler, *Jesus und die Sünder* (BBET 3; Frankfurt/Bern: Lang, 1976); L. Oberlinner, *Todeserwartung und Todesgewissheit Jesu* (SBB 10; Stuttgart: Kath. Bibelwerk, 1980).

3. Cf. H. Schürmann, *Jesu ureigener Tod* (Freiburg et al.: Herder, 1975); H. Schürmann, *Gottes Reich — Jesu Geschick* (Freiburg et al.: Herder, 1983); H. Schürmann, *Jesus — Gestalt und Geheimnis* (ed. K. Scholtissek; Paderborn: Bonifatius, 1994); A. Vögtle, "Jesus von Nazareth," in R. Kottje/B. Moeller (eds.), *Ökumenische Kirchengeschichte, Bd. I* (Mainz/Munich: Matthias-Grünewald-Verl., 1970), pp. 3-24; A. Vögtle, "Todesankündigungen und Todesverständnis Jesu," in K. Kertelge (ed.), *Der Tod Jesu — Deutungen im Neuen Testament* (QD

that Schürmann saw Jesus himself, faced with the rejection of his message and the consequent threat of the failure of his mission, not only expecting a violent death, but regarding this as laying down his life in place of others.[4] He thus consciously exposed himself to the crisis of his message, applying his Kingdom *(basileia)* message and his death to each other. By contrast, Vögtle intensified his questioning of the strained relationship between Jesus' proclamation of and claim to salvation on the one hand, and a death that he understood in this way as mediating salvation, on the other. Vögtle argued that, if Jesus had seen his death as an atonement, this would have contradicted both his claim to stand for the Kingdom *(basileia)* of God and to initiate it, and also his unconditional requirement that people follow his message. It would have meant redefining his message to such an extent that it would inevitably have led to a self-contradiction.[5]

Helmut Merklein then entered the debate and added a new element to it.[6] He does not take the proclaiming of Jesus' message and its inherent *basileia* claim as his starting-point, but rather approaches the question *starting from the end*. He argues that Jesus saw his death as giving his life "for many" in the sense of Isaiah 53, originally having Israel in mind. God asserted himself in spite of Israel's rejection by making atonement for that very Israel through the death of his eschatological messenger; the death of Jesus thus appeared as an integral part of the proclamation of God's work of salvation by Jesus.[7] Merklein took fully into account the fact that one cannot speak of a blanket rejection of Jesus by the whole of Israel, but

---

74; Freiburg et al.: Herder, 1976), pp. 51-113; A. Vögtle, "Der verkündigende und verkündigte Jesus 'Christus,'" in J. Sauer (ed.), *Wer ist Jesus Christus?* (Freiburg et al.: Herder, 1977), pp. 27-91; A. Vögtle, "Hat sich Jesus als Heilsmittler offenbart?" in *BK* 34 (1979): 4-11; A. Vögtle, "Grundfragen der Diskussion um das heilsmittlerische Todesverständnis Jesu," in *Offenbarungsgeschehen und Wirkungsgeschichte* (Freiburg et al.: Herder, 1985), pp. 141-67.

4. Cf Schürmann, *Jesu ureigener Tod*, pp. 26-33; H. Schürmann, "Jesu Tod als Heilstod im Kontext seiner Basileia-Verkündigung," in Schürmann, *Jesus*, pp. 168-85.

5. Cf. Vögtle, "Jesus von Nazareth," pp. 21-22.

6. Cf. H. Merklein, *Die Botschaft Jesu von der Gottesherrschaft* (SBS 111; Stuttgart: Kath. Bibelwerk 3. Aufl., 1989), esp. pp. 133-46; H. Merklein, "Der Tod Jesu als stellvertretender Sühnetod," in *Studien zu Jesus und Paulus* (WUNT 43; Tübingen: Mohr Siebeck, 1987), pp. 181-91; "Wie hat Jesus seinen Tod verstanden?" in *Studien zu Jesus und Paulus II* (WUNT 105; Tübingen: Mohr Siebeck, 1998), pp. 174-89.

7. Cf. Merklein, "Der Tod Jesu," p. 184.

stressed the repercussions of the rejection of Jesus by the high priests among the majority of the people.[8]

> The . . . theological problem [of the incompatibility of the proclamation of salvation by Jesus with the acceptance of his death as an atonement] turns out on closer examination to be only a seeming problem. It is resolved if we see Jesus' death of atonement not as an *additional* factor of salvation apart from the salvation of the kingdom of God, but as an event that is part of what happens in the kingdom of God.[9]

The interpretation of the death of Jesus as a death of atonement is so much a consequence of his message "that the possibility should seriously be considered that this interpretation goes back to Jesus himself and that he had expressed it to his disciples at the Last Supper."[10] Merklein also assumes that the crisis in Jesus' mission had intensified, when he concedes that God's action in choosing the whole of Israel must have seemed an obviously inoperative event with the execution of Jesus.[11]

It is no accident that Merklein speaks of a "possibility." Merklein draws the theological conclusion that God has asserted himself against Israel's rejection of Jesus by means of the death of atonement.[12] This is a legitimate conclusion in theological terms if one looks back at Jesus' ministry, but it is not a historical demonstration that Jesus himself attached this meaning to his death; it is an opinion established on a different level than the historical one. The problem remains of the contrast between the claim to salvation in Jesus' message and the efficacy for salvation of his violent death (which he may have articulated).

Recently, Gerd Häfner, the New Testament scholar from Munich, has raised this issue once again[13] and taken the debate further by adding another point of view. Häfner stresses that the assumption Jesus saw his fail-

---

8. Cf. Merklein, "Wie hat Jesus," p. 185.

9. Merklein, "Wie hat Jesus," p. 184; cf. also Merklein, *Botschaft*, p. 142. Italics are Merklein's.

10. Merklein, *Botschaft*, p. 144.

11. Cf. Merklein, "Wie hat Jesus," p. 185.

12. Cf. Merklein, "Der Tod Jesu," p. 184.

13. Gerd Häfner, "Nach dem Tod Jesu fragen. Brennpunkte der Diskussion aus neutestamentlicher Sicht," in Gerd Häfner/H. Schmid (eds.), *Wie heute vom Tod Jesu sprechen? Neutestamentliche, systematisch-theologische und liturgiewissenschaftliche Perspektiven* (Freiburg: Kath. Akad. der Erzdiözese Freiburg, 2002), pp. 139-90.

ure does not much help us as a starting-point for an interpretation made by him of a death of atonement. For the crucial factor was not "that Jesus himself had doubts about his message, but that this message must have seemed to be refuted *to those he was addressing.*"[14] The notion of atonement on Jesus' part would have been a very inadequate answer to this problem, for those who thought Jesus' message had no future because of the fate he met "would not have been impressed by the news that in this death an atonement for the sins of the people had been made. The alleged problem (failure of the *basileia* message) and solution (death in atonement) do not fit together."[15]

The discussion cannot be presented here in its entirety. The points outlined here have been placed as markers in order to describe the problem, and also to draw attention to a lack of conceptual clarity on certain points. In the scholarly discussion phrases have been used such as "Jesus had to," "Jesus could," and "people must have thought Jesus was. . . ." But it is not a question — and this is a consequence that can be drawn from Häfner's contribution — of how Jesus himself *"understood"* his death, of what attitude *he himself* took to any perceived failure of his message. It is a question of how, in expectation of his violent death, he assessed the viability of the message he had formulated during his public ministry, and what arguments he used to present that message. In other words, what is important is not how Jesus understood *himself,* but what he presented *to the outside world.*

My intention here is to concentrate on just one aspect of the problem, without any pretension to completeness. A consensus can more or less be reached — on which Vögtle, Schürmann and Merklein would also agree — on the fact that the eschatological prospect in Mark 14:25 ("I tell you the truth, I will not drink again of the fruit of the vine until that day when I drink it anew in the kingdom of God") was decisive for Jesus' expectation of, and interpretation of, his death with a view to the coming *basileia.* Together with the fundamental statement in Mark 1:15, this saying forms "the material framework for the proclamation of Jesus' message according to Mark,"[16] for Jesus himself as well. The parables in Mark 4:3-9; 4:26-29; 4:30-32 pick up the proclamation of 1:15 once more, on the level of the second

14. Häfner, "Nach dem Tod Jesu fragen," p. 154; my italics.

15. Häfner, "Nach dem Tod Jesu fragen," p. 154.

16. J. Blank, "Der 'eschatologische Ausblick' Mk 14,25," in P. G. Müller/W. Stenger (eds.), *Kontinuität und Einheit* (FS F. Mussner; Freiburg et al.: Herder, 1981), pp. 508-18, here p. 515.

Gospel, connecting proclamation and eschatological prospect together. This also applies to the authentic proclamation of Jesus' message. With the handing down of the parables, therefore, it is possible to relate the *basileia* message proclaimed by Jesus to its intention and claim as proclamation, on the one hand, and to Jesus' attitude to the fate of death that awaits him and that he has articulated, on the other hand.[17] Following on from this, a reference to the banquet parable that lies outside the Markan tradition provides a still broader basis for establishing the contours of a plausible picture.

There are of course a number of hermeneutical problems connected with the evaluation of the parables in terms of the search for the historical Jesus. But it should be possible to reach a consensus on the assumption that in the parables that have been passed down we can find the essential features of the sayings that Jesus proclaimed. C. Kähler rightly claimed that if we are able to observe the preacher, largely unknown to us, at work, then it is above all in the parables.[18] It can therefore be considered at least legitimate to look for a reliable trace of what Jesus intended to proclaim in the parables.[19]

The Parables in Mark 4 as *Basileia* Parables

As is well known, Mark 4 contains three parables, of which 4:26-29 and 4:30-32 are explicit βασιλεία-parables and take up once more the βασιλεία-proclamation of Mark 1:15. They are preceded by the parable of the sower,

---

17. Cf. Schürmann, *Jesus*, p. 272.

18. Cf. C. Kähler, *Jesu Gleichnisse als Poesie und Therapie* (WUNT 78; Tübingen: Mohr Siebeck, 1995), p. 69. On the hermeneutic issues relating to interpretation of the parables, cf. also the contribution by M. Wolter in this volume.

19. Cf. the firm attempts by Schürmann, "Die Basileia als mögliches Todesgeschick Jesu: Das Missgeschick des Basileia-Engagements Jesu," in Schürmann, *Jesus*, pp. 157-67. The fact that Jesus launched a "movement" and formed a circle of disciples in which all tendencies of contemporary Judaism were represented, and that his enterprise thus became dangerous "from outside, too" (p. 161), does not help establish whether Jesus integrated the concept of the violent end to his plans and claims being effective for salvation into his mission in a way that is historically verifiable from the records that are available to us. The question is not whether Jesus thought about his death as a martyr (cf. p. 162), but whether he himself related the levels "salvation qua basileia effect" and "salvation qua death as a martyr" to one another. The question then at least needs to be asked whether Jesus only developed the thought of the potential failure of his mission as a result of the reaction to his movement. The issue therefore remains unresolved.

which thus also acquires the character of a *basileia* parable. This is not to say that the three parables can all be reduced to *one* level; each of them has its own place as an expression of the *basileia* message, and each of them should be understood on the basis of its own life events. However, certain common features can be recognized in them. In terms of the search for the historical Jesus I am assuming that all three parables have gone through a transmission process that can still be approximately retraced.[20]

The Parable of the Sower (Mark 4:3-9)

THE PARABLE OF JESUS AND HIS MESSAGE

The parable of the sower should in principle be separated from the other two parables in this chapter of Mark (4:26-29 and 4:30-32), even though the three parables may have formed one collection in a pre-Mark stage.[21]

An essential element in judging how the parable was passed down is

20. There is a general consensus on this in research into Mark, regardless of all other individual issues that remain open. L. Schenke, *Das Markusevangelium* (Stuttgart: Kohl-hammer, 1988), pp. 49-53, is skeptical about tracing back a pre-Mark tradition, but he, too, does not of course contest the fact that "Mark used material that had been handed down, the history of whose form and tradition could hypothetically (!) be profitably reproduced for exegesis of Mark" (p. 52). However, if one wants to go back to Jesus himself, then an attempt to make the history of the handing down of the texts transparent cannot be avoided.

21. On the issue of how the parables may have been handed down prior to Mark there is admittedly considerable divergence of opinion. While some support the idea of a pre-Mark collection and believe the three parables 4:3-9; 4:26-29; 4:30-32 have all been passed down from the same level and had a previous form that has been further reconstructed (cf. H. Weder, *Die Gleichnisse Jesu als Metaphern* [FRLANT 120; Göttingen: Vandenhoeck & Ruprecht, 1980], pp. 99-138; H. J. Klauck, *Allegorie und Allegorese in synoptischen Gleichnistexten* [NTAbh 13; Münster: Aschendorff, 1986], pp. 185-227), there are also those who ascribe a literary level to the parable of the sower and its interpretation, and only allocate 4:26-29 and 4:30-32, together with 4:21-25, to an older tradition (G. Sellin, "Textlinguistische und semiotische Erwägungen zu Mk 4,1-34," *NTS* 29 [1983]: 508-30, here p. 519). G. Dautzenberg, "Mk 4,1-34 als Belehrung über das Reich Gottes," *BZ* 34 (1990): 38-62, here p. 47, makes a further distinction between 4:14-15 (more recent stage) and 4:16-20 (earlier stage). For the issue we are examining here, it is not the history of how Mark 4 was handed down as a whole that is important, but primarily the question of whether the narrative of 4:3-9 can be ascribed to Jesus and his proclamation of *basileia*, or whether it has its origin in a later, post-Jesus stage. The question of whether it has its origin with Jesus can certainly be judged optimistically.

an examination of the fixed form that shapes the narrative.[22] Here we need only to outline it briefly:

The narrative consists of the exposition, i.e., the statement that sowing is taking place, and four parts; the first three parts illustrate a negative result of the sowing, and the fourth a positive result. Each of the parts has a structure containing three elements, describing (1) the seed falling on the ground, (2) the emergence of an adverse threat, and (3) the destruction of the seed. This structure is also effectively maintained in the fourth part, except that there of course the result is positive instead of negative. This triple structure also forms the basis of the exposition (ὁ σπείρων — σπεῖραι — ἐν τῷ σπείρειν) and of verse eight (triple repetition of ἐν).

The whole of the narrative is directed towards the fourth part, as the beginning of each of the parts makes clear (ὃ μὲν — ἄλλο — ἄλλο — ἄλλα). This is reinforced by the grammar; the action verbs in vv. 4, 6 and 7, expressing the negative reaction to the influences on the seed (κατεσθίειν, ξηραίνειν, καυματίζειν, συμπνίζειν), are in the aorist, while the action verbs in the fourth part (ἐδίδου, ἔφερεν) are in the imperfect. The difference in the narrative is confirmed by the transformation of the seed from passive object in the first three parts to active subject in the fourth part.[23]

The descriptions in v. 5 stand out because they do not fit into this structure with its set form aimed at the conclusion. This has again and again given rise to doubts about their originality. The parable therefore probably originally consisted of the introduction, the description of each process that occurs with the seed (it falls along the path, on stony ground, among thorns, and on good soil), the threat (birds, the sun, thorns), and the destruction of the seed or its bearing fruit.[24] In spite of all due reservations about literal reconstructions, this assumed stage of the handing down of the text can be ascribed to the authentic proclamation of Jesus.[25]

22. On critical findings on the form, cf. G. Lohfink, "Das Gleichnis vom Sämann," BZ 30 (1986): 36-69, especially pp. 36-45.

23. Cf. αὐτό in elements 1 and 3, and ἐκαυματίσθη and ἐξηράνθη in element 2 compared with ἐδίδου/ἔφερεν in element 4.

24. While arguments can admittedly be advanced for the change from ἐκαυματίσθη to ἐκαυμάτισεν proposed by Klauck, Allegorie, pp. 187-88, in my view it goes beyond what can be demonstrated with certainty.

25. This does not necessarily mean that Mark 4:3-8 was introduced in a similar way to 4:26-29 or 4:30-32; this is possible, but cannot be demonstrated. At all events, it was understood in this way by the time of Mark, at the latest (cf. Dautzenberg, "Mk 4,1-34," p. 39; Sellin,

It is against this background that the question of the situation and intention of Jesus' original proclamation should be raised. Although no explicit comparison of the *basileia* is made with the world in the narrative, it can be assumed that Jesus places the parable in the context of his *basileia* proclamation.[26] The imagery undergirding the narrative arouses this association, and the comparable instances in contemporary Judaism also suggest this connection.[27]

We may assume that the person telling the parable, while being influenced by his addressees in his choice of content and means of presentation, nevertheless through the use of the parable form himself appears as an authority forcing his hearers to reflect and thus provoking them into agreement or rejection. Working from this assumption, it is important for him that his words convince his audience of the effectiveness and future prospects for his message, which is closely related to his person, in spite of the apparently superior negative effect of the opposition that has been experienced. It is important for the narrator, Jesus, that on the metaphorical level the yield is introduced in such a positive way that his hearers *can be convinced* of the validity of his message and of its final confirmation.

Researchers have so far failed to reach a consensus on how to classify the parable of the sower. Different aspects of it can be used to support arguments for both the category of "parable"[28] and of "similitude."[29] The general use of the aorist in vv. 3-7 argues, but not conclusively, for the category of "parable," as do the stylization and the device of alienation. This is not an everyday story that can be understood from direct experience, but the individual case of an agricultural worker whose actions leading to a thirty-, sixty-, and hundredfold yield have an effect transcending all natural expectations. In the proclamation of Jesus' message this effect serves to make the

---

"Erwägungen," p. 522; if Mark 4:3-9, 26-29, 30-32 did indeed form a pre-Mark collection (cf. H. W. Kuhn, *Ältere Sammlungen im Markusevangelium* [SUNT 8; Göttingen: Vandenhoeck & Ruprecht, 1971], pp. 99-146), then this stage of editing would have also already created the *basileia* relationship. Here we are primarily concerned with the possible allocation to the authentic proclamation of Jesus.

26. Cf. the relevant commentaries; cf. Dautzenberg, "Mk 4,1-34," pp. 46-48.

27. Cf. U. Luck, "Das Gleichnis vom Sämann und die Verkündigung Jesu," *WD* 11 (1971): 73-92, esp. 80-88.

28. Cf. Klauck, *Allegorie*, pp. 188-89.

29. Cf. Lohfink, "Gleichnis," pp. 50-51; J. Gnilka, *Das Evangelium nach Markus: 1. Teilband Mk 1–8,26* (EKKNT II/1; Zürich/Neukirchen-Vluyn: Benzinger/Neukirchener, 1978), p. 157.

audience react positively to the end of the story, and thus to make acceptable the underlying claim that the kingdom of God can be established. It is precisely the form of the parable that reinforces this underlying statement.

THE LIFE STORY OF THE PARABLE

F. Mussner advanced the argument some time ago that, in addition to a "Galilean spring" in Jesus' proclamation of his message, there was also a "Galilean crisis."[30] Mussner believed that Jesus' message had followed a path leading from an initial acceptance to rejection, leading to his being conscious of himself as the "suffering Messiah."[31] L. Oberlinner disputed Mussner's thesis of the progression from agreement with Jesus to rejection on the grounds that it could not be historically verified. He opposed this "division into two parts," pointing to the continuing polarity of Jesus' call to repentance, and arguing that Jesus' public ministry was marked "right from the beginning by the tension between acceptance and rejection."[32]

If one considers Mussner's thesis to be plausible, then one can assert that the story of the sower is an indication of this crisis situation (something Mussner, however, does not do). But in this case it would rather run counter to the assumption of the "consciousness of a suffering Messiah," in view of the positive prospects that the parable suggests.

If the intention of what Jesus is saying is indeed to reinforce the *basileia* proclamation in spite of manifest adversity, then it would make sense to place the story in a phase of Jesus' preaching ministry when it was exposed to the threat of opposition, and when Jesus himself, with his claim, was under threat. This could be at the end of Jesus' public ministry, although it does not have to be.[33] From this we can conclude that the Nazarene had not only been consistent in maintaining his claim to stand for the coming of the *basileia* of God in word and practice, but had emphatically underlined that claim. Based on the parable of the sower, we nowhere see for Jesus any qualitative reorientation in the tense relationship between, on the one hand, the

---

30. Cf. F. Mussner, "Gab es eine 'galiläische Krise'?," in P. Hoffmann (ed.), *Orientierung an Jesus: zur Theologie der Synoptiker* (FS J. Schmid; Freiburg: Herder, 1973), pp. 238-52, here pp. 242-48.

31. Cf. Mussner, "'Krise,'" p. 249.

32. L. Oberlinner, *Todeserwartung,* p. 83.

33. The argument for the end of Jesus' public ministry is put forward by Gnilka, *Mk I,* p. 161.

enforceability of God's will for salvation that he had represented and proclaimed, and, on the other, the experience of the failure of his own mission. Looking at it in these terms, and even if we assume that the parable was told at an earlier stage of Jesus' public ministry, we can say that a positive impetus is being asserted here, which hardly makes it likely that Jesus could have withdrawn it without his cause suffering a setback, and that in addition there is no indication that he did withdraw it.

Mark 4:26-29

The basic line that we have indicated in Jesus' concept of proclamation can be shown to take on more concrete form in the two parables that follow in Mark 4. Regardless of whether the parable of the seed that grows by itself is part of a pre-Mark collection together with the other two parables, it should be looked at on its own and evaluated on the basis of what it says itself. In other words, it is not necessary to assume that Jesus himself had already established a connection with the parables of the mustard seed or of the sower.

In the original form the teller of the parable draws a comparison between the *basileia* and a man who scatters seed on his field, who then lets the seed grow day and night, quite normally, and who finally takes the sickle to it when harvest time comes. Together with other interpreters,[34] I would argue that this parable, too, has gone through a process of transmission, in that Mark 4:28 reflects a later formation of the text, although I would leave open the question of the phase of this later formation. Reasons of both content and language can be advanced to support the argument of a secondary expansion of the text.[35] If this is correct, the contrast will be placed in the centre of this parable, too; it is here that the life story of the parable is played out. The original parable is concerned less with the growing, less with a process, and far more with the *inevitability of the end when the time has come for the harvest.* We should be skeptical of the hypothesis that the reception of Joel 3:13 means the parable's message includes the idea of judgment.[36] It is the ending, when the time has come for the harvest, that is the primary point whereby Jesus links this story with his *basileia* message:

---

34. Cf. Klauck, *Allegorie*, pp. 218-20; Weder, *Gleichnisse*, pp. 117-20.

35. The subject of ἀποστέλλει in v. 29 is the ἄνθρωπος in v. 26. V. 28 makes this connection unclear, at the least.

36. Cf. Dautzenberg, "Mk 4,1-34," pp. 54-55.

the *basileia* will come certainly and inevitably, even if the apparent circumstances do not necessarily indicate this to be the case. In this sense, G. Dautzenberg is correct in suspecting that the critical question of the "when?" of the kingdom of God underlies this parable.[37] There is no exact answer to this question, but there is a definite assertion that the kingdom of God is not far off and will not be long in coming. We do not have to see Jesus himself in the ἄνθρωπος scattering seed on the ground. We can limit ourselves to finding Jesus clearly attempting to convince his listeners of the certainty of the eschatological establishment of the *basileia* in the story.

Mark 4:30-32

The element of contrast is even more strongly emphasized in the parable of the mustard seed than in the parable of the growing seed. Here, too, it is necessary to first mention the process of how this short narrative was handed down. Behind the double passing down of the story in Mark/Q lies the original and still relatively traceable form of the comparison of the *basileia* with a mustard seed that is planted in the ground and puts out such large branches that birds can nest in them. The statement about its growth was probably present in an intermediate version, but not to the extent of the process narrated in Mark. Here, too, it is not the *growth* that the narrator focuses on, but rather the *contrast* between the inconspicuous beginning that has nevertheless been made and the huge, overwhelming end. In his comparison Jesus bears in mind the experience of his listeners, for whom his proclamation in Mark 1:15 has so far not shown itself to be real, but who nevertheless need to be convinced that the fundamental power of the *basileia* will be demonstrated.

Matt 22:1-10/Luke 14:16-24

To complete the picture we will look at the parable of the banquet in Matt 22:1-10/Luke 14:16-24, which can reasonably be traced back to Jesus himself,[38] and which can be classified in the context of the *basileia* proclama-

---

37. Dautzenberg, "Mark 4:1-34," p. 55.

38. Cf. R. Hoppe, "Das Gastmahlgleichnis Jesu (Mt 22,1-10; Lk 14,16-24) und seine vorevangelische Traditionsgeschichte," in: R. Hoppe and U. Busse (eds.), *Von Jesus zum*

tion. The assumption here is that the versions in Matthew and Luke that have come down to us are based on a previous Q tradition. I have myself attempted to reconstruct this possible process of handing down prior to the Gospels,[39] and the result does not greatly differ from the attempt by the international Q project.[40] Admittedly, U. Luz raises doubts about the text being handed down through Q.[41] But even this possible form of the parable as preserved by Q can hardly be identical with the proclamation by Jesus. Here I will confine myself to the essential content of the parable of the banquet, regardless of its allocation to a particular tradition.

The authentic parable probably contained the following elements: the comparison of the *basileia* to the invitation by an ἄνθρωπος to a banquet, carried out by messengers, the rejection of the invitation by all those who had been invited on the grounds of their own interests, the consequent invitation of other guests and their positive reaction, and the successful assembling of a group of guests and the holding of the banquet feast. Unlike in the reception of the parable by Matthew or Luke, in the story as told by Jesus the refusal of those who were originally invited had a primarily functional significance, aimed at emphasizing the fact that *the banquet would take place no matter what.* The sending out of the renewed invitation and the announcement that it had been successfully carried out underline the certainty that the banquet will be held. This is where the reaction of the story's addressees comes into play. Jesus' listeners are supposed to identify with the reaction of the second group of invitees and share in their spontaneous acceptance of the invitation. It is essential for the construction and development of the narrative that the holding of the banquet and the invitation in themselves are not affected by the rejection by the first group of invitees, but that the *existing* invitation for the same banquet is now directed at the new group of invitees. In terms of the issues we are dealing with, it is the aspect of keeping to the intention of holding the banquet that is of primary significance.

If this basic line has been correctly identified and the metaphor of the banquet is to be connected with the kingdom of God, this means that Jesus is expressing two things: (1) that the coming of God's *basileia,* in spite of all

Christus. Christologische Studien (FS Paul Hoffmann; Berlin and New York: de Gruyter, 1998), pp. 277-93, esp. pp. 290-92.

39. Cf. Hoppe, "Gastmahlgleichnis," p. 290.

40. Cf. J. M. Robinson, P. Hoffmann, J. S. Kloppenborg (eds.), *The Critical Edition of Q* (Leuven: Peeters, 2000), pp. 432-49.

41. U. Luz, "Mt und Q," in Hoppe and Busse, *Von Jesus,* pp. 201-15, esp. p. 204.

skepticism and rejection, is inevitable, and (2) that he puts the choice between approval and rejection before his listeners and presses them to become directly involved in the coming event.

Preliminary Conclusions

An examination of the parables in Mark 4 and of Jesus' banquet parable
provides a very uniform picture: These parables describe what are obviously the limits to the addressees' acceptance of the message of the rule of
God. In this respect we can certainly speak of Jesus experiencing a crisis in
the proclamation of the *basileia*. We cannot, on the other hand, speak of
thoughts of a *failure of the message,* however they may be articulated. The
leitmotif throughout the parables told by Jesus is the expectation and certainty of the coming event of the *basileia,* and thus the validity of the claim
he makes in the message he proclaims. We are left with the question of
how to relate this *leitmotif,* based on a constructive stimulus, to Jesus' expectation of his death, expressed indirectly in Mark 14:25, and what consequences are to be drawn from this.

The "Eschatological Prospect" (Mark 14:25)

The "Death Prophecy" (v. 25a)

The saying in Mark 14:25 consists of two parts: a death announcement or
death "prophecy," and the "eschatological prospect" which is connected
with ἕως τῆς ἡμέρας, i.e. the day of the revelation of the *basileia*. In terms
of the history of the form of the saying, we are dealing with a prophetic
saying. It is introduced by the phrase ἀμὴν λέγω ὑμῖν, which replaces the
Old Testament prophetic messenger formula. The prophetic saying form is
reinforced by the double negation οὐ μή. The emphasis of the saying lies
on drinking the fruit of the vine for the last time and not on a re-
establishment of the banquet in the future.[42] In favor of the saying being a
very old one — whether the ἀμὴν λέγω ὑμῖν is considered to be original or
not is another question — is the fact that there is a tension between the
motif of drinking and the phrase of interpretation about the cup, and it is

---

42. Cf. K. Berger, *Die Amen-Worte Jesu* (BZNW 39; Berlin: de Gruyter, 1970), p. 55.

possible that the former came earlier.[43] At any rate the saying expresses the certainty of the decision made against Jesus, and sees this development — evident by the prophetic character of the saying — as an expression of the divine will, to which Jesus is prepared to submit, because he is able to interpret this fate as coming from God. This in no way lessens Jesus' certainty that with an imminent end of his drinking "from the fruit of the vine," the current fellowship with his followers will also come to an end. The future of this fellowship is not dealt with in the prophetic saying. The saying does however show quite clearly that what is at stake is the fate and the cause of *Jesus,* and thus their validity in the face of the threat to the end of his ministry. But no realistic expectation of a renewal of the table fellowship underlies the style of Jesus' statement as handed down in Mark — which is incidentally different from the reception in Matthew (μεθ' ὑμῶν). This idea is simply sometimes read into this saying of Jesus.[44]

From what has been said it follows that the principal idea in Mark 14:25a is the reference to the inevitability of a violent death, and not, for example — even if we take into account the continuation in v. 25b — the comforting prospect of the re-establishment of the fellowship with the disciples, in whatever form that might take. It would seem that this "prophetic knowledge" of Jesus and his interpretation of it might certainly be historically substantiated in the final phase of his appearance in Jerusalem.[45] So, although it cannot be excluded that the "Amen introduction" is a secondary formulation, it is still more than likely that the core of the first part of the verse is authentic, especially as it is functionally essential for v. 25b.

The Expectation of the Basileia (V. 25b)

This leads us to consider v. 25b. If we do not believe that the aforementioned explication of Mark 14:25b in Matthew[46] is already present in the Mark text

---

43. Cf. A. Vögtle, "Der verkündigende und der verkündigte Jesus 'Christus,'" in J. Sauer (ed.), *Wer ist Jesus Christus?* (Freiburg: Herder, 1977), pp. 68-69; A. Vögtle, "Jesus von Nazareth," pp. 23-24; E. Grässer, *Die Naherwartung Jesu* (SBS 61; Stuttgart: Kath. Bibelwerk, 1973), pp. 113-18.

44. Cf. H. Merklein, "Erwägungen zur Überlieferungsgeschichte der neutestamentlichen Abendmahlstradition," *BZ* 21 (1977): 88-101, 235-44, here p. 238.

45. Cf. Oberlinner, "Todeserwartung," p. 132.

46. Matt 26:29: μεθ' ὑμῶν.

— and the text itself is against this[47] — then v. 25b expresses Jesus' expectation of drinking anew in the kingdom of God.[48] Possible parallels such as *1 En.* 62.14 (table fellowship of the Son of Man with his own) or 1QSa 2.11-22 (eschatological banquet with the priest-messiah) are of only limited usefulness in clarifying the intention of the text, because the statements that are being compared are not on the same level; the tradition underlying Mark 14:25 is not concerned with the future banquet, but with the resolution of a conflict situation existing in the present. Nothing more can be found stated in the text than that Jesus, in line with the theocentricity of what he proclaims, continues to maintain that the *basileia* is coming and expects himself to have a part in that coming. He is convinced that his proclamation of the rule of God will be vindicated and will finally be put into practice, and implicitly then equally links the participation of his addressees in the *basileia* with their affirmation of his person. The emphasis of the entire saying lies on the *certainty* of the future establishment of the *basileia* in all its fullness and Jesus' expectation that he himself will be an integral part of this event, in other words the articulated prospect of his own vindication in spite of his imminent violent death. This view suggests itself in particular when we see that the common feature linking the two parts of the verse is the *certainty* and *reality* of the coming event in each case.[49]

The Validity of the Claim Made in the Message Proclaimed by Jesus

J. Gnilka sees the present meal and the eschatological banquet in Mark 14:25 as so closely related to each other that the present meal conceals

---

47. But see J. Gnilka, "Wie urteilte Jesus über seinen Tod?", in K. Kertelge (ed.), *Der Tod Jesu — Deutungen im NT* (QD 74; Freiburg: Herder, 1976), pp. 13-50, here p. 34.

48. Of course Jesus cannot be seen in isolation from the disciples, especially as the relationship between speaker and addressees has to be taken into consideration here. The fact that Jesus points out that he is an integral part of the *basileia* shows that he has his disciples in mind, and indeed all those who receive his message. But this has a *functional* significance: Jesus expresses the certainty of his imminent death, and refers to the confirmation of his message in the rule of God, which in turn has consequences for the circle of disciples. In my view, the specific announcement of a re-establishment of the fellowship would effectively amount to a qualitative shift in Jesus' proclamation of salvation that cannot be backed up by the text.

49. Cf. D. Zeller, "Prophetisches Wissen um die Zukunft in synoptischen Jesusworten," *TP* 52 (1977): 258-71, here p. 266.

within it the coming of the heavenly banquet. "This occurs through the revelation of the royal rule of God, which is imminent and cannot take place without Jesus. The saying thus expresses his future hope and his certainty of his resurrection."[50] If this can also be said for the stage of editing by Mark,[51] then caution seems to be called for in terms of the historical Jesus. An insinuated statement of the resurrection can hardly be deduced from the difference from what is said in the prophetic saying. The tradition underlying Mark 14:25 hardly goes much further than the prophetic saying that contrasts the present predominance of the fate of death with the coming of the *basileia*. And here we come to Jesus' basic concept, which should also be asserted for the pre-Mark tradition:

When analyzing the parables in Mark 4, and also the parable of the banquet in Q 14:16-24, we saw that the intention of the narrator Jesus was to maintain the viability of what he was preaching in spite of all actual or potential destructive opposition. The narrator of these parables was thus claiming that his message would be acknowledged as valid in the future, no matter how much it might be threatened, and it would thus prove the superiority of that message. Here lies the inner unity between the different traditions. Fom this insight it follows that the starting-point for the idea of Jesus possibly seeing his death as being necessary for salvation may be found as early as the original message preached by Jesus himself. Yet, this assumption can, at the very least, not be supported by texts whose statement structure is comparable with the parables that we have discussed.

If, however, it can be agreed that Jesus' teaching in parables lies at the core of his message, and that he therefore emphasizes the validity of that message precisely through his parables, then we can probably forego the line that during his public ministry Jesus asserts a qualitatively new orientation in his proclamation of salvation through himself. Rather, the man from Nazareth proclaims unshakeably the God who is with him even during negative experiences and who will uphold and implement his cause.

---

50. J. Gnilka, *Das Evangelium nach Markus. 2. Teilband Mk 8,27–16,20* (EKKNT II/2; Zürich/Neukirchen-Vluyn: Benzinger/Neukirchener, 1979), p. 246.

51. Cf. the internal relationship between Mark 14:28 and Mark 16:7.

Demoniac and Drunkard: John the Baptist and Jesus According to Q 7:33-34

Petr Pokorný

Survey and Methodology

Scholars devoted to Jesus Research work with several clusters of traditions and texts: Jesus' teaching on the Kingdom of God, materials gathered in the Passion story, Jesus' healings and miracles, Jesus' symbolic acts, Jesus' self-understanding, Son of Man sayings, Jesus' expected return, Jesus tradition in Pauline letters and — last but not least — Jesus and John the Baptist.

In the New Testament, John the Baptist appears in the shadow of Jesus. Except for information from Josephus in his book on Jewish History[1] and some traditions like that about John's instructions from Luke 3:10-14, the accounts regarding John the Baptist are influenced by Christian confessions about Jesus. Telling or writing about John the Baptist, the followers of Jesus tried to express the significance of their Master and Lord. It was not easy, since in his time John the Baptist was more popular among the Jews than Jesus. In fact John and Jesus were both reformers of Israel, both unsuccessful, since after the fall of Jerusalem in 70 CE the successful project was the Pharisaic one. However, both were successful outside Israel. John was proclaimed Messiah by some of the Jewish Baptist groups (*Ps.-Clem., Recogn.* 1.60) and later became one of the most important representative personalities of Mandaean religion in its semi-mythical and semi-speculative texts, whereas the mission of Jesus' disciples led to the formation of the Christian Church. Jesus became a member of the Trinity. These

---

1. *Ant.* 18.5.2 paragraph 116-19; about the authenticity of this text see Robert L. Webb, *John the Baptizer and Prophet* (JSNTSup 62; Sheffield: Sheffield Academic Press, 1991).

are incommensurable careers, and today, at least in the West, John is much more known as the precursor of Jesus than as a Mandaean saint.[2]

The Christian tradition emphasized the importance of Jesus by saying that he was more important than John. In the sayings concerning John the Baptist from the opening part of Mark and from Q (Mark 1:2-8; QLk 3:7-9, 17), John is clearly the predecessor of Jesus, even if we can deduce from those traditions John considered himself to be the forerunner for a mighty figure, maybe for the Son of God, or even for God himself coming in judgment.[3] Similar function has the discussion about Elijah from Mark 9:9-13, where Elijah (= John) is the predecessor of the Son of Man (= Jesus), or the saying about John as the last prophet, who inaugurated the period of proclaiming the Kingdom of God (QLk 16:16 par.).[4] The tendency towards interpreting John the Baptist from a Christian view culminated in the reshaping of various popular accounts and hymns from the Baptist groups into a legend about Jesus' pre-history in Luke 1:54-80.[5]

Nevertheless, from the pericope about the baptism of Jesus we may learn that at the beginning Jesus was a disciple of John (Mark 1:9-11 par.). However, in Matthew 3:13-17, as well as in the *Gospel of the Ebionites* (Frg. 3), John maintains that he should be baptized by Jesus; and in John 1:29-34 he does not dare to baptize Jesus at all and proclaims only that he is the lamb of God. According to Luke 3:20, *John was imprisoned* when Jesus was baptized (3:21-22). The ecclesiastical tendency is clear. The legendary account of John's death in Mark 6:17-29 par. is not interpreted in a Christian way except by its position and function in the Gospel of Mark. Also, in his death John is Jesus' predecessor, suggesting to the reader that Jesus faces a similar fate.

This ecclesiastical image of John the Baptist may include some splinters of historical truth, but the whole is a post-Easter construct, illustrating in-

2. W. Barnes Tatum, *John the Baptist and Jesus: A Report of the Jesus Seminar* (Sonoma, Calif.: Polebridge, 1994).

3. Mark 1:3 (= Isa 40:3); see Luke 1:76a; Mark 1:2 (Mal 3:1; see the context); Q (Luke) 3:15-16, cf. John 1:24-28. See Hartwig Thyen, *Studien zur Sündenvergebung* (FRLANT 96; Göttingen: Vandenhoeck & Ruprecht, 1970); W. Barnes Tatum, *John the Baptist and Jesus*, pp. 128ff.

4. See C. R. Kazmierski, *John the Baptist: Prophet and Evangelist* (Collegeville: Liturgical Press, 1996), pp. 79ff.

5. For the differences of John the Baptist's image in the individual Gospels and other sources see Webb, *John the Baptizer*, pp. 47ff.

Petr Pokorný

directly the power of Easter experience and, directly, the role of John in Christian tradition and piety (his *Wirkungsgeschichte*). However, every impact has to be tested as to its adequacy to the original impulse from which it derives its authority. So, it is understandable that we ask about the "John the Baptist of history." In the present context, we are not so much interested in John alone as in his very relation to Jesus and Jesus' relation to him. Our main topic for consideration will be why Jesus divided the group of John's students. What is the difference in their teaching? This is the question.

Q 7:33-34 (Matt 11:18-19) as a Source of Information about John and Jesus

We begin with a biblical text not yet mentioned. It is the second largest cluster of sayings about John the Baptist from QLk 7:18-35 (Matt 11:18-19). Here the pivotal segment of tradition reports about John sending his disciples to Jesus and asking him whether he is "the one who is to come" (Gr. ὁ ἐρχόμενος, QLk 7:19; cf. 3:16). This saying reflects the real relation between these two men better than the ecclesiastical interpretation. However, the uncertainty or tension in John's relation toward Jesus represented in this account is authentic. If John's question were authentic, it might be an argument for his expectation of another God-inspired mediating person before the end of this age,[6] even if the Q source makes Jesus' answer clear that he is the one who is to come (QLk 13:35).[7] The authenticity of this tradition is probable, but it cannot be proved.[8]

Yet there is one sentence whose reliability can scarcely be doubted. It is from QLk 7:33-34, a slander against John the Baptist and Jesus of Nazareth. The wording of the saying according to Matthew is:

> For John came neither eating nor drinking, and they say, "He has a demon." The Son of Man came eating and drinking, and they say, "Look,

---

6. G. Theissen and A. Merz, *Der historische Jesus* (Göttingen: Vandenhoeck & Ruprecht, 1996), pp. 189-90; Webb, *John the Baptizer*, p. 288. Another possibility — as we mentioned — is that John expected the coming of God himself; see also n. 2 above.

7. J. Schröter, *Erinnerung an Jesu Worte. Studien zur Rezeption der Logienüberlieferung bei Markus, Q und Thomas* (WMANT 76; Neukirchen: Neukirchener Verlag, 1997), p. 470.

8. See the discussion of this problem in U. Luz, *Das Evangelium nach Matthäus: Mt 8–17* (EKKNT 1/2; Zürich/Neukirchen-Vluyn: Benzinger/Neukirchener, 1990), pp. 183-84.

a glutton and a drunkard, a friend of tax collectors and sinners!" (Matt 11:18-19a)[9]

Generally, we consider the information as authentic which is witnessed by at least two independent testimonies. About eighty percent of the sayings and accounts about Jesus included in the canonical Gospels cannot be authenticated this way. Yet there is another rule of historical criticism stating that a second witness is unnecessary, if those providing the witness (a unit of tradition in the form of a saying, story, hymn, etc.) had no interest in creating such a text. In the case of this logion it is clear that both those who translated it and those who gathered it into a larger unit of tradition were adherents of Jesus who would never have invented such a saying slandering Jesus.

This insight does not mean that this is a Greek translation of an authentic saying of Jesus. This possibility is not excluded, but what we can say for sure is only that the saying is reliable and valuable, since it includes information about Jesus and John which is not influenced by the post-Easter tendency to depict Jesus as Saviour and Son of God, and to present John the Baptist as his predecessor.

Jesus' followers preserved the saying obviously since in the oral tradition it was linked with some other sayings of their Lord and since they expected that its context might help readers to cope with similar slanders in their time.

In Luke we find the saying in a slightly different version: ". . . neither eating *bread* nor drinking *wine*. . . ." This may mean that John ate only raw food (according to Mark 1:6b par. this was locusts and wild honey),[10] but it may be a post-Easter hint indicating that the Eucharist (Lord's Table)[11] cannot be derived from John. Therefore we will concentrate on Matthew's version.

The information is important, since it is a characteristic of Jesus from the mouth of his opponents. It is all the more valuable since he is compared here with John the Baptist. The advantages of our having such a reliable text from Jesus' time are counterbalanced by a drawback: the text is a

---

9. The translation is from the NRSV.

10. François Bovon, *Das Evangelium nach Lukas 1,1–9,50* (EKKNT 3/1; Zürich: Benzinger; Neukirchen-Vluyn: Neukirchener Verlag, 1989), *ad loc.*

11. Joseph A. Fitzmyer, *The Gospel According to Luke (I–IX): Introduction, Translation, and Notes* (AB 28; Garden City, N.Y.: Doubleday, 1981), *ad loc.*

polemic, and only through a mirror-reading can we learn something about the two persons mentioned here.

John and Jesus

The first surprising discovery is that John the Baptist and Jesus are referred to as two persons on the same level. John is (already) named "the Baptist," but he is not (yet) playing the role of Jesus' precursor.[12] He is named first, since he obviously was older and had been imprisoned before Jesus started to teach, and maybe also because he was Jesus' teacher. The Gospel writers did not harmonize this information with what they took over from Mark's Gospel, where John is presented as Jesus' precursor.

In Q the slander is a part of Jesus' speech to the crowds (ὄχλοι, QLk 7:24). The crowds are addressed in the second person ("What did you go out in the desert to see?"), but in Matt 11:18 the slanderers are mentioned in the third person. They are not identical with the crowds. According to Matt 14:5 the crowd supported John the Baptist and according to Q 11:14 the crowds were obviously also on the side of Jesus. The slanderers are identical with "this generation" from QLk 7:31 (Matt 11:16) which does not accept the prophetic message of Jesus and John. According to Matt 23:2-3, Jesus warned the crowds against the Pharisees, and it is very probable that they are the immediate addressees of Jesus' criticism in QLk 7:33-34, formulated here in the second person, since according to Luke 7:30 the Pharisees and Scribes "rejected God's purpose." The disputation of QLk 7:18-35 may have received its present form post-Easter, during the conflicts between Jesus' adherents and Pharisees. But in its inner logic, the saying in verses 33-34 reflects the problems of Jesus' time, not the disputations during the middle of the first century. The reasons for this statement are clear: it reflects neither the post-Easter Christology nor Soteriology, and together with Jesus it also rejects John the Baptist. Even in the introductory dialogue with John's messengers the argument for Jesus' messiahship does not mention or reflect any Easter experience.[13]

QLk 7:33-34 is in fact a double-logion. The two parts of QLk 7:33-34 are analogically structured. Each of the two parts has two segments. The

---

12. Morton J. Enslin, "John and Jesus," *ZNW* 66 (1975): 1-18, here p. 5.
13. Theissen/Merz, *Der historische Jesus*, p. 191: the dialogue has historical core.

first is Jesus' characterization of John the Baptist and of the "Son of Man" (his indirect self-designation). The second part of each of these twin-sayings is the thesis of the opponents, in both cases a slander. The first part of each of the twin sayings revealed the second one as false. Both functioned analogically and the hearer discovered the inconsistency in the views of the opponents — their opinion was negative irrespective of the striking differences in behavior of those criticized. Jesus' argument is clear: The negative judgment is in both cases a prejudice.

John is being criticized because of his ascetic way of life, which is similar to that of some prophets. John's opponents claimed that "he has a demon (δαιμόνιον)" (Luke 7:33). This accusation was very serious slander, since the person criticized was declared to be on the side of Satan, the Evil One. According to Deut 21:20-21, such a person should be stoned to death in order for the evil to be purged from Israel. "Friend of tax collectors and sinners" was also clearly a slander (Luke 7:34).

The Difference in Their Strategy

In our context it is most interesting to compare the characteristics of both men that can be deduced from QLk 7:33-34. John's ascetic life was obviously a prophetic sign for the society of his time. He was dressed like the prophet Elijah (2 Kgs 1:8), and his fasting, like the wailing of the children from QLk 7:32, exhorted the people to repent, to "mourn" (cf. Jonah 3:5). This is a characteristic that corresponds to his preaching as reported in QLk 3:7 (God's coming judgment), 3:8 (repentance), 3:9 (an axe at the root of the bare tree), and 3:17 (the chaff will be burned). John announced the wrath of God against all sinners. In Mark judgment is not mentioned, but repentance and confession of sins are demanded (1:4-5).[14] Baptism (in the Jordan; Luke 3:3) was obviously an anticipation of God's judgment and a reminder of the flood by which God destroyed sinful humankind (Gen 6-9; cf. 1 Pet 3:21),[15] not only an additional demonstrative cleaning of the body, as may be deduced from the account of Josephus (*Ant.* 18.117).

14. Flavius Josephus does not mention God's judgment in his report on John (*Ant.* 18.117) either. Josephus interpreted John the Baptist's activity from the point of its results in ethics. His baptism was a means to achieve righteousness (δικαιοσύνη) through purification (ἁγνεία) of the soul.

15. Webb, *John the Baptizer,* pp. 214-16.

John's obvious intention was to change the life of his Jewish contemporaries by shocking them. He confronted them with God's impending punishment and thereby he intended to bring about their purification. In some respects we may compare it with the *katharsis* in classical Greek tragedy. *Katharsis* of the spectators in the theatre was caused by a fatal catastrophe in the life story of the heroes. Unlike in Greek tragedy, the end of John's purification was clearly ethical. In this point the report of Josephus is reliable. Just like Jesus, John intended to save the people. The means he used to change their behaviour was, however, predominantly the fear of punishment.[16] The saying about fire (QLk 3:17) does not symbolize purification, but clearly the Last Judgment (Mal 3:1-7).[17]

Unlike John, Jesus is described as one who eats and drinks too much, as a "glutton and drunkard, a friend of tax collectors and sinners." From the synoptic tradition we know that Jesus often participated in table fellowships (συμπόσια) in the manner of Socrates.[18] Some of his crucial sayings were pronounced in such a setting. For example, in the story of his dinner in a Pharisee's house, which in Luke immediately follows the pericope we are discussing (Luke 7:36-50 par.; cf. John 12:1-8), Jesus said to the sinful woman, "Your sins are forgiven" (Luke 7:48). In the house of Zacchaeus, where Jesus was a guest according to Luke 19:1-10, Jesus proclaimed, "Today salvation has come to this house" (19:9a). The tradition of the Last Supper (1 Cor 11:23-26; Mark 14:22-25 par.; Luke 22:15-20) contains not only sayings expressing the meaning of Jesus' suffering for other people ("for you"), but also sayings about the Last Supper anticipating the joy of the Kingdom of God: Mark 14:25 par. (at the end of the pericope), in Luke 22:15-18 (at the beginning) and also in 1 Cor 11:26, where Paul mentioned the second coming of Jesus Christ, as it was a typical expectation in the post-Easter time.

16. See Helmut Merklein, "Die Umkehrspredigt bei Johannes dem Täufer und Jesus von Nazareth," *BZ* 25 (1981): 29-46.
17. For a profiled discussion see: Paul W. Hollenbach, "John the Baptist," *ABD* (New York/London: Doubleday, 1992), vol. 3, pp. 887-99, esp. section B.2, pp. 893-98.
18. J. Bolyki, *Jesu Tischgemeinschaften* (WUNT 2/96; Tübingen: Mohr Siebeck, 1998), pp. 70-74, 228-29; M. Klinghardt, *Gemeinschaftsmahl und Mahlgemeinschaft: Soziologie und Liturgie frühchristlicher Mahlfeiern* (TANZ 13; Tübingen/Basel: Francke Verlag, 1996), discussed the social function of common meals in Early Christianity (523ff.); however, he does not analyze the theology (eschatology) as it is included in the so-called "Institution" of the Lord's Supper.

In light of these observations we can understand why in Jesus' sayings a banquet is often used as an image of the Kingdom of God (of the "age to come") as in the parable of the great banquet (Matt 22:1-14; Luke 14:16-24;[19] *Gos. Thom.* 64), in the logion about people from East and West coming to the feast in the Kingdom of God (QLk 13:28-29), or in the beatitudes of the poor and hungry (QLk 6:20-21).

In all cases this is an image whose main features are: (a) the human fellowship sealed at the fellowship table, (b) the dependence of all participants on God, and (c) the fact that the participants are not qualified to receive such a privilege because of their own moral qualities, but only through God's intention and mercy. It is the invitation itself that changed their lives.

Since such a fellowship is part of Jesus' proclamation of the Kingdom of God, it is obvious that his strategy of salvation was different from that of John the Baptist. This conclusion fits the other information we have about John the Baptist and Jesus from Mark, the Gospel of John, and the other available sources. Jesus considered his time as a time of joy, as was common at a wedding feast (Mark 2:19), as a time full of signs pointing towards God's mercy in the messianic age (QLk 7:22).[20]

In QLk 7:31-32 (Matt 11:16-17) the slander against Jesus and John is introduced by a metaphor from the world of children. There the addressees are compared to children who (a) do not dance, when the flute is being played (they do not enter the wedding feast), and who (b) do not weep, when the others wail (they do not enter the world of a funeral feast).[21] Case (a) obviously represents the proclamation of Jesus, and case (b) that of John the Baptist. On the literary surface, QLk 7:31-34 has a chiastic structure: a-b-b-a. More important than this observation is the pragmatics of the two ways of reforming God's people: The wailing or the playing of the flute. Playing the flute is the way of Jesus' proclamation, his "Good News." The fact that the early church, and most probably Jesus himself, summarized his message as "good news" (εὐαγγέλιον) corresponds to our findings derived from the views of Jesus' opponents.

19. The two versions are so different that the origin of this parable in the source Q is often questioned.

20. On the difference between John the Baptist and Jesus see Joachim Gnilka, *Jesus von Nazareth: Botschaft und Geschichte* (HTKNT.S 3; Freiburg i. Br.: Herder 1990), pp. 85-86.

21. Matt 11:17 has better preserved the shape of the saying reflecting the Jewish setting. Instead about "weeping" we read here about "beating the breast" (NRSV: "mourning").

It is good to have such a clear and simple (and simplifying) image of the difference between Jesus and John as their contemporaries would have seen it. The deepest reason for Jesus' parting from John was obviously here, in the general strategy of salvation and reform.[22]

The Anchoring of Jesus' Proclamation

However, this does not mean that Jesus' preaching was a meek sentiment and the opposite of John's proclamation of the judgment of God.

First, it is apparent that according to the saying from QLk 7:33-34 John and Jesus are principally seen as allies, both presenting solutions to Israel's problems that were dangerous in the eyes of political as well as of priestly representatives of Jewish (limited) autonomy. The proclamation of the judgment as well as the proclamation of the Kingdom of God stressed that their positions were relative. Jesus declared John to be a person opening the Age to Come — as a prophet (QLk 16:16 and 7:28; Codex A etc.),[23] and as a new bearer of God's spirit, considered absent from Israel (see Ps 74:9) since the period after Zechariah and Malachi (*b. Sanh.* 11a) and expected only as a prelude of a new age. QLk 7:33-34 as well as the popular fame that Jesus was identical with the presumed resurrected John (Mark 6:14 par.; Codex B etc.),[24] indicates that many Jews perceived Jesus and John as allies.

Second, Jesus and John obviously shared a kind of apocalyptic expectation. This is what German scholars described in the twentieth century: Jesus' teaching about the Kingdom of God cannot be understood without the apocalyptic myth about God's universal judgment and the coming of the Age to Come. Jesus' mysterious logion about fire and suffering (Luke 12:49-50; *Gos. Thom.* 10)[25] reflects the awareness of an apocalyptic rupture in human history (Luke 12:52; *Gos. Thom.* 16).

22. According to J. Dominic Crossan, *The Historical Jesus: The Life of a Mediterranean Jewish Peasant* (San Francisco: Harper, 1991), p. 259, the reason for Jesus' emancipation from John was that he no longer accepted his apocalyptic message. I would rather say that there was a deep difference in their interpretation of the apocalyptic. Cf. P. Hollenbach, "The Conversion of Jesus: From Jesus the Baptizer to Jesus the Healer," *ANRW* 2.25.1, pp. 196-219.

23. See C. H. Kraeling, *John the Baptist* (New York/London: Charles Scribner's Sons, 1951), pp. 137ff.

24. According to Codex Aleph, A, etc. it was an assumption of Herod (Antipas).

25. Mysterious statements preserved in the tradition originate obviously in a layer older than the final shape of the text.

The apocalyptic background of Jesus' preaching has been questioned in recent decades. Some scholars interpreted Jesus in a non-apocalyptic way, in some cases even as a teacher of wisdom, similar to the itinerant cynic philosophers.[26] Without supra-individual expectation, Jesus' self-understanding would not be understandable. In addition to it, in his sayings we discover a strong motif of apocalyptic judgment against individual groups in Israel (e.g. QLk 10:13-15) as well as against Israel as a whole (QLk 11:31-32 par.; Matt/Q 8:11-12 par.). Even the logion we are discussing now is obviously a declaration of judgment against his Jewish contemporaries and compatriots. Numerous scholars stressed the proclamation of God's eschatological judgment as a constant element of all Jesus' traditions.[27] This is (1) because Jesus proclaimed the Kingdom of God against the background of an apocalyptic judgment, but also (2) because the rejection of his message in Jerusalem and probably already in Galilee obviously evoked a special series of sayings about judgment. This does not mean that the "good news" in Jesus' proclamation reflects only the post-Easter success of Christian mission among the pagans. More probably it was the rejection of God's grace (i.e. of the promise transcending the definitions of the very people of God), that motivated Jesus' pronouncing of judgment against Israel and especially against some of its influential groups. It was necessary to mention this discussion before we analyze the difference between Jesus and John the Baptist as it is expressed in Luke (Q) 7:33-34.

The difference between Jesus and John is also understandable against this background: Instead of stressing the catastrophe at the end of This Age, Jesus concentrated on the Kingdom of God as the Age to Come.[28] In-

26. Those interpreting Jesus in a non-apocalyptic way are mentioned by M. Borg, *Conflict, Holiness and Politics in the Teaching of Jesus* (SBEC 5; New York/Toronto: Edwin Mellen Press, 1984); F. G. Downing, *The Christ and the Cynics* (JSOTSup 4; Sheffield: Sheffield Academic Press, 1988); Crossan, *The Historical Jesus*, esp. pp. 76, 103. For the critique see M. Ebner, *Jesus — ein Weisheitslehrer? Synoptische Weisheitslogien im Traditionsprozess* (HBS 15; Freiburg i. Br.: Herder, 1998), esp. p. 428.

27. M. Reiser, *Die Gerichtspredigt Jesu* (NTAbh NF 2; Münster: Aschendorff, 1990); W. Zager, *Gottesherrschaft und Endgericht in der Verkündigung Jesu* (BZNW 2; Berlin/New York: de Gruyter, 1996); E. Rau, *Jesus, Freund von Zöllnern und Sündern: Eine methodologische Untersuchung* (Stuttgart: Verlag W. Kohlhammer, 2000), pp. 96ff.

28. Undoubtedly, there are numerous sayings about the last judgment in the Jesus tradition. The most striking example is Jesus' exclamation of "woe" to the unrepentant cities in QLk 10:13-15. But even here it is evident that this is not the center of his message. Tyre and Sidon will be better off than Capernaum and other unrepentant Jewish towns.

deed, Jesus also suggested alternative projects framing his proclamation; he did not stick with apocalyptic. His anticipation of the Kingdom of God in QLk 7:33-34 is even explicitly linked with the term wisdom (σοφία) in verse 35: "Nevertheless, wisdom is vindicated by all her children." However here the wisdom is not the teaching of Jesus; it is Jesus himself.[29] The term "wisdom" here describes Jesus in his relation to God, not the genre of his speeches.

All of this does not mean Jesus' teaching is typically apocalyptic. It means only that he re-interpreted the wisdom tradition at least as deeply as the apocalyptic. His concept of the Kingdom of God has its eschatological key dimension: Jesus interpreted it as a harvest, the coming of a thief, an assault, and a great banquet introducing a social change. This meant that the Kingdom of God was coming near (ἐγγίζειν, e.g. Mark 1:15 par.) with a supra-individual power — as a social and even cosmic phenomenon. Otherwise it could not be proclaimed as a guarantee of Jesus' promises (e.g. as expressed in the Beatitudes). Without a supra-individual expectation, John's self-understanding as a forerunner of the Stronger One would not be understandable.

Apocalyptic eschatology was not a common horizon of that time, but it was a social, religious and cultural background of several Jewish groups of Jesus' day (apocalyptic authors and their readers, Jesus' adherents, John's disciples, Qumran sect) and Jesus' proclamation of the Kingdom of God. Instead of speaking about punishment, Jesus revealed what survives the judgment, what is the connecting link between the present and eternity. Instead of shocking the people by proclaiming the judgment of God, he interpreted God's ultimate judgment positively. Since the Kingdom of God is the ultimate prospect, human beings are free from the heaviest burden of worry: "Do not worry about your life. . . . Who of you by worrying can add a single hour to his life . . . ? But seek his Kingdom, and these things will be given to you as well" (QLk 12:22, 25, 27-28, 31).[30] Jesus' vision is apocalyptic in the basic eschatological sense: It is not built upon moral exhortation and moral effort, but upon the coming of the Kingdom of God. It was a hope that was based supra-ethically and anchored in the very structure of the

29. Cf. the personification of Wisdom in Proverbs (ch. 8).

30. One anachronistic observation should be mentioned here. Jesus' sayings about care (μέριμνα, μεριμνάω) could be interpreted as a kind of counterbalance of Martin Heidegger's philosophy in which the mortality is the source of everyday human "Sorge" (care and sorrow).

Kingdom, in which God's justice will prevail and the poor will be the co-regents. Here the opponents of Jesus disagreed: "A friend of tax collectors and sinners" was their answer to Jesus' Good News (QLk 7:22-23).

If we look in the synoptic tradition for some analogy to the Pauline teaching about the priority of God's grace, it is precisely this reinterpretation of apocalyptic eschatology from Q. This teaching was so typical of Jesus' message that even the distorted interpretation of his opponents was not able to suppress its inner power.

"Have You Not Read . . . ?"
Jesus' Subversive Interpretation of Scripture

Craig A. Evans

The scholars of the North American Jesus Seminar tend to disregard the presence of Old Testament Scripture in the dominical tradition, assuming that its presence is due to apologetic interests of the Palestinian Jesus Movement.[1] It must be acknowledged, of course, that the early community embellished the scriptural witness, especially as seen in proof-texting. But many other scholars rightly recognize that the very essence of Jesus' proclamation sprang from the "good news" of God's reign promised in Isaiah, while the mighty deeds of Jesus were interpreted as also fulfilling the expectation enunciated by the great prophet of old.[2] Studies have also rightly

1. For example, R. W. Funk and R. W. Hoover (eds.), *The Five Gospels: The Search for the Authentic Words of Jesus* (Sonoma, Calif.: Polebridge; New York: Macmillan, 1993), p. 68: "Jesus taught on his own authority and seems not to have invoked scripture to justify his pronouncements." Throughout, dominical quotations and allusions to Scripture are judged inauthentic. I have no special interest in the Jesus Seminar, headquartered in California and for years led by the late Robert Funk. The Seminar has received far more attention in the popular media than it deserves, but — happily — has been largely ignored in scholarly publications. I cite the Seminar here because its skepticism with regard to Jesus' eschatology and use of Scripture is helpfully illustrative for the present purposes. So far as the Seminar's overall program is concerned, I can say nothing more pertinent than what Professor Gerd Theissen has already said, when he remarks humorously that the "'non-eschatological Jesus' [of the Seminar] seems to have more Californian than Galilean local colouring." See G. Theissen and A. Merz, *The Historical Jesus: A Comprehensive Guide* (Minneapolis: Fortress, 1998), p. 11.

2. The "good news" or "gospel" of God's reign springs from Isa 40:9; 52:7; and 61:1-2, while the "works" that accompany and provide evidence of the reality of this rule are delineated in Isa 26:19; 29:18-19; 35:5-6; and 61:1-2. Appeals to these scriptures were made not only

and productively compared Jesus' style and method of interpretation to what we find in rabbinic and targumic literature.[3]

Half a century ago the British New Testament scholar C. H. Dodd investigated the function of the Old Testament in the theology of the early community of Jesus' followers. At the end of his study he remarked: "This is a piece of genuinely creative thinking. Who was responsible for it? . . . Whose was the originating mind here?" Dodd believed that the creative approach to the Old Testament found in the Gospels and elsewhere in the writings of the New Testament originated with Jesus himself.[4] In a study published two decades later, R. T. France agreed with Dodd, adding: "The source of the distinctive Christian use of the Old Testament was not the creative thinking of the primitive community, but that of its founder."[5]

In my opinion the conclusions reached by Dodd and France are fully justified. The purpose of the present investigation is to explore one aspect of Jesus' creative use of Scripture. This aspect appears to be a deliberately subversive interpretation of Scripture. We may see this in Jesus' remarkable subversions of passages and themes from Daniel and Zechariah, as well as in cases involving legal materials. Because this was not a tendency in the early Church, where proof-texting emphasized correspondence and agreement, not dissonance, we may have here an important point of entry into Jesus' understanding of scripture and of his own mission.[6]

---

by Jesus' followers but by Jesus himself, as his reply to the imprisoned and questioning John the Baptist makes clear (cf. Matt 11:2-6 = Luke 7:18-23). The message and activity of Jesus cannot be properly understood apart from this prophetic background. I develop this line of interpretation in C. A. Evans, "From Gospel to Gospel: The Function of Isaiah in the New Testament," in C. C. Broyles and C. A. Evans (eds.), *Writing and Reading the Scroll of Isaiah: Studies of an Interpretive Tradition* (VTSup 70/2; FIOTL 1/2; Leiden: Brill, 1997), pp. 651-91, esp. pp. 653-74.

3. See B. D. Chilton, *God in Strength: Jesus' Announcement of the Kingdom* (SNTSU 1; Freistadt: Plöchl, 1979; repr. BibSem 8; Sheffield: JSOT Press, 1987); idem, *A Galilean Rabbi and His Bible: Jesus' Use of the Interpreted Scripture of His Time* (GNS 8; Wilmington: Glazier, 1984).

4. C. H. Dodd, *According to the Scriptures: The Sub-Structure of New Testament Theology* (London: Nisbet, 1952), pp. 109-10.

5. R. T. France, *Jesus and the Old Testament* (London: The Tyndale Press, 1971), p. 226.

6. I am invoking here a form of the criterion of dissimilarity. This criterion functions helpfully when used with caution and usually with positive application. The problem is in its negative application, by which it is believed that whatever the Gospels say Jesus said or did that is not dissimilar to Christian belief or Jewish thought must be rejected. We should assume that Jesus in fact did and said many things that other Jewish teachers said and did and

Craig A. Evans

More than twenty-five years ago the late Bishop John Robinson asked if Jesus had a distinctive use of Scripture. He concluded that he did, and he described it as a "challenging use" of Scripture.[7] This use of Scripture often appears with a challenging question: "Have you never read what David did?" (Mark 2:25); or "Have you not read this scripture?" (Mark 12:10); or "Have you not read in the book of Moses?" (Mark 12:26). Other examples are introduced with "how" (πῶς): "How is it written of the Son of man?" (Mark 9:12); or "How can the scribes say?" (Mark 12:35). Very intriguing is the series of counter-questions we find in Luke 10, where the legal authority asks what he must do to inherit eternal life. Jesus asks him in turn: "What is written in the law? How do you read?" (Luke 10:26). In essence, Jesus has asked this man to think about his hermeneutics. What is in Scripture, and how does he interpret it? Robinson concludes his essay by calling attention to Jesus' distinctive use of amen ("truly," "certainly").

At about the same time that Robinson's essay appeared, Bruce Chilton published his stimulating A Galilean Rabbi and His Bible.[8] Although the burden of this important study is to show the relevance and meaning of the emerging targumic tradition for understanding Jesus' use of the Scriptures, he too called attention to the distinctive, asseverative usage of amen. For Chilton it was symptomatic of Jesus' experience of Scripture as fulfilled, as referring to "divine activity in the present."[9]

Here, Chilton seems to have put his finger on a very important feature of the larger question of how Jesus understood and used Scripture. Elsewhere Chilton argues that for Jesus "[S]cripture is fulfilled in the sense that it mediates a fresh perception of God."[10] In my opinion, Chilton's most interesting conclusion is seen in this statement: "Jesus completes or fulfills

---

that many things he taught his followers accepted without revision. The misuse of the criterion of dissimilarity has been subjected to trenchant criticism in recent years. For example, see M. D. Hooker, "On Using the Wrong Tool," *Theol* 75 (1972): 570-81; T. Holmén, "Doubts about Double Dissimilarity: Restructuring the Main Criterion of Jesus-of-History Research," in C. A. Evans and B. Chilton (eds.), *Authenticating the Words of Jesus* (NTTS 28/1; Leiden: Brill, 1999), pp. 47-80.

7. J. A. T. Robinson, "Did Jesus Have a Distinctive Use of Scripture?" in *Twelve More New Testament Studies* (London: SCM Press, 1984), pp. 35-43; originally appeared in R. F. Berkey and S. A. Edwards (eds.), *Christological Perspectives: Essays in Honor of Harvey K. McArthur* (New York: Pilgrim, 1982), pp. 49-57.

8. Cited in n. 3 above.

9. Chilton, *A Galilean Rabbi and His Bible*, p. 174.

10. Chilton, *A Galilean Rabbi and His Bible*, p. 186.

what is lacking in the text itself by the introduction of his own insight; he alters the text so that it becomes a reflection of his experience of God."[11]

It is this intriguing observation that Jesus "alters the text so that it becomes a reflection of his experience of God" that seems to be the key to understanding Jesus' subversive interpretation of Scripture.[12] Let me hasten to say that Jesus' interpretation and usage of Scripture are not always subversive. Neither is every instance of creative interpretation of Scripture — whether altered or not — subversive. More often than not, Jesus presupposes the conventional interpretation of Scripture, especially the Law.[13] One of the examples cited by Professor Klaus Haacker is a case in point.[14] In Luke 10:25 the legal authority asks Jesus, "What must I do to inherit eternal life?" When queried by Jesus, he cites the great Double Commandment. Jesus commends him and assures him: "Do this and you will live" (Luke 10:28: τοῦτο ποίει καὶ ζήσῃ). This is an unmistakable allusion to Lev 18:5, which in its early context refers only to life in the Promised Land and Israel's possession of it — as Professor Haacker rightly notes. So how does Lev 18:5 reassure the legal authority concerning eternal life? According to the Targum, Lev 18:5 promises life *in the world to come,* as well as life in the land of Israel. The antiquity of this Aramaic interpretation is attested in column 3 of the *Damascus Document,* as preserved in the genizah text from the Cairo synagogue.

> 15bThe desires of his will — which a human should carry out 16and so have life in them [Lev 18:5] — he opened up to them. So they "dug a well," yielding much water. 17Those who reject this water he will not allow to live. . . . 20But those who hold firm to it shall receive everlasting life, and all human honor is rightly theirs. (CD 3:15b-20)

Thus, Jesus' usage of Lev 18:5 is supportive of the saving value of the Law, specifically agreeing with contemporary interpretation of this important passage of Scripture. What is particularly striking is that Jesus' posi-

11. Chilton, *A Galilean Rabbi and His Bible,* p. 185.

12. I should note that N. T. Wright also speaks of the presence of "deeply subversive" elements in the dominical tradition, which he views as indications of authentic material. See N. T. Wright, *Jesus and the Victory of God* (Minneapolis: Fortress, 1996), p. 132.

13. This point is made by France, *Jesus and the Old Testament,* p. 201: "[H]e was in general unusually faithful to its intended meaning" (in contrast to interpretive approaches seen in Philo, the Dead Sea Scrolls, and early rabbinic literature).

14. See the chapter by Klaus Haacker in the present volume.

tive appeal to Lev 18:5 stands in tension with Paul's negative use of it in Rom 10:5 and Gal 3:12, in polemical contexts in which the apostle emphatically asserts that by the works of the Law no one can be saved. In this particular case, Jesus' exegesis does not subvert Jewish interpretation, but later "Christian" — or at least Pauline — exegesis![15]

Jesus' subversive interpretation of Scripture manifests itself in at least five important areas: (1) revelation, (2) authority, (3) service and mission, (4) divine wrath, and (5) law and obligations. Examples in these areas will be treated briefly. My purpose here is suggestive only; my treatment is by no means definitive.

Revelation

In a tradition preserved in Q (Matt 11:25-27 = Luke 10:21-22) Jesus thanks God for special revelation. The Matthean version reads as follows:

> I thank you, Father, Lord of heaven and earth, because you have hidden these things from the eyes of the wise and discerning and revealed them to babes [ἐξομολογοῦμαί σοι, πάτερ, κύριε τοῦ οὐρανοῦ καὶ τῆς γῆς, ὅτι ἔκρυψας ταῦτα ἀπὸ σοφῶν καὶ συνετῶν καὶ ἀπεκάλυψας αὐτὰ νηπίοις]. (Matt 11:25)

In favor of authenticity is reference to Jesus' followers as "babes," suggesting naiveté. Indeed, the implication is that the disciples are not "wise and discerning" (cf. Wis 12:24; 15:14, where "babes" occurs with "fools"). This is hardly a saying generated by the early church.[16]

Commentators have heard in this prayer allusions to various passages of Scripture.[17] Discussing the form we have in Matthew, Dale Allison and W. D. Davies suggest possible dependence on Isa 29:14 (". . . the wisdom of their wise men shall perish, and the discernment of their discerning men

15. For this reason, I believe that it is almost certain that Jesus appealed to the Torah in such a positive fashion. Christian apologetic may go so far as to assert Jesus' compliance with Jewish law (as we see in Matt 5:17-20), but it is very doubtful that a tradition that affirms life through obedience to Torah was generated by the primitive community.

16. See the perceptive comments in U. Luz, *Matthew 8–20* (Hermeneia; Minneapolis: Fortress, 2001), pp. 157-58, 161-64.

17. See the helpful discussion in J. Nolland, *Luke 9:21–18:34* (WBC 35b; Dallas: Word, 1993), pp. 571-72; Luz, *Matthew 8–20*, pp. 163-64.

shall be hidden"), which Paul quotes in 1 Cor 1:19. However, they acknowledge that "the thought is common enough in Jewish texts."[18]

In a series of studies Werner Grimm has called our attention to Dan 2:19-23, in which Daniel thanks God for making known his mysteries and giving wisdom and discernment to the wise.[19] The most relevant part of the passage reads as follows:

> 20Daniel said: "Blessed be the name of God for ever and ever, to whom belong wisdom and majesty. 21He changes times and seasons; he removes kings and sets up kings; he gives to the wise wisdom [σοφοῖς σοφίαν] and to those with discernment [καὶ σύνεσιν] understanding; 22he reveals [ἀνακαλύπτων] deep and mysterious things; he knows what is in the darkness, and the light dwells with him. 23To you, O God of my fathers, I give thanks [ἐξομολογοῦμαι][20] and praise, for you have given me wisdom and intelligence [σοφίαν καὶ φρόνησιν], and have now made known to me what we asked of you, for you have made known to us the king's matter." (Dan 2:20-23)

Two principal factors support Grimm's suggestion that Jesus' prayer does indeed allude to Daniel 2: (1) The concentration of common vocabulary, and (2) the subversive relationship between Jesus' prayer and Daniel's prayer. By "subversive relationship" I mean that Jesus thanks God for not revealing his mysteries to the "wise and discerning," by which is probably meant the educated and professional, that is, the professional wise man, such as Daniel and his colleagues.[21] No, God has not revealed his deepest truths to such as these; he has revealed his truth to the followers of Jesus,

---

18. W. D. Davies and D. C. Allison, Jr., *A Critical and Exegetical Commentary on the Gospel according to Saint Matthew.* Volume II: *Commentary on Matthew VIII–XVIII* (ICC; Edinburgh: T&T Clark, 1991), p. 275.

19. W. Grimm, "Selige Augenzeugen, Luk. 10,23f: Alttestamentlicher Hintergrund und ursprünglicher Sinn," *TZ* 26 (1970): 172-83; idem, "Der Dank für die empfangene Offenbarung bei Jesus und Josephus," *BZ* 17 (1973): 249-56; idem, *Jesus und das Danielbuch.* Band I: *Jesu Einspruch gegen das Offenbarungssystem Daniels (Mt 11,25-27; Lk 17,20-21)* (ANTJ 6.1; Frankfurt am Main: Peter Lang, 1984), pp. 1-69.

20. The verb "give thanks" renders the Aramaic ידא, whose cognate ידה was chosen by Franz Delitzsch in his Hebrew translation of *exomologoumai* in Matt 11:25. ידה, of course, is the verb that regularly appears in 1QHᵃ, the Hodayot, or Thanksgiving Hymns.

21. Luz, *Matthew 8–20,* p. 163: "Especially noticeable is the contrast with Dan 2:20-23. . . ."

who in another context are described as unlettered and untrained (Acts 4:13). Jesus' followers are mere "babes" in expertise in religion, but thanks to God, who reveals his truth to the innocent, they now have a deeper understanding of the divine will than do the professionals.

There are also two minor factors that lend additional support to Daniel 2 as the primary scriptural backdrop to Jesus' prayer. The first is seen in Jesus' addressing of God as "Lord of heaven and earth" (κύριε τοῦ οὐρανοῦ καὶ τῆς γῆς). This epithet occurs in Tobit and 1Q20 (the *Genesis Apocryphon*). Both of these works originated in Aramaic and were in circulation in the time of Jesus and his contemporaries.[22] Jesus' use of an Aramaic epithet for God encourages us to look to an Aramaic source, such as Daniel, for other components in his prayer.

The second minor factor is the observation that the author of Qumran's *Thanksgiving Hymns* addresses God in a similar way.[23] Several times the author says, "I give thanks to you, O Lord," for wisdom, understanding, insight, and truth (cf. 1QH[a] 4.21; 6.19, 38; 15.29 [= 4Q428 Frg. 9 line 1]). This author, who may well have been the Righteous Teacher, perhaps also the founder of the movement, seems to have been influenced by Daniel, a book popular at Qumran. As will Jesus a few generations later, the author of the *Thanksgiving Hymns* extols God for revealing his truth. Unlike Jesus, however, the author of the *Thanksgiving Hymns* thanks God for revealing his truth to those well studied in Scripture. Jesus' subversive use of Daniel's prayer contrasts both with Daniel and with similar prayers of thanksgiving found in the *Thanksgiving Hymns*.[24]

---

22. In 1Q20 22.16 and 22.21 the Aramaic reads: מרה שמיא וארעא. Tobit 7:17 (Eng. 7:18) is not extant in the Aramaic fragments from Qumran (i.e., 4Q196-199). The Greek translation reads: ὁ κύριος τοῦ οὐρανοῦ καὶ τῆς γῆς.

23. Observed long ago in J. Carmignac and P. Guilbert, *Les textes de Qumran: Traduits et annotés*. Vol. 1: *La Règle de la Communauté, la Règle de la Guerre, les Hymnes* (Paris: Letouzey et Ané, 1961), p. 157 n. 1. See also R. H. Gundry, *Matthew: A Commentary on His Handbook for a Mixed Church under Persecution* (Grand Rapids: Eerdmans, 1994 [2nd ed.]), pp. 216-18.

24. This is not to discount the possible influence of Isa 29:14, as Allison and Davies suggested. Isaiah seems to have made important contributions to Jesus' teaching and language in many contexts. In the present case, the subversion of Daniel 2 may well have been encouraged by Isaiah's oracle against the wise.

Authority

Criticized for permitting his disciples to pluck grain on the Sabbath, Jesus asserts his authority over the Sabbath (Mark 2:23-28). His reply is as follows:

> The Sabbath was made for man, not man for the Sabbath; so the son of man is lord even of the Sabbath. (vv. 27-28)

Jesus' self-reference as "son of man" almost certainly derives from Dan 7:13-14, where the figure, who is "like a son of man," receives from God royal authority. Invested with this divine authority, Jesus as son of man may announce God's rule,[25] pronounce sins forgiven (as in Mark 2:1-12), and even assert lordly authority over the Sabbath itself.

This is an amazing statement, which I believe authentically derives from Jesus.[26] It flies in the face of the high regard in which Jews in late antiquity, including early "Christians," held the Sabbath. The sacredness of the Sabbath reaches back to creation itself, as seen in the following selection of texts:

> 2And on the seventh day God finished his work, which he had done, and he rested on the seventh day from all his work, which he had done. 3So God blessed the seventh day and sanctified it, because on it God rested from all his work that he had done in creation. (Gen 2:2-3)

> 10But the seventh day is a Sabbath to the LORD your God; in it you shall not do any work, you, or your son, or your daughter, your manservant, or your maidservant, or your cattle, or the sojourner who is within your gates; 11for in six days the LORD made heaven and earth, the sea, and all that is in them, and rested the seventh day; therefore the LORD blessed the Sabbath day and hallowed it. (Exod 20:10-11)

---

25. See J. Schröter ("The Son of Man as the Representative of God's Kingdom: On the Interpretation of Jesus in Mark and Q," in M. Labahn and A. Schmidt (eds.), *Jesus, Mark and Q: The Teaching of Jesus and Its Earliest Records* [JSNTSup 214; Sheffield: Sheffield Academic Press, 2001], pp. 34-68), who rightly emphasizes the linkage between the epithet "son of man" and the proclamation of the kingdom of God. This point will not be pursued further in the present study, but it is presupposed throughout.

26. For discussion of linguistic and cultural details, see M. Casey, *Aramaic Sources of Mark's Gospel* (SNTSMS 102; Cambridge: Cambridge University Press, 1998), pp. 138-92, esp. pp. 148-51. Casey rightly argues for a *Sitz im Leben Jesu*. I follow Casey on most points.

> Blessed is the man who does this, and the son of man who holds it fast, who keeps the Sabbath, not profaning it, and keeps his hand from doing any evil. (Isa 56:2)

In the face of traditions such as these, Jesus' claim to have the authority to make pronouncements concerning what is allowed and not allowed on the Sabbath is extraordinary. But even more than this, Jesus says that as "son of man" he is the "lord of the Sabbath." On what basis can Jesus or anyone else possess this kind of authority? The answer lies in the interesting epithet "son of man," which in my opinion — despite some loud and influential voices to the contrary[27] — derives from the vision of Daniel 7, a vision which in his own way Jesus experienced and applied to himself. Accordingly, as "son of man" he "has authority *on earth* to forgive sins" (Mark 2:10). The curious prepositional phrase "on earth" is not otiose, but stands in contrast to the *heavenly* setting, in which the Danielic son of man received his authority.[28] Possessing this authority, Jesus the son of man may now forgive sins and make Sabbath pronouncements. Jesus has in effect subverted a major teaching of Scripture, but has done so through his dynamic appropriation of other Scripture.

---

27. For examples, see G. H. Boobyer, "Mark II.10a and the Interpretation of the Healing of the Paralytic," *HTR* 47 (1954): 115-20; C. P. Ceroke, "Is Mark 2:10 a Saying of Jesus?" *CBQ* 22 (1960): 369-90; L. S. Hay, "The Son of Man in Mark 2:10, and 2:28," *JBL* 89 (1970): 69-75; K. Kertelge, "Die Vollmacht des Menschensohnes zur Sündenvergebung (Mk 2, 18)," in P. Hoffmann, N. Brox, and W. Pesch (eds.), *Orientierung an Jesus: Zur Theologie der Synoptiker* (J. Schmid Festschrift; Freiburg: Herder, 1973), pp. 205-13, here pp. 208-11; N. Perrin, *A Modern Pilgrimage in New Testament Christology* (Philadelphia: Fortress, 1974), pp. 88-89.

28. The epithet "son of man" is not a title, nor is it messianic. It means *human* (as opposed to beast or angel). But its consistent articular usage on the lips of Jesus, throughout the Gospels, is in reference to a *specific* human figure — the one described in Daniel 7. Jesus understood himself as this figure, who from God, *in heaven,* received authority; and now, *on earth,* exercises that authority. On Jesus' employment of the articular "son of man," see B. Chilton, "The Son of Man: Human and Heavenly," in F. Van Segbroeck, C. M. Tuckett, G. van Belle, and J. Verheyden (eds.), *The Four Gospels 1992: Festschrift Frans Neirynck* (3 vols.; BETL 100; Leuven: Peeters and Leuven University Press, 1992), vol. 1, pp. 203-18. M. Casey (*Son of Man: The Interpretation and Influence of Daniel 7* [London: SPCK, 1979]; idem, *Aramaic Sources,* pp. 117-21), following a long line of interpretation, argues that it was Jesus' use of "Son of Man" that encourages early followers of Jesus to appeal to Daniel 7. This, of course, does not explain the ubiquitous appearance in the Gospels of the definite article(s): "The Son of (the) Man" (ὁ υἱὸς τοῦ ἀνθρώπου).

Service and Mission

We have just seen how appeal to the authority of the son of man figure in Daniel 7 provided the rationale for claiming authority over the Sabbath itself. In the present example we see Jesus subverting Daniel 7, almost in effect denying the authority of the son of man. In a saying of uncertain context but probable authenticity, Jesus says to his disciples:

> The son of man has come not to be served, but to serve (ὁ υἱὸς τοῦ ἀνθρώπου οὐκ ἦλθεν διακονηθῆναι ἀλλὰ διακονῆσαι) and give his life a ransom for many. (Mark 10:45)

We have here an unmistakable allusion to Dan 7:13-14:

> 13I saw in the night visions, and behold, with the clouds of heaven there came one like a son of man [υἱὸς ἀνθρώπου ἤρχετο], and he came to the Ancient of Days and was presented before him. 14And to him was given dominion and glory and kingdom, *that all peoples, nations, and languages should serve him* [πάντα τὰ ἔθνη τῆς γῆς κατὰ γένη καὶ πᾶσα δόξα αὐτῷ λατρεύουσα/יִפְלְחוּן]; his dominion is an everlasting dominion, which shall not pass away, and his kingdom one that shall not be destroyed. (emphasis added)

The saying in Mark 10:45, which I believe does derive from Jesus, though it was probably uttered in a different context (perhaps in the context of the Last Supper), is quite remarkable.[29] It seemingly contradicts Dan 7:14, in which it is emphatically stated that "all peoples, nations, and languages should serve" the son of man figure described in v. 13. No, Jesus says, the son of man has not come to be served, but to serve.

Many critics, of course, have interpreted Mark 10:45 as a community formulation, which gave expression to the post-Easter understanding of the saving significance of Jesus' death. This line of interpretation is plausible and may well be correct. But I have my doubts. Elsewhere I have argued for its setting in the *Sitz im Leben Jesu*.[30] Here I only wish to point out that

29. For discussion of linguistic and cultural issues, see Casey, *Aramaic Sources,* pp. 193-218.

30. C. A. Evans, *Mark 8:27–16:20* (WBC 34b; Nashville: Thomas Nelson, 2001), pp. 114, 119-25. See also C. K. Barrett, "The Background of Mark 10:45," in A. J. B. Higgins (ed.), *New Testament Essays: Studies in Memory of Thomas Walter Manson 1893-1958* (Manchester:

Craig A. Evans

Jesus' tendency to subvert Scripture provides a context for understanding the ransom saying as yet one more instance of this tendency. Contrary to popular beliefs, in which the Lord's anointed was expected to crush Israel's enemies (as seen, for example, in 4Q285, in which the armies of the Kittim will be slaughtered and the king of the Kittim, that is, the Roman Emperor, will be slain by the Branch of David), Jesus states that the son of man will give his life in exchange for the lives of others.[31]

The events of Passion Week may well have colored the form of the saying that we have in Mark 10:45, but the subversion of Dan 7:13-14 in all probability derives from Jesus. The ransom idea, which may well reflect Isaiah 53, is what encouraged the subversion.

Divine Wrath

Another instance in which Jesus subverts Scripture is his appeal to the stricken shepherd of Zechariah 13.[32] According to the version in Mark, Jesus tells his disciples: "I will strike the shepherd, and the sheep will be scattered [πατάξω τὸν ποιμένα, καὶ τὰ πρόβατα διασκορπισθήσονται]" (Mark 14:27).

Manchester University Press, 1959), pp. 1-18; W. Grimm, *Weil ich dich liebe: Die Verkündigung Jesu und Deuterojesaja* (ANTJ 1; Bern and Frankfurt am Main: Lang, 1976), pp. 231-77; M. D. Hooker, *The Son of Man in Mark: A Study of the Background of the Term 'Son of Man' and Its Use in St Mark's Gospel* (London: SPCK, 1967), pp. 140-47; P. Stuhlmacher, "Vicariously Giving His Life for Many, Mark 10:45 (Matt. 20:28)," in *Reconciliation, Law, and Righteousness* (Philadelphia: Fortress, 1986), pp. 16-29.

31. Jesus' allusive, subversive use of Dan 7:13-14 in Mark 10:45 stands in contrast to his more conventional use of the passage, in combination with Ps 110:1, in Mark 14:62. The combination of Daniel 7 and Psalm 110 coheres with Jewish expectations of the appearance of a Messiah who will judge Israel's enemies (*Pss. Sol.* 17:21-25, 30, 35, 43; cf. *Midr. Ps.* 2.9 [on Ps 2:7], where Ps 110:1 and Dan 7:13 are combined). What is shocking — and from the aristocratic-priestly perspective quite subversive — is the implication that the ruling priests will be among Messiah's enemies.

32. On the function of Zechariah in Jesus and the Gospels, see R. M. Grant, "The Coming of the Kingdom," *JBL* 67 (1948): 297-303; F. F. Bruce, "The Book of Zechariah and the Passion Narrative," *BJRL* 43 (1960-61): 336-53; S. Kim, "Jesus — The Son of God, the Stone, the Son of Man, and the Servant: The Role of Zechariah in the Self-Identification of Jesus," in G. F. Hawthorne and O. Betz (eds.), *Tradition and Interpretation in the New Testament* (E. E. Ellis Festschrift; Grand Rapids: Eerdmans, 1987), pp. 134-42; and C. A. Evans, "Jesus and Zechariah's Messianic Hope," in C. A. Evans and B. Chilton (eds.), *Authenticating the Activities of Jesus* (NTTS 28/2; Leiden: Brill, 1998), pp. 373-88.

The dominical utterance alludes to a judgmental saying in Zechariah:

"Awake, O sword, against my shepherd, against the man who stands next to me," says the LORD of hosts. "Strike the shepherd, that the sheep may be scattered [הַךְ אֶת־הָרֹעֶה וּתְפוּצֶיןָ הַצֹּאן/πατάξατε τοὺς ποιμένας καὶ ἐκσπάσατε τὰ πρόβατα]; I will turn my hand against the little ones." (Zech 13:7)

Some scholars think the quotation of Zech 13:7 comes from the evangelist Mark, not from Jesus.[33] I disagree. I think it is unlikely that early "Christians," including the Markan Evangelist, would appeal to Zech 13:7 as a prophetic reference to Jesus, because the prophecy speaks of divine judgment *directed against* the shepherd: "'Awake, O sword, against my shepherd, against the man who stands next to me,' says the LORD of hosts. 'Strike the shepherd, that the sheep may be scattered; I will turn my hand against the little ones.'" Not only is the prophecy directed against the shepherd, it is directed against the flock itself.[34] Would early "Christians" be inclined to cite such a text, even though it admittedly fits some of the details of the Passion story?[35]

We have an intriguing interpretation of Zech 13:7 in the *Damascus Covenant* (in col. 19, or col. 1 in the parallel "B" version). It reads as follows:

7When the oracle of the prophet Zechariah comes true, "O sword, be lively and smite 8My shepherd and the man loyal to me — so says God. If you strike down the shepherd, the flock will scatter. 9Then I will turn my power against the little ones" [Zech 13:7]. But those who give heed to God are "the poor of the flock" [Zech 11:7] — 10they will escape in the time of punishment, but all the rest will be handed over to the sword when the Messiah of 11Aaron and of Israel comes, just as it happened

33. As, for example, in A. Suhl, *Die Funktion der alttestamentlichen Zitate und Anspielungen im Markusevangelium* (Gütersloh: Mohn, 1965), pp. 62-64; M. Wilcox, "The Denial-Sequence in Mark xiv.26-31, 66-72," *NTS* 17 (1970-71): 426-36, esp. pp. 429-30.

34. On the meaning of Zech 13:7-9, see D. L. Petersen, *Zechariah 9–14 and Malachi* (OTL; Louisville: Westminster John Knox, 1995), pp. 130-31; R. L. Smith, *Micah-Malachi* (WBC 32; Dallas: Word, 1984), pp. 282-84.

35. Jesus' understanding of himself as in some sense Israel's shepherd coheres with dominical tradition, most of which has reasonable claim to authenticity (e.g., Mark 6:34; Q: Matt 10:16 = Luke 10:3; Matt 18:12 = Luke 15:4-6; L: Luke 12:32). It also coheres with contemporary messianic ideas, as seen in *Pss. Sol.* 17:40, where the Davidic Messiah is expected to "shepherd faithfully and righteously the Lord's flock."

during the time of the first punishment, as 12Ezekiel said, "Make a mark on the foreheads of those who moan and lament" [Ezek 9:4], 13but the rest were given to the sword that makes retaliation for covenant violations. And such is the verdict on all members of 14His covenant who do not hold firm to these laws: they are condemned to destruction by Belial.[36] (CD 19:7-14)

The author has developed a typology, in which the ancient disaster that overtook Ephraim in 721 BCE, resulting in the survival of a remnant, is about to recur.[37] The "shepherd" who will be struck down by the sword could be a Hasmonean king (Jannaeus?),[38] whereas the sheep that will be scattered are probably his princes. The typology is qualified by a phrase taken from Zech 11:7, "the poor of the flock." These are the members of the Qumran community "who give heed to God." They "will escape in the time of punishment" and can look forward to the restoration in the messianic age. The apostate of Israel, however, will be given to the sword.

Not all critics interpret the midrash in this fashion. The shepherd could be the high priest (again, possibly in reference to Jannaeus, or perhaps in reference to one of his sons). The shepherd has also been identified with the Righteous Teacher,[39] but given the way the midrash develops, I find this option doubtful.[40] It is probable that the stricken shepherd in the midrash of the *Damascus Document* is an apostate king,[41] just as he was

36. M. O. Wise, M. G. Abegg Jr., and E. M. Cook, *The Dead Sea Scrolls: A New Translation* (San Francisco: HarperCollins, 1996), p. 58.

37. See P. R. Davies, *The Damascus Covenant: An Interpretation of the "Damascus Document"* (JSOTSup 25; Sheffield: JSOT Press, 1982), pp. 150-55. CD 19:7-14 (or B 1:7-14) appears to be an interpretation that supplements the similar midrash in CD 7:9-15.

38. The Targum at Zech 13:7 renders shepherd as "king."

39. C. Rabin, *The Zadokite Documents* (rev. ed., Oxford: Clarendon, 1958), p. 31.

40. I doubt too that the evangelists Matthew and Mark, in citing part of Zech 13:7, had in mind Qumran's Righteous Teacher. The possibility is raised by A. Dupont-Sommer, *The Essene Writings from Qumran* (Gloucester: Peter Smith, 1973), p. 137 n. 4. It is rightly rejected by J. Carmignac, É. Cothenet, and H. Lignée, *Les textes de Qumran: Traduits et annotés*. Vol. 2: *Règle de la Congrégation, etc.* (Paris: Letouzey et Ané, 1963), p. 171 n. 14. See the brief but very helpful comments in J. C. VanderKam, "Messianism in the Scrolls," in E. Ulrich and J. C. VanderKam (eds.), *The Community of the Renewed Covenant: The Notre Dame Symposium on the Dead Sea Scrolls* (CJA 10; Notre Dame: University of Notre Dame Press, 1994), pp. 211-34, here pp. 230-31.

41. In contrast to the righteous king, of the Davidic line, whom God someday will raise up (cf. Ezek 34:24; 37:25; *Pss. Sol.* 17:40-42).

when Zechariah 13 was originally composed. Those who rally to him, even if this group appears to be the majority, will be destroyed (i.e., the "two-thirds" that will be cut off, according to Zech 13:8-9). Those who stand aloof and remain faithful to God's law, though small in number and subjected to refining fire, will be delivered.

Both the original meaning of Zechariah 13 and its later application in the *Damascus Document* understand the shepherd as deserving of divine judgment. In view of this tradition of interpretation, it is quite surprising that the text is applied to Jesus. Contrary to conventional interpretation, Jesus anticipates that the wrath of God will fall *on himself,* possibly as part of his role as the righteous sufferer (Mark 10:45; 14:22-25), whose death will benefit Israel.

A second example may be mentioned briefly. Jesus bases his parable of the Wicked Vineyard Tenants (Mark 12:1-9) on Isaiah's Song of the Vineyard (Isa 5:1-7). Isaiah's song is clearly judgmental. God planted a vineyard, cared for it, sparing no cost, but the vineyard did not produce worthy fruit. Stated in plain language, God complains that his people have not produced justice: "he looked for justice, but behold, bloodshed; for righteousness, but behold, a cry!" (Isa 5:7).

In the Aramaic tradition, the focus shifts to the temple establishment. Details in the parable are changed to accommodate the modified perspective. Instead of a watchtower, God has given his vineyard a sanctuary; instead of a wine vat, God has given an altar. When judgment comes, it will not be the wall and hedge that are destroyed (Isa 5:5); it will be the holy places and the altar that are destroyed.

What is fascinating in Jesus' version of the parable is that the vineyard itself, that is, the people of Israel (cf. Isa 5:7 "the vineyard of the LORD of hosts is the house of Israel, and the men of Judah are his pleasant planting"), is exculpated. They do not face judgment. Rather, the threat of judgment is directed specifically against the caretakers of the vineyard, that is, the ruling priests. Jesus has taken a further provocative step in the cultic interpretive orientation that we see in the later targumic and rabbinic interpretation (*t. Me'il.* 1.16; *t. Sukkah* 3.15), and in the much earlier interpretation attested in the small fragment identified as 4Q500.[42]

---

42. On the coherence of Jesus' parable with targumic and rabbinic interpretation, see Chilton, *A Galilean Rabbi and His Bible,* pp. 111-16. On the parable's coherence with 4Q500, see G. J. Brooke, "4Q500 1 and the Use of Scripture in the Parable of the Vineyard," *DSD* 2

Craig A. Evans

Law and Obligations

We also encounter dominical tradition that stands in tension with legal and ethical teaching in Jewish Palestine of late antiquity. For example, Jesus declares: "If any one comes to me and does not hate his own father and mother and wife and children and brothers and sisters, yes, and even his own life, he cannot be my disciple" (Luke 14:26). This remarkable statement flies in the face of many commandments in the Jewish law:

> Whoever curses his father or his mother shall be put to death. (Exod 21:17)

> You shall not hate your brother. . . . (Lev 19:17)

> For every one who curses his father or his mother shall be put to death; he has cursed his father or his mother, his blood is upon him. (Lev 20:9)

> If one curses his father or his mother, his lamp will be put out in utter darkness. (Prov 20:20)

Even when allowance is made for the rhetorical and hyperbolic nature of Jesus' statement (as well as a measure of coherence with Exod 32:27-29), it is quite remarkable and not likely a community product.[43]

We might also consider Jesus' pronouncement regarding what defiles:

(1995): 268-94. On the coherence between 4Q500 and rabbinic interpretation, see J. M. Baumgarten, "4Q500 and the Ancient Conception of the Lord's Vineyard," *JJS* 40 (1989): 1-6. I review the evidence in *Mark 8:27–16:20*, pp. 222-39. For debate over the question of the degree to which the vineyard parable depends on the Greek tradition (as opposed to the Hebrew or Aramaic), see J. S. Kloppenborg, "Egyptian Viticultural Practices and the Citation of Isa 5:1-7 in Mark 12:1-9," *NovT* 44 (2002): 134-59; C. A. Evans, "How Septuagintal Is Isa 5:1-7 in Mark 12:1-9?" *Novum Testamentum* 45 (2003): 105-10; and, as a rejoinder to Evans, J. S. Kloppenborg, "Isa 5:1-7 LXX and Mark 12:1, 9," *NovT* 46 (2004): 12-19. See now Kloppenborg's massive study *The Tenants in the Vineyard: Ideology, Economics, and Agrarian Conflict in Jewish Palestine* (WUNT 195; Tübingen: Mohr Siebeck, 2006).

43. Early followers of Jesus emphasized love of the community, and even love of enemies. This emphasis no doubt grew out of dominical teaching, which again makes it unlikely that Luke 14:26 is a community product. One should recall that Qumran teaches that its members "hate all the sons of darkness" (1QS 1:10 [= 4Q256 1:9]; 9:21-22 [= 4Q256 18:5]), that is, outsiders. For discussion of underlying Semitic thought, as well as comparison with related sayings in the Greco-Roman world, see Nolland, *Luke 9:21–18:34*, pp. 762-63.

Hear me, all of you, and understand: There is nothing outside a man, which by going into him can defile him; but the things that come out of a man are what defile him. (Mark 7:15).

Such a remarkable statement strains against the Levitical code (cf. Lev 18:24 "Do not defile yourselves by any of these things, for by all these the nations I am casting out before you defiled themselves"). The saying of Mark 7:15 originated with Jesus, even if the related discussion, which applied this teaching to food (as in Mark 7:19; Acts 15; and various passages in Paul's letters), clearly reflects debate within the Palestinian Jesus Movement.[44]

One thinks also of Jesus' startling injunction given to the man who wishes first to bury his father, before he can follow Jesus:

Leave the dead to bury their own dead; but as for you, go and proclaim the kingdom of God. (Luke 9:60 = Matt 8:22)

Jesus' statement strains against family responsibilities and the importance of seeing to proper burial, especially with reference to one's father. One thinks of several pertinent scriptural passages (Gen 23:13; 50:5-14; cf. Tob 1:18-20; 2:3-8; 4:3-4; 6:15; 14:10-13; Philo, *Ios.* 5 §22-25).

Of course, I think in saying, "leave the dead to bury their own dead," Jesus has alluded to ossilegium, that is, the Jewish practice of reburying the bones of the deceased. He has not heartlessly required the would-be disciple to abandon his father on his sickbed. Rather, he has suggested that the proclamation of the kingdom of God takes precedence over reburial. After all, the would-be follower's deceased father is already safe in his family tomb; let his dead relatives see to what needs remain.[45] For now, the man must undertake the mission of the kingdom to the living. Nevertheless, even on this understanding, Jesus' startling command would have struck many of his contemporaries as straining against pious convention and filial obligation.

Another failed would-be disciple occasions another surprising remark:

---

44. See the discussion in R. A. Guelich, *Mark 1–8:26* (WBC 34a; Dallas: Word, 1989), pp. 374-79.

45. See B. R. McCane, "'Let the Dead Bury Their Own Dead': Secondary Burial and Matt 8:21-22," *HTR* 83 (1990): 31-43.

61Another said, "I will follow you, Lord; but let me first say farewell to those at my home." 62Jesus said to him, "No one who puts his hand to the plow and looks back is fit for the kingdom of God." (Luke 9:61-62)

Jesus' reply clearly alludes to 1 Kings 19:19-21 (where Elisha is plowing, turns back, and bids his family farewell). In this case, Jesus' allusion to Elijah's call of Elisha suggests that what Elijah permitted, Jesus will not. The mere suggestion that Elijah's example is somehow deficient, especially in reference to something that relates in some way to the eschatological hour, would have struck Jesus' contemporaries as quite strange indeed.

Conclusion

The early members of the Palestinian Jesus Movement augmented, embellished, and interpreted the story of Jesus with various scriptures. These Jews searched the scriptures for fulfillment and for clarification. But the subversive, challenging use of scripture that we find here and there in the dominical tradition authentically reflects, it seems to me, the creative, authoritative mind of Jesus. One might say that Jesus was *informed* by scripture, but was not *confined* by it. The authority of scripture and the experience of the Spirit seem to have provided the framework in which Jesus formulated some of his most distinctive teaching.

A Contagious Purity:
Jesus' Inverse Strategy for
Eschatological Cleanliness

Tom Holmén

Introduction

Jesus' attitude toward purity matters is certainly one of the most intriguing and entangling questions in current research of the historical Jesus. The difficulties stem from Jesus' dealings with people who were considered ritually impure, his table fellowship with sinners and his granting them the legitimacy of having a share in God's kingdom, as well as some sayings displaying oddity in his view on purity.[1] In the present article, I shall concentrate on one conspicuous thread of this tangled skein of problems, namely Jesus' dealings with the unclean. The curious thing about the dealings that has often attracted scholars' attention is the unreservedness with which Jesus seems to give himself to these situations. He is not hesitant to come into close contact with people who would communicate severe impurities to him, even intentionally touching them. According to a common scholarly interpretation of the dealings, by this activity Jesus purposed to make the unclean clean.[2] In my view, this interpretation

---

1. See below. The activities here mentioned display a characteristic behavior of Jesus. For a more in-depth discussion of purity and related themes in Judaism and in the teaching of Jesus see T. Holmén, *Jesus and Jewish Covenant Thinking* (BibInt Series 55; Leiden: Brill, 2001), pp. 200-251. The present article adds a further perspective to my treatment of the issue in the book.

2. See, for instance, M. D. Hooker, "Interchange in Christ," *JTS* 22 (1971): 349-61, esp. p. 351; M. J. Borg, *Conflict, Holiness & Politics in the Teachings of Jesus* (SBEC 5; New York: Edwin Mellen, 1984), pp. 134-36; K. Berger, "Jesus als Pharisäer und frühe Christen als Pharisäer," *NovT* 30 (1988): 231-62, esp. pp. 245-47; R. Guelich, *Mark 1–8:26* (WBC 34a; Dal-

should have some remarkable corollaries to understanding Jesus' purity thinking, and perhaps to understanding his mission and message more generally. I shall therefore study the grounds for sustaining this interpretation. The foundation laid here will then serve in seeking out the corollaries by considering the dealings in Jesus' Jewish context, in the context of other Jesuanic material pertaining to purity, and in the context of Jesus' overall message.

Jesus' Way with the Unclean

We will first highlight this interpretation of Jesus' making the unclean clean. The basic historicity of Jesus' dealings with the unclean as a regular pattern of his behavior should not be doubted. All in all, this material is almost as prevalent as that pertaining to Jesus' miracles.[3] The picture of Jesus as an exorcist and a healer is strongly attested to in the sources.[4] No matter what origin or role in Jesus' ministry one ascribes to these characteristics, they form an integral part of the tradition and are currently regarded as one of the most reliable facts about Jesus.[5] Naturally, this statement is not an automatic endorsement of the authenticity of every individual tradition exhibiting these characteristics. Further indications of authenticity will be welcome, but the burden of proof lies with those denying the authenticity of these individual traditions.

---

las: Word, 1989), p. 74; C. A. Evans, "'Who Touched Me?' Jesus and the Ritually Impure," in B. Chilton and C. A. Evans (eds.), *Jesus in Context: Temple, Purity, and Restoration* (AGJU 93; Leiden: Brill, 1997), pp. 353-76, esp. pp. 368-69; J. Marcus, *Mark 1–8: A New Translation with Introduction and Commentary* (AB 27; New York: Doubleday, 1999), p. 209; somewhat hesitantly, J. D. G. Dunn, "Jesus and Purity: An Ongoing Debate," *NTS* 48 (2002): 449-67, esp. p. 461.

3. We can disregard the so-called nature miracles (Mark 4:35-41; 6:32-44; 6:45-52; 11:12-14, 20-21; Matt 17.24-27; Luke 5:1-11; John 2:1-11).

4. Cf. J. P. Meier, *A Marginal Jew: Rethinking the Historical Jesus*, 3 vols. Vol. 2: *Mentor, Message and Miracles* (ABRL; New York: Doubleday, 1994), pp. 619-30, 646-1039.

5. Cf. B. L. Blackburn, "The Miracles of Jesus," in B. Chilton and C. A. Evans (eds.), *Studying the Historical Jesus: Evaluations of the State of Current Research* (NTTS 19; Leiden: Brill, 1994), pp. 353-94, esp. p. 392; J. H. Charlesworth, "Jesus Research Expands with Chaotic Creativity," in J. H. Charlesworth and W. P. Weaver (eds.), *Images of Jesus Today* (FSC 3; Valley Forge, Pa.: Trinity, 1994), pp. 1-41, esp. pp. 12-13; C. A. Evans, *Jesus and His Contemporaries: Comparative Studies* (AGJU 25; Leiden: Brill, 1995), p. 213.

The issue of purity is most evident in the prevalent reports of Jesus' contacts with lepers[6] and the dead,[7] but also in the story of the woman who had a hemorrhage (Mark 5:25-34 par.) and the story of the prostitute (Luke 7:36-50). Jesus' contacts with people with unclean spirits, which appear recurrently in the tradition, are no doubt also relevant.

Indeed, the expulsions of "unclean spirits" are reported almost throughout the Jesus tradition and cannot really be removed from the bedrock elements of Jesus' activity.[8] Πνεῦμα ἀκάθαρτον[9] represents a known Jewish designation for a demon,[10] and reflects the evil spirits' work of either causing uncleanness and leading to it, or their possession of people as a consequence of an impure life.[11] The latter thought is discernible especially in later rabbinic literature.[12] The term "unclean spirit" appropriately marks off spirits which are not to be associated with God, who is holy.[13] Comparable in a way are expressions such as, "a lying spirit" (1 Kgs 22:22-

---

6. Mark 1:41; Matt 11:5 par. Luke 7:22 (= Q); Luke 17:11-19 (= Luke's special source); cf. also Mark 14:3.

7. Mark 5:21-43; Matt 11:5 par. Luke 7:22 (= Q); Luke 7:11-17 (= Luke's special source); cf. also John 11:1-44.

8. G. Theissen, *Urchristliche Wundergeschichten: Ein Beitrag zur formgeschichtlichen Erforschung der synoptischen Evangelien* (SNT 8; Gütersloh: Gütersloher Verlagshaus Mohn, 1974), pp. 274-77; J. D. G. Dunn, *Jesus and the Spirit: A Study of the Religious and Charismatic Experience of Jesus and the First Christians as Reflected in the New Testament* (Grand Rapids: Eerdmans, 1997), p. 44.

9. See Mark 1:23, 26-27; 3:11, 30; 5:2, 8, 13; 6:7; 7:25; 9:25; Matt 10:1; 12:43; Luke 4:33, 36; 6:18; 8:29; 9:42.

10. W. Foerster, "δαίμων κτλ.," *TWNT* vol. 2, pp. 1-21, esp. p. 16; Guelich, *Mark*, p. 56; J. Reiling, "Unclean Spirits," in K. van der Toorn, B. Becking and P. W. van der Horst (eds.), *Dictionary of Deities and Demons in the Bible* (Leiden: Brill, 1999 [2nd ed.]), p. 882.

11. See, for instance, *Jub.* 10.1; 11.4; *1 En.* 19.1; 1QM 13.5; *T. Benj.* 5.1-3; cf. already Zech 13:2: רוח הטמאה, "the unclean spirit," in a cultic context; F. Hauck, "καθαρός κτλ.," *TWNT* vol. 3, pp. 416-21, 427-34, esp. pp. 431-32. For the close association of demons and impurity in Judaism, see further T. Kazen, *Jesus and Purity Halakhah: Was Jesus Indifferent to Impurity?* (ConBNT 38; Stockholm: Almqvist & Wiksell, 2002), pp. 301-13; C. Wahlen, *Jesus and the Impurity of Spirits in the Synoptic Gospels* (WUNT 2.185; Tübingen: Mohr Siebeck, 2004), pp. 24-59.

12. See H. L. Strack and P. Billerbeck, *Kommentar zum Neuen Testament aus Talmud und Midrasch: Exkurse zu einzelnen Stellen des Neuen Testaments: Erster Teil* (Munich: C. H. Beck'sche Verlagsbuchhandlung, 1928), pp. 503-4.

13. Strack and Billerbeck, *Kommentar*, p. 503; R. H. Gundry, *Mark: A Commentary on His Apology for the Cross* (Grand Rapids: Eerdmans, 1993), p. 83; cf. 1QM 13.2-5; see Mark 1:24; 3:11, 29-30; 5:7, and parallels.

23), "a spirit of affliction" (1QapGen 20.16), "a spirit of purulence" (1QapGen 20.26), and "a spirit of weakness" (Luke 13:11). The condition of being possessed is aptly depicted by Joel Marcus, who comments on Mark 1:23 (and the Markan expression ἐν πνεύματι ἀκαθάρτῳ, which is probably a Semitism):[14] "This picture of 'a man in an unclean spirit,' enclosed by that which contaminates him, is horrifying."[15]

There is no reason to doubt that Jesus shared this common understanding of the nature of these spirits.[16] The sources suggest he had no objections to the notion that the spirits are unclean, nor to seeing them as having contaminated the people they had taken into possession (or who had them in their possession). In fact, both Mark and Q tell of Jesus himself referring to the spirits as unclean (Mark 5:8; Matt 12:43 par. Luke 11:24). Implications on the question of cleaning the unclean should also be clear. The removal of an unclean spirit denotes almost by definition the removal of uncleanness.[17]

Most germane to the question are naturally the situations in which Jesus is expressly said to have cleansed people from impurity. In these cases, while authenticity may be less obvious there is still reason to trust the basic historicity of this pattern of Jesus' behavior. In Matt 11:5 par. Luke 7:22 (= Q: καθαρίζονται), Jesus refers to his own work by mentioning, *inter alia*, the cleansing of lepers. Actual instances of such cleansing are mentioned in Mark 1:40-45 par. (v. 41, καθαρίσθητι) and Luke 17:11-19 (v. 17, ἐκαθαρίσθησαν; cf. v. 15, ἰάθη).[18] These three traditions thus manifoldly attest that Jesus saw his activity as resulting in the purification of uncleanness. That is, we can appeal to the criterion of multiple attestation in arguing for the authenticity of this common idea in these passages. A few words are perhaps needed regarding the two actual in-

---

14. See also Mark 5:2.

15. Marcus, *Mark*, p. 192.

16. See Kazen, *Purity Halakhah*, pp. 332-38. Wahlen, *Impurity of Spirits*, p. 68, points out early Judaism's "growing interest in spirits and their relation to impurity which . . . is manifest also in the Synoptic Gospels." Further, he states that "the earliest Palestinian community and perhaps Jesus himself were very concerned with the notions of purity and impurity in connection with demon possession, so much so that expelling these spirits is remembered as a significant part of his work" (Wahlen, *Impurity of Spirits*, p. 174).

17. That is, just as the expulsion of a mute spirit results in a removal of the muteness of the possessed person; see Matt 9:32-33/Luke 11:14.

18. See also Guelich, *Mark*, p. 74; Marcus, *Mark*, p. 209.

stances of cleansing, although they are not easily verified to be authentic individually.[19] As the stories in Mark 1:40-45 and Luke 17:11-19 report, Jesus sends the lepers to the priests and in Mark he even gives the order to sacrifice περὶ τοῦ καθαρισμοῦ σου. This appears to be according to the law, which prescribes: "Thus [referring to various purification rites and sacrifices] the priest shall make atonement on his behalf and he shall be clean" (Lev 14:20). However, in both New Testament stories the lepers in reality become both cured and cleansed already before they get to the priests for the sacrifice (cf. Mark 1:42; Luke 17:14). The procedure of sacrifice is undertaken for merely pragmatic reasons, which, as such, are of course important: the procedure was needed for the reintegration of the lepers into the ordinary social and religious life of the community.[20] But the acts of cleansing occur independently of this procedure.

In the cases of the other acts of healing mentioned above, there is no easy way to ferret out indications of authenticity. At any event, what the sources put forward is rather obvious. Consider, for example, the story of the woman who had a hemorrhage. The nature of the woman's disease makes implications of purity inescapable.[21] She had been seriously unclean for all of the large breadth of time she had suffered from her illness, and this must have prevented her from leading a normal life.[22] That is why she is prepared to sneak in the crowd and secretly touch Jesus' cloak. Then she is made healthy again. The natural thought evoked by this scene is that,

19. Cf. Meier, *A Marginal Jew,* vol. 2, pp. 698-705. This does not invalidate the general conclusion drawn about Jesus cleansing people from impurity. See Meier, *A Marginal Jew,* vol. 2, p. 706.

20. For the contagiousness of leprosy impurity, see *Apion* 1.281; *m. Zab* 5:6; T. Frymer-Kensky, "Pollution, Purification, and Purgation in Biblical Israel," in C. L. Meyers and M. O'Connor (eds.), *The Word of the Lord Shall Go Forth* (FS D. N. Freedman; ASOR 1; Winona Lake, Ind.: Eisenbrauns, 1983), pp. 399-414, esp. pp. 399-400; D. P. Wright, *The Disposal of Impurity: Elimination Rites in the Bible and in Hittite and Mesopotamian Literature* (SBLDS 101; Atlanta: Scholars Press, 1987), pp. 209-10. Cf. also Lev 5:3 and 13:45-46.

21. Dunn, "Jesus and Purity," p. 461.

22. The discharge would have continuously kept her in a state of impurity (Lev 15:25-30). Earlier such impurities with high communicability (cf. Lev 15:19-24 which appears to describe even a fourth level impurity for a woman with a regular discharge of blood) were to be removed from the "camp"; see Num 5:1-4 which lists people with leprosy, abnormal sexual discharge, and corpse contamination. Later expulsion was reduced to apply only to people having leprosy; Wright, *Disposal of Impurity,* pp. 168-78. Cf., however, *War* 5.227, where Josephus also mentions gonorrhea as resulting in expulsion from the city.

just as she became healed, she was also cleansed from her impurity. Accordingly, she is also recognized as part of Israel once more.[23] In the case of the lepers, purification is explicitly said to have taken place before they get to the rites that should officially assure their reintegration into the community. Here the woman's reintegration is implied as a *fait accompli,* thus *presupposing* her purification.

Similar ideas are called forth by the stories about Jesus' touching dead people.[24] A dead human body carries grave ritual impurity, the removal of which from those contaminated would require elaborate procedures over a lengthy period of time.[25] When the girl of Mark 5 and the boy of Luke 7 were made alive by Jesus, what would have happened to their impurity? It is difficult to imagine that Jesus understood himself to have raised these people from the dead but not to have restored their purity as well. There may, however, be a further point that could be advanced here. A corpse is very much impure, but if it ceases to be a corpse, would not its impurity also cease to be? After all, a corpse has not been rendered impure by being *touched* by a corpse but rather by *being* one. Such a situation differs from all the cases where a recovery had been anticipated. There are regulations for instance for the case that a leper has become cured,[26] that is, how such people should deal with the impurity their ailment had given them. With respect to corpse impurity, however, the comparable regulations concern only those who have collected impurity by having somehow been in contact with a corpse, not those who have regained their lives.[27] I am under the impression that if a human corpse regains its life, its purity is as if it had lived the whole time, that is, it is no

---

23. Cf. Mark 5:34. See J. A. Fitzmyer, *The Gospel According to Luke (I-IX): Introduction, Translation, and Notes* (AB 28; Garden City, N.Y.: Doubleday, 1981), p. 747; Evans, "Jesus and the Ritually Impure," p. 368.

24. Mark 5:35-43; Luke 7:12-16; cf. also John 11:17-44. In Luke 7:14, Jesus is said to touch the bier on which the corpse is lying. This act was almost equally serious, for a human corpse could create first-level impurities (by contact, overshadowing etc.) — that is, new sources of impurity. Hence the rabbinic term "father of fathers of uncleanness."

25. Corpse-impurity makes persons (or objects) unclean for seven days (Num 19). The impurity should be removed by sprinkling water especially blended for this purpose on the third and seventh days. The mixture consists of water and the ashes of the red cow (Num 19:2-9). On the seventh day, impure persons are to bathe and wash their clothes (Num 19:19; cf. 31:24).

26. See Lev 13:1-46.

27. See n. 25 above.

longer unclean.[28] If this is the case, the restored purity of the girl and the boy in Mark 5 and Luke 7 would have been evident precisely by the token of their restored life.

To a certain extent, we can add to this argument the instances of lame and blind people. 2 Sam 5:8b reads: "The blind and the lame shall not come into the house." One can think of two slightly differing reasons as to why the blind and the lame should not enter the Temple: either they are regarded as unclean and thus capable of polluting the Temple, or they are simply seen as being able to profane the Temple's holiness by virtue of their defects.[29] Interestingly, in 11QT 45.12-14, a passage elaborating on 2 Sam 5:8,[30] the blind are to be excluded so that they "shall not defile the city in the centre of which I dwell." In other words, the blind are regarded as unclean.[31] Further, 1QSa 2.9b-10(11) establishes that, together with other people with physical blemishes, the lame and the blind (deaf, dumb, etc.; see the lengthy list in vv. 3-7) should be regarded as contaminated.[32] For those who shared the view represented by these texts,[33] Jesus' cures of disabilities would have carried important purity connotations.[34] The restoration of sight and capability of movement *(inter alia)* would at the same time have meant a visible and inarguable restoration of purity.[35]

28. Communication with Professor Jacob Neusner and with my Rabbi. Cf. the First Temple stories 1 Kgs 17:17-24; 2 Kgs 4:18-37.

29. S. M. Olyan, "The Exegetical Dimensions of Restrictions on the Blind and the Lame in Texts from Qumran," *DSD* 8 (2001): 38-50, esp. p. 41.

30. See Olyan, "The Blind and the Lame," pp. 38-43, who argues for 2 Sam 5:8b and a tandem reading of other Old Testament texts such as Isa 52:1 and Num 5:3b as the background of 11QT 45.12-14.

31. The lame are not mentioned in 11QT 45.12-14.

32. D. Barthélemy and J. T. Milik (eds.), *Qumran Cave I* (DJD 1; Oxford: Clarendon Press, 1955), p. 116, translate "contaminé"; F. García Martínez, *The Dead Sea Scrolls Translated: The Qumran Texts in English* (trans. W. G. E. Watson; Leiden: Brill, 1996 [2nd ed.]), p. 127, translates "defiled." This meaning of מנוגע in v. 10 is motivated by the context (especially v. 3). Hence L. Schwienhorst, "נגע," *ThWAT* 5 (1986): 219-26, esp. p. 226, gives the verb נגע in 1QSa 2.3-6, 10 the rendering "mit einer Unreinheit geschlagen sein."

33. See also 4QMMT 55-57 which reasons that those who do not see nor hear cannot know how to apply regulations concerning purity. Cf. even Acts 3:2, 8, 10.

34. The cures of *(inter alia)* lame and blind people are related in, for example, Mark 3:1-5, Matt 11:5 par. Luke 7:22 (= Q), and Luke 13:11-13 (lame) as well as in Mark 8:22-25; 10:46-52; Matt 11:5 par. Luke 7:22 (= Q); Matt 12:22; 15:29-31 (blind).

35. A cultic defectiveness along the lines of 2 Sam 5:8, be it uncleanness or power to profane, seems to be presupposed in Matt 21:12-14. See D. Hagner, *Matthew 14–28* (WBC 33b;

The natural conclusion regarding Jesus' healings is that along with the restored health came also restored purity. This is expressly suggested by the cleansing of the lepers and is clear in the exorcisms of the unclean spirits. And as much as the other acts of healing with apparent overtones of purity provide historically reliable information, they yield not a disharmonious but, rather, a corroborating picture.

One more point deserves to be observed. Purity could naturally be lost for a good cause and then regained through appropriate means. In Jesus' dealings with the unclean such causes are clear, although perhaps not altogether obvious. For instance, Jesus is not a close relative to the dead girl and boy, and in the case of the woman with a hemorrhage he does not even take the initiative. But one was not to gratuitously delay undertaking purification measures even when not planning to enter the Temple.[36] Delaying purification was considered a sin.[37] But the sources remarkably bear no mention of Jesus engaging the means of purification. This is not attested or alluded to in the data at any point where Jesus' contamination would have been evident. Similarly, Jesus is nowhere depicted as behaving as if he would have sought not to communicate the impurities he had gathered.

This silence is not surprising, for these activities of Jesus seem by their very nature to exclude the idea that he had temporarily sacrificed his state of purity only to restore it again, and to restore it with the ordinary means of purification. For why would he have needed to implement these for his own purification when he did not need to resort to them for others?[38] We

---

Dallas: Word, 1995), p. 601; cf. U. Luz, *Das Evangelium nach Matthäus: 3. Teilband Mt 18–25* (EKKNT 1.3; Neukirchen-Vluyn: Neukirchener Verlag, 1997), p. 188.

36. S. Westerholm, *Jesus and Scribal Authority* (ConBNT 10; Lund: Gleerup, 1978), p. 64; E. P. Sanders, *Judaism: Practice and Belief 63 BCE–66 CE* (London: SCM Press, 2nd impr., 1994), p. 218. For evidence for extra-Temple purity, see J. C. Poirier, "Purity Beyond the Temple in the Second Temple Era," *JBL* 122 (2003): 247-65, esp. pp. 256-59. He states (p. 265) in conclusion: "The notion that the ritual purity laws of Second Temple Judaism existed solely for the sake of the temple is a scholarly construct with little basis in reality." Cf. also the case of the *miqvaot* discussed below. See further J. Milgrom, "Israel's Sanctuary: The Priestly 'Picture of Dorian Gray,'" *RB* 83 (1976): 390-99.

37. See Lev 5:1-6, which speaks of an unintentional delay; in Lev 17:15-16 we find an intentional delay; cf. *Ant.* 3.262; D. P. Wright, "Unclean and Clean: Old Testament," *ABD* 6 (1992): 729-41, esp. pp. 737-38; Sanders, *Practice and Belief*, p. 219.

38. The silence is also broken in a way that supports the conclusion drawn from it here. *Papyrus Oxyrhynchus* 840 lets a Pharisee accuse Jesus precisely of what we have above suggested, namely that Jesus did not regularly go through the proper means of purification. What-

can also account for the silence on the basis of what has been suggested all along: Jesus saw himself as being able to restore people's purity. Impurity did not threaten Jesus' state of purity; it was simply overcome by him.[39]

This purity material is part of the miracle and exorcism tradition which, as a whole, comes with high claims to authenticity. A closer look at instances of the tradition where the question of purity is most evident has produced quite a consistent result. The sources clearly put forward that Jesus purposed to make the unclean clean. Sometimes this intention of his is made explicit, sometimes it appears as the natural implication of the stories. Nothing contesting this impression is discerned; there appear no deviating, competing or contradicting ideas. The inevitable conclusion thus seems to be that just as Jesus demonstrated power over diseases, demons, and death, he thought he could even reverse impurity. Of course, if one completely mistrusts what the sources suggest, one can question this conclusion. From that perspective, however, all conclusions must remain questionable.

Thus, in my view, there are good grounds for understanding Jesus' dealings with the unclean along the lines of the common interpretation — that is, Jesus making the unclean clean.[40] This is foundational for the following discussion about the corollaries of this interpretation. The settings within which the interpretation will be studied, prompting and beckoning

---

ever one may make of the papyrus, it does reflect the conditions of the Temple and purity discussions at Jesus' time fairly accurately; see Kazen, *Purity Halakhah*, pp. 256-60. Very suggestive, for example, is the Pharisee's statement that he has "gone down by the one stair and come up by the other." The description is strikingly illuminated by the last decades' archaeological findings of numerous *miqvaot* with both divided and double staircases; see for instance Sanders, *Practice and Belief*, p. 225. Grenfell and Hunt, who originally published the papyrus, ascribed this statement of the Pharisee to the author's imagination; see B. P. Grenfell and A. S. Hunt (eds.), *The Oxyrhynchus Papyri: Part 5* (London: Egypt Exploration Fund, 1908), p. 3. Less understandable is how F. Bovon, "Fragment *Oxyrhynchus 840*, Fragment of a Lost Gospel, Witness of an Early Christian Controversy over Purity," *JBL* 119 (2000): 705-28, still comments on the statement only by referring to the structure of an early Christian baptistery (p. 717).

39. Kazen, *Purity Halakhah*, p. 255, is right to maintain that even if Jesus and his disciples had immersed when attending important festivals together with other pilgrims (John 13:10 probably belongs to such a context), this "is not equal to regular immersions after contact with different types of impurity bearers."

40. All in all, we can disassemble the interpretation as follows: (a) prior to his dealings with these people, Jesus perceived them as unclean; (b) he affirmed their regained state of purity after his dealings with them; (c) he saw himself as having caused the change that had occurred and (d) interpreted this as cleansing.

the corollaries, are Jesus' Jewish context, the context of other Jesuanic material pertaining to purity, and the context of Jesus' overall message.

An Inverse Strategy of Purity

Jewish Context

Intriguingly, in his dealings with the unclean Jesus seems to construe (im)purity in a way that presupposes an *inversion* of a basic rule. The rule is succinctly expressed by the Old Testament prophet Haggai:

> Thus says the Lord of hosts: Ask the priests for a ruling: If one carries consecrated meat in the fold of one's garment, and with the fold touches bread, or stew, or wine, or oil, or any kind of food, does it become holy? The priests answered, "No." Then Haggai said, "If one who is unclean by contact with a dead body touches any of these, does it become unclean?" The priests answered, "Yes, it becomes unclean." (Hag 2:11-13)

As stated by commentators, "an obvious point has been made by this series of inquiries."[41] "Although defilement is contagious, . . . holiness in contrast is not."[42] *Uncleanness* was transferable, cleanness was not, and the mere act of touching sufficed to defile. There was only one exception to this general rule of the transferability of (im)purity: the altar of the temple (and some of its utensils) could render those of clerical parentage pure or holy.[43] They, however, could not communicate their purity further.

41. D. L. Petersen, *Haggai and Zechariah 1-8: A Commentary* (OTL; London: SCM Press, 1985), p. 79.
42. C. L. Meyers and E. M. Meyers, *Haggai, Zechariah 1-8: A New Translation with Introduction and Commentary* (AB 25; Garden City, N.Y.: Doubleday, 1987), p. 56. See even, for example, Petersen, *Haggai*, p. 79; R. L. Smith, *Micah-Malachi* (WBC 32; Waco: Word, 1984), p. 160; D. Kellermann, "Heiligkeit II: Altes Testament," *TRE* 14 (1985): 697-703, esp. p. 702. B. A. Levine, *Leviticus* ויקרא: *The Traditional Hebrew Text with the New JPS Translation* (The JPS Torah Commentary; Philadelphia: The Jewish Publication Society, 1989), p. 38, states: "The point is that whereas impurity is transferred through physical contact alone, substances do not become holy merely through contact with sacred materials. An act of consecration is required."
43. Exod 29:37; 30:29. See Petersen, *Haggai*, pp. 75-76, 78-79. However, it is probable that יקדש in the referred verses (as in Lev 6:11, 20) merely implies that those who touch the

In this way, purity needed protection, and the higher the purity, the more it had to be guarded. Therefore everything sacred was to be carefully kept free from defilement. This applied particularly to the Temple, but even to other "areas,"[44] such as the holy feasts of Israel (e.g., the Sabbath),[45] priests,[46] and theophanic experiences.[47] The different attitudes in handling corpse impurity illuminate the point in question:

Ordinary people were allowed to touch and be in close contact with their deceased relatives in order to bury them. Though a human corpse was regarded as the most serious of all sources of impurity, and rigorous purification was required after contacting a corpse, the living had an imperative duty to give a person a decent burial.[48] By comparison, priests, holy men as they were, could take care of the dead bodies of only the closest of their kin, such as their parents.[49] And the high priest, logically, was denied even this deed,[50] which was otherwise considered an indispensable act of piety and reverence.[51] Hence, impurity transferred to the pure and holy, contaminating them. Not even the high priest could communicate

---

holy things must themselves be in a holy state; Levine, *Leviticus*, pp. 37-38, 40; *Tg. Ps.-J. ad loc.*; *Tg. Onq. ad loc.*; cf. N. M. Sarna, *Exodus* שמות: *The Traditional Hebrew Text with the New JPS Translation* (The JPS Torah Commentary; Philadelphia: The Jewish Publication Society, 1991), p. 191; but see *idem*, p. 259.

44. See Kellermann, "Heiligkeit," pp. 700-702.

45. Neh 13:19, 22.

46. Lev 21; Ezek 4:14; 44:31.

47. Of these, we have a prime example in the people at Sinai receiving the commandments (Exod 19:10-25). The list could go on with blood, the product of trees in their first three years, etc.

48. In the Old Testament, being denied burial is pictured as the ultimate punishment and horror (Deut 28:26; Jer 7:33; 8:1-2; Ezek 6:5; 29:5). Tobit is mocked because of his eagerness to bury all the dead "brothers" he comes across (Tob 1:16-19; 2:3-8). And Josephus says that the Jews "were so careful about funeral rites" that even crucified criminals used to be taken down and buried (*War* 4.317; cf. 3.377). See also *4 Ezra* 2:22-23.

49. Lev 21:1-2. The exact list also encompasses the priest's son, daughter, brother, and virgin sister (who is without a husband to care for her in the case of her death).

50. Lev 21:10-11. A temporary denial to bury even the closest relatives was also issued to Nazirites (Num 6:5-12).

51. Especially the parents were worthy of burial, and this was the imperative duty of the son. For example Abraham and Isaac are favored by their sons' arrangement of their burials (Tob 4:3-4; 14:11-12; *Jub.* 23:7; 36:1-2, 18-19). Being denied this service is seen as a particular misfortune (Tob 6:14; 2 Macc 5:10; *War* 5.545; see also *1 En.* 98:13). See even, for instance, *m. Ber* 3.1.

his holiness to render even the most slightly unclean thing, let alone a human corpse, pure. On the contrary, he had to be protected all the more.

Jesus thus seems to have dealt with (im)purity in a way that utterly inverts the general rule described by Haggai. Coming into contact with unclean people does not make Jesus impure; that is, their uncleanness is not transferred to him. Instead, it is the unclean who become clean; purity is transferred to them.[52] With regards to Jesus, *purity* has become contagious.[53] In these deeds of purification, Jesus appears to be pursuing a kind of *inverse strategy*, which, in reality, holds two remarkable notions: (a) the diametrical change of the transferability of (im)purity and (b) Jesus' special role as the catalyst through whom the change takes place — in other words, his purity has become contagious.

Alterations and new viewpoints were nothing unusual in early Judaism. Matters of purity, in particular, aroused a multitude of varying interpretations. Debates concerning purity were a central factor in the history of Jewish sectarianism.[54] Different groups defined themselves to a significant degree through their exposition of purity regulations.[55] Even within

---

52. Similarly Borg, *Holiness*, p. 135, explaining the healing of the leper: "it was not Jesus who was made unclean by touching the leper — rather, the leper was made clean. . . . holiness was understood to overpower uncleanness rather than the converse"; Evans, "Jesus and the Ritually Impure," p. 368, expounding the story about the woman with hemorrhage: "[i]nstead of conveying uncleanness to Jesus, whom she touches, cleanness is conveyed to her"; and Berger, "Pharisäer," p. 240: "offensive Reinheit/Heiligkeit ist . . . eine Reinheit, die sich von ihrem Träger aus verbreitet, die 'ansteckend' ist, die Unreines rein machen kann. . . . Diese Reinheit/Heiligkeit wirkt so, wie früher Unreinheit wirkte. Die Machtverhältnisse sind jetzt und hier umgekehrt worden." See also n. 2 above for other proponents of this interpretation.

53. Nothing suggests that Jesus had thought of someone else as possessing capabilities similar to his own or that he had seen the inversion of the transferability of (im)purity as a general phenomenon taking place through and through at his time. If Mark 6:7-13 can be utilized in a historical assessment, it rather reveals the "authority over the unclean spirits" as an ability of individuals and of exceptionally bestowed people other than Jesus himself (see esp. v. 7). The pericope may, however, have had further meaning for the Palestinian Jesus movement. See the discussion below.

54. See M. Smith, "The Dead Sea Sect in Relation to Ancient Judaism," *NTS* 7 (1961): 347-60, esp. p. 352. See also depictions of the course of events in B. Chilton, *A Feast of Meanings: Eucharistic Theologies from Jesus Through Johannine Circles* (NovTSup 72; Leiden: Brill, 1994), pp. 15-24; in E. Regev, "Abominated Temple and a Holy Community: The Formation of the Notions of Purity and Impurity in Qumran," *DSD* 10 (2003): 243-78.

55. J. Neusner, *The Idea of Purity in Ancient Judaism: The Haskell Lectures 1972-1973*

this diversity, however, the view of purity implied by Jesus' dealings with the unclean must be characterized as exceptional and radical. Instead of the common model of how the state of purity should be restored (dealings with the means of purification → pure), we must assume another kind of scheme (dealings with Jesus → pure). But one should notice that in contacts with Jesus, uncleanness is not actually dealt with as with the means of purification. Jesus does not act as a priest attending to the means of purification.[56] Neither does he gather impurity so that he needed to dispose of it afterwards. Instead, purity simply conquers impurity; it behaves contagiously, in the way impurity had used to do. Jesus thus seems to be a holy man without a correspondent in the living representatives of Israel's holiness.[57] As a matter of fact, he appears to function just like the altar of the temple which by mere touch could render people clean, but I do not wish to press this analogy too much now.

Hence, the inverse strategy entails a major change in the purity thinking of Judaism. At issue here are not merely questions such as what are the substances that defile, how contagious can different substances be, how long does the defilement caused by them last, how are various defilements to be purged, etc. Instead, it is the fundamental view of how ritual (im)purity behaves, i.e., the basic idea of the contagiousness of impurity, that undergoes a radical change. This was precisely what made impurities so threatening: their ability to multiply themselves, some more easily than others.[58] This was why questions of (im)purity kept surfacing in the debates of the learned as well as in the daily lives of common people. Close to the Temple, the elaborate system of *miqvaot*, ritual baths, served precisely to work against the contagiousness of impurity.[59] However, such structures (both *miqvaot* and various stone vessels meant for purification) have been

---

(SJLA 1; Leiden: Brill, 1973), p. 108; Westerholm, *Jesus and Scribal Authority*, p. 62; M. Newton, *The Concept of Purity at Qumran and in the Letters of Paul* (SNTSMS 53; Cambridge: Cambridge University Press, 1985), p. 49. "In a way, it seems that during the Hasmonean and Herodian periods there was competition within Judean society for who was the most scrupulous observer of purity" (Regev, "Abominated Temple," p. 243).

56. Cf. Dunn, "Jesus and Purity," p. 459.

57. Cf. Job 14:4: "Who can make the unclean into the clean? No one!" The translation is according to D. J. A. Clines, *Job 1-20* (WBC 17; Dallas: Word, 1989), p. 277.

58. See n. 22 above.

59. E. P. Sanders, *Jewish Law from Jesus to the Mishnah: Five Studies* (London: SCM Press, 1990), pp. 214-27.

found not only in the vicinity of the Temple, but even at greater distances.[60] This strongly suggests that the *miqvaot* in question were used for maintaining purity for its own sake. We may gather that delays in purification, particularly in the case of severe and highly communicable impurities, would have begun to threaten the purity of entire communities; the impurities would have had more time to spread and multiply.[61] Hence, even when not aiming to enter the Temple, people tried to retain their state of purity and to regain it if lost. For this constant concern, the *miqvaot* furnished an indispensable help.[62]

Against this background, it is easy to fathom the remarkable change the inverse strategy of (im)purity would anticipate. For someone believing he had the ability to invert the transferability of (im)purity, the abundance of *miqvaot*, and more the way of life they represented, would have begun to appear as irrelevant. Indeed, can we avoid thinking that the inverse strategy holds the potential of bringing about a major transformation of Judaism? In my view, some sort of eschatological and messianic ideas need to be regarded as lying behind Jesus' purity thinking. Otherwise, it would be difficult to account for the radicalness of the change of the transferability of (im)purity on the one hand, and, on the other, the particular role in this change Jesus assumes for himself. I shall return to these considerations later on.

In the eyes of beholders not belonging to Jesus' close followers, his unreserved dealings with the unclean could have remained obscure. Outside observers would have had difficulty anticipating other possible motivations behind this unreservedness. Therefore, as I have put forward elsewhere, within the framework of contemporary covenant thinking, where the purity paradigm played an integral role, this behavior of Jesus could have appeared as suspicious and most readily explainable as laxity.[63] The Gospel reports do, however, suggest that Jesus' own aims with the behavior were not derivative of indifference or negligence but rather of a view of the

60. R. Reich, "Ritual Baths," in E. M. Meyers (ed.), *The Oxford Encyclopedia of Archaeology in the Near East: Volume 4* (Oxford: Oxford University Press, 1997), pp. 430-31; A. Negev and S. Gibson, *Archaeological Encyclopedia of the Holy Land* (New York: Continuum, 2003 [2nd ed.]), p. 71; Poirier, "Purity Beyond the Temple," p. 257.

61. Frymer-Kensky, "Pollution, Purification, and Purgation," p. 403.

62. Kazen, *Purity Halakhah*, p. 75: "The fairly widespread use of *miqvaot* made an expansionist view of impurity possible to implement."

63. Holmén, *Jesus and Jewish Covenant Thinking*, p. 251.

inversion of the transferability of ritual (im)purity that he sees as taking place in his person and mission. Naturally, with such a conception of transferability, impurity also loses much of its threatening character. Deprived of its ability to multiply itself, it becomes easily manageable and conquerable, and can therefore be approached with a more relaxed attitude. Hence, it is not so much what comes outside a person that can defile.[64]

Jesus Traditions Pertaining to Purity

By this remark I have begun to consider the inverse strategy in the context of other Jesuanic material which carries purity overtones. I shall be content with two examples.[65]

First, the saying in Mark 7:15, often regarded as historically reliable,[66] is clearly compatible with the inverse strategy. In fact, the strategy remarkably illuminates the saying. How can defilement from outside — that is, forbidden foods and general ritual impurity[67] — not defile, in contrast to defilement from the inside,[68] probably meaning moral contamination?[69] The answer is that, since Jesus is now able to invert the transferability of (im)purity, nothing from the outside, not even unclean foods, can pose the kind of threat they once did. On the other hand, with respect to moral impurities, the situation is different, for their communication does not take place in the same manner! The morally defiling acts mentioned in the Torah are sexual sins (Lev 18), idolatry (Lev 19:31; 20:1-3), and murder (Num

64. Cf. Mark 7:15.

65. For the Temple as obviously relevant to purity, see the following section.

66. For an analysis, see Holmén, *Jesus and Jewish Covenant Thinking*, pp. 237-49.

67. Food seems to be implied by the phrase "going into"; H. Räisänen, "Jesus and the Food Laws: Reflections on Mark 7.15," in A.-M. Enroth (ed.), *The Torah and Christ: Essays in German and English on the Problem of the Law in Early Christianity* (SESJ 45; Helsinki: Raamattutalo, 1986), pp. 219-41, esp. p. 223. Though food is in focus only by implication, the context (even if not originally the present one) may have made it explicit. At any event, reference to food can also be interpreted as a *pars pro toto* case, hence denoting ritual or thus "outside" impurity in general.

68. For these alternatives, see shortly below in the text.

69. R. P. Booth, *Jesus and the Laws of Purity: Tradition History and Legal History in Mark 7* (JSNTSup 13; Sheffield: JSOT Press, 1986), p. 210; Holmén, *Jesus and Jewish Covenant Thinking*, pp. 238-39.

35:33-34),[70] though Jesus or other contemporary Jews need not have restricted moral defilement to these deeds alone.[71] While ritual impurity, as it was commonly thought, was communicated by touching, moral impurity came through *doing* the sins in question. Moral impurity did not spread by physical contact! Still, it created a longer standing state of impurity and was impervious to the rites of purification.[72] In other words, moral impurity was not conceived as being contagious in the way that ritual impurities were, and it also required different means of purification. In consequence of this, the inversion of the contagiousness of (im)purity did not apply to moral defilement and did not warrant a relaxed attitude in that respect.[73]

There is also another way that the inverse strategy of ritual (im)purity can illumine Mark 7:15. As is known, the saying can be read either as an absolute denial of the defiling power of what comes from outside or as a relative statement stressing the greater significance of moral issues (while devaluing ritual impurities). The latter reading has gained popularity as of late. The tone of Mark 7:15 is clearly remindful of Old Testament prophetic oracles such as Jer 7:22-23 and Hos 6:6, which by stressing what is now urgently needed seemingly dismiss the opposite. Grammatically speaking, Mark 7:15 (as well as the Old Testament passages) may be understood as a "dialectic negation."[74] As a Semitic idiom, the formula "not A, but B" (οὐ ... ἀλλά) can be rendered "not so much A, but rather B,"[75] hence, "a man is not so much defiled by that which enters him from outside as he is by that which comes from within."[76]

70. Wright, "Unclean and Clean," pp. 733-35.

71. See J. Klawans, *Impurity and Sin in Ancient Judaism* (Oxford: Oxford University Press, 2000), pp. 43-60; Regev, "Abominated Temple," pp. 250-51.

72. Frymer-Kensky, "Pollution, Purification, and Purgation," pp. 404-9; Klawans, *Impurity and Sin*, pp. 26-31; Regev, "Abominated Temple," p. 245.

73. The inverse strategy of ritual (im)purity illuminates in a similar way the Q saying Matt 23:25-26/Luke 11:39-41 as well.

74. See H. Kruse, "Die 'dialektische Negation' als semitisches idiom," *VT* 4 (1954): 385-400.

75. F. Blass, A. Debrunner and F. Rehkopf, *Grammatik des neutestamentlichen Griechisch* (Göttingen: Vandenhoeck & Ruprecht, 1990 [17th ed.]), p. 378 (§448 n. 1); M. Zerwick, *Biblical Greek Illustrated by Examples* (English edition adapted from the 4th Latin ed. by J. Smith; SPIB 114; Roma: Editrice Pontificio Istituto Biblico, 6th repr., 1994), p. 150 (§445).

76. For similar interpretation see, for instance, Westerholm, *Jesus and Scribal Authority,*

At the same time, the absolute (and literal) interpretation has run into difficulties because of the emphasis in current research on the Jewishness of Jesus. The idea that Jesus would have abrogated the food laws, or even denied the distinction between sacred and secular so fundamental to Judaism, was earlier found appealing and, since it attests to an obvious uniqueness, also suggesting authenticity.[77] Nowadays, however, such radicalness is perceived as unsuited to Jesus the Jew, and the authenticity of the saying is often made dependent on the acceptance of the relative interpretation.[78]

It is clear that the relative interpretation fits well with the inverse strategy of (im)purity. Ritual impurity has not vanished, but because Jesus has the power to ward it off and revert it easily, it does not require so much attention any longer. Instead, moral uncleanness stays untouched by the in-

---

p. 83; Booth, *Laws of Purity*, pp. 68-71; H. Merklein, *Jesu Botschaft von der Gottesherrschaft: Eine Skizze* (SBS 111; Stuttgart: Katholisches Bibelwerk, 1989 [3rd ed.]), p. 98; Holmén, *Jesus and Jewish Covenant Thinking*, pp. 239-41; J. D. G. Dunn, *Jesus Remembered* (CM 1; Grand Rapids: Eerdmans, 2003), pp. 574-75.

77. See, for instance, E. Käsemann, *Exegetische Versuche und Besinnungen: Erster Band* (Göttingen: Vandenhoeck & Ruprecht, 1960 [2nd ed.]), p. 238; N. Perrin, *Rediscovering the Teaching of Jesus* (New York: Harper & Row, 1967), p. 150; H. Hübner, *Das Gesetz in der synoptischen Tradition: Studien zur These einer progressiven Qumranisierung und Judaisierung innerhalb der synoptischen Tradition* (Witten: Lutter-Verlag, 1973), pp. 165-75. Even more recently, see W. Weiss, *"Eine neue Lehre in Vollmacht": Die Streit- und Schulgespräche des Markus-Evangeliums* (BZNW 52; Berlin: Walter de Gruyter, 1989), pp. 70-71; R. W. Funk and R. W. Hoover, *The Five Gospels: The Search for the Authentic Words of Jesus* (New York: Scribner, 1996), p. 69. For the use and misuse of the criteria of authenticity in assessing Mark 7:15, see T. Holmén, "Doubts about Double Dissimilarity," in B. Chilton and C. A. Evans (eds.), *Authenticating the Words of Jesus* (NTTS 28.1; Leiden: Brill, 1999), pp. 47-80, esp. pp. 70-73.

78. See, for instance, Sanders, *Jewish Law*, p. 28. Cf., however, J. P. Meier, *A Marginal Jew: Rethinking the Historical Jesus: The Roots of the Problem and the Person* (ABRL; New York: Doubleday, 1991), vol. 1, p. 173. Further, J. Riches, *Jesus and the Transformation of Judaism* (London: Darton, Longman & Todd, 1980), p. 112; J. D. G. Dunn, "Jesus and Ritual Purity: A Study of the Tradition History of Mark 7:15," in *Cause de l'Évangile: Études sur les Synoptiques et les Actes* (FS J. Dupont; LD 123; Paris: Cerf, 1985), pp. 251-76, esp. p. 254. For my solution to the dilemma, see T. Holmén, "Doubts about Double Dissimilarity," pp. 59-62. This is also G. Theissen's assessment of the current research; see G. Theissen, "Das Reinheitslogion Mark 7,15 und die Trennung von Juden und Christen," in A. Merz (ed.), *Jesus als historische Gestalt: Beiträge zur Jesusforschung* (FS G. Theissen; FRLANT 202; Göttingen: Vandenhoeck & Ruprecht, 2003), pp. 73-89, esp. pp. 73-76. However, Theissen himself interprets the saying absolutely *and* sustains its authenticity. He points out that the saying is indicatively formulated, not imperatively as later in early Christianity (*idem*, pp. 80-84).

verse strategy since that type of defilement has had nothing to do with contact-contagion in the first place. However, the strategy also affords an absolute reading of the saying which eschews being non-Jewish or too radical. If the straightforward inability of any outside impurity to defile — as it is literally put forward in Mark 7:15[79] — is understood against the background of Jesus' imperviousness to such impurities and his contagious, "defiling purity," we obtain an absolute reading which by no means abrogates the laws of ritual (im)purity. According to it, ritual (im)purity does not cease to exist but — seen strictly from Jesus' perspective — simply can no longer do any harm, i.e., defile.[80]

As a second example, I shall consider the theme of Jesus' table fellowship with toll collectors and sinners. Ed Sanders argues for the historicity of the theme on the following grounds: (a) the extent of the material bearing on this question is large; (b) there is a multiple attestation in forms: "parables, other sayings, flat declarations of purpose, reports of Jesus' activity, and reported accusations against him"; (c) a high tolerance of sinners is dissimilar to the practice of the early Church as we know it.[81] Sanders also maintains that the main offense of Jesus' table fellowship was not that he ate with common people unobservant of the specific food regulations of the *haverim* or the Pharisees, but that he granted unrepentant sinners the legitimacy of the people of God.[82] I think Sanders is right on both points. Accordingly, the theme provides authentic information, and it provides information about Jesus' message about the kingdom of God. Sharing the table was a cheerful event suitable for a cheerful message. In other words, here Jesus imparted his message and made sinners and outcasts heirs of the kingdom.[83]

79. Cf. οὐδέν ἐστιν ἔξωθεν . . . ὃ δύναται κοινῶσαι. See Theissen, "Das Reinheitslogion Mark 7,15," pp. 76-77. Cf. Holmén, *Jesus and Jewish Covenant Thinking*, p. 241.

80. The relative interpretation perhaps sees the issue from a wider perspective, taking into account that the inversion of the transferability of (im)purity concerned only Jesus and was applied to those with whom he had dealings.

81. E. P. Sanders, *Jesus and Judaism* (London: SCM Press, 1985), p. 174. For the authenticity of this motif see also, for instance, Meier, *A Marginal Jew*, vol. 2, pp. 149-51; D. E. Smith, "Table Fellowship and the Historical Jesus," in L. Bormann, K. Del Tredici and A. Standhartinger (eds.), *Religious Propaganda and Missionary Competition in the New Testament World: Essays honoring Dieter Georgi* (NovTSup 74; Leiden: Brill, 1994), pp. 135-62.

82. Sanders, *Jesus and Judaism*, pp. 174-211.

83. For a recent re-evaluation of the historicity of the table fellowship as Jesus' means of imparting his message about the kingdom, see D.-A. Koch, "Jesu Tischgemeinschaft mit

However, as noted above, I do believe that matters of purity, though perhaps less focally, were also involved in these situations of Jesus' mission. The involvement of purity questions has been suggested for instance by Bruce Chilton and more recently by James D. G. Dunn,[84] and I share their opinion in that the presence of mixed interests can by no means be excluded. Purity questions arose at the table at least because, in general, sinners were no better than pagans,[85] and in particular, toll collectors were defiled because in their profession they likely came into contact with Gentiles.[86] Therefore the table fellowship theme is also apt for probing the applicability of the inverse strategy of (im)purity.

Indeed, the strategy can well be seen as operative even behind this conspicuous feature of Jesus' behavior. Table fellowship naturally brought people into close physical contact with each other. The purity of food is certainly relevant here as well.[87] The unreservedness towards the looming impurities that Jesus displayed by this activity can again be explained by the ability to invert the transferability of (im)purity which he assumed to possess. However, the inverse strategy of (im)purity cannot account for the entire situation of table fellowship. As stated, purity was not the only question arising from this fellowship. Together with Sanders, I hold that the inclusion of sinners in the kingdom attracted a foremost attention. How could Jesus treat them with such an openness? This falls outside the scope of the ritual (im)purity strategy, if only because the sinners would have likely also committed deeds resulting in

---

Zöllnern und Sündern: Erwägungen zur Entstehung von Mark 2,13-17," in D.-A. Koch, G. Sellin and A. Lindemann (eds.), *Jesu Rede von Gott und ihre Nachgeschichte im frühen Christentum: Beiträge zur Verkündigung Jesu und zum Kerygma der Kirche* (Gütersloh: Gütersloher Verlagshaus Mohn, 1989), pp. 57-73.

84. B. Chilton, "Jesus and the Repentance of E. P. Sanders," *TynBul* 39 (1988): 1-18. Dunn, "Jesus and Purity," p. 465. So also Sanders, *Jesus and Judaism*, pp. 187, 210.

85. Booth, *Laws of Purity*, p. 110, correctly observes that through being in contact with these sorts of people Jesus was liable to be defiled.

86. Antipas' main toll collectors were probably located in Tiberias, which was not only a prominently Greek city but was also founded on an old graveyard (*Ant.* 18.36-38).

87. Josephus tells of at least two groups who so strictly kept to their own table fellowship that, when this became impossible, they starved; they refused to touch other people's food. See *War* 2.143-44 about some Essenes and *Ant.* 20.181, 206-7 about some other priests. The same pattern is behind the prohibition that a *haber* should not eat together with the "people of land" (see *m. Demai*). The above interpretation(s) of Mark 7:15 would work purposefully in the table fellowship practiced by Jesus.

moral defilement.[88] The conclusive answer lies in understanding Jesus' message about the kingdom of God. Somehow this enabled him to include even sinners.[89] That the inverse strategy of (im)purity was part of the kingdom message seems clear, but it was not the whole message.[90]

Hence, the inverse strategy represents ritual (im)purity as a matter relevant to Jesus, while at the same time explaining his seemingly indifferent behavior in various situations and the relaxed attitude he voices. Though ritual impurity was a real and relevant issue to Jesus, it was not a problem or a danger, since, for him, its sting (i.e., its contagiousness) had fallen away. Moreover, the inverse strategy also illuminates the fact that the relaxed attitude never applies to moral issues. Since moral defilement was "contagiousless," it could not be dealt with by means of Jesus' contagious purity. Some other strategy was needed instead.

The Overall Message of Jesus

The obvious question emerging from these formulations is how Jesus had arrived at such a view of ritual (im)purity. As I stated earlier, it seems requisite to engage with the issues of the eschatological message of Jesus and the specific role within that message which he adopted for himself. In Jewish restoration eschatology, the task of the agent of God was to bring about God's rule, thereby at last establishing purity and

---

88. In the Gospels, the designation "sinners" (ἁμαρτωλοί), given of the group Jesus kept company with (a deviant use for instance in Luke 5:8), denotes those who had intentionally broken God's commandments, as these were understood by Jews in general, not just by some isolated group or association. The designation is advanced by many kinds of people: By the evangelist (Mark 2:15), by the Pharisees (Mark 2:16), by Jesus himself (Mark 2:17), and by people in general (Luke 19:7; Matt 11:19 par. Luke 7:34 = Q). Especially the last point shows that the people designated ἁμαρτωλοί were sinners in general respect, i.e., they were regarded as sinners by Jews in general. In fact, here probably lies the function of "the toll collectors," the regular adherent of the very designation. Because everyone disliked "the toll collectors," it conveniently serves to indicate that ἁμαρτωλοί is not meant just as some special grouping's judgment of other people. Further on this see, for instance, J. Jeremias, "Zöllner und Sünder," ZNW 13 (1931): 293-300; Westerholm, Jesus and Scribal Authority, pp. 70-71; H. Merklein, Die Gottesherrschaft als Handlungsprinzip: Untersuchung zur Ethik Jesu (FzB 34;Würzburg: Echter Verlag, 1981 [2nd ed.]), pp. 200-201; Sanders, Jesus and Judaism, pp. 177-79.

89. See the remarks in the next section.

90. See the short remark on the table fellowship in the next section.

righteousness.[91] The restoration of the purity of the Land, the people, and/or Jerusalem, envisaged by prophets, was longed for in many Second Temple writings and was usually pictured as involving the exclusion of sinners and ritually unclean people.[92] Maybe, in Jesus' view, it was this eschatological purity that through him now began to rule over impurity. In his view, however, the restoration of purity would not take place by excluding the ritually unclean people, but through the efficient expurgation of their uncleanness by means of the inversion of the transferability of (im)purity. Hence the statement "O Jerusalem . . . the unclean shall enter you no more" (Isa 52:1) would indeed hold true, but because those with impurities have been made clean.

Would such a hypothesis find support in Jesus' overall message? It would be illuminating to see whether motifs reminiscent of the inverse strategy of (im)purity could be located elsewhere in the Gospel's Jesus tradition. Actually, there are quite a number of traditions that display the feature of inversion. First, the "parables of reversal":[93]

The Pharisee and the Publican (Luke 18:10-14), the Good Samaritan (Luke 10:30-37), the Rich Man and Lazarus (Luke 16:19-31), the Wedding Guests (Luke 14:7-11), the Proper Guests (Luke 14:12-14), the Great Supper (Matt 22:1-10 par. Luke 14:16-24), and the Prodigal Son (Luke 15:11-32).

Secondly, some short statements clearly apply here:

The tax collectors and the prostitutes are going into the kingdom of God ahead of you (Matt 21:32)

Whoever wishes to be great among you must be your servant (Matt 20:26)

For the Son of Man came not to be served but to serve (Mark 10:45)

---

91. See, for example, Isa 42:1-7; Jer 23:5-6; Ezek 37:22-28; *Pss. Sol.* 17.

92. Ps 24:3-4; Isa 35:8; 52:1; *Pss. Sol.* 17.22-23. Sometimes a powerful removal of the *uncleanness* of the people was envisioned; Isa 4:3-4; Ezek 36:25, 29; *Jub.* 4.26; 50.5; *Pss. Sol.* 17.26; 1QS 4.20-22. However, many of these passages can also be understood as referring to the removal of the unclean people themselves.

93. See here J. D. Crossan, *In Parables: The Challenge of the Historical Jesus* (New York: Harper & Row, 1973), pp. 53-78.

I tell you, many will come from east and west and will eat with Abraham and Isaac and Jacob in the kingdom of heaven, while the heirs of the kingdom will be thrown into the outer darkness (Matt 8:11-12)

I have come to call not the righteous but sinners (Mark 2:17).

All these texts put forward ideas that invert traditional beliefs and notions. As a third group, some paradoxical sayings could be mentioned:

But many who are first will be last, and the last will be first (Mark 10:31)

Those who find their life will lose it, and those who lose their life for my sake will save it (Matt 10:39; cf. Mark 8:35)

I came into this world for judgment so that those who do not see may see, and those who do see may become blind (John 9:39; cf. Mark 4:11-12).

Naturally, the Beatitudes of the Sermon on the Mount or on the Plain can also be seen as based on inversion.[94]

The relation of the statements in the third group with those in the second is obvious, no doubt because they all involve playing with opposites. However, their relationship lies deeper. For "paradox is to language as eschaton is to world."[95] The sayings in the second group express in a more informative guise how eschatology means a radical change (or inversion) in the issues and beliefs in question. The sayings of the third group use a paradoxical way of speech to accentuate the radicalness of the change.

I do not suggest that every item in the above lists exhibits an authentic saying of Jesus. Similarly, the explicit Christological motif found in some of them is probably secondary. Nonetheless, seeing how firmly rooted in the tradition is the conviction of Jesus inverting some basic conceptions of salvation, it is difficult to avoid concluding that the conviction begins in the genuine teaching of Jesus.[96] In fact, this conclusion presents itself as in-

---

94. Dunn, *Jesus Remembered*, pp. 412-13.

95. Crossan, *In Parables*, p. 76.

96. So also for instance D. L. Bock, *Luke, Volume 2: 9:51–24:53* (BECNT 3b; Grand Rapids: Baker, 1996), p. 1232; Dunn, *Jesus Remembered*, pp. 412-17; J. P. Meier, *A Marginal Jew: Rethinking the Historical Jesus: Companions and Competitors* (ABRL; New York: Doubleday, 2001), vol. 3, pp. 56-64.

evitable, if we choose to follow the methodological principle suggested by James Dunn in his recent major work on Jesus, namely that one should above all accept the basic historicity of the general and recurrent motifs of the Jesus tradition.[97] Actually, there are quite a few scholars in whose views such motifs merit a high claim to authenticity.[98] In addition, however, some items from the lists merit claims to authenticity even as individual traditions, such as the oracle about people coming from the east and west to dine with Abraham, Isaac and Jacob.[99]

As we can see, the inverse strategy of (im)purity appears not to have been a solitary phenomenon in Jesus' message. It forms part of a *general motif of inversion* that imperatively goes through the tradition, being best characterized as eschatological and closely connected to the message about the kingdom of God. It ought to have a scriptural counterpart in texts which underline God's sovereignty over human fortunes, as for example in Ezek 17:24: "I bring low the high tree, I make high the low tree; I dry up the green tree and make the dry tree flourish."[100] We may note that Jesus' table fellowship with sinners and outcasts discussed above displays many themes that are central here: the imparting of the kingdom message, inversed purity concerns as well as inversed apprehension of whom the kingdom belongs to, and Jesus' particular role of being the mediator in all of this. We can also hear echoes of the table fellowship in the oracle concerning the consummation of the kingdom where wholly unexpected kinds of people feast with Abraham and the patriarchs.

However, the inverse strategy of (im)purity clearly operates on a more particular level than the general motif of inversion. Perhaps the best way to

---

97. Dunn, *Jesus Remembered*, pp. 332-35.

98. See, for instance, H. K. McArthur, "A Survey of Recent Gospel Research," *Int* 18 (1964): 39-55, esp. p. 48; Perrin, *Rediscovering*, p. 46; N. J. McEleney, "Authenticating Criteria and Mark 7:1-23," *CBQ* 34 (1972): 431-60, esp. p. 434; S. E. Porter, *The Criteria for Authenticity in Historical-Jesus Research: Previous Discussion and New Proposals* (JSNTSup 191; Sheffield: Sheffield Academic Press, 2000), p. 86; Holmén, *Jesus and Jewish Covenant Thinking*, pp. 34-36; G. Theissen and D. Winter, *The Quest for the Plausible Jesus: The Question of Criteria* (trans. M. E. Boring; Louisville: Westminster John Knox, 2002), pp. 177-79.

99. See J. Schlosser, *Le règne de Dieu dans les dits de Jésus: Deuxième partie* (EBib; 2 vols.; Paris: Gabalda, 1980), pp. 603-24; Meier, *A Marginal Jew*, vol. 2, pp. 309-17. G. Theissen and A. Merz, *Der historische Jesus: Ein Lehrbuch* (Göttingen: Vandenhoeck & Ruprecht, 1996), p. 233.

100. See also for example 1 Sam 2:1-8 (see Luke 1:46-53; cf. even Jas 5:1-3); Pss 75:8; 113:7-9; Ezek 21:27; Dan 2:21.

describe this difference is to say that the inverse strategy of (im)purity is one of the things that *enable* for Jesus the general pursuit of inversion. It makes it possible for him to bring his message about the last being first (cf. Mark 10:31) to a certain group of those last, the ritually unclean.[101] Indeed, I earlier pointed out the certain restrictedness of the inverse strategy of (im)purity. It could not account for the openness Jesus showed towards the sinners in granting them the legitimacy of the people of God. Closely related to this, moral defilement also falls outside its sphere of influence. Hence, other such strategies (or "specific viewpoints")[102] need to be fixed if one wishes to explain the general pursuit of inversion witnessed in the lists above of parables, sayings, paradoxes and Beatitudes. Naturally, I cannot attempt a full clarification of that here. Nonetheless, I wish to take a look at an issue which should have functioned in a close proximity to the inverse strategy of (im)purity and which could guide us to seeing how further viewpoints of inversion were connected to each other: the Temple.

Issues of the Temple and purity were closely connected with each other in early Judaism. The holiness of the Temple was the central concern of all Jews at every period of the building.[103] In particular, the Temple not only demanded purity but was the source of it.[104] The purity of the Temple

101. Of course, temporary states of ritual uncleanness were largely an everyday matter for people. Usually, they did not give rise to any greater tragedies. When I characterize the ritually impure as the "last," I obviously mean those states of impurity which would more or less completely have prevented a person from leading a normal life. Examples of such states seen in this article are: people possessed by unclean spirits, lepers, and the woman with the hemorrhage.

102. If one wants to avoid the word "strategy." E. P. Sanders' position ("ancients in general and ancient Jews in particular formulated aims and shaped their actions so as to accomplish them . . . on my reading, the evidence points towards Jesus' having a definite programme" [Sanders, *Jesus and Judaism*, pp. 20-21; see further *idem*, 18-22]), already preceded by B. F. Meyer, *The Aims of Jesus* (London: SCM Press, 1979), has been fully appropriated by the "Third Quest." I would call the means implemented to fulfill a program "strategies." See also B. Chilton, *The Temple of Jesus: His Sacrificial Program Within Cultural History of Sacrifice* (University Park: Pennsylvania State University Press, 1992) and appendix 3, "Jesus' Program within Early Judaic Pluralism" (pp. 181-90).

103. The Halakhic Letter 4QMMT elaborates on the purity of the offerings; the purity and appropriateness of the priesthood concerns many writers of the Second Temple period (cf., for instance, *T. Mos.* 5-7); and Josephus describes how only pure Israelites could enter the temple (*Apion* 2.193-96).

104. S. Safrai, "The Temple," in S. Safrai and M. Stern (eds.), *The Jewish People in the First Century: Historical Geography, Political History, Social, Cultural and Religious Life and*

granted the purity of the chosen people gathering there to serve their God. Notwithstanding the modesty of Zerubbabel's temple referred to in Haggai (2:9), its altar functioned as a distributor of purity; it was accepted as the "fountain opened for . . . the inhabitants of Jerusalem to cleanse them from sin and impurity" (Zech 13:1; cf. Ezek 47:1).

Jesus' relationship to the Temple and its cult was, however, "notoriously problematic."[105] Though there is no unanimity among scholars about the exact nature of the problem, many would agree that Jesus predicted and awaited the destruction of the Temple.[106] Probably, then, for whatever reason, Jesus saw the Temple as not being up to its tasks. Why else would he have awaited its fall? Granted then that there was a linkage between the Temple and purity, both in early Judaism generally and in Jesus' thinking, his conviction that the Temple did not work and would disappear could offer at least one of the reasons why he adopted the role of himself as a distributor of purity. Some kind of parallel can be found in the Qumran Community's way of regarding itself as a collective Temple, in its residing in the desert in order to atone for the land and maintaining purity within the Community.[107] And we should not forget to consider John the Baptist either.[108]

Institutions. Volume Two (CRINT 1; 2 vols.; Assen: Van Gorcum, 1976), pp. 865-907, esp. pp. 876-77; Frymer-Kensky, "Pollution, Purification, and Purgation," p. 406. Many rites of purification included sacrifices as their integral component.

105. See Chilton, *A Feast of Meanings*, p. 34.

106. Holmén, *Jesus and Jewish Covenant Thinking*, pp. 300-301. Cf., for example, Mark 13:1-2; 14:57-58; Matt 23:37-39 par. Luke 13:34-35; Luke 19:41-44; Acts 6:13-14. For a more detailed discussion on the theme "Jesus and the temple," see Holmén, *Jesus and Jewish Covenant Thinking*, pp. 275-329. See also T. Holmén, "The Temple Action of Jesus (Mark 11:15-17) in Historical Context," in K.-J. Illman, T. Ahlbäck, S.-O. Bäck and R. Nurmela (eds.), *A Bouquet of Wisdom: Essays in Honour of Karl-Gustav Sandelin* (RS 48; Åbo: Åbo Akademi University Printing House, 2000), pp. 99-127. For contemporary parallels to seeing the Temple as doomed, see for instance 1 *En*. 89.54, 56; *Sib. Or*. 3.270-76 (dated 163-145 BCE by J. J. Collins, "Sibylline Oracles," in *OTP* vol 1, pp. 317-472, esp. p. 355); T. *Levi* 15.1; *War* 6.250, 301.

107. See, for instance, 1QS 8.4-10; 1QSa 2.2-10; L. H. Schiffman, "Community Without Temple: The Qumran Community's Withdrawal from the Jerusalem Temple," in B. Ego, A. Lange and P. Pilhofer (eds.), *Gemeinde ohne Tempel/Community without Temple: Zur Substituierung und Transformation des Jerusalemer Tempels und seines Kults im Alten Testament, antiken Judentum und frühen Christentum* (WUNT 118; Tübingen: Mohr Siebeck, 1999), pp. 267-84, esp. pp. 272-74.

108. As Dunn, "Jesus and Purity," p. 459, states, John "offered his own ritual as an alternative to the Temple ritual." See the references for this view in Dunn, "Jesus and Purity," nn. 48 and 49.

Jesus' view of the Temple would thus fittingly accompany the inverse strategy of (im)purity in explaining (at least partly) why there was a need for such a strategy. There is also an intriguing detail which connects Jesus' views of the Temple with Haggai's aforementioned purity saying (Hag 2:11-13) in a way characteristic of the (im)purity strategy — that is, by way of inversion. In Mark 13:1, one of Jesus' disciples is reported to have been amazed by the large stones and buildings of the Temple. As can be gathered, the overwhelming grandeur of the Temple could easily bring into mind the words of Hag 2:9: "the latter splendor of this house shall be greater than the former." Immediately after these words in Haggai follows the regulation concerning the contagiousness of impurity (2:10-14). And Haggai continues, "so is it with this people, and with this nation . . . and so with every work of their hands; and what they offer there is unclean" (Hag 2:14). Nevertheless, there is now a better hope with which Haggai can console himself. Though modest, the Temple initiated by Zerubbabel is there, and times of blessings will come. How different indeed was the time — and now come words that are unique to Haggai in the Old Testament[109] — "before a stone was placed upon a stone in the Lord's temple" (Hag 2:15). "Stone on another" probably refers "to the ritual manipulation of the 'former' stone" mentioned specifically in Zech 4:7 and laid (יסדו) by Zerubbabel (4:9), "a stone designed to guarantee *ritual continuity* with the earlier holy building."[110] Intriguingly, in Mark 13:2, Jesus is said to have replied to his disciple's awe with an inversion of Haggai's words about the stone: "there will not be left here one stone upon another."[111] However, the inversion hardly applies to the verbal level alone. Jesus' disbelief in the current Temple's capacity to do what people (as once Haggai) expected may even be conflated with a disbelief in a temple "made with hands," thus a human one (cf. Hag 2:14 quoted above; see also Mark 14:58).[112] The inver-

---

109. H. W. Wolff, *Dodekapropheton 6: Haggai* (BKAT 14.6; Neukirchen-Vluyn: Neukirchener Verlag, 1986), p. 44.

110. Petersen, *Haggai,* p. 90 (emphasis added). See also D. L. Petersen, "Zerubbabel and Jerusalem Temple Reconstruction," *CBQ* 36 (1974): 366-72, esp. pp. 368-69. See further in Holmén, *Jesus and Jewish Covenant Thinking,* pp. 294-96, 301-3.

111. For the arguments for regarding this tradition as authentic, see Holmén, *Jesus and Jewish Covenant Thinking,* pp. 292-96, 301. These words can easily be seen as referring to the passage in Haggai; J. Schlosser, "La parole de Jésus sur la fin du Temple," *NTS* 36 (1990): 398-414, esp. pp. 407-8.

112. Hag 2:14: **מעשה ידיהם**, "work of their hands." The *terminus technicus* χειρο-

sion of the words about the ritual stone could then imply the coming divine (i.e., *not* made with hands) Temple's *discontinuity* from the current one. Such discontinuity would be necessary for signaling and/or enforcing the remarkable change in the transferability of ritual (im)purity already anticipated in Jesus' work.

Irrespective of the "stone" words, however, the above depiction of Jesus' view of the Temple would fittingly cooperate with his view of the inversion of (im)purity. The analogy of the altar of the Temple again suggests itself. At the same time, if we grant that the very sketchy depiction is basically accurate and catches the gist of the issue,[113] Jesus' view of the Temple may approximate the matrix of the general pursuit of inversion and furnish the link combining many specific viewpoints (or strategies) that, together with the inverse strategy of (im)purity, need to cooperate to make up the pursuit. For, obviously, purity was not the only function of the Temple. Jesus' openness towards the sinners in granting them the legitimacy of the people of God, for example, could be explained by the assumption that he considered himself to have the authority to forgive sins regardless of the Temple institutions. In fact, if the present Temple was already sentenced for destruction,[114] he would have judged his authority greater than that of the Temple. Hence, although the sinners would not go to the Temple,[115] forgiveness comes to them.[116] And ultimately, it would be the sinners (who

---

ποίητος, "made with hands" (both χειροποίητος and ἀχειροποίητος appear in Mark 14:58), is Septuagintal (see Lev 26:1; 26:30; Isa 2:18; 10:11; 16:12; 19:1; 21:9; 31:7; 46:6; Dan 5:4, 23; Jdt 8:18; Wis 14:8; Bel 1:5) and has no exact Hebrew or Aramaic equivalent. Cf. Hag 2:14 LXX: τὰ ἔργα τῶν χειρῶν αὐτῶν. However, the formulation of Hag 2:14 can quite well have evoked the same notion. In my view, D. J. A. Clines, "Haggai's Temple: Constructed, Deconstructed and Reconstructed," *SJOT* 7 (1993): 51-77, has shown that the discussed passages from Haggai can also invite a pessimistic interpretation of the Temple's state; see especially Clines, "Haggai's Temple," pp. 61-66. Clines does not, however, point out the possibility of seeing Hag 2:14 as a critique of a temple "made with hands."

113. For a more in-depth discussion of the issue see Holmén, *Jesus and Jewish Covenant Thinking*, pp. 275-328.

114. As thus is above proposed as Jesus' view.

115. Out of laxity or due to exclusion; Num 15:27-31 (see Milgrom, "Israel's Sanctuary," p. 393); Ps 15 (see A. Weiser, *The Psalms: A Commentary* [OTL; London: SCM Press, 1962], p. 170); 24:3-5; Isa 33:14-16.

116. In this respect, I think Sanders' (see Sanders, *Jesus and Judaism*, pp. 174-211) characterization of the people who ate together with Jesus as unrepentant sinners is important. The characterization should be qualified, however, with B. Chilton's suggestion that at the

eat with Jesus) and not the righteous (who sacrifice in the Temple) who would come first.

For now, these last suggestions must remain what they are, i.e., possibilities for further research. It seems clear, though, that Jesus' dealings with the unclean presuppose an eschatological vision on his part, a vision that reveals itself as all the more thoroughgoing the further we follow the tracks left by the dealings. The hypothesis about an eschatological purity program sketched in the beginning of this section reveals itself to be well-founded. Eschatological purity formed an integral part of Jesus' mission and message.

Conclusions (Corollaries) and Future Questions

Jesus' dealings with the ritually unclean attest to a mode of behavior which can best be explained by an assumption of an eschatological vision on his part. This vision proposed that, with regard to Jesus, a radical change in the ways purity and impurity behave had taken place. It proposed a view of an inversion of the transferability of (im)purity that rendered Jesus capable of cleaning the unclean without resorting to ordinary means of purification: the impurities of the unclean do not transfer to Jesus; instead, Jesus' purity transfers to the unclean. From now on, through him, this eschatological purity would start ruling over impurity. Even the ritually unclean would become part of God's kingdom.

Jesus' eschatological vision, the inverse strategy of (im)purity, did not lead him to oppose the ritual purity paradigm. Nor did he aim at devaluing it. On the contrary, Jesus can be said to have had a positive and appreciative disposition to ritual purity. A gradually increasing devaluation was effectuated, however, since the inverse strategy radically diminished the threat posed by impurity. Its contagiousness being ruled out, it demanded decisively less attention. On the other hand, the contagiousness of Jesus' purity worked in the same direction. Thus a conspicuously relaxed attitude had become possible, and a major transformation was on its way. For outside observers all this would easily have appeared as indifference and/or laxity.

The inverse strategy of (im)purity did not apply to moral defilement, for this was not conceived as contact-contagious. Hereby we can explain the im-

---

background here lies the pattern of forgiveness leading to reformation (Matt 18:23-35; Luke 7:36-50; 16:1-9; thus, an inversion of the more common order of reformation leading to forgiveness). See Chilton, "Jesus and the Repentance," pp. 8, 10-12.

pression given by the Jesus traditions pertaining to purity that he stressed the moral dimensions of the law at the cost of downplaying the ritual ones. In reality, both were important for him but different strategies were required to handle them. In this respect it is informative that the overall teaching of Jesus reveals the inverse strategy of (im)purity to form part of a general motif of inversion inherent to Jesus' kingdom message: the first will come last and the last will come first. The scope of the present article did not yield an ascertainment of what other strategies or specific viewpoints contributed to the general inversion pursuit. The statements put forward about the Temple and the forgiveness of sins remain suggestions at present. Still, these issues can quite naturally be linked with the (im)purity strategy. Jesus' view of the Temple would appear to offer a nexus for several viewpoints of inversion. Likewise, an authority to revert sins would feature a convenient complement to the power to revert ritual impurity he assumed to possess.

Hence, while we have obtained some notable results, the need for further research is also clearly indicated. Almost as an affirmation of the need, I shall lastly propose a fresh set of questions. I can now address them only briefly. What happened in the long run to those who became clean through Jesus? Did they still continue to collect impurities with the same susceptibility as earlier, or should we think of some more permanent change? As will be seen, these questions connect to the following: How did the early Christians reflect upon the Jesuanic inverse strategy of (im)purity? I shall approach this chain of questions from its end.

Klaus Berger has studied some texts which, being illuminative of a purity that has turned contagious, could represent a further development of Jesus' (im)purity strategy.[117] Most peculiar is 1 Cor 7:14:

> For the unbelieving husband is made holy (ἡγίασται) through his wife, and the unbelieving wife is made holy (ἡγίασται) through her husband. Otherwise, your children would be unclean (ἀκάθαρτα), but as it is, they are holy (ἄγια).

With some other texts pointing in the same direction,[118] there might be reason to maintain that the early Christians assumed they had become part

---

117. See Berger, "Pharisäer," pp. 240-45. Berger's thesis rests mainly on the assessment of the motif of the "offensive cleanness/holiness" (see n. 52 above) in early Christianity. He considers Jesus as the last of his five points; see Berger, "Pharisäer," p. 246.

118. E.g., Rom 11:16; Tit 1:15; *1 Clem.* 46.2.

of Jesus' contagious purity. Hence, once they had become pure through him, they would not be contaminated any more, at least not through the same channels as before; moreover, they could even themselves become communicators of purity. This would explain the rather rapid fading of a way of life considerably centered around the warding off of impurity (as suggested earlier)[119] without the need to postulate a categorical turning against the purity paradigm on the part of the early Christians.

However, an important question concerns the bridge from the idea of Jesus' contagious purity to the idea that even his followers had the same or similar capability. What could have furnished the early Christians with a link to Jesus in this respect — that is, how did they think that they had come to have the same or similar contagious purity? There are a couple of passages that could offer some clarification.

In Mark 6:7, Jesus grants "the twelve" an "authority over the unclean spirits." In effect, this means that they can proclaim, cast out demons, and cure the ailing by anointing them with oil (6:12-13). Matthew puts somewhat more stress on purity, and lets Jesus command: "Cure the sick, raise the dead, cleanse the lepers, cast out demons" (10:8).[120] It is difficult to see either version as a conscious statement put forward to justify the view that Christians have been bestowed with Jesus' power to make the unclean clean. Still, the tradition may have secondarily offered some help to that end.

There is, however, another way by which the early Christians could have justified that they had been granted Jesus' contagious purity, a way which derives from the logic of contemporary purity thinking itself. I have already mentioned Luke 7:12-15 and the case where Jesus is said to touch the bier on which the dead boy lies (7:14). What makes this move astonishing is the fact that unlike other sources of impurity,[121] a human corpse could generate new sources of impurity. For this reason it was called by the rabbis "father of fathers of uncleanness." Therefore, though touching only the bier, Jesus would not have been safe, but since the bier had become a source of impurity he would have collected corpse impurity even by this act. All with elementary knowledge of the Jewish purity regulations would

119. See pp. 208-13 above.

120. The demons are called "unclean spirits" in Matthew as well (10:1). Luke (9:1-6) completely ignores the language of purity.

121. Besides dead human bodies, the main sources of impurity were leprosy, human discharges, and dead animal bodies. See "Purity and Impurity, Ritual," *EncJud* 13 (1978): 1405-14, esp. p. 1405.

have understood this when seeing (if the story calls upon a historical reminiscence) or when reading what happened.

It is difficult to say whether the story about the woman with a hemorrhage in Mark 5:25-34 can be argued to have an authentic core. For my present purpose, however, this is irrelevant. What is important now is the observation that purity is communicated to the woman from Jesus' cloak. This would suggest that Jesus' contagious purity could create new sources of purity, thereby emulating the logic of corpse impurity! It may well be that the story about the woman does not particularly emphasize its inherent purity aspects. Still, for any Jew telling or hearing the story, the purity implications would have been inescapable.[122] Furthermore, what the story does emphasize is the fact that the woman touches only Jesus' cloak. In Mark this is stated first by the narrator, then by the woman herself, and lastly by Jesus.[123] Matthew and Luke reduce the times the cloak is mentioned but make the point conspicuous by speaking about the "fringe" (κράσπεδον) of the cloak.[124] Those with some knowledge of the problematic communication of impurity, as in the case of corpse impurity, would have heard this so: look, his cloak had turned into a source of purity.

If some applied thinking was allowed, this case would have offered a good starting-point for reasoning that those cleansed by Jesus had themselves become sources of purity. Hence, to the pure all things are pure.[125] This means that they would not have got exactly the same capability as Jesus had, but they would still be understood as having obtained a permanent state of purity.[126]

Was this also Jesus' view? I cannot see why it should not be. However, this issue, and even the prospect of being able to argue it, will need to be studied in some later work.

---

122. Slightly modifying Dunn's (see Dunn, "Jesus and Purity," p. 461) testimony of the four stories in Mark 5:1-20; 5:21-24, 35-43; 5:25-34; and Luke 7:11-17.

123. Cf. Mark 5:27, 28, 30.

124. Matt 9:20 (9:21 only "cloak"); Luke 8:44. One would not sit or lie on the "fringe" (or "tassel"). See the "fringe" mentioned in Mark 6:56 par. Matt 14:36 and having similar effects.

125. Tit 1:15. The locus to become part of this purity for those unable to touch Jesus physically would obviously be the baptism. Cf. Rom 6 esp. v. 19.

126. As I remarked earlier (see n. 53 above), Jesus had probably not regarded anyone else as possessing capabilities similar to his. Neither had he seen the inversion of the transferability of (im)purity as a general phenomenon taking place through and through at his time.

Founding Christianity: Comparing Jesus and Japanese "New Religions"

Ulrich Luz

Introduction

My general interest in this paper is to understand historically and contextually the birth of Christianity as a new religion. Thus, I shall compare Jesus with the new religions in Japan. More specifically I have three interests:

My first interest is to understand the significance and function of so called "founder-figures" of religions. This term was one of the key terms in an earlier epoch of religious studies. Gustav Mensching, for example, distinguished between "grown" and "founded" religions. "Grown" religions are for him popular religions, traditional religions of tribes or peoples. "Founded" religions are religions at the origin of which there was "a historical personality with a specific religious vision" who remained fundamentally influential for the later stages of their development;[1] they are at the same time universal and individualizing.[2] It was on the basis of this general theory of religions that Mensching wrote his important comparative study *Buddha und Christus*.[3] In a similar way in a newer book Theo Sundermeier distinguishes between "primary" and "secondary" experience of religion: "secondary" religions are shaped by a new experience of religion by "figures of founders, charismatics, prophets or reformators"

---

1. Gustav Mensching, *Vergleichende Religionswissenschaft* (Heidelberg: Quelle-Meyer, 1949), p. 151 (translation by U.L.).
2. Mensching, *Vergleichende*, p. 155.
3. Gustav Mensching, *Buddha und Christus* (Stuttgart: Deutsche Verlagsanstalt, 1978; new ed., Udo Tworuschka, Freiburg: Herder, 2001).

and absorb, integrate and reject elements of "primary" religion in different ways.[4]

However, in the present discourse of religious studies the term "founder of religion" does not play a significant role. Why not? One of the reasons might be that many of the so-called "founder-figures" did not intend to "found" a new religion; rather, they were outstanding "charismatics," "prophets," or "teachers" of their religion and became "founders" of a new religion only in their post-history through the process of their reception-history among their followers. In this respect, the term "founder of religion" has a reception-historical dimension.[5] The same is true for another term I am going to use following Mark R. Mullins, namely "minor founder."[6] This is a helpful designation for charismatic persons that became "founders" of new religious movements, schools, or sects in a tradition which already had its "main" founder. In Christianity figures like St. Francis of Assisi, Luther, Simon Kimbangu, or, in Japan, Uchimura Kanzo, the founder of Mukyôkai, belong to this category; in Japanese Buddhism Shinran and Nichiren might be called "minor founders." A third term that I want to propose is "final revealer" in order to designate founder-figures who wanted to surpass previous religions with their own founder figures. Examples in the West are Mani or Mohammed; one of many examples in the history of new Japanese religions is Kotama Okada, the founder of Mahikari. This term has no reception-historical dimensions, but it refers to the way founder figures saw themselves.

My second interest lies in a more general way in the similarities and differences in the earliest stage of development of religious movements[7] that later became a "new" religion.[8] Such similarities can include: (1) a de-

---

4. Theo Sundermeier, *Was ist Religion? Religionswissenschaft im theologischen Kontext* (ThB 96; Gütersloh: Chr. Kaiser, 1999), pp. 34-42, quotation p. 37.

5. Cf. Günter Risse, "Religionsstifter," in Hans Gasper et al. (eds.), *Lexikon der Sekten, Sondergruppen und Weltanschauungen* (Freiburg: Herder, 1990), p. 905.

6. Mark R. Mullins, "Christianity as a New Religion: Charisma, Minor Founders and Indigenous Movements," in idem, Susumu Shimazono, and Paul L. Swanson (eds.), *Religion and Society in Modern Japan* (Nanzan Institute for Religion and Culture; Berkeley: Asian Humanities Press, 1993), pp. 257-72.

7. I use the term "religious movement" in the very broad sense as it is used in modern sociology of religion; cf. e.g. Hubert Knoblauch, *Religionssoziologie* (SG 2094; Berlin: de Gruyter, 1999), esp. pp. 153-69.

8. More specific terms of Western sociology of religion, such as "church," "sect" (in the

velopment from a charismatic or prophetic beginning to a more institutionalized continuation; (2) a development from radical beginnings to a more adapted second stage; (3) the rise of a religion in a situation of social change, when new needs required new answers; (4) the mythologization or divinization of the founder; (5) a great missionary activity in the first phase; (6) a gradually growing interest in tradition, often resulting in the writing of a canon or the fixation of a doctrine; (7) the formation of institutionalized social forms of community that allowed the adherents to survive for a longer period; (8) the formation of basic rituals that were constitutive for the identity of the new community and its members, and the like.

Comparative studies of early Christianity with other nascent religions are important. They lead to the question of what kind of impacts different historical, social and cultural situations have on the birth of religions, and what could be more or less general in the process of the birth and early development of a new religion. For Christian theology, with its implicit tendencies to see Christianity as something unique, such a comparison offers important correctives.

My third interest has to do with Japan and the situation of Christian theology there. In order to explain this I have to make some basic explanations for a Western readership. Why do I choose newer Japanese religions for such a comparative study? Naturally, Japan is a wonderful country for this kind of study because the last two centuries have seen the rise of many really *new* religions. In this respect the situation in Japan is rather different both from Western Christian countries and from other countries in Eastern Asia. In Europe and partly also in North America most new religious movements[9] have a much more tradition-shaped identity. Most of them are either Christian or Muslim. Less self-evident is the fact that the situa-

---

sense of Ernst Troeltsch, Max Weber and Brian Wilson) or "denomination" should be applied to Japanese (or other non-European) religions only with great caution.

9. It is a question of interpretation whether the new forms of Christianity and the European forms of Islam should be called "new religions" or not. There are some analogies between religious developments in East Asia, Africa and Europe after the Second World War. Their basis is the decreasing strength of traditional institutionalized religions, increasing individualization and intensified global contacts. For the sake of clarity I propose to speak about a "new" religion only if there is: (1) a set of basic beliefs in a new composition; (2) a self-understanding of its adherents of being a new and different religion; (3) distinctive rituals. Most of these "new religions" have their "founders" or "minor founders," whose religious experiences have a lasting formative influence upon them.

tion in Japan is also very different from South Korea or China. Roughly speaking, one can say that in South Korea Christianity filled a similar religious vacuum to the one filled by the so-called "new religions" in Japan; today in China Christianity has excellent prospects of doing the same. Christianity started its modern history in Japan in the Meji era, around the middle of the nineteenth century, at about the same time when the successful history of the so-called "new religions" started. But unlike the "new religions," the history of the Christian mission in Japan cannot be called a success. The membership of Christian Churches hardly exceeds one percent of the population while the membership of "new religions" is estimated to be between 10 and 20% even by skeptics,[10] that is, by scholars distrusting the membership figures given by the new religions themselves.

What are the reasons for this development? They are complex. The main reason cannot be that Christianity requires an exclusive membership and traditional Japanese religions, Shinto and Buddhism, do not. There are successful new religions with a conversionist attitude that do demand an exclusive membership too, like Sôka Gakkai, and most new religions have something like a "soft" claim for exclusive membership, because they are basically monolatric. The main reason can also not be that Christianity was indigenized only to a comparatively small extent and basically remained a "foreign," "Western" religion. In Japan those Christian movements that tried to indigenize like "Mukyôkai" or "Christ Heart Church" were not successful either,[11] whereas in Korea the conservative Christians sticking faithfully to their Western mother-doctrines seem to be very successful. What is important is that, in Korea, Christianity had a great advantage because it was not Japanese and could form an oppositional identity over against the dominating colonial power Japan, whereas in Japan it was politically disadvantageous not to be "Japanese." Maybe the most important reason is that Christianity started as a middle- and upper-class religion of educated samurais and intellectuals looking for a new orientation,

10. Susumu Shimazono, *From Salvation to Spirituality: Popular Religious Movements in Modern Japan* (Melbourne: Trans Pacific Press, 2004), p. 4.

11. Cf. M. R. Mullins, "Christianity as a New Religion"; Mullins, "Christianity Transplanted: Towards a Sociology of Success and Failure," in Mullins and Richard F. Young (eds.), *Perspectives on Christianity in Korea and Japan: The Gospel and Culture in East Asia* (Lewiston etc.: Edwin Mellen, 1995), pp. 61-77, esp. pp. 65-68. Cf. also his comprehensive monograph: *Christianity Made in Japan: A Study of Indigenous Movements* (Honolulu: University of Hawaii, 1998).

whereas the new religions of the nineteenth century had their roots in the villages among the farmers. The social background of the clientele of new religions changed considerably in the twentieth century; they became predominantly urban religions, but Christianity remained the same. Yet another reason might be a mental one: Experts believe "this-worldly salvation" to be a basic characteristic of all new Japanese religions,[12] although this is not typically Japanese but also a widespread characteristic of modern Western mainstream Christianity. More accurate seems to me a formulation of a Japanese Christian observer: "The basic question of Japanese people encountering a religion is not: 'Is it true?' but 'what is it good for?'"[13] There could be many reasons for Christian theologians in Japan to study the phenomenon of the new native religions. However, hardly anyone does so; Japanese theology is almost exclusively occupied with studying its Mediterranean and European roots.

For me this was an incentive to do some research in this field during my four-month stay in Japan in 2004. But what a naive and unscholarly undertaking! How could I dare to do such a thing? I am neither an expert on Japan, nor on religious studies. Worse than this, I do not read Japanese. Only some sources and very little secondary literature exist in English, and practically nothing in any other Western language.[14] Many of my insights are based upon conversations with Japanese experts and with representatives of new religions, with or without translators. Among these experts I would particularly like to mention Prof. Susumu Shimazono of Tokyo University who devoted much of his time to satisfying my curiosity and answering my questions.[15]

But I have to repeat: What I am presenting here cannot claim to be a serious scholarly work. But this is the third reason why I dare to write such

---

12. E.g. Shimazono, *From Salvation to Spirituality*, p. 5.

13. Yasuo Furuya (orally).

14. In German, Werner Kohler, *Die Lotus-Lehre und die modernen Religionen in Japan* (Zürich: Atlantis, 1962) concentrates on neo-Buddhist new religions. A very helpful newer survey can be found in Johannes Laube (trans. and ed.), *Neureligionen: Stand ihrer Erforschung in Japan: Ein Handbuch* (StOR 31; Wiesbaden: Harrassowitz, 1995), pp. 238-69 (this is a partly updated German translation of a corresponding Japanese "handobukku" of 1981).

15. Besides him, I want to thank Mr. Shinji Yamada (Konkôkyô-Center Tôkyô), Prof. Migaku Sato (Rikkyo University Tokyo), Dr. Katsumi Shimada (Tenri University) and Prof. Axel Michaels (Heidelberg) for reading my manuscript and making helpful comments.

a comparative study: I think that I am doing things that Japanese theologians should do, but they do not. So let me be their unworthy forerunner and encourage them to do what I now try to do, in a better and more academically grounded way than I am able to do.

It soon became clear to me that I had to concentrate upon the oldest of the "new" religions, those originating in the nineteenth century, namely Nyoraikyô, Tenrikyô, and Konkôkyô. The reasons are the following:

1. In the new religions of the nineteenth century we find a full analogy to what we call "religion" in the West, namely comprehensive, holistic systems of beliefs, rituals, piety, and praxis based upon the experience of a transworldly reality and encompassing the whole of human existence and world-interpretation.[16]

2. In the new religions, from the nineteenth century on, the normal social form is that of a local *"kô,"* i.e. a community based upon personal commitment and individual and voluntary membership.[17] This "community" tends to be responsible for all the religious needs of its members and tends to shape the whole of their lives. This was different in earlier centuries; to belong to a Buddhist "shu"[18] was mainly a matter of family tradition. To belong to a Shinto-shrine depends only on the geographical proximity of a shrine. With the new religions a new social form of membership comes into being.

3. In the "new religions" of the nineteenth century, there is not yet a visible Christian influence. This is different in many of the twentieth-century new religions, particularly in those that came into being after the Second World War.

4. The new religions, from the nineteenth century on, tend to divinize their founder or foundress and share the idea that he or she is "present" in

16. According to Migaku Sato, the Japanese word used presently for "religion," namely "shûkyô" (originally "the most important teaching"), was not used in this way before 1870/1880. It was only after that time that the "Way of Buddha" (Jap. Butsudô) and the "Way of the Gods" (Jap. Shintô) were interpreted as "religion" and Buddhism was now called "Bukkyô."

17. Prof. Michihito Tsushima (Kwansei Gakuin University, Nishinomiya) characterizes (orally) a "kô" as association on a local level, with usually no entrance requirements; however, commitment and "exercise" by the members is demanded that sometimes gives the "kô" type of religions a conversionist character. This comes close to the "sect" type of Western sociology of religion, but is not identical with it.

18. The usual translation with "sect" is not very appropriate. A "shu" is rather a traditional religious "school" which includes ritual functions.

their communities till the present day. I have the impression (but I am not sure) that the relation to the founder in the new religions is different from the significance a founder-figure like Dogen or Shinran had for the various Buddhist schools in earlier times.[19] This provides a strong analogy to Christianity and its divinization of Jesus, in spite of the fact that the transcendence of God in Jewish/Christian contexts is different from what the Japanese call "kami."

5. As a general rule we can say that new religions that are primarily based upon Shinto traditions do have their own canon, while new religions that are primarily based upon Buddhist, mostly Nichiren-shu, traditions have one of the classical Buddhist texts, mostly the Lotus-Sutra, as a canonical text and their own literature has rather a "commentary-like" character in the widest possible sense. Because Christianity did develop its own canon the former group of new religions will provide closer analogies than the latter.

These are the reasons why I concentrated my interest primarily on Nyoraikyô, Tenrikyô, and Konkôkyô. Let me start with some general remarks.

Nyoraikyô, Tenrikyô, and Konkôkyô

Nyoraikyô is the oldest of the so-called new religions. Its foundress was a simple and poor servant woman named Kino Isson (1756-1826) who lived in a village in the Nagoya region. She experienced a very hard life and became a medium of the Supreme Being, Nyorai. Following the summary of Shimazono, Kino "ended her days in the world as the sin-redeeming Lord . . . who suffered tribulations and . . . is now worshiped, revered and prayed to as 'Ryuzen Nyorai.'"[20] Nyoraikyô is characterized by a strong consciousness of original sin, a negative outlook towards this world, a transworldly concept of salvation into a Paradise, and the concept of vicarious salvation through others, not self-salvation. It is not surprising that the analogies to Christianity were felt to be very striking when scholars discovered this se-

19. Susumu Shimazono, "The Living Kami Idea in the New Religions of Japan," *JJRS* 6 (1979): 389-412, finds a reduced importance of the salvific function of the founder in the time after his death. However, according to my observations it remains very high.

20. Shimazono, *Salvation to Spirituality*, p. 14; more information in: Hideo Kanda, "Religious Thought of Nyoraikyo," *TJR* 22 (1988): 59-89.

cluded religious group early in the twentieth century. However, Kirishitan[21] influence is rather unlikely in these early pre-Meji years when the surviving Kirishitan lived in secrecy. Nyoraikyô would have been very interesting for me; however, I had to abandon the idea of including it in this study because I could not establish any contacts with its "churches."

The foundress of *Tenrikyô*[22] is also a woman, Miki Maegawa (*1798), known after her marriage as Miki Nakayama. Her family was a middle-class farmer's family living in the area of Yamato, south of Nara. Her father taught her to write and she visited an elementary school; this was far from usual, not only because she was a girl, but also because literacy among the farmers was looked at rather negatively by the ruling daimyo class in the Tokugawa era. After her marriage to the farmer Zenbei Nakayama at the age of twelve, she became a devoted housewife and mother. In 1838, when both her eldest son and her husband were seriously ill and the local shaman was not available, Miki became "the shrine" of the supreme God "Tsukihi" (Moon-Sun) and from that time on she acted as a mediator of God for family members and villagers. Upon the command to "fall into the depths of poverty" she gave away all her personal possessions and eventually even dismantled their family-house. Later she practiced a ritual of "safe child birth" and other rituals of healing.

It was not until the early 1860s that Miki attracted a greater number of followers and started to construct a new religion. Fellowships of followers in different places came into being, the construction of a place of service started, and the songs and rituals for two fundamental ritual services,

21. Kirishitan = the "hidden" Christians whose existence goes back to the mission of the sixteenth and earlier seventeenth century, living mainly in Kyushu.

22. Official biography of the foundress: *The Life of Oyasama, foundress of Tenrikyô* (Tenri: Tenrikyô Church Headquarters, 1996), mainly based upon a biography written by her successor. The canon of Tenrikyô: *Ofudesaki: The Tip of the Writing Bush* (Tenri: Tenrikyô Church Headquarters, 1993); *Mikagura-uta: The Songs for the Service* (Tenri: Tenrikyô Church Headquarters, 1999). History, doctrine and theology: Tenrikyô Church Headquarters (ed.), *The Doctrine of Tenrikyô* (Tenri, 2002 = translation of Tenrikyô Kyoten, 1984, the official doctrine of Tenrikyô); Tenrikyô Overseas Mission Department (ed.), *An Introduction to Tenrikyô: Its History and Teachings* (Tenri: Tenrikyô Church Headquarters, 1966); Oyasato Research Institute, Tenri University (ed.), *The Theological Perspectives of Tenrikyô* (Tenri: Tenri University Press, 1986); *Tenrikyô: The Path to Joyousness* (Tenri: Tenrikyô Overseas Mission Department, 1998); *Tenrikyô-Christian Dialogue* (Tenri: Tenri University Press, 1999 = documents of a Symposium held at the Gregorian University in Rome).

kagura[23] and *teodori,* were composed and collected in the *Mikagura-uta,* one of the canonical books of Tenrikô.

From 1869 on Miki started to write the *Ofudesaki,* a collection of Divine utterances in metaphorical language and poetical form. In 1875 she identified the place of the *kanrodai,* the holy stone marking the place from which the world was created. Through followers who came to visit Miki from far away and through active mission, the new religion spread as far as Tokyo during the lifetime of Miki. The last years were marked by persecutions and harassments by the police.

Miki insisted on public celebration of the basic rituals that she thought to be essential for the salvation of the world even without official recognition. At the time of her death in 1887 all the basic institutions of the new religion were completed and her grandson was appointed as her successor. Official recognition as a Shinto sect was reached in 1908. Today there are about two million members of Tenrikô in Japan and other, mainly Asian, countries. After a first period of a dual leadership by a charismatic and an institutional leader,[24] Tenrikô now has become a centralized religious body under the sole leadership of the "Shimbashira" (a descendant of the foundress) with the central sanctuary in Tenri (at the site of the former Nakayama family home) where the salvation-bringing rituals are performed.

Bunjirô is the founder of *Konkôkyô.*[25] He was born in 1814 as the son of a small farmer in a village in Western Honshu, and was adopted by the Kawate (Akazawa) family, also farmers, and given his name. His father

---

23. A "re-enactment . . . of God the Parent's workings during creation" (*Teachings* [n. 22], p. 14).

24. In the first decades after Miki's death there was a spiritual leader besides the Shimbashira, the "honseki" (= "true seat") Iburi Izo, whose mediations with God were collected in the *Osashizu.* However, this dual leadership system was later discontinued.

25. Official biography of the founder: *Konko Daijin: A Biography* (Konko Churches of America, San Francisco: Morosi, 1981). The canon of Konkôkyô : (1) *Oshirase-goto oboe-cho,* revelations received by Konko Daijin (Konko: Konkôkyô honbu, 1996); (2) *Konko Daijin oboegaki,* memoirs of Konko Daijin (Konko: Konkôkyô honbu, 1989); (3) *Gorikai I,* teachings of Konko Daijin, recorded by his disciples (Konko: Konkôkyô honbu, 1987); (4) *Gorikai II* (Konko: Konkôkyô honbu, 1987); (5) *Gorikai III* (Konko: Konkôkyô honbu, 1983). An earlier book is Delwin B. Schneider, *Konkôkyô: A Japanese Religion* (Tokyo: ISR, 1962); the author is Christian. Cf. also Willis Stoesz, "The Universal Attitude of Konko Daijin," *JJRS* 13 (1986): 3-29.

died early. Bunji took over responsibility for the family, married, and had children.

Their life was more or less typical until 1855, when Bunji Akazawa came to realize, during a critical illness, that a deity named Konjin, generally thought to be an evil demon, is in reality the loving and helping parent- and creator-God. From 1858 on Bunji began to speak the words of "Tenchi Kane no Kami," the parent God of the universe. He developed more and more a very personal relation to this God. Instead of ritual prescriptions about directions and purities, a personal relationship with God, faith, prayers, and "single-heartedness" became the center of his piety.[26]

Gradually Bunji retired from farming and acted as a mediator to God. Many villagers and more and more people from far away visited him in a special room of his house *(hiromae)* where he mediated their questions and problems to God and God's answers to them *(toritsugi)*. The Divine answers were sober, clear, practical, always insisting on sincerity, confidence, gratitude to God and patience. In modern terminology, we might call what Bunji did "counseling."

In 1868, he was allowed to have the name "Ikigami (= living god) Konko Daijin," which is explained in the official biography not as mythical deification, but as a "description given to one who expressed divine virtue through his deeds."[27] In 1883, Bunji died peacefully. His third surviving son, Ieyoshi, became his successor in performing toritsugi. The canon of Konkôkyô consists of five parts; two of them were written by Konko-Daijin himself in a very simple prosaic style (records of revelations and memoirs), the other three are memoirs by his pupils in the form of sayings and apophthegms. Today, Konkôkyô is a religious body with 400,000-500,000 members, family-based, open and tolerant, with an emphasis on collective leadership, democratic structures and a church life which — except for some ceremonies — resembles that of a Protestant parish in many respects.

---

26. Cf. Gorikai III Konko Kyoso Gorikai 26: "You do not need anyone else to practice faith with. You should practice faith on your own."

27. *Konko Daijin* (n. 25), p. 69.

Ulrich Luz

Analogies to Jesus in the Lives and Teachings of the Founders

Social Background

Like the historical Jesus, Miki and Bunji come from the lower classes of their societies; they were farmers, but not from the poorest segment of the farmer-class.[28] Farmers, the large majority of the Japanese population, were severely oppressed in the Tokugawa period, and afterwards they passed through a very difficult time of transition in the Meji period. Their oppression with high taxation (40-50% of the harvest), other taxes, forced labor, duty of residence, conscriptions, strict prescriptions concerning cultivation, clothes and food, etc., reached its peak in the late Tokugawa period and led to frequent famines and revolts.[29]

The new central Meji-government was formally a liberation for farmers; the rigid class system was abolished and freedom of residence was introduced. Even so, taxation became even harsher because now taxes had to be paid in money according to the size of land owned, regardless of the size of the harvest, and not in kind. Many farmers lost their land and became tenants or urban proletariat.[30] Mikiso Hane characterizes the situation of the farmers in the Meji period as one of "pain, bewilderment and anger."[31]

The parallels between their situation and that of the small farmers and tenants in Roman Palestine in the time of Jesus — also a time of transition and growing economic prosperity and urbanization whose victims were the small farmers — are obvious. Like Jesus, Miki and Bunji do not belong to the well-educated elites, but some kind of literacy on a lower level was available to them. I assume this is also possible in the case of Jesus in spite of the fact that we have only legendary Lukan testimonies to it — Luke 2:41-52; 4:16-21. Like Jesus, Miki and Bunji were natives of small villages.

Both Miki and Bunji can be understood against the background of a process of growing self-awareness of the farmers, who became conscious

28. This is true for Jesus too, who as son of a carpenter did not belong to the poorest of the poor.

29. Mikiso Hane, *Peasants, Rebels and Outcasts: The Underside of Modern Japan* (New York: Pantheon Books, 1982), pp. 6-9. Hane reckons with about 2800 bigger or smaller revolts of farmers in the Tokugawa period between 1590 and 1867.

30. Hane, *Peasants,* pp. 17-23.

31. Hane, *Peasants,* p. 21.

of the necessity to make individual decisions and tended to emancipate themselves from traditional value systems towards greater individuation and higher self-esteem. In the case of Konkôkyô the social background is very clear: all kinds of everyday problems for ordinary people, such as sickness, family problems, child-birth, problems of harvest and small businesses, were brought before Konko Daijin and became the subject of prayer.

A large part of the canon consists of concrete memories of toritsugi recorded by clients who became pupils of Bunji (Gorikai I-III). In the canon of Tenrikyô this is less directly visible, but the importance of a safe birth and of healings in Tenrikyô is evident. Both Tenrikyô and Konkôkyô were new religious groups, where everyone was accepted and where everyone could take over responsibility and leadership.

Voluntary Poverty

In terms of voluntary poverty, only Miki Nakayama provides an analogy to Jesus. Following the divine commandment, she gave away all her possessions in a very impressive way for the sake of the poor, even dismantling her own house, an action that met much resistance from her family. Particularly after the death of her husband she lived with her children in extremely penurious conditions. The interpretation of her life in extreme poverty in Tenrikyô is not unilinear and includes both the dimension of charity and turning away from worldly things.[32] A certain antagonism towards rich and powerful people, symbolized as "high mountains," is to be felt in many words:

> Until now, the high mountains, boastful, have thrived and done as they pleased in every matter. But from now on, I, Tsukihi, shall do as I please instead.[33]

The mission among rich people had evidently been unsuccessful,[34] but they will not be excluded, because "all people in the world are my children."[35]

32. Cf. *Path to Joyousness* (n. 22), pp. 7-8.
33. Ofudesaki VI 72-73; cf. also XV 56.
34. Ofudesaki III 140.
35. Ofudesaki XV 68.

Ulrich Luz

The affinities with and differences from the Palestinian Jesus Movement are obvious. Most notable among the differences is that there is hardly any eschatological dimension in Tenrikyô[36] and that Miki's voluntary poverty did not take the form of itinerancy. Indeed, quite the opposite: the place where she lived has an extremely high religious significance for her and Tenrikyô.

Women Founded Nyoraikyô, Kino Isson, and Tenrikyô

Rural women were almost totally unprivileged in Japan until the twentieth century. They were under the authority of the elder and male members of the families into which they had been married. Their duty was to work, to serve, and to give birth to as many children as possible (but only to a limited extent to educate them!).[37] Women are totally equal as disciples in Tenrikyô:

> Of these trees, I do not say whether male pine or female pine.
> Tsukihi has an intention for any tree.[38]

The first missionary of Tsukihi was Miki's daughter Kokan who went to Osaka as a street-missionary. Among those who visited Konko Daijin, asking for advice and help, were many women.[39] Note this saying: "Women are closer to Kami. Faith starts with a woman."[40]

However, both in Konkôkyô and Tenrikyô the successors of the founders were male members of the founder's family. In the case of Tenrikyô the change from the female foundress to male dominance is particularly conspicuous, in spite of the fact that female priesthood is main-

---

36. Comment by Dr. Katsumi Shimada, Tenri: "I would say that there is no clear eschatology in Miki's thought itself, but some people who were influenced by Miki's thought did seem to have eschatological views after Miki's death and some of them . . . left Tenrikyô for their eschatological views and eventually started their own factional activities."

37. For the situation of Japanese rural women in the twentieth century, cf. Hane, *Peasants*, pp. 78ff.

38. Ofudesaki 7:21.

39. According to checks by Shinji Yamada about one third. "Considering the transportation, travel expense and other conditions in these times I think that it is not a low rate" (letter of March 31, 2005).

40. Gorikai I. Shimamura Hachitaro 20.

tained in local churches and female participation is maintained in rituals on all levels. It is possible to interpret the first history of Nyoraikyô and Tenrikyô as part of an emancipation history of underprivileged women who find their own ways of expression. The analogies in the history of Jesus and early Christianity are obvious.

Healings

For Miki and Bunji — and after them for many new Japanese religions up until today — healings were a central part of their mission. "Healing" does not necessarily mean spectacular and complete healings in one moment, but more often the inauguration of a process of healing through prayer and in sincere faith. In the case of Miki Nakayama a blessing-ritual for safe childbirth was the origin of her healing mission; the "sazuke," a kind of empowerment-ritual for members entitled to heal, plays an important role in Tenrikyô.[41] Diseases were widely believed to be the result of demonic possession in the popular religious belief of the time; however in the Ofudesaki, Miki Nakayama expresses a new understanding: sickness for her has an educational purpose and is ultimately an expression of God's love:

> Illness and pain of whatever kind do not exist.
> They are none other than the hastening and guidance of God.[42]

Bunji Akazawa healed many people through prayers which initiated a healing process.

> Since we have been created by Kami, isn't asking Kami to cure our illnesses a natural way to practice faith?[43]

Except for "toritsugi," the ritual of mediation to God, and the use of sacred sake and sacred rice by many believers, there seems to be little emphasis on special healing rituals in Konkôkyô. God's messages to those seeking cures

41. *Life* (n. 22), pp. 28ff.
42. Ofudesaki II 7, cf. I 25 (illness = anger of God); II 22 (illnesses are road signs of guidance by God); III 78 (illness = regret of God, when people neglect works of salvation); IV 25 (illness = God's call to service); XIV 21 (illness = care of Tsukihi).
43. Gorikai I Yamamoto Sadajiro 21,4.

for sick people in the canonical text document an impressive combination of realism and optimism expressed in prayers from sincere hearts.[44]

In contrast to the Evangelists' reports of Jesus' exorcisms, I did not find any stories of exorcisms in Japan's new religions (although the "administration of Sazuke" in Tenrikyô has some similarity to exorcisms). This corresponds to the fact that illnesses are never interpreted in dualistic categories as possessions by evil powers.

Teachings

In their teachings there are remarkable affinities between Konko Daijin and Jesus. For both, rituals are only of secondary importance; both advocate inner and not external purity.[45] In the ethical teaching of Konko Daijin there are many parallels with the Gospels, especially the Sermon on the Mount.[46] In comparison to this, the ritual-centered piety of Miki Nakayama is rather different from Jesus.

Persecutions

It seems a rather common experience that founders and foundresses of religions meet resistance and are persecuted. In Japan the Meji government wanted to control all religious movements and was very restrictive in recognizing new religions as Shinto sects. In the case of Miki Nakayama, she met severe resistance from government officials. She was imprisoned several times, and her model of steadfastness was very effective for her followers.[47] Bunjiro Akazawa met some resistance too, but he generally tended to be more submissive.

---

44. An example is Gorikai II Akiyama Kinoe 1.

45. Cf. Gorikai I Ichimura Mitsugoro 2:2; Gorikai I Yamamoto Sadajiro 22:2.

46. Compare Matt 5:21-22 with Gorikai II Sato Mirusjiro 27:1-2; Matt 5:38ff. with Gorikai II Kataoka Jiroshiro 3; Matt 5:42 with Gorikai II Kashiwara Toku 6; Matt 6:7-8 with Gorikai III Konko Kyoso Gorikai 68:2; Matt 10:39 with Gorikai I Shimamura Hachitaro 28; Matt 15:1ff. with Gorikai I Shimamura Hachitaro 25; Matt 25:31ff with Gorikai III Jinkyu Kyogoroku 168; Mark 11:23 with Gorikai I Ogihara Sugi 17; Mark 12:41ff. with Gorikai III Naiden 2:2.

47. *Life* (n. 22), p. 170ff.

Divine Indwelling in the Founders

The point of departure in both religions is a type of shamanistic belief in the divine power of Shamans who were responsible, e.g., for healing possessed people. In the life of both Miki Nakayama and Bunji Akazawa this concept was transformed in an interesting but different way. Miki Nakayama became the permanent "shrine" for Tsukihi. Her possession by God was very intensive; seemingly, when God did speak through her she was not conscious of herself.[48]

> These thoughts of Tsukihi are spoken through her:
> The mouth is human, the mind is that of Tsukihi.[49]

In Ofudesaki there is an interesting mixture between I-words of Tsukihi, words where the I of the speaker is different from Tsukihi, and I-words full of divine authority where Tsukihi is not mentioned.[50] My impression is that Miki did write down her messages in a spirit of full functional identity of herself with Tsukihi. She was dressed very unusually in red clothes:

> What do you think of these red clothes?
> Tsukihi dwells within.[51]

The official "Teaching" of Tenrikyô formulates: "Oyasama is Tsukihi on earth and the Parent of humankind."[52]

The case of Bunji Akazawa is different. His first fundamental experience, that the presumed evil demon Konjin is in reality a loving and gracious universal God, is not the result of an inspiration, but of a reflection. Bunji, during a severe illness, opposed the opinion of a relative.[53] I have the impression that his later revelations do not have a primarily ecstatic character, in spite of an "unusual behavior" while he spoke in the name of Kami.[54] In Oboegaki and Oshirase-goto,[55] Konko Daijin never formulates Kami's

---

48. *Life* (n. 22), p. 6.
49. Ofudesaki XII:67.
50. Cf. e.g. 6:73 with 6:74-75 or 6:67-69 or with 6:78-81.
51. Ofudesaki VI 63.
52. Doctrine (n. 22), p. 11.
53. *Konko Daijin* (n. 25), pp. 16-18.
54. *Konko Daijin* (above n. 25), p. 20.
55. Cf. above n. 25.

words as his own words, but makes a clear distinction as in Old Testament prophecy. In many sayings he is addressed in the second person by God. In Gorikai II a resistance against his divinization is visible. He himself says:

> I am not an ikigami. I am a manure carrier. Praying to Tenchi Kane No Kami is fine. I just mediate to Kami.

But in the following revelation of Kami we hear different accents:

> It is only because of Konko Daijin that Tenchi Kane No Kami's blessings can now be received.

Because Konko Daijin has revealed to the people that Konjin is a benevolent and gracious deity,

> Kami is indebted to Konko Daijin. . . . Konko Daijin is the savior for Kami and people. Give your requests to Konko Daijin.

Interestingly enough in this dialogue the founder has the last word. He protests openly against God:

> Though you have just heard the words of Kami-Sama, I am only Kami's caretaker. So even if you pray to me, you will not receive divine blessings.[56]

In spite of the fact that he is mediator and revealer of Kami, Bunji remains a very sober and clear person. The center of his piety is prayer and faith in a God who is different from him. The realization of the benevolent nature of the deity Konjin — his basic religious experience — was not the result of any kind of special experience or inspiration, but an insight gained from a dialogue: "Kami thinks only of saving people, nothing else."[57] This is the basis of his personal piety and of what one could call his "pious optimism."

I think that there is an affinity between Bunji Akazawa and Old Testament prophets, in spite of the fact that the content of their messages is very different. Miki Nakayama is comparable with various types of inspiration in Hellenism and Hellenistic Judaism, but also with New Testament

56. Gorikai II Kondo Fujimori 3:1-4.
57. Gorikai III Jinkyu Kyogoroku 12.

prophets, who occasionally use the "I" of the exalted Lord, and with the concept of inspiration in the *Odes of Solomon*.[58]

Families

Finally, I want to add one point where the difference between the lives of our founders and Jesus is a total one. This is their relation to their families. Miki Nakayama is embedded in family structures. She is a wonderful wife, a perfect mother, and always surrounded by her family. All her decisions have to be supported by her family. Her succession after her death is regulated within her family. All her children become her adherents. The same is true for Bunji Akazawa, and later for most Japanese new religions. The case of Jesus is quite different. He is a runaway son of his family (Mark 3:31-35) and not married. Following Jesus could involve the rupture of family ties in different forms (Mark 1:20; 10:29-30; Q 9:59; 14:26). In light of the strong family ties of Mediterranean culture in antiquity this is extraordinary. This is also one of the main reasons why the process of institutionalizing the new religions in Japan was rather different from early Christianity; both in Konkôkyô and Tenrikyô, and in almost all other Japanese new religions, the leadership of the religious body remained in the hands of the family of the founder.

Postmortal Existence of the Founders and "Founder-ology"

The Death of the Founder

Only in Tenrikyô is there a faint analogy to an atoning force that is analogous to Jesus and the force of his death upon his followers. Because Miki had prophesied that she would live to the age of 115, her "early" death at the age of 90 had to be explained by her followers. One explanation was that God had shortened her life in order to save his children in the whole world.[59] But there is no further explanation of Miki's failure to live to 115.

---

58. Cf. 42:6: "Then I arose and am with them/and will speak by their mouths." Translation by Charlesworth in *OTP* 2.771.

59. *Life* (n. 22), p. 240 = Osahizu 18.2.1887; Shimazono, *Salvation* (n. 10), 137.

Ulrich Luz

The Afterlife of the Founders

In "Doctrine of Tenrikyô," we read about the foundress: "She withdrew from physical life, yet remains alive now and forever at the Residence of Origin, with the portals open, protecting humankind day and night and shedding Her infinite, parental love on each of us."[60] That Miki remains spiritually at her residence of origin is characteristic for Tenrikyô, for which the central sanctuary in Tenri with the holy place kanrodai is of extreme importance.[61] A visit to Tenri shows that this permanent presence of the foundress in the central shrine of Tenrikyô is thought about very concretely: she keeps her room, gets her meals every day, etc. This does not exclude a kind of omnipresence, at least in popular belief.[62]

In Konko faith, there is no idea of a continuing physical presence of the founder at one specific place. Konko Daijin himself expects a kind of omnipresence for his afterlife: "Having a physical body makes it difficult for me to see people's suffering in the world. When my body is gone, I can go to where I am requested and save people."[63] He also expects a deification after his death, which goes beyond his being "kami" already during his earthly existence; he will be "true kami" after his death.[64] Konkôkyô adherents believe "that the founder is alive as a kami of Toritsugi and . . . recite his name 'Konko-Sama' to ask for his Toritsugi when they are in need (at anytime, any places, and for any matters)."[65] This corresponds to the early Christian concept of the exalted Christ as heavenly intercessor (Rom 8:34; 1 John 2:1 etc.).

How does all this relate to early "Christian" ideas about the resurrection of Jesus and the continuing presence of the exalted Lord within the Jesus Movement in and outside Palestine? There are differences, naturally. One difference is that the transition of the founder to a new quality of existence is not conceived of as a special "event" after his death. There also seems to be no idea of spatial transcendence of the founders in the sense of

60. *Doctrine* (n. 22), 11.

61. "Sah, sah, I am still living here. I have not gone anywhere, not gone anywhere!" (Osashizu, 17.3.1890, in *Life*, pp. 241-42).

62. Theologians in Tenri told me hesitatingly that some people even buy an additional train ticket for Miki Nakayama when they undertake a missionary journey.

63. Gorikai II, Karahi Tsunezo 4.

64. Gorikai I, Shimamura Hachitaro 11.

65. Shinji Yamada, letter of March 31, 2005.

248

an ascension to an otherworldly heaven. In spite of this, the similarities are striking. Both in early Christianity and in these new Japanese religions we find a belief in a very special everlasting presence of the founder which is an expression of his unique salvific function.

Founder as Model

A very significant analogy between Tenrikyô and the early Jesus Movement is that the life of the founder became a model. Tenrikyô has edited an official biography of Miki Nakayama in order "to appreciate and practice the Divine Model of Oyasama, which is the aim of our faith."[66] This is a kind of "Tenrikyô-Gospel." It contains many legends and apophthegms illustrating her loving kindness, her mercy, her generosity, her devotion to her husband and parents-in-law, her faithfulness in persecution and trials, etc. A further striking analogy is that the model-function of the foundress is extended back to her childhood, long before the time of her activity as a shrine of Tsukihi. This has an analogy in the Infancy Gospels in Matthew and Luke.

In Konkôkyô, it is less the model character of the life of Konko Daijin that is emphasized[67] than his central function as a revealer: "Listening to him and following his words are the same as listening to and following Kami's words."[68]

Titles

The fourth point is the titles of Jesus and of the founders of new religions. Miki Nakayama is normally called "Oyasama" which is translated as "our beloved Parent." Since the name of her Kami, Tsukihi, was later changed into "Oya" (parents) the proximity, if not identity, between God and his shrine Miki is very clear in this title.

Bunji Akazawa was addressed as "Ikigami Konko Daijin" which desig-

---

66. *Life* (n. 22), preface.

67. The Japanese original of the official biography of Konko Daijin was only published in 1953 and has the character of a popular historical biography. It is not "sacred scripture."

68. Gorikai I, Kondo Fujimori 71:2.

Ulrich Luz

nates Bunji as living God and mediator. This title was given to him in 1868 by Kami, the last of several honorific divine titles.[69] I am not fully informed about the significance of such honorific titles in Japanese religious culture, and therefore I simply want to point to one important difference: all Christological titles attributed to Jesus were attributed to him after his death and resurrection.[70] The Japanese founders received their titles during their lifetime.

Missionary Religions

The next point is not directly related to the after-life of the founder and will be touched on only briefly: both Tenrikyô and Konkôkyô were missionary religions from their beginnings. Universalism in their understanding of the parent-God and missionary activity are closely related.

The Intent to Found a New Religion

Let me add one last remark which I cannot omit, concerning a point I find extremely puzzling: Kino Isson, Miki Nakayama, and Bunjiro Akazawa really wanted to found a new religion,[71] and this is true for all founders of Japanese new religions. They installed their successors and institutionalized the rituals and the structure of their movements. Miki Nakayama even wrote the Ofudesaki with the intention of writing a canonical text. This is very striking, because neither Jesus nor Buddha Shakyamuni wanted to be "founders" of a new religion; they only became so after their deaths. How did Miki, Bunji and their predecessor Kino Isson come to "found" a new religion? This is for me something quite extraordinary and

69. Oshirase goto 8:5; 10:5; 12:14. "Konko" seems to be an artificial word-construction, consisting of "kon" (from "Tenchi *kane* no kami," the name under which Konjin is venerated, and "ko" = light; Gorikai II Konko Hagio 21). "Konko" was already used as a family name by Bunji and became the name of Otani, his village, also.

70. I assume that "the son of the man" did not function as a title either for Jesus himself, or for the Post-Easter Church.

71. I note a critical objection by Prof. Shimazono to this point: "This seems to me an exaggeration. Here the concept of 'religion' must be considered critically. This may not be their own concept but our own."

far from being self-evident. The experience of the "newness" of their encounter with God must have been extremely strong.[72] In the case of Kino Isson her God was a hitherto insignificant deity of the Buddhist pantheon. In the case of Bunji, his God was an evil demon who became something entirely different in Bunji's interpretation. Miki's God Tsukihi seems to have been a new deity. The case of Jesus is very different: he proclaimed a new message from the well-known and faithful God of Israel. The historical Jesus, by no means, intended to found a new religion.

Concluding Remarks and Questions

Analogies between Jesus and his movement and the two Japanese founders of new religions are evident on the socio-historical level in their origin in a situation of transition and social tension and in their roots among ordinary lower-class people. The experiences of "crisis" which are encountered by all three religions are not only and probably not primarily on a cognitive or emotional level,[73] but on a very concrete level of ordinary daily life.

Analogies between Jesus and the two Japanese founder figures and their religious movements exist also on the level of beliefs, piety and praxis. Here I would like to mention:

The monolatric faith: Miki Nakayama and Bunji Akazawa are advocates of a *functional monotheism;* other Gods are, according to Miki Nakayama, only "instruments of the one true God."[74] Konko Dajin does not deny the existence of other deities, but prays only to Kenchi Kane No Kami.

Together with this goes their *universalism:* because God is the Lord, or the body of the whole world, *all* human beings are children of God. God is the parent of all people according to Tenrikyô and Konkôkyô.[75]

---

72. Cf. Miki Nakayama/Tsukihi about Kagura-Service: "I shall begin a Service which has never existed since I began this world" (Ofudesaki 6:8).

73. Cf. Gerd Theissen, *Die Religion der ersten Christen* (Gütersloh: Gütersloher Verlagshaus, 2000), p. 30. Theissen points to cognitive experiences of crisis met by religions such as border-line experiences like death or to emotional experiences of crisis such as fear or guilt. However for early Christianity, Konkôkyô and Tenrikyô the significance of the new religion for dealing with various forms of external experiences of crisis, such as sickness, poverty etc., should not be underestimated.

74. Ofudesaki 6:50.

75. Ofudesaki 4:62.79; cf. 13:43; Gorikai II Sato Mitsujiro 12; 14:3; Gorikai II Shinkun 1:5.

Corresponding with the new religious experience is an *emphasis on individual and personal piety:* in Konkôkyô "faith" is emphasized, in Tenrikyô "sincerity," and in both religions "single-heartedness." The new religions — and Christianity in its beginnings and in various later stages of its history — played an eminent role in what I would call the conscientization- and individuation-process of so-called ordinary people.

In all three religions the *person of the founder became an integral and constitutive part of their faith and life.*

In all three religions the social body of a *"community"* ("kô") with close fellowship, based upon individual decision[76] and personal commitment, was the result of the founder's or foundress's mission. In all three religious movements a subsequent development towards something like an "established sect" and a "denomination" took place.[77]

All three religions developed very strong *missionary activities* as a consequence of the newness and the universal claim of their basic religious experience.

And finally: In all three cases the experiences, the biography and the teaching of the founder or foundress became the basis of a *comprehensive system of beliefs, rituals, and praxis* which formed the "new" identity of its followers and made other "religions" virtually superfluous.[78]

All these analogies are not identities, but they are conspicuous. Therefore I close this reflection with an open question: Can the seven analogies mentioned here be taken as characteristics of a special type of religion, called "founded religions" by Gustav Mensching and others?[79] This term is not highly valued in today's religious studies, but it seems to be important in order to understand many religions, including Christianity, and for inter-religious dialogue.

Jesus, Miki Nakayama and Bunji Akazawa were "founders" of new religions in similar, but not identical, senses. The main difference between Jesus and our two Japanese charismatic figures is that the latter institutu-

---

76. In the categories of Brian Wilson, a "sect" of the evangelistic and conversionist type.

77. For the terms cf. Günter Kehrer, "Religionssoziologie," *Handbuch religionswissenschaftlicher Grundbegriffe* (5 vols.; ed. Hubert Cancik et al.; Stuttgart: Kohlhammer, 1988), vol. 1, p. 85.

78. Naturally the attitude to other religions is very different, mainly exclusive and intolerant in the case of early Christianity, and mainly tolerant and "co-existent" in the case of Konkôkyô and Tenrikyô.

79. Cf. Mensching, *Vergleichende Religionswissenschaft* (n. 1), pp. 150ff.

tionalized their religious movements themselves, whereas Jesus the Jew was far from founding a "new" religion. The differences, however, are not absolute: there are good reasons to assume that Jesus wanted the circle of his disciples and followers to continue their task of the proclamation of the Kingdom of God beyond his own death.[80] Neither of the three can be called a "final redeemer" in the proper sense of the word, but at least Miki and Jesus seem to have had a (very different!) consciousness of the "final" and unsurpassable character of their own mission.[81]

Another important question is when and where in the history of religions charismatic persons who wanted to be founder figures or were taken as such in their post-history do appear. My guess is that this is often the case in situations where traditional religious institutions (e.g. temples, shrines, traditional churches, and denominations) and collective bearers of religious identity (e.g. "nations," families) could no longer meet the needs of people becoming conscious of their own identity. This could be true for the Japanese farmers in relation to the "family-religion" Buddhism and the rituals performed in traditional "Shinto" piety in the nineteenth century and for the Galilean "people of the land" in their relation to Jewish institutions and their representatives.

Beyond these remarks I want to close with the personal note that Bunji Akazawa has become a very impressive person for me as a Protestant theologian. Not only his discovery of the grace of God[82] as the basis of his very personal faith- and prayer-centered piety, but also his very liberal and open attitude towards other religions,[83] his emphasis on inner purity, his rejection of sacred places,[84] his ethics, his institutionalization of the system of toritsugi (which is a nineteenth-century anticipation of modern counseling and pastoral care), and the combination of his personal piety and

80. What if Jesus' activity had not found an early and abrupt end through his crucifixion?

81. Cf. for Jesus Matt 5:21-22; 12:41-42. But Jesus does not fully fit into the category of the "final redeemer" because he surpasses only previous religious figures in Israel and does not intend to found a new religion different from the religion of Israel.

82. Gorikai III Konko Kyoso Gorikai 7:1-2; Gorikai I Kondo Fujimori 10; Gorikai I Ichimura Mitsugoro 6; Gorikai I Yamamoto Sadajiro 17:3.

83. Gorikai II Sato Mitsujiro 14:1-2; idem, Sato Norio 4:4-5. Gorikai II Ichimura Mitsugoro 17:1: "Tenchi Kane No Kami does not discriminate between kamis and buddhas. Kami protects Shintoists as well as Buddhists."

84. "The whole world is Tenchi Kane No Kami's hiromae" (Gorikai III Konko kyoso Gorikai 6. Cf. also Gorikai II Fukushima Gihe 10; Gorikai II Tomita Tomi 1:1-3).

human common sense lead me to think of this simple farmer as a great religious personality who deserves to be known outside the limited circle of his believers.

Summary

The focus of this paper is a comparison between the historical Jesus and a foundress and a founder of two new Japanese religions of the nineteenth century, Miki Nakayama, foundress of Tenrikyô, and Bunji Akazawa, founder of Konkôkyô. The births of these two religions provide many analogies to the birth of Christianity. Jesus' life is paralleled by their social background among lower-class people. Jesus' message and life are often similar to their teachings and lives. Finally, belief in Jesus' resurrection is comparable to the after-life of the founders in these Japanese religions. Like Jesus, the Palestinian Jesus Movement, and early Christianity, these religions are characterized by functional monotheism, universalism, individuation, healings, mission and an "early-church-like" social body. In the conclusion of the paper the question is posed as to whether the category "founded religions" could be a relevant category, in spite of the fact that it is not popular in religious studies today.

SELECTED BIBLIOGRAPHY:
The First Princeton-Prague Symposium
on the Historical Jesus

Brian Rhea

Allison, Dale C., Jr. *Jesus of Nazareth: Millenarian Prophet.* Minneapolis: Fortress, 1998.

Anderson, Paul N. *The Christology of the Fourth Gospel: Its Unity and Disunity in the Light of John 6.* Valley Forge, Pa.: Trinity, 1996.

Aus, Roger. *Water into Wine and the Beheading of John the Baptist: Early Jewish-Christian Interpretation of Esther 1 in John 2:1-11 and Mark 6:17-29.* Brown Judaic Studies 150. Atlanta: Scholars Press, 1988.

———. "The Release of Barabbas (Mark 15:6-15 par.; John 18:39-40), and Judaic Traditions on the Book of Esther." Pages 1-27 in *Barabbas and Esther and Other Studies in the Judaic Illumination of Earliest Christianity.* Edited by Roger Aus. South Florida Studies in the History of Judaism 54. Atlanta: Scholars Press, 1992.

Aviam, Mordechai. *Jews, Pagans and Christians in the Galilee: 25 Years of Archaeological Excavations and Surveys: Hellenistic to Byzantine Periods.* Land of Galilee 1. Rochester, N.Y.: University of Rochester Press, 2004.

Barrett, Charles Kingsley. "The Background of Mark 10:45." Pages 1-18 in *New Testament Essays: Studies in Memory of Thomas Walter Manson, 1893-1958.* Edited by A. J. B. Higgins. Manchester: Manchester University Press, 1959.

———. *The Gospel According to St. John: An Introduction with Commentary and Notes on the Greek Text.* 2nd ed. Philadelphia: Westminster, 1978.

Barthélemy, Jean-Dominique, and Józef T. Milik, eds. *Qumran Cave I.* Discoveries in the Judean Desert 1. Oxford: Clarendon, 1955.

Batey, Richard A. *Jesus and the Forgotten City: New Light on Sepphoris and the Urban World of Jesus.* Grand Rapids: Baker Book House, 1991.

Baumgarten, Joseph M. "4Q500 and the Ancient Conception of the Lord's Vineyard." *Journal of Jewish Studies* 40 (1989): 1-6.

Baur, Ferdinand Christian. *Das Christenthum und die christliche Kirche der drei ersten Jahrhunderte.* Tübingen: L. F. Fues, 1853. English: *The Church History of the First*

Brian Rhea

Three Centuries. Translated by Allan Menzies. 2 vols. 3rd ed. London: Williams and Norgate, 1878-79.

Beasley-Murray, George R. *John.* 2nd ed. Word Biblical Commentary 36. Nashville: Thomas Nelson, 1999.

Bebbington, David W. *Patterns in History: A Christian View.* Downers Grove, Ill.: InterVarsity, 1979.

Becker, Jürgen. "Wunder und Christologie: Zum literarkritischen und christologischen Problem der Wunder im Johannesevangelium." *New Testament Studies* 16 (1969/70): 130-48.

———. *Das Evangelium nach Johannes: Kapitel 1–10.* Ökumenischer Taschenbuch-Kommentar 4/2. 3rd ed. Gütersloh: Gütersloher, 1991.

Belle, Gilbert van. *The Signs Source in the Fourth Gospel: Historical Survey and Critical Evaluation of the Semeia Hypothesis.* Bibliotheca ephemeridum theologicarum lovaniensium 116. Leuven: Leuven University Press, 1994.

Berger, Klaus. *Die Amen-Worte Jesu.* Beihefte zur Zeitschrift für die neutestamentliche Wissenschaft 39. Berlin: de Gruyter, 1970.

———, "Jesus als Pharisäer und frühe Christen als Pharisäer." *Novum Testamentum* 30 (1988): 231-62.

Berger, Klaus, and Carsten Colpe. *Religionsgeschichtliches Textbuch zum Neuen Testament.* Texte zum Neuen Testament: Das Neue Testament Deutsch, Textreihe 1. Göttingen: Vandenhoeck & Ruprecht, 1987.

Berger, Peter L., and Thomas Luckmann, *The Social Construction of Reality: A Treatise in the Sociology of Knowledge.* Garden City, N.Y.: Doubleday, 1966. German: P. L. Berger and T. Luckmann, *Die gesellschaftliche Konstruktion der Wirklichkeit.* 3rd ed. Frankfurt: Fischer, 1994.

Berkey, Robert F., and Sarah A. Edwards, eds. *Christological Perspectives: Essays in Honor of Harvey K. McArthur.* New York: Pilgrim, 1982.

Black, Matthew. *An Aramaic Approach to the Gospels and Acts.* 3rd ed. Oxford: Clarendon, 1967.

Blackburn, Barry L. "The Miracles of Jesus." Pages 353-94 in *Studying the Historical Jesus: Evaluations of the State of Current Research.* Edited by Bruce Chilton and Craig A. Evans. New Testament Tools and Studies 19. Leiden: Brill, 1994.

Blank, Josef. "Der 'eschatologische Ausblick' Mk 14,25." Pages 508-18 in *Kontinuität und Einheit: für Franz Mussner.* Edited by Paul-Gerhard Müller and Werner Stenger. Freiburg et al.: Herder, 1981.

Blass, Friedrich, Albert Debrunner, and Friedrich Rehkopf. *Grammatik des neutestamentlichen Griechisch.* 17th ed. Göttingen: Vandenhoeck & Ruprecht, 1990.

Blomberg, Craig L. *The Historical Reliability of John's Gospel: Issues & Commentary.* Downers Grove, Ill.: InterVarsity, 2001.

———. Review of S. E. Porter, *Criteria for Authenticity in Historical-Jesus Research: Previous Discussion and New Proposals. Themelios* 26.2 (2001): 83-84.

Bock, Darrell L. *Luke*. Baker Exegetical Commentary on the New Testament 3a-b. 2 vols. Grand Rapids: Baker, 1994-96.

Bolyki, János. *Jesu Tischgemeinschaften*. Wissenschaftliche Untersuchungen zum Neuen Testament, Second Series 96. Tübingen: Mohr Siebeck, 1998.

Boobyer, G. H. "Mark II.10a and the Interpretation of the Healing of the Paralytic." *Harvard Theological Review* 47 (1954): 115-20.

Booth, Roger P. *Jesus and the Laws of Purity: Tradition History and Legal History in Mark 7*. Journal for the Study of the New Testament Supplement Series 13. Sheffield: JSOT Press, 1986.

Borchert, Gerald L. *John 1–11*. New American Commentary 25A. Nashville: Broadman & Holman, 1996.

Borg, Marcus J. *Conflict, Holiness & Politics in the Teachings of Jesus*. Studies in the Bible and Early Christianity 5. New York: Edwin Mellen, 1984.

Bornkamm, Günther. *Jesus von Nazareth*. Stuttgart: Kohlhammer, 1956. English: *Jesus of Nazareth*. Translated by Irene and Fraser McLuskey with James M. Robinson. Foreword by Helmut Koester. Minneapolis: Fortress, 1995.

Botterweck, Gerhard Johannes, and Helmer Ringgren, eds. *Theologisches Wörterbuch zum Alten Testament*. Stuttgart: W. Kohlhammer, 1970-.

Bousset, Wilhelm. *Kyrios Christos: Geschichte des Christusglaubens von den Anfängen des Christentums bis Irenaeus*. Göttingen: Vandenhoeck & Ruprecht, 1913 (2nd ed., 1921). English: *Kyrios Christos: A History of the Belief in Christ from the Beginnings of Christianity to Irenaeus*. Translated by John E. Steely. Nashville: Abingdon, 1970.

Bovon, François. *Das Evangelium nach Lukas 1,1–9,50*. Evangelisch-katholischer Kommentar zum Neuen Testament 3/1. Zürich: Benzinger; Neukirchen-Vluyn: Neukirchener, 1989.

———. "Fragment *Oxyrhynchus 840*, Fragment of a Lost Gospel, Witness of an Early Christian Controversy over Purity." *Journal of Biblical Literature* 119 (2000): 705-28.

Bowersock, Glen W. *Hellenism in Late Antiquity: Thomas Spencer Jerome Lectures*. Ann Arbor, Mich.: University of Michigan Press, 1990.

Braund, D. C. "Philip." Pages 310-11 in vol. 5 of *The Anchor Bible Dictionary*. Edited by David Noel Freedman. New York: Doubleday, 1992.

Bremond, Claude. *Logique du récit*. Paris: Ed. du Seuil, 1973.

Broer, Ingo. "Noch einmal: Zur religionsgeschichtlichen 'Ableitung' von Joh. 2,1-11." *Studien zum Neuen Testament und seiner Umwelt Serie A* 8 (1983): 103-23.

———. "Das Weinwunder zu Kana (Joh 2,1-11) und die Weinwunder der Antike." Pages 291-308 in *Das Urchristentum in seiner literarischen Geschichte: Festschrift für Jürgen Becker zum 65. Geburtstag*. Edited by Ulrich Mell and Ulrich B. Müller. Beihefte zur Zeitschrift für die neutestamentliche Wissenschaft 100. Berlin and New York: Walter de Gruyter, 1999.

Brooke, George J. "4Q500 1 and the Use of Scripture in the Parable of the Vineyard." *Dead Sea Discoveries* 2 (1995): 268-94.

Brown, Raymond E. *The Gospel According to John I–XII: A New Translation with Introduction and Commentary.* Anchor Bible 29. New York: Doubleday, 1966.

Bruce, Frederick Fyvie. "The Book of Zechariah and the Passion Narrative." *Bulletin of the John Rylands University Library of Manchester* 43 (1960-61): 336-53.

Buchanan, George W. *The Consequences of the Covenant.* Leiden: Brill, 1970.

Bultmann, Rudolf. *History of the Synoptic Tradition.* Translated by J. Marsh. 1921. Repr., Oxford: Blackwell, 1963.

———. *Jesus.* Berlin: Deutsche Bibliothek, 1926. Repr., Tübingen: Mohr Siebeck, 1983.

———. "The New Approach to the Synoptic Problem." Pages 35-54 in *Existence and Faith: Shorter Writings of Rudolf Bultmann.* Edited by S. Ogden. New York: Meridian, 1960. Repr. from *Journal of Religion* 6 (1926): 337-62.

———. *Das Evangelium des Johannes.* Göttingen: Vandenhoeck & Ruprecht, 1941. English: *The Gospel of John: A Commentary.* Edited by Rupert W. N. Hoare and John K. Riches. Translated by George R. Beasley-Murray. Philadelphia: Westminster, 1971.

———. *Theologie des Neuen Testaments.* Tübingen: J. C. B. Mohr, 1953. English: *Theology of the New Testament.* Translated by Kendrick Grobel. 2 vols. New York: Scribners, 1951-55.

Burchard, Christoph. "Jesus von Nazareth." Pages 12-58 in *Die Anfänge des Christentums: Alte Welt und neue Hoffnung.* Edited by Jürgen Becker. Stuttgart: Kohlhammer, 1987.

Burkett, Delbert Royce. *The Son of Man Debate: A History and Evaluation.* Society for New Testament Studies Monograph Series 107. Cambridge: Cambridge University Press, 1999.

Burney, Charles Fox. *The Poetry of Our Lord.* Oxford: Clarendon, 1925.

Burridge, Richard A. *What Are the Gospels? A Comparison with Graeco-Roman Biography.* 2nd ed. Grand Rapids: Eerdmans, 2004.

Carmignac, Jean, and P. Guilbert. *La Règle de la Communauté, la Règle de la Guerre, les Hymnes.* Vol. 1 of *Les textes de Qumran: Traduits et annotés.* Paris: Letouzey et Ané, 1961.

Carmignac, Jean, É. Cothenet, and H. Lignée. *Règle de la Congrégation, etc.* Vol. 2 of *Les textes de Qumran: Traduits et annotés.* Paris: Letouzey et Ané, 1963.

Case, Shirley Jackson. *Jesus: A New Biography.* Chicago: University of Chicago, 1927.

Casey, Maurice. *Son of Man: The Interpretation and Influence of Daniel 7.* London: SPCK, 1979.

———. *Aramaic Sources of Mark's Gospel.* Society for New Testament Studies Monograph Series 102. Cambridge: Cambridge University Press, 1998.

———. "An Aramaic Approach to the Synoptic Gospels." *Expository Times* 110.7 (1999): 175-78.

Ceroke, C. P. "Is Mark 2:10 a Saying of Jesus?" *Catholic Biblical Quarterly* 22 (1960): 369-90.

Chancey, Mark A. "The Cultural Milieu of Ancient Sepphoris." *New Testament Studies* 47 (2001): 127-45.

———. *The Myth of a Gentile Galilee.* Society for New Testament Studies Monograph Series 118. Cambridge: Cambridge University Press, 2002.

Charlesworth, James H. *Jesus Within Judaism: New Light from Exciting Archaeological Discoveries.* Anchor Bible Reference Library. Garden City, N.Y.: Doubleday, 1988.

———. "The Jewish Background of the Lord's Prayer." *Abstracts: American Academy of Religion/Society of Biblical Literature* (1989): 115-16.

———. "The Righteous Teacher and the Historical Jesus: A Study of the Self-Understanding of Two Jewish Charismatics." Pages 73-94 in *Perspectives on Christology.* Edited by Walter P. Weaver. Nashville: Exodus, 1989.

———. "Jewish Prayers in the Time of Jesus." Pages 36-55 in *The Lord's Prayer: Perspectives for Reclaiming Christian Prayer.* Edited by Daniel L. Migliore. Grand Rapids: Eerdmans, 1993.

———. "Jesus Research Expands with Chaotic Creativity." Pages 1-41 in *Images of Jesus Today.* Edited by James H. Charlesworth and Walter P. Weaver. Faith and Scholarship Colloquies 3. Valley Forge, Pa.: Trinity, 1994.

———. "Jesus in the Agrapha and Apocryphal Gospels." Pages 479-533 in *Studying the Historical Jesus: Evaluations of the State of Current Research.* Edited by Bruce Chilton and Craig A. Evans. Leiden: Brill, 1994.

———. *The Beloved Disciple.* Valley Forge, Pa.: Trinity, 1995.

———. "The Son of David: Solomon and Jesus." Pages 72-87 in *The New Testament and Hellenistic Judaism.* Edited by P. Borgen and S. Giversen. Aarhus: Aarhus University Press, 1995.

———. *Jesus and the Dead Sea Scrolls: What Do We Know After Fifty Years?* The Loy H. Witherspoon Lectures in Religious Studies. The University of North Carolina at Charlotte, 1998.

———. "John the Baptizer and Qumran Barriers in Light of *The Rule of the Community.*" Pages 353-75 in *The Provo International Conference on the Dead Sea Scrolls.* Edited by Donald W. Parry and Eugene Ulrich. Studies on the Texts of the Desert of Judah 30. Leiden: Brill, 1999.

———. "The Qumran Beatitudes (4Q525) and the New Testament (Mt 5:3-11, Lk 6:20-26)." *Revue d'Histoire et de Philosophie Religieuses* 80 (2000): 13-35.

———. "The Historical Jesus: Sources and a Sketch." Pages 84-128 in *Jesus Two Thousand Years Later.* Edited by James H. Charlesworth and Walter P. Weaver. Faith and Scholarship Colloquies. Harrisburg, Pa.: Trinity, 2000.

———. "The Historical Jesus and Exegetical Theology." *Princeton Seminary Bulletin* 22 (2001): 45-63.

———. "Jesus Research and the Appearance of Psychobiography." Pages 55-84 in *Revelation, Reason and Faith: Essays in Honor of Truman G. Madsen.* Edited by Donald W. Parry, D. C. Peterson, and S. D. Ricks. Provo, Utah: Foundation for Ancient Research and Mormon Studies, 2002.

Brian Rhea

────. "Can One Recover Aramaic Sources behind Mark's Gospel?" *Review of Rabbinic Judaism* 5.2 (2002): 249-58.

────. "The Priority of John? Reflections on the Essenes and the First Edition of John." Pages 73-114 in *Für und wider die Priorität des Johannesevangeliums: Symposium in Salzburg am 10. März 2000.* Edited by P. L. Hofrichter. Theologische Texte und Studien 9. Hildesheim, Zürich, New York: Georg Olms Verlag, 2002.

────. "Jesus Research and Near Eastern Archaeology: Reflections on Recent Developments." Pages 37-70 in *Neotestamentica et Philonica: Studies in Honor of Peder Borgen.* Edited by David E. Aune, Torrey Seland, and Jarl H. Ulrichsen. Supplements to *Novum Testamentum* 106. Leiden: Brill, 2003.

────. "Did the Fourth Evangelist Know the Enoch Tradition?" Pages 223-39 in *Testimony and Interpretation: Early Christology and Its Judeo-Hellenistic Milieu: Studies in Honor of Petr Pokorný.* Edited by Jiří Mrázek and Jan Roskovec. London and New York: T&T Clark, 2004.

────. *An Essential Guide to the Historical Jesus.* Abingdon Essential Guides. Nashville: Abingdon, in press.

────. *The Good & Evil Serpent.* Anchor Bible Reference Library. New York: Doubleday, in press.

────. "The Jesus of History and the Topography of the Holy Land." *Handbook on the Historical Jesus,* in press.

Charlesworth, James H., Casey D. Elledge, James L. Crenshaw, Hendrikus Boers, and W. Waite Willis, Jr. *Resurrection: The Origin and Future of a Biblical Doctrine.* Faith and Scholarship Colloquies Series. New York and London: T&T Clark International, 2006.

Charlesworth, James H., ed. *The Old Testament Pseudepigrapha.* 2 vols. Garden City, N.Y.: Doubleday, 1983-85.

────, ed. *John and the Dead Sea Scrolls.* Christian Origins Library. New York: Crossroad, 1990.

────, ed. *Jesus' Jewishness: Exploring the Place of Jesus within Early Judaism.* Shared Ground Among Jews and Christians 2. New York: American Interfaith Institute, Crossroad, 1991.

────, ed. *Jesus and the Dead Sea Scrolls.* Anchor Bible Reference Library. New York: Doubleday, 1992.

────, ed. *Jesus and Archaeology.* Grand Rapids: Eerdmans, 2006.

────, ed. *The Bible and the Dead Sea Scrolls.* 3 vols. Waco, Tex.: Baylor University Press, 2006.

Charlesworth, James H., et al., eds. *Damascus Document II, Some Works of the Torah, and Related Documents.* Vol. 3 of *The Dead Sea Scrolls: Hebrew, Aramaic and Greek Texts with English Translations.* PTSDSSP 3. Tübingen: Mohr Siebeck; Louisville: Westminster John Knox, 2006.

Charlesworth, James H., with J. Brownson, M. T. Davis, S. J. Kraftchick, and A. F. Segal, eds. *The Messiah: Developments in Earliest Judaism and Christianity.* Minneapolis: Fortress, 1992.

Charlesworth, James H., and Loren L. Johns, eds. *Hillel and Jesus.* Minneapolis: Fortress, 1997.

Charlesworth, James H., and Walter P. Weaver, eds. *What Has Archaeology to Do with Faith?* Philadelphia: Trinity, 1992.

————, eds. *Images of Jesus Today.* Valley Forge, Pa.: Trinity, 1994.

————, eds. *Earthing Christologies: From Jesus' Parables to Jesus the Parable.* Valley Forge, Pa.: Trinity, 1995.

————, eds. *Jesus Two Thousand Years Later.* Harrisburg, Pa.: Trinity, 2000.

Chilton, Bruce D. *A Galilean Rabbi and His Bible: Jesus' Use of the Interpreted Scripture of His Time.* Good News Studies 8. Wilmington, Del.: Michael Glazier, 1984.

————. *God in Strength: Jesus' Announcement of the Kingdom.* Studien zum Neuen Testament und seiner Umwelt 1. Freistadt: Plöchl, 1979. Repr., The Biblical Seminar 8. Sheffield: JSOT Press, 1987.

————. "Jesus and the Repentance of E. P. Sanders." *Tyndale Bulletin* 39 (1988): 1-18.

————. "The Son of Man: Human and Heavenly." Pages 203-18 in vol. 1 of *The Four Gospels 1992: Festschrift Frans Neirynck.* Edited by F. Van Segbroeck, C. M. Tuckett, Gilbert van Belle, and J. Verheyden. 3 vols. Bibliotheca ephemeridum theologicarum lovaniensium 100. Leuven: Peeters and Leuven University Press, 1992.

————. *The Temple of Jesus: His Sacrificial Program Within Cultural History of Sacrifice.* University Park: Pennsylvania State University Press, 1992.

————. *A Feast of Meanings: Eucharistic Theologies from Jesus through Johannine Circles.* Novum Testamentum Supplements 72. Leiden: Brill, 1994.

————. *Rabbi Jesus: An Intimate Biography.* New York: Doubleday, 2000.

Chilton, Bruce D., and Craig A. Evans, eds. *Authenticating the Words of Jesus.* New Testament Tools and Studies 28.1. Leiden: Brill, 1999.

Christ, Felix. *Jesus Sophia: Die Sophia-Christologie bei den Synoptikern.* Abhandlungen zur Theologie des Alten und Neuen Testaments 57. Zürich: Zwingli, 1970.

Claussen, Carsten. *Versammlung, Gemeinde, Synagoge: Das hellenistisch-jüdische Umfeld der frühchristlichen Gemeinden.* Studien zur Umwelt des Neuen Testaments 27. Göttingen: Vandenhoeck & Ruprecht, 2002.

Clemen, Carl. *Religionsgeschichtliche Erklärung des Neuen Testaments: die Abhängigkeit des ältesten Christentums von nichtjüdischen Religionen und philosophischen Systemen.* 4th ed. Giessen: Töpelmann, 1924.

Clines, David J. A. *Job 1-20.* Word Biblical Commentary 17. Dallas: Word, 1989.

————. "Haggai's Temple: Constructed, Deconstructed and Reconstructed." *Scandinavian Journal of the Old Testament* 7 (1993): 51-77.

Coenen, Lothar, and Klaus Haacker, eds. *Theologisches Begriffslexion zum Neuen Testament.* 2 vols. Wuppertal: Brockhaus/Neukirchen-Vluyn: Neukirchener 1997.

Cohen, O. ". . . ein Schiff wird kommen . . . Die Bergung und Restaurierung eines 2000

Brian Rhea

Jahre alten Bootes am See Gennesaret." Pages 147-52 in *Leben am See Gennesaret: Kulturgeschichtliche Entdeckungen in einer biblischen Region.* Edited by Gabriele Fassbeck, et al. Zaberns Bildbände zur Archäologie: Sonderbände der antiken Welt. Munich: von Zabern, 2002.

Collingwood, Robin George. *The Idea of History.* Oxford: Oxford University Press, 1946.

Collins, John J. "Sibylline Oracles: A New Translation and Introduction." Pages 317-472 in *Apocalyptic Literature and Testaments.* Vol. 1 of *The Old Testament Pseudepigrapha.* Edited by James H. Charlesworth. New York: Doubleday, 1983.

Crossan, John Dominic. *In Parables: The Challenge of the Historical Jesus.* New York: Harper & Row, 1973.

———. *The Historical Jesus: The Life of a Mediterranean Jewish Peasant.* San Francisco: Harper, 1991.

Crossan, J. Dominic, and Jonathan L. Reed. *Excavating Jesus: Beneath the Stones, Behind the Texts.* San Francisco: HarperSanFrancisco, 2001. German: *Jesus ausgraben: Zwischen den Steinen — hinter den Texten.* Düsseldorf: Patmos, 2003.

Culpepper, R. Alan. *The Gospel and the Letters of John.* Nashville: Abingdon, 1998.

Dalman, Gustaf. *Grammatik des jüdisch-palästinischen Aramäisch.* Leipzig: Hinrichs, 1894.

———. *The Words of Jesus Considered in the Light of Post-Biblical Jewish Writings and the Aramaic Language.* Translated by David Miller Kay. 1898. Edinburgh: T&T Clark, 1909.

———. *Jesus-Jeshua: Studies in the Gospels.* Translated by Paul P. Levertoff. 1922. London: SPCK, 1929.

Daniélou, Jean. *Les manuscrits de la Mer Morte et les origins du Christianisme.* Paris: Editions du Seuil, 1957.

Dautzenberg, Gerhard. "Mk 4,1-34 als Belehrung über das Reich Gottes." *Biblische Zeitschrift* 34 (1990): 38-62.

Davies, Margaret. *Rhetoric and Reference in the Fourth Gospel.* Journal for the Study of the New Testament Supplement Series 69. Sheffield: Sheffield Academic, 1992.

Davies, Philip R. *The Damascus Covenant: An Interpretation of the "Damascus Document."* Journal for the Study of the Old Testament: Supplement Series 25. Sheffield: JSOT Press, 1982.

Davies, William D., and Dale C. Allison, Jr. *A Critical and Exegetical Commentary on the Gospel according to Saint Matthew.* International Critical Commentary. 3 vols. Edinburgh: T&T Clark, 1987-97.

Deines, Roland. *Jüdische Steingefässe und pharisäische Frömmigkeit: ein archäologisch-historischer Beitrag zum Verständnis von Joh 2,6 und der jüdischen Reinheitshalacha zur Zeit Jesu.* Tübingen: J. C. B. Mohr, 1993.

Dibelius, Martin. *Die Formgeschichte des Evangeliums.* Tübingen: Mohr, 1919. English: *From Tradition to Gospel.* Translated by B. Woolf. London: Ivor Nicholson & Watson, 1934.

Dodd, Charles Harold. *According to the Scriptures: The Sub-Structure of New Testament Theology.* London: Nisbet, 1952.

———. *The Interpretation of the Fourth Gospel.* Cambridge: Cambridge University Press, 1958.

———. *Historical Tradition in the Fourth Gospel.* Cambridge: Cambridge University Press, 1965.

Downing, Francis Gerald. "Cynics and Christians." *New Testament Studies* 30 (1984): 584-93.

———. *Christ and the Cynics.* Journal for the Study of the Old Testament Supplement Series 4. Sheffield: Academic, 1988.

———. *Cynics and Christian Origins.* Edinburgh: Clark, 1992.

———. "The Jewish Cynic Jesus." Pages 184-214 in *Jesus, Mark and Q: The Teaching of Jesus and Its Earliest Records.* Edited by Michael Labahn and Andreas Schmid. Journal for the Study of the New Testament: Supplement Series 214. Sheffield: Academic, 2001.

Dray, William H. *Philosophy of History.* Englewood Cliffs, N.J.: Prentice-Hall, 1964.

Dunn, James D. G. *The Evidence for Jesus: The Impact of Scholarship on Our Understanding of How Christianity Began.* London: SCM, 1985.

———. "Jesus and Ritual Purity: A Study of the Tradition History of Mark 7:15." Pages 251-76 in *Cause de l'Évangile: Études sur les Synoptiques et les Actes: offertes au P. Jacques Dupont, O.S.B. à l'occasion de son 70e anniversaire.* Edited by R. Gantoy. Lectio divina 123. Paris: Cerf, 1985.

———. *Jesus and the Spirit: A Study of the Religious and Charismatic Experience of Jesus and the First Christians as Reflected in the New Testament.* Grand Rapids: Eerdmans, 1997.

———. "Jesus and Purity: An Ongoing Debate." *New Testament Studies* 48 (2002): 449-67.

———. *Jesus Remembered.* Christianity in the Making 1. Grand Rapids: Eerdmans, 2003.

Dupont-Sommer, André. *The Essene Writings from Qumran.* Gloucester: Peter Smith, 1973.

Du Toit, David S. "Redefining Jesus: Current Trends in Jesus Research." Pages 82-124 in *Jesus, Mark and Q: The Teaching of Jesus and Its Earliest Records.* Edited by Michael Labahn and Andreas Schmid. Journal for the Study of the New Testament: Supplement Series 214. Sheffield: Sheffield Academic, 2001.

Ebertz, Michael N. *Das Charisma des Gekreuzigten: Zur Soziologie der Jesusbewegung.* Wissenschaftliche Untersuchungen zum Neuen Testament 45. Tübingen: Mohr, 1987.

Ebner, Martin. *Jesus — ein Weisheitslehre? Synoptische Weisheitslogien im Traditionsprozess.* Herders biblische Studien 15. Freiburg: Herder, 1998.

———. *Jesus von Nazaret in seiner Zeit. Sozialgeschichtliche Zugänge.* Stuttgarter Bibelstudien 196. Stuttgart: Katholisches Bibelwerk, 2003.

Eco, Umberto. *Lector in fabula: la cooperazione interpretativa nei testi narrativi.* Milan: Bompiani, 1979. German: *Lector in fibula: Die Mitarbeit der Interpretation in erzählenden Texten.* 3rd ed. Munich: dtv, 1998.

Edwards, D. E. "The Socio-Economic and Cultural Ethos of the Lower Galilee in the First Century: Implications for the Nascent Jesus Movement." Pages 53-73 in *The Galilee in Late Antiquity.* Edited by Lee I. Levine. New York and Jerusalem: The Jewish Theological Seminary of America, 1992.

Edwards, Douglas R. "Khirbet Qana: From Jewish Village to Christian Pilgrim Site." Pages 101-32 in vol. 3 of *The Roman and Byzantine Near East.* Edited by John H. Humphrey. Journal of Roman Archaeology Supplementary Series 49. Portsmouth, R.I.: JRA, 2002.

Edwards, Douglas R., and C. Thomas McCullough. *Archaeology and the Galilee: Texts and Contexts in the Graeco-Roman and Byzantine Periods.* South Florida Studies in the History of Judaism 143. Atlanta: Scholars Press, 1997.

Egger, Wilhelm. *Nachfolge als Weg zum Leben. Chancen neuerer exegetischer Methoden dargelegt an Mk 10,17-31.* Österreichische biblische Studien 1. Klosterneuburg: Österreichisches Katholisches Bibelwerk, 1979.

———. *Methodenlehre zum Neuen Testament.* Freiburg/Basel/Vienna: Herder, 1987.

Ehrman, Bart D. *Jesus: Apocalyptic Prophet of the New Millennium.* New York: Oxford University Press, 1999.

Eichholz, Georg. *Gleichnisse der Evangelien.* Neukirchen-Vluyn: Neukirchener, 1971.

Encyclopaedia Judaica. 16 vols. Jerusalem: Encyclopaedia Judaica; New York: Macmillan, 1971-72. "Purity and Impurity, Ritual." 13:1405-14.

Enslin, Morton J. "John and Jesus." *Zeitschrift für die neutestamentliche Wissenschaft und die Kunde der älteren Kirche* 66 (1975): 1-18.

Erlemann, Kurt. *Gleichnisauslegung: Ein Lehr- und Arbeitsbuch.* Tübingen/Basel: Francke, 1999.

Evans, Craig A. *Jesus and His Contemporaries: Comparative Studies.* Arbeiten zur Geschichte des antiken Judentums und des Urchristentums 25. Leiden: Brill, 1995.

———. "'Who Touched Me?' Jesus and the Ritually Impure." Pages 353-76 in *Jesus in Context: Temple, Purity, and Restoration.* Edited by Bruce Chilton and Craig A. Evans. Arbeiten zur Geschichte des antiken Judentums und des Urchristentums 93. Leiden: Brill, 1997.

———. "From Gospel to Gospel: The Function of Isaiah in the New Testament." Pages 651-91 in *Writing and Reading the Scroll of Isaiah: Studies of an Interpretive Tradition.* Edited by Craig C. Broyles and Craig A. Evans. 2 vols. Supplements to Vetus Testamentum 70, 72. Formation and Interpretation of Old Testament Literature 1 and 2. Leiden: Brill, 1997.

———. "Jesus and Zechariah's Messianic Hope." Pages 373-88 in *Authenticating the Activities of Jesus.* Edited by Craig A. Evans and Bruce Chilton. New Testament Tools and Studies 28/2. Leiden: Brill, 1998.

―――. *Mark 8:27–16:20*. Word Biblical Commentary 34B. Nashville: Thomas Nelson, 2001.

―――. "How Septuagintal is Isa 5:1-7 in Mark 12:1-9?" *Novum Testamentum* 45 (2003): 105-10.

Fander, Monika. *Die Stellung der Frau im Markusevangelium*. Münsteraner theologische Abhandlungen 8. Münster: Telos-Verlag, 1989.

Fiedler, Peter. *Jesus und die Sünder*. Beiträge zur biblischen Exegese und Theologie 3. Frankfurt/Bern: Lang, 1976.

Fiensy, David A. "Leaders of Mass Movements and the Leader of the Jesus Movement." *Journal for the Study of the New Testament* 74 (1999): 3-27.

Fine, Steven. "Gamala." Page 382 in vol. 2 of *The Oxford Encyclopedia of Archaeology in the Near East*. Edited by Eric M. Meyers. New York: Oxford University Press, 1997.

Fischer, David Hackett. *Historians' Fallacies: Toward a Logic of Historical Thought*. New York: Harper, 1970.

Fitzmyer, Joseph A. "The Languages of Palestine in the First Century A D." *Catholic Biblical Quarterly* 32 (1970): 501-31.

―――. *The Gospel According to Luke I–IX: Introduction, Translation, and Notes*. Anchor Bible 28. Garden City, N.Y.: Doubleday, 1981.

Fortna, Robert T. *The Gospel of Signs: A Reconstruction of the Narrative Sources Underlying the Fourth Gospel*. Society for New Testament Studies Monograph Series 11. Cambridge: Cambridge University Press, 1970.

―――. *The Fourth Gospel and Its Predecessor: From Narrative Source to Present Gospel*. Philadelphia: Polebridge, 1988.

France, Richard Thomas. *Jesus and the Old Testament*. London: Tyndale, 1971.

Fredriksen, Paula. *From Jesus to Christ: The Origins of the New Testament Images of Jesus*. New Haven: Yale University Press, 1988.

―――. *Jesus of Nazareth, King of the Jews: A Jewish Life and the Emergence of Christianity*. New York: Knopf, 1999.

Frey, Jörg. *Die johanneische Eschatologie*. 3 vols. Wissenschaftliche Untersuchungen zum Neuen Testament 96, 110, 117. Tübingen: Mohr Siebeck, 1997-2000.

―――. "Das Vierte Evangelium auf dem Hintergrund der älteren Evangelienliteratur: Zum Problem: Johannes und die Synoptiker." Pages 60-118 in *Johannesevangelium — Mitte oder Rand des Kanons? Neue Standortbestimmungen*. Edited by T. Söding. Quaestiones disputatae 203. Freiburg: Herder, 2003.

Freyne, Seán. *Galilee from Alexander the Great to Hadrian, 323 B.C.E. to 135 C.E.: A Study of Second Temple Judaism*. Wilmington, Del.: Michael Glazier, 1980.

―――. *Galilee, Jesus, and the Gospels: Literary Approaches and Historical Investigations*. Philadelphia: Fortress, 1988.

―――. "The Geography, Politics, and Economics of Galilee and the Quest for the Historical Jesus." Pages 75-121 in *Studying the Historical Jesus: Evaluations of the State of Current Research*. Edited by Bruce Chilton and Craig A. Evans. New Testament Tools and Studies 19. Leiden: Brill, 1994.

———. "Galilee." Pages 370-76 in vol. 2 of *The Oxford Encyclopedia of Archaeology in the Near East*. Edited by Eric M. Meyers. 5 vols. New York: Oxford University Press, 1997.

———. *Galilee and Gospel: Collected Essays*. Wissenschaftliche Untersuchungen zum Neuen Testament 125. Tübingen: Mohr Siebeck, 2000.

———. "The Geography of Restoration: Galilee–Jerusalem Relations in Early Jewish and Christian Experience." *New Testament Studies* 47 (2001): 289-311.

———. *Jesus, a Jewish Galilean: A New Reading of the Jesus-Story*. New York: T&T Clark International, 2004.

Frymer-Kensky, Tikva S. "Pollution, Purification, and Purgation in Biblical Israel." Pages 399-414 in *The Word of the Lord Shall Go Forth: Essays in Honor of David Noel Freedman in Celebration of His Sixtieth Birthday*. Edited by Carol L. Meyers and M. O'Connor. American Schools of Oriental Research 1. Winona Lake, Ind.: Eisenbrauns, 1983.

Funk, Robert W., and Roy W. Hoover, eds. *The Five Gospels: The Search for the Authentic Words of Jesus*. New York: Macmillan, 1993.

Gadamer, Hans-Georg. *Wahrheit und Methode: Grundzüge einer philosophischen Hermeneutik*. 1960. Repr., Tübingen: Mohr Siebeck, 1986.

Gal, Zvi. *Lower Galilee During the Iron Age*. American Schools of Oriental Research Dissertation Series 8. Winona Lake, Ind.: Eisenbrauns, 1992.

———. "Galilee: Chalcolithic to Persian Periods." Pages 450-53 in vol. 2 of *The New Encyclopedia of Archaeological Excavations in the Holy Land*. Edited by Ephraim Stern. 4 vols. New York: Simon & Schuster, 1993.

———. "Galilee in the Bronze and Iron Ages." Pages 369-70 in vol. 2 of *The Oxford Encyclopedia of Archaeology in the Near East*. Edited by Eric M. Meyers. 5 vols. New York: Oxford University Press, 1997.

Gathercole, Simon J. "The Critical and Dogmatic Agenda of Albert Schweitzer's *The Quest of the Historical Jesus*." *Tyndale Bulletin* 51 (2000): 261-83.

Gaventa, Beverly Roberts. *Mary: Glimpses of the Mother of Jesus*. Minneapolis: Fortress, 1999.

Gemünden, Petra von. "'Draw near to me, you unlearned' (Sirach 51:23): Concepts of Wisdom in Biblical Times." *Annual of the Japanese Biblical Institute* 31 (2005): 63-106.

Gerhardsson, Birger. *Memory and Manuscript: Oral Tradition and Written Transmission in Rabbinic Judaism and Early Christianity*. Lund: Gleerup, 1961. Rev. ed., Grand Rapids: Eerdmans, 1998.

Giblin, Charles H. "Suggestion, Negative Response, and Positive Action in St John's Portrayal of Jesus (John 2:1-11; 4:46-54; 7:2-14; 11:1-44)." *New Testament Studies* 26 (1980): 197-211.

Glasson, Thomas Francis. "Schweitzer's Influence: Blessing or Bane?" *Journal of Theological Studies* 28 (1977): 289-302. Repr. pages 107-20 in *The Kingdom of God*. Edited by Bruce Chilton. London: SPCK, 1984.

Gnilka, Joachim. "Wie urteilte Jesus über seinen Tod?" Pages 13-50 in *Der Tod Jesu — Deutungen im NT*. Edited by Karl Kertelge. Quaestiones disputatae 74. Freiburg: Herder, 1976.

———. *Das Evangelium nach Markus*. 2 vols. Evangelisch-katholischer Kommentar zum Neuen Testament 2.1, 2.2. Zürich/Neukirchen-Vluyn: Benzinger/Neukirchener, 1978-79.

———. *Jesus von Nazareth: Botschaft und Geschichte*. Herders Theologischer Kommentar zum Neuen Testament, Supplement 3. Freiburg: Herder, 1990.

Grant, R. M. "The Coming of the Kingdom." *Journal of Biblical Literature* 67 (1948): 297-303.

Grässer, Erich. *Die Naherwartung Jesu*. Stuttgarter Bibelstudien 61. Stuttgart: Kath. Bibelwerk, 1973.

Grenfell, Bernard P., and Arthur S. Hunt, eds. *The Oxyrhynchus Papyri: Part 5*. London: Egypt Exploration Fund, 1908.

Grimm, Werner. "Selige Augenzeugen, Luk. 10,23f: Alttestamentlicher Hintergrund und ursprünglicher Sinn." *Theologische Zeitschrift* 26 (1970): 172-83.

———. "Der Dank für die empfangene Offenbarung bei Jesus und Josephus." *Biblische Zeitschrift* 17 (1973): 249-56.

———. *Weil ich dich liebe: Die Verkündigung Jesu und Deuterojesaja*. Arbeiten zum Neuen Testament und Judentum 1. Bern and Frankfurt am Main: Lang, 1976.

———. *Jesus und das Danielbuch*. Vol. I: *Jesu Einspruch gegen das Offenbarungssystem Daniels (Mt 11,25-27; Lk 17,20-21)*. Arbeiten zum Neuen Testament und Judentum 6.1. Frankfurt am Main: Peter Lang, 1984.

Guelich, Robert A. *Mark 1–8:26*. Word Biblical Commentary 34A. Dallas: Word, 1989.

Gundry, Robert H. *Mark: A Commentary on His Apology for the Cross*. Grand Rapids: Eerdmans, 1993.

———. *Matthew: A Commentary on His Handbook for a Mixed Church under Persecution*. Rev. ed. Grand Rapids: Eerdmans, 1994.

Gunkel, Hermann. *The Legends of Genesis: The Biblical Saga and History*. Translated by W. H. Carruth. Chicago: Open Court, 1901. Repr., New York: Schocken, 1964.

Gutman, Shmaryahu. "Gamala." Pages 459-63 in vol. 2 of *The New Encyclopedia of Archaeological Excavations in the Holy Land*. Edited by Ephraim Stern. 4 vols. New York: Simon & Schuster, 1993.

Haacker, Klaus. *Neutestamentliche Wissenschaft: Eine Einführung in Fragestellungen und Methoden*. 2nd ed. Wuppertal: Brockhaus, 1985.

———. "Die moderne historische Jesus-Forschung als hermeneutisches Problem." *Theologische Beiträge* 31 (2000): 60-74.

Häfner, Gerd. "Nach dem Tod Jesu fragen: Brennpunkte der Diskussion aus neutestamentlicher Sicht." Pages 139-90 in *Wie heute vom Tod Jesu sprechen? Neutestamentliche, systematisch-theologische und liturgiewissenschaftliche Perspektiven*. Edited by Gerd Häfner and H. Schmid. Freiburg: Kath. Akad. der Erzdiözese Freiburg, 2002.

Brian Rhea

Hagner, Donald A. *Matthew 14–28*. Word Biblical Commentary 33B. Dallas: Word, 1995.

———. "An Analysis of Recent 'Historical Jesus' Studies." Pages 81-106 in *Religious Diversity in the Graeco-Roman World: A Survey of Recent Scholarship*. Edited by D. Cohn-Sherbok and J. M. Court. Sheffield: Sheffield Academic, 2001.

Hahn, Ferdinand. "Sehen und Glauben im Johannesevangelium." Pages 125-41 in *Neues Testament und Geschichte: historisches Geschehen und Deutung im Neuen Testament: Oscar Cullmann zum 70. Geburtstag*. Zürich: Theologischer/Tübingen: Mohr, 1972.

Hane, Mikiso. *Peasants, Rebels and Outcasts: The Underside of Modern Japan*. New York: Pantheon Books, 1982.

Hanhart, Karel. "The Structure of John I 35–IV 54." Pages 22-46 in *Studies in John: Presented to Professor Dr. J. N. Sevenster on the Occasion of His Seventieth Birthday*. Novum Testamentum Supplements 24. Leiden: Brill, 1970.

Hay, Lewis Scott. "The Son of Man in Mark 2:10, and 2:28." *Journal of Biblical Literature* 89 (1970): 69-75.

Heekerens, Hans-Peter. *Die Zeichen-Quelle der johanneischen Redaktion: Ein Beitrag zur Entstehungsgeschichte des vierten Evangeliums*. Stuttgarter Bibelstudien 113. Stuttgart: Katholisches Bibelwerk, 1984.

Heininger, Bernhard. *Metaphorik, Erzählstruktur und szenisch-dramatische Gestaltung in den Sondergutgleichnissen bei Lukas*. Münster: Aschendorff, 1991.

Heitmüller, Wilhelm. "Jesus Christus I." Pages 34-35, cols. 343-62, in vol. 3 of *Die Religion in Geschichte und Gegenwart: Handwörterbuch im gemeinverständlicher Darstellung*. Edited by Friedrich Michael Schiele. 5 vols. Tübingen: Mohr Siebeck, 1912.

Hengel, Martin. *Nachfolge und Charisma: Eine exegetisch-religionsgeschichtliche Studie zu Mt 8,21f. und Jesu Ruf in die Nachfolge*. Beihefte zur Zeitschrift für die neutestamentliche Wissenschaft 34. Berlin: de Gruyter, 1968.

———. *Die Zeloten: Untersuchungen zur jüdischen Freiheitsbewegung in der Zeit von Herodes I. bis 70 n. Chr*. Arbeiten zur Geschichte des antiken Judentums und des Urchristentums 1. Leiden: Brill, 1976.

———. "The Interpretation of the Wine Miracle at Cana: John 2:1-11." Pages 83-112 in *The Glory of Christ in the New Testament: Studies in Christology in Memory of George Bradford Caird*. Edited by L. D. Hurst and N. T. Wright. Oxford: Clarendon, 1987.

———. "Das Johannesevangelium als Quelle für die Geschichte des antiken Judentums." Pages 293-334 in *Judaica, Hellenistica et Christiana: Kleine Schriften II*. Wissenschaftliche Untersuchungen zum Neuen Testament 100. Edited by M. Hengel, J. Frey, and D. Betz, with H. Bloedhorn and M. Küchler. Tübingen: Mohr Siebeck, 1999.

———. "Jesus als messianischer Lehrer der Weisheit und die Anfänge der Christologie." Pages 147-90 in *Sagesse et Religion*. Edited by Edmond Jacob. Paris:

Presses Univ. de France, 1979. Revised as pages 81-131 in *Der messianische Anspruch Jesu und die Anfänge der Christologie* by Martin Hengel and Anna Maria Schwemer. Wissenschaftliche Untersuchungen zum Neuen Testament 138. Tübingen: Mohr, 2001.

Hoegen-Rohls, Christina. *Der nachösterliche Johannes: Die Abschiedsreden als hermeneutischer Schlüssel zum vierten Evangelium.* Wissenschaftliche Untersuchungen zum Neuen Testament, Second Series 84. Tübingen: Mohr Siebeck, 1996.

Hoehner, Harold W. *Herod Antipas.* Society for New Testament Studies Monograph Series 17. Cambridge: Cambridge University Press, 1972.

Hoffmann, Paul. *Studien zur Theologie der Logienquelle.* Neutestamentliche Abhandlungen 8. Münster: Aschendorf, 1972.

Hollenbach, Paul W. "John the Baptist." Pages 887-99 in vol. 3 of *The Anchor Bible Dictionary.* Edited by David Noel Freedman. New York: Doubleday, 1992.

———. "The Conversion of Jesus: From Jesus the Baptizer to Jesus the Healer." *ANRW* 25.1:196-219. Part 2, *Principat,* 25.1. Edited by H. Temporini and W. Haase. Berlin, 1972-.

Holmén, Tom. "Doubts about Double Dissimilarity: Restructuring the Main Criterion of Jesus-of-History Research." Pages 47-80 in *Authenticating the Words of Jesus.* Edited by Bruce Chilton and Craig A. Evans. New Testament Tools and Studies 28.1. Leiden: Brill, 1999.

———. "The Temple Action of Jesus (Mark 11:15-17) in Historical Context." Pages 99-127 in *A Bouquet of Wisdom: Essays in Honour of Karl-Gustav Sandelin.* Edited by Karl-Johan Illman, Tore Ahlbäck, Sven-Olav Bäck, and Risto Nurmela. Religionsvetenskapliga skrifter 48. Åbo: Åbo Akademi University Printing House, 2000.

———. *Jesus and Jewish Covenant Thinking.* Biblical Interpretation Series 55. Leiden: Brill, 2001.

Hooker, Morna D. *The Son of Man in Mark: A Study of the Background of the Term 'Son of Man' and Its Use in St Mark's Gospel.* London: SPCK, 1967.

———. "Interchange in Christ." *Journal of Theological Studies* 22 (1971): 349-61.

———. "On Using the Wrong Tool." *Theology* 75 (1972): 570-81.

Hoppe, Rudolf. "Das Gastmahlgleichnis Jesu (Mt 22,1-10; Lk 14,16-24) und seine vorevangelische Traditionsgeschichte." Pages 277-93 in *Von Jesus zum Christus. Christologische Studien: Festgabe für Paul Hoffmann zum 65. Geburtstag.* Edited by Rudolf Hoppe and Ulrich Busse. Berlin and New York: de Gruyter, 1998.

———. "Galiläa — Geschichte, Kultur Religion." Pages 42-58 in L. Schenke et al., *Jesus von Nazaret — Spuren und Konturen.* Edited by Ludger Schenke, et al. Stuttgart: Kohlhammer, 2004.

Horn, Friedrich W. "Die synoptischen Einlasssprüche." *Zeitschrift für die neutestamentliche Wissenschaft und die Kunde der älteren Kirche* 87 (1996): 187-203.

Horsley, Richard A. *Galilee: History, Politics, People.* Valley Forge, Pa.: Trinity, 1995.

———. *Archaeology, History, and Society in Galilee: The Social Context of Jesus and the Rabbis.* Valley Forge, Pa.: Trinity, 1996.

Brian Rhea

Hübner, Hans. *Das Gesetz in der synoptischen Tradition: Studien zur These einer progressiven Qumranisierung und Judaisierung innerhalb der synoptischen Tradition.* Witten: Lutter, 1973.

Isler, Hans-Peter. "Acheloos [2]." Page 72 in vol. 1 of *Der neue Pauly: Enzyklopädie der Antike.* Edited by Hubert Cancik and Helmuth Schneider. Stuttgart: J. B. Metzler, 1996-.

Jenkins, Philip. *Hidden Gospels: How the Search for Jesus Lost Its Way.* Oxford: Oxford University Press, 2001.

Jeremias, Joachim. *Jesus als Weltvollender.* Beiträge zur Förderung christlicher Theologie 33/4. Gütersloh: Bertelsmann, 1930.

————. "Zöllner und Sünder." *Zeitschrift für die neutestamentliche Wissenschaft und die Kunde der älteren Kirche* 13 (1931): 293-300.

————. *Die abendmahlsworte Jesu.* Göttingen: Vandenhoeck & Ruprecht, 1935. English: *The Eucharistic Words of Jesus.* Translated from the 2nd German ed. by Arnold Ehrhardt. Oxford: Blackwell, 1955.

————. *Die Gleichnisse Jesu.* Göttingen: Vandenhoeck & Ruprecht, 1947. English: *The Parables of Jesus.* Translated by S. H. Hooke. 3rd ed. London: SCM, 1972.

————. "Characteristics of the *Ipsissima Vox Jesu.*" Pages 108-15 in *The Prayers of Jesus.* Translated by J. Bowden, C. Burchard and J. Reumann. London: SCM, 1967.

————. *Neutestamentliche Theologie: Erster Teil: Die Verkündigung Jesu.* Gütersloh: Gütersloher, 1971. English: *New Testament Theology: The Proclamation of Jesus.* Translated by J. Bowden. London: SCM, 1971.

Kähler, Christoph. *Jesu Gleichnisse als Poesie und Therapie.* Wissenschaftliche Untersuchungen zum Neuen Testament 78. Tübingen: Mohr Siebeck, 1995.

Kähler, Martin. *Der sogenannte historische Jesus und der geschichtliche, biblische Christus.* Leipzig: Deichert, 1892. English: *The So-Called Historical Jesus and the Historic, Biblical Christ.* Translated by C. E. Braaten. Philadelphia: Fortress, 1964.

Kanda, Hideo. "Religious Thought of Nyoraikyo." *Tenri Journal of Religion* 22 (1988): 59-89.

Käsemann, Ernst. "Das Problem des historischen Jesus." *Zeitschrift für Theologie und Kirche* 51 (1954): 125-53. English: "The Problem of the Historical Jesus." Pages 15-47 in *Essays on New Testament Themes.* Translated by W. J. Montague. London: SCM, 1964.

————. *Exegetische Versuche und Besinnungen: Erster Band.* 2nd ed. Göttingen: Vandenhoeck & Ruprecht, 1960.

————. *Jesu letzter Wille nach Johannes 17.* Tübingen: Mohr Siebeck, 1966. English: *The Testament of Jesus: A Study of the Gospel of John in the Light of Chapter 17.* Translated by Gerhard Krodel. Philadelphia: Fortress, 1968.

Kazen, Thomas. *Jesus and Purity Halakhah: Was Jesus Indifferent to Impurity?* Coniectanea biblica: New Testament Series 38. Stockholm: Almqvist & Wiksell, 2002.

Kazmierski, Carl R. *John the Baptist: Prophet and Evangelist.* Collegeville, Minn.: The Liturgical Press, 1996.

Kee, Howard Clark. *Miracle in the Early Christian World: A Study in Socio-historical Method.* New Haven.: Yale University Press, 1983.

Keener, Craig S. *The Gospel of John: A Commentary.* 2 vols. Peabody, Mass.: Hendrickson, 2003.

Kehrer, Günter. "Religionssoziologie." *Handbuch religionswissenschaftlicher Grundbegriffe.* Edited by Hubert Cancik, et al. 5 vols. Stuttgart: Kohlhammer, 1988.

Kellermann, Diether. "Heiligkeit II: Altes Testament." Pages 697-703 in vol. 14 of *Theologische Realenzyklopädie.* Edited by Gerhard Krause and Gerhard Müller. 36 vols. Berlin: W. de Gruyter, 1977-.

Kertelge, Karl. "Die Vollmacht des Menschensohnes zur Sündenvergebung (Mk 2,18)." Pages 205-13 in *Orientierung an Jesus: Zur Theologie der Synoptiker.* Edited by Paul Hoffmann, N. Brox, and W. Pesch. Freiburg: Herder, 1973.

Kim, S. "Jesus — The Son of God, the Stone, the Son of Man, and the Servant: The Role of Zechariah in the Self-Identification of Jesus." Pages 134-42 in *Tradition and Interpretation in the New Testament: Essays in Honor of E. Earle Ellis for His 60th Birthday.* Edited by Gerald F. Hawthorne and Otto Betz. Grand Rapids: Eerdmans, 1987.

Kirk, Geoffrey Stephen. *The Songs of Homer.* Cambridge: Cambridge University Press, 1962.

Kittel, Gerhard, and Gerhard Friedrich, eds. *Theologisches Wörterbuch zum Neuen Testament.* 10 vols. Stuttgart: W. Kohlhammer, 1932-79.

Klauck, Hans-Josef. *Allegorie und Allegorese in synoptischen Gleichnistexten.* Neutestamentliche Abhandlungen 13. Münster: Aschendorff, 1986.

Klawans, Jonathan. *Impurity and Sin in Ancient Judaism.* Oxford: Oxford University Press, 2000.

Klinghardt, Matthias. *Gemeinschaftsmahl und Mahlgemeinschaft: Soziologie und Liturgie frühchristlicher Mahlfeiern.* Texte und Arbeiten zum neutestamentlichen Zeitalter 13. Tübingen/Basel: Francke, 1996.

Kloppenborg Verbin, John S. *Excavating Q: The History and Setting of the Saying Gospel.* Edinburgh: T&T Clark, 2000.

———. "Egyptian Viticultural Practices and the Citation of Isa 5:1-7 in Mark 12:1-9." *Novum Testamentum* 44 (2002): 134-59.

———. "Isa 5:1-7 LXX and Mark 12:1, 9." *Novum Testamentum* 46 (2004): 12-19.

———. *The Tenants in the Vineyard: Ideology, Economics, and Agrarian Conflict in Jewish Palestine.* Wissenschaftliche Untersuchungen zum Neuen Testament 195. Tübingen: Mohr Siebeck, 2006.

Knoblauch, Hubert. *Religionssoziologie.* Sammlung Göschen 2094. Berlin: de Gruyter, 1999.

Koch, Dietrich-Alex. "Jesu Tischgemeinschaft mit Zöllnern und Sündern: Erwägungen zur Entstehung von Mark 2,13-17." Pages 57-73 in *Jesu Rede von Gott und ihre*

Nachgeschichte im frühen Christentum: Beiträge zur Verkündigung Jesu und zum Kerygma der Kirche. Edited by D.-A. Koch, G. Sellin and A. Lindemann. Gütersloh: Gütersloher, 1989.

Koester, Craig R. *Symbolism in the Fourth Gospel: Meaning, Mystery, Community.* Minneapolis: Fortress, 1995.

Kohler, Werner. *Die Lotus-Lehre und die modernen Religionen in Japan.* Zürich: Atlantis, 1962.

Konko Churches of America. *Konko Daijin: A Biography.* San Francisco: Morosi, 1981.

————. *Gorikai.* 3 vols. Konko: Konkôkyô honbu, 1983-87.

————. *Konko Daijin oboegaki.* Konko: Konkôkyô honbu, 1989.

————. *Oshirase-goto oboe-cho.* Konko: Konkôkyô honbu, 1996.

Koselleck, Reinhart. *Vergangene Zukunft: Zur Semantik geschichtlicher Zeiten.* Frankfurt: Suhrkamp, 1979.

Kraeling, Carl H. *John the Baptist.* New York: Charles Scribner's Sons, 1951.

Kruse, H. "Die 'dialektische Negation' als semitisches idiom." *Vetus Testamentum* 4 (1954): 385-400.

Kuhn, Heinz-Wolfgang. *Ältere Sammlungen im Markusevangelium.* Studien zur Umwelt des Neuen Testaments 8. Göttingen: Vandenhoeck & Ruprecht, 1971.

Labahn, Michael. *Jesus als Lebensspender: Untersuchungen zu einer Geschichte der johanneischen Tradition anhand ihrer Wundergeschichten.* Beihefte zur Zeitschrift für die neutestamentliche Wissenschaft 98. Berlin and New York: Walter de Gruyter, 1999.

Lapide, Pinchas. *Ist die Bibel richtig übersetzt?* 2 vols. Gütersloh: Mohn, 1987-94.

Laube, Johannes, ed. and trans. *Neureligionen: Stand ihrer Erforschung in Japan: Ein Handbuch.* Studies in Oriental Religions 31. Wiesbaden: Harrassowitz, 1995.

Lausberg, Heinrich. "Der Johannes-Prolog: Rhetorische Befunde zu Form und Sinn des Textes." Pages 189-279 in vol. 1 of *Nachrichten der Akademie der Wissenschaften in Göttingen. Philologisch-Historische Klasse* 5. Göttingen: Vandenhoeck & Ruprecht, 1984.

————. "Der Vers J 1,27." Pages 281-96 in vol. 1 of *Nachrichten der Akademie der Wissenschaften in Göttingen. Philologisch-Historische Klasse* 6. Göttingen: Vandenhoeck & Ruprecht, 1984.

————. "Die Verse J 2,10-11 des Johannes-Evangeliums: Rhetorische Befunde zu Form und Sinn des Textes." Pages 113-25 in vol. 3 of *Nachrichten der Akademie der Wissenschaften in Göttingen. Philologisch-Historische Klasse* 3. Göttingen: Vandenhoeck & Ruprecht, 1986.

————. "Der Vers J 1,19 im Rahmen des 'redaktionellen Kapitels' J 1,19–2,11: Rhetorische Befunde zu Form und Sinn des Textes." Pages 9-19 in vol. 2 of *Nachrichten der Akademie der Wissenschaften in Göttingen. Philologisch-Historische Klasse.* Göttingen: Vandenhoeck & Ruprecht, 1987.

Lefkovits, Etgar. "2nd Temple Pool Found." Page 5 of *Jerusalem Post.* 10 June 2004.

Levine, Baruch A. *Leviticus* ויקרא: *The Traditional Hebrew Text with the New JPS*

Translation. The JPS Torah Commentary. Philadelphia: The Jewish Publication Society, 1989.

Levine, Lee I., ed. *The Galilee in Late Antiquity*. New York: Jewish Theological Seminary of America, 1992.

Linnemann, Eta. "Die Hochzeit zu Kana und Dionysos." *New Testament Studies* 20 (1974): 408-18.

Little, Edmund. *Echoes of the Old Testament in The Wine of Cana in Galilee (John 2:1-11) and The Multiplication of the Loaves and Fish (John 6:1-15): Towards an Appreciation*. Cahiers de la Revue biblique 41. Paris: J. Gabalda, 1998.

Lohfink, Gerhard. "Das Gleichnis vom Sämann." *Biblische Zeitschrift* 30 (1986): 36-69.

Lohse, Eduard. "Missionarisches Handeln Jesu nach dem Evangelium des Lukas." *Theologische Zeitschrift* 10 (1954): 1-13.

Luck, Ulrich. "Das Gleichnis vom Sämann und die Verkündigung Jesu." *Wort und Dienst* 11 (1971): 73-92.

Lütgehetmann, Walter. *Die Hochzeit von Kana (Joh 2,1-11): zu Ursprung und Deutung einer Wundererzählung im Rahmen johanneischer Redaktionsgeschichte*. Biblische Untersuchungen 20. Regensburg: Friedrich Pustet, 1990.

Luz, Ulrich. *Das Evangelium nach Matthäus*. 4 vols. Evangelisch-katholischer Kommentar zum Neuen Testament 1.1-4. Zürich/Neukirchen-Vluyn: Benzinger/ Neukirchener, 1985-2002.

———. "Mt und Q." Pages 201-15 in *Von Jesus zum Christus: Christologische Studien: Festgabe für Paul Hoffmann zum 65. Geburtstag*. Edited by Rudolf Hoppe and Ulrich Busse. Berlin and New York: de Gruyter, 1998.

———. *Matthew*. Edited by Helmut Koester. Translated by James E. Crouch. 3 vols. Hermeneia. Minneapolis: Fortress, 1989-2005.

Luz, Ulrich, and Pinchas Lapide. *Jesus in Two Perspectives: A Jewish-Christian Dialog*. Translated by Lawrence W. Denef. Minneapolis: Augsburg, 1985.

Mack, Burton L. *A Myth of Innocence: Mark and Christian Origins*. Philadelphia: Fortress, 1988.

Marcus, Joel. *Mark 1-8: A New Translation with Introduction and Commentary*. Anchor Bible 27. New York: Doubleday, 1999.

Martínez, F. García. *The Dead Sea Scrolls Translated: The Qumran Texts in English*. Translated by W. G. E. Watson. 2nd ed. Leiden: Brill, 1996.

Martyn, J. Louis. *History and Theology in the Fourth Gospel*. 3rd ed. Louisville: Westminster John Knox, 2003.

McArthur, Harvey K. "A Survey of Recent Gospel Research." *Interpretation* 18 (1964): 39-55.

McCane, Byron R. "'Let the Dead Bury Their Own Dead': Secondary Burial and Matt 8:21-22." *Harvard Theological Review* 83 (1990): 31-43.

McEleney, Neil J. "Authenticating Criteria and Mark 7:1-23." *Catholic Biblical Quarterly* 34 (1972): 431-60.

Brian Rhea

Meier, John P. *A Marginal Jew: Rethinking the Historical Jesus.* 3 vols. Anchor Bible Reference Library. New York: Doubleday, 1991-2001.

Meister, Klaus. "M(emnon) aus Herkleia." Pages 1205-6 in vol. 7 of *Der neue Pauly: Enzyklopädie der Antike.* Edited by Hubert Cancik and Helmuth Schneider. Stuttgart: J. B. Metzler, 1996-.

Mensching, Gustav. *Vergleichende Religionswissenschaft.* Heidelberg: Quelle-Meyer, 1949.

———. *Buddha und Christus.* Stuttgart: Deutsche Verlagsanstalt, 1978. Repr., edited by Udo Tworuschka. Freiburg: Herder, 2001.

Merklein, Helmut. "Erwägungen zur Überlieferungsgeschichte der neutestamentlichen Abendmahlstradition." *Biblische Zeitschrift* 21 (1977): 88-101, 235-44.

———. *Die Gottesherrschaft als Handlungsprinzip: Untersuchung zur Ethik Jesu.* 2nd ed. Forschung zur Bibel 34. Würzburg: Echter, 1981.

———. "Die Umkehrspredigt bei Johannes dem Täufer und Jesus von Nazareth." *Biblische Zeitschrift* 25 (1981): 29-46.

———. "Der Tod Jesu als stellvertretender Sühnetod." Pages 181-91 in *Studien zu Jesus und Paulus.* Wissenschaftliche Untersuchungen zum Neuen Testament 43. Tübingen: Mohr Siebeck, 1987.

———. *Jesu Botschaft von der Gottesherrschaft: Eine Skizze.* 3rd ed. Stuttgarter Bibelstudien 111. Stuttgart: Katholisches Bibelwerk, 1989.

———. "Wie hat Jesus seinen Tod verstanden?" Pages 174-89 in *Studien zu Jesus und Paulus II.* Wissenschaftliche Untersuchungen zum Neuen Testament 105. Tübingen: Mohr Siebeck, 1998.

Meyer, Arnold. *Jesu Muttersprache: Das galiläische Aramäisch in seiner Bedeutung für die Erklärung der Reden Jesu und der Evangelien überhaupt.* Freiburg: Mohr Siebeck, 1896.

Meyer, Ben F. *The Aims of Jesus.* London: SCM, 1979.

———. *Critical Realism and the New Testament.* Allison Park, Pa.: Pickwick Publications, 1989.

Meyers, Carol L., and Eric M. Meyers. *Haggai, Zechariah 1–8: A New Translation with Introduction and Commentary.* Anchor Bible 25. Garden City, N.Y.: Doubleday, 1987.

Meyers, Eric M. "Sepphoris on the Eve of the Great Revolt (67-68 C.E.): Archaeology and Josephus." Pages 109-22 in *Galilee Through the Centuries: Confluence of Cultures.* Edited by Eric M. Meyers. Duke Judaic Studies Series 1. Winona Lake, Ind.: Eisenbrauns, 1999.

Meyers, Eric M., ed. *The Oxford Encyclopedia of Archaeology in the Near East: Prepared under the Auspices of the American Schools of Oriental Research.* 5 vols. New York: Oxford University Press, 1997.

———, ed. *Galilee Through the Centuries: Confluence of Cultures.* Duke Judaic Studies Series 1. Winona Lake, Ind.: Eisenbrauns, 1999.

Milgrom, Jacob. "Israel's Sanctuary: The Priestly 'Picture of Dorian Gray.'" *Revue biblique* 83 (1976): 390-99.

Mödritzer, Helmut. *Stigma und Charisma im Neuen Testament und seiner Umwelt: Zur Soziologie des Urchristentums.* Novum Testamentum et Orbis Antiquus 28. Freiburg, Switz.: Universitätsverlag/Göttingen: Vandenhoeck, 1994.

Moloney, Francis J., SDB. "The Fourth Gospel and the Jesus of History." *New Testament Studies* 46 (2000): 42-58.

Montanari, Franco. "Apollodorus 7, aus Athen." Pages 857-80 in vol. 1 of *Der neue Pauly: Enzyklopädie der Antike.* Edited by Hubert Cancik and Helmuth Schneider. Stuttgart: J. B. Metzler, 1996-.

Moore, Carey A. *Esther: Introduction, Translation and Notes.* Anchor Bible 7B. Garden City, N.Y.: Doubleday, 1971.

Moule, Charles Francis Digby. "The Individualism of the Fourth Gospel." *New Testament Studies* 5 (1962): 171-90.

Moxness, Halvor. "The Construction of Galilee as a Place for the Historical Jesus — Part I." *Biblical Theology Bulletin* 31 (2001): 26-37.

——. "The Construction of Galilee as a Place for the Historical Jesus — Part II." *Biblical Theology Bulletin* 31 (2001): 64-77.

——. *Putting Jesus in His Place: A Radical Vision of Household and Kingdom.* Louisville: Westminster John Knox, 2003.

Mrázek, Jiří, Jan Roskovec, and Petr Polorný, eds. *Testimony and Interpretation: Early Christology in Its Judeo-Hellenistic Milieu: Studies in Honor of Petr Pokorný.* Journal for the Study of the New Testament Supplement Series 272. New York: T&T Clark International, 2004.

Mullins, Mark R. "Christianity as a New Religion: Charisma, Minor Founders and Indigenous Movements." Pages 257-72 in *Religion and Society in Modern Japan.* Edited by Mark R. Mullins, Susumu Shimazono, and Paul L. Swanson. Nanzan Studies in Asian Religions. Berkeley: Asian Humanities Press, 1993.

——. "Christianity Transplanted: Towards a Sociology of Success and Failure." Pages 61-77 in *Perspectives on Christianity in Korea and Japan: The Gospel and Culture in East Asia.* Edited by Mark R. Mullins and Richard F. Young. Lewiston: Edwin Mellen, 1995.

——. *Christianity Made in Japan: A Study of Indigenous Movements.* Honolulu: University of Hawaii, 1998.

Mussner, Franz. *Die Johanneische Sichtweise und die Frage nach dem Historischen Jesus.* Quaestiones disputatae 28. Freiburg: Herder, 1965.

——. "Gab es eine 'galiläische Krise'?" Pages 238-52 in *Orientierung an Jesus: zur Theologie der Synoptiker.* Edited by Paul Hoffmann. Freiburg: Herder, 1973.

Negev, Avraham, and Shimon Gibson, eds. *Archaeological Encyclopedia of the Holy Land.* 2nd ed. New York: Continuum, 2003.

Neill, Stephen, and Tom Wright. *The Interpretation of the New Testament, 1861-1986.* 2nd ed. Oxford: Oxford University Press, 1988.

Netzer, Ehud. "Herod's Building Program." Pages 169-72 in vol. 3 of *The Anchor Bible Dictionary*. Edited by David Noel Freedman. New York: Doubleday, 1992.

Neusner, Jacob. *The Idea of Purity in Ancient Judaism: The Haskell Lectures 1972-1973*. Studies in Judaism in Late Antiquity 1. Leiden: Brill, 1973.

Newton, Michael. *The Concept of Purity at Qumran and in the Letters of Paul*. Society for New Testament Studies Monograph Series 53. Cambridge: Cambridge University Press, 1985.

Nicol, W. *The Semeia in the Fourth Gospel*. Novum Testamentum Supplements 32. Leiden: Brill, 1972.

Noetzel, Heinz. *Christus und Dionysos: Bemerkungen zum religionsgeschichtlichen Hintergrund von Johannes 2,1-11*. Stuttgart: Calwer, 1960.

Nolland, John. *Luke 9:21–18:34*. Word Biblical Commentary 35B. Dallas: Word, 1993.

Oakman, Douglas E. *Jesus and the Economic Question of His Day*. Studies in the Bible and Early Christianity 8. Lewiston/Queenston: Edwin Mellen, 1986.

Oberlinner, Lorenz. *Todeserwartung und Todesgewissheit Jesu*. Stuttgarter biblische Beiträge 10. Stuttgart: Kath. Bibelwerk, 1980.

Olsson, Birger. *Structure and Meaning in the Fourth Gospel: A Text-linguistic Analysis of John 2:1-11 and 4:1-42*. Lund: CWK Gleerup, 1974.

Olyan, Saul M. "The Exegetical Dimensions of Restrictions on the Blind and the Lame in Texts from Qumran." *Dead Sea Discoveries* 8 (2001): 38-50.

Onuki, Takashi. "Zur literatursoziologischen Analyse des Johannesevangeliums — auf dem Wege zur Methodenintegration." *Annual of the Japanese Biblical Institute* 8 (1982): 162-216.

———. *Gemeinde und Welt im Johannesevangelium: Ein Beitrag zur Frage nach der theologischen und pragmatischen Funktion des johanneischen 'Dualismus.'* Wissenschaftliche Monographien zum Alten und Neuen Testament 56. Neukirchen-Vluyn: Neukirchener, 1984.

Osten-Sacken, Peter von der. "Zur Christologie des lukanischen Reiseberichts." *Evangelische Theologie* 33 (1973): 476-96.

Ostmeyer, Karl-Heinrich. "Armenhaus und Räuberhöhle? Galiläa zur Zeit Jesu." *Zeitschrift für die neutestamentliche Wissenschaft und die Kunde der älteren Kirche* 96 (2005): 147-70.

Perrin, Norman. *Rediscovering the Teaching of Jesus*. New York: Harper & Row, 1967.

———. *What Is Redaction Criticism?* Philadelphia: Fortress, 1970.

———. *A Modern Pilgrimage in New Testament Christology*. Philadelphia: Fortress, 1974.

Petersen, David L. "Zerubbabel and Jerusalem Temple Reconstruction." *Catholic Biblical Quarterly* 36 (1974): 366-72.

———. *Haggai and Zechariah 1–8: A Commentary*. Old Testament Library. Louisville: Westminster John Knox, 1984.

———. *Zechariah 9–14 and Malachi: A Commentary*. Old Testament Library. Louisville: Westminster John Knox, 1995.

Poirier, J. C. "Purity Beyond the Temple in the Second Temple Era." *Journal of Biblical Literature* 122 (2003): 247-65.

Pokorný, Petr. *Genesis of Christology.* Translated by Marcus Lefébure. Edinburgh: T&T Clark, 1987.

———. *Jesus in the Eyes of His Followers: Newly Discovered Manuscripts and Old Christian Confessions.* Dead Sea Scrolls and Christian Origins Library 4. North Richland Hills, Tex.: BIBAL, 1998.

———. *Theologie der Lukanischen Schriften.* Forschungen zur Religion und Literatur des Alten und Neuen Testaments. Göttingen: Vandenhoeck & Ruprecht, 1998.

Pokorný, Petr, et al. *Hermeneutika jako teorie porozumění: od základních otázek jazyka k výkladu bible.* Prague: Vyšehrad, 2006.

Pokorný, Petr, and Jan Roskovec, eds. *Philosophical Hermeneutics and Biblical Exegesis.* Wissenschaftliche Untersuchungen zum Neuen Testament 153. Tübingen: Mohr Siebeck, 2002.

Popper, Karl J. *The Poverty of Historicism.* London: Routledge, 1957.

———. *Conjectures and Refutations: The Growth of Scientific Knowledge.* London: Routledge and Kegan Paul, 1963.

Porter, Stanley E. *The Criteria for Authenticity in Historical-Jesus Research: Previous Discussion and New Proposals.* Journal for the Study of the New Testament Supplement Series 191. Sheffield: Sheffield Academic, 2000.

———. "Luke 17.11-19 and the Criteria for Authenticity Revisited." *Journal for the Study of the Historical Jesus* 1 (2003): 201-24.

———. "Reading the Gospels and the Quest for the Historical Jesus." Pages 27-55 in *Reading the Gospels Today.* Edited by Stanley E. Porter. McMaster New Testament Studies. Grand Rapids: Eerdmans, 2004.

———. Review of Gerd Theissen and Dagmar Winter, *Quest for the Plausible Jesus.* *Journal of the Evangelical Theological Society* 47 (2004): 507-10.

Rabin, Chaim. *The Zadokite Documents.* Rev. ed. Oxford: Clarendon, 1958.

Räisänen, Heikki. "Jesus and the Food Laws: Reflections on Mark 7.15." Pages 219-41 in *The Torah and Christ: Essays in German and English on the Problem of the Law in Early Christianity.* Edited by Anne-Marit Enroth. Suomen Eksegeettisen Seuran julkaisuja, Publications of the Finnish Exegetical Society 45. Helsinki: Raamattutalo, 1986.

Ranke, Leopold von. *Geschichten der romanischen und germanischen Völker von 1494 bis 1514.* 2nd ed. Collected Works 33/34. Leipzig: Duncker und Humblot, 1874.

Rappaport, Uriel. "How Anti-Roman Was the Galilee?" Pages 95-102 in *The Galilee in Late Antiquity.* Edited by Lee I. Levine. New York: Jewish Theological Seminary of America, 1992.

Rau, Eckhard. *Jesus, Freund von Zöllnern und Sünder: Eine methodologische Untersuchung.* Stuttgart: Kohlhammer, 2000.

Reed, Jonathan L. *Archaeology and the Galilean Jesus: A Re-examination of the Evidence.* Harrisburg, Pa.: Trinity, 2000.

———. "Stone Vessels and Gospel Texts: Purity and Socio-Economics in John 2." Pages 381-401 in *Zeichen aus Text und Stein: Studien auf dem Weg zu einer Archäologie des Neuen Testaments*. Edited by Stefan Alkier and Jürgen Zangenberg. Texte und Arbeiten zum neutestamentlichen Zeitalter 42. Tübingen: Francke, 2003.

———. *The HarperCollins Visual Guide to the New Testament: What Archaeology Reveals about the First Christians*. New York: HarperCollins, 2007.

Regev, Eyal. "Abominated Temple and a Holy Community: The Formation of the Notions of Purity and Impurity in Qumran." *Dead Sea Discoveries* 10 (2003): 243-78.

Reich, Ronny. "Ritual Baths." Pages 430-31 in vol. 4 of *The Oxford Encyclopedia of Archaeology in the Near East*. Edited by Eric M. Meyers. 5 vols. New York: Oxford University Press, 1997.

Reicke, Bo. "Instruction and Discussion in the Travel Narrative." *Texte und Untersuchungen zur Geschichte der altchristlichen Literatur* 73 (1959): 206-14.

Reiling, J. "Unclean Spirits." Page 882 in *Dictionary of Deities and Demons in the Bible*. Edited by Karel van der Toorn, Bob Becking, Pieter W. van der Horst. 2nd ed. Leiden: Brill, 1999.

Reiser, Marius. *Syntax und Stil des Markusevangeliums im Licht der hellenistischen Volksliteratur*. Wissenschaftliche Untersuchungen zum Neuen Testament, Second Series 11. Tübingen: Mohr Siebeck, 1984.

———. *Die Gerichtspredigt Jesu*. Neutestamentliche Abhandlungen: Neue Folge 2. Münster: Aschendorff, 1990.

Renan, Ernest. *Das Leben Jesu*. Leipzig: Reclam, 1929.

Rhoads, David M. *Israel in Revolution 6-74 CE: A Political History Based on the Writings of Josephus*. Philadelphia: Fortress, 1976.

Richardson, Peter. *Building Jewish in the Roman East*. Waco, Tex.: Baylor University Press, 2004.

Riches, John K. *Jesus and the Transformation of Judaism*. London: Darton, Longman & Todd, 1980.

Riesner, Rainer. "Das Boot vom See Gennesaret." *Bibel und Kirche* 41 (1986): 135-38.

———. "Neues vom See Gennesaret." *Bibel und Kirche* 42 (1987): 171-73.

Ripley, Jason. *Behold, the Lamb of God: Johannine Christology and the Martyrdoms of Isaac*. Ph.D. diss., Princeton Theological Seminary, 2005.

Risse, Günter. "Religionsstifter." Page 905 in *Lexikon der Sekten, Sondergruppen und Weltanschauungen*. Edited by Hans Gasper, et al. Freiburg: Herder 1990.

Ritmeyer, Leen. *The Quest: Revealing the Temple Mount in Jerusalem*. Jerusalem: Carta: The Lamb Foundation, 2006.

Rivkin, Ellis. *What Crucified Jesus?* Nashville: Abingdon, 1984.

Robinson, James M. "The Johannine Trajectory." Pages 232-68 in *Trajectories through Early Christianity*. Edited by James M. Robinson and Helmut Koester. Philadelphia: Fortress, 1971.

Robinson, James M., P. Hoffmann, and J. S. Kloppenborg, eds. *The Critical Edition of Q*. Leuven: Peeters, 2000.

Robinson, John A. T. "Did Jesus Have a Distinctive Use of Scripture?" Pages 49-57 in *Christological Perspectives: Essays in Honor of Harvey K. McArthur*. Edited by R. F. Berkey and S. A. Edwards. New York: Pilgrim, 1982. Repr., pages 35-43 in *Twelve More New Testament Studies*. London: SCM, 1984.

Roh, Taeseong. *Die "familia dei" in den synoptischen Evangelien*. Novum Testamentum et Orbis Antiquus 37. Freiburg, Switz.: Universitätsverlag/Göttingen: Vandenhoeck, 2000.

Safrai, Shemuel. "The Temple." Pages 865-907 in vol. 2 of *The Jewish People in the First Century: Historical Geography, Political History, Social, Cultural and Religious Life and Institutions*. Edited by S. Safrai and M. Stern. 2 vols. Compendia rerum iudaicarum ad Novum Testamentum 1. Assen: Van Gorcum, 1976.

Salier, Willis Hedley. *The Rhetorical Impact of the Semeia in the Gospel of John*. Wissenschaftliche Untersuchungen zum Neuen Testament, Second Series 186. Tübingen: Mohr Siebeck, 2004.

Sanders, E. P. *The Tendencies of the Synoptic Tradition*. Society for New Testament Studies Monograph Series 9. Cambridge: Cambridge University Press, 1969.

———. *Jesus and Judaism*. Philadelphia: Fortress, 1985.

———. *Jewish Law from Jesus to the Mishnah: Five Studies*. London: SCM, 1990.

———. *Judaism: Practice and Belief, 63 BCE–66 CE*. London: SCM, 1992.

———. *The Historical Figure of Jesus*. London and New York: Allen/Penguin, 1993. German: *Sohn Gottes: Eine historische Biographie Jesu*. Stuttgart: Klett-Cotta, 1996.

———. "Jesus' Galilee." Pages 3-41 in *Fair Play: Diversity and Conflicts in Early Christianity. Essays in Honour of Heikki Räisänen*. Edited by Ismo Dunderberg, Christopher Tuckett, and Kari Syreeni. Leiden: Brill, 2002.

Sarna, Nahum M. *Exodus שמות: The Traditional Hebrew Text with the New JPS Translation*. The JPS Torah Commentary. Philadelphia: The Jewish Publication Society, 1991.

Schenke, Ludgar. *Das Markusevangelium*. Stuttgart: Kohlhammer, 1988.

Schiffman, Lawrence H. "Community Without Temple: The Qumran Community's Withdrawal from the Jerusalem Temple." Pages 267-84 in *Gemeinde ohne Tempel/ Community without Temple: Zur Substituierung und Transformation des Jerusalemer Tempels und seines Kults im Alten Testament, antiken Judentum und frühen Christentum*. Edited by Beate Ego, Armin Lange and Peter Pilhofer. Wissenschaftliche Untersuchungen zum Neuen Testament 118. Tübingen: Mohr Siebeck, 1999.

Schlosser, Jacques. *Le règne de Dieu dans les dits de Jésus: Deuxième partie*. 2 vols. *Etudes bibliques*. Paris: Gabalda, 1980.

———. "La parole de Jésus sur la fin du Temple." *New Testament Studies* 36 (1990): 398-414.

Schmeller, Thomas. "Jesus im Umland Galiläas: Zu den markinischen Berichten vom Aufenthalt Jesu in den Gebieten von Tyros, Cäsarea Philippi und der Dekapolis." *Biblische Zeitschrift* 38 (1994): 44-66.

Schmiedel, Paul W. "Gospels." Cols. 1761-1898 in vol. 2 of *Encyclopaedia Biblica*. Edited by Thomas K. Cheyne and J. Sutherland Black. 4 vols. London: A. & C. Black, 1899-1907.

Schnackenburg, Rudolf. *Das erste Wunder Jesu (Joh. 2,1-11)*. Freiburg: Herder, 1951.

————. *Das Johannesevangelium*. 4 vols. Herders Theologischer Kommentar zum Neuen Testament 4. Freiburg: Herder, 1965-84.

Schneider, Delwin B. *Konkôkyô: A Japanese Religion*. Tokyo: ISR, 1962.

Schneider, Gerhard. *Das Evangelium nach Lukas*. 2 vols. Ökumenischer Taschenbuchkommentar zum Neuen Testament 3. Gütersloh: Gütersloher, 1977.

Schnelle, Udo. *Das Evangelium nach Johannes*. 2nd ed. Theologischer Kommentar zum Neuen Testament 4. Leipzig: Evangelische Verlagsanstalt, 2000.

Schnelle, Udo, with Michael Labahn and Manfred Lang, eds. *Neuer Wettstein: Texte zum Neuen Testament aus Griechentum und Hellenismus I/2: Texte zum Johannesevangelium*. Berlin: Walter de Gruyter, 2001.

Schottroff, Luise. *Der Glaubende und die feindliche Welt: Beobachtungen zum gnostischen Dualismus und seiner Bedeutung für Paulus und das Johannesevangelium*. Wissenschaftliche Monographien zum Alten und Neuen Testament 37. Neukirchen-Vluyn: Neukirchener, 1970.

Schröter, Jens. *Erinnerung an Jesu Worte. Studien zur Rezeption der Logienüberlieferung bei Markus, Q und Thomas*. Wissenschaftliche Monographien zum Alten und Neuen Testament 76. Neukirchen: Neukirchener, 1997.

————. "The Son of Man as the Representative of God's Kingdom: On the Interpretation of Jesus in Mark and Q." Pages 34-68 in *Jesus, Mark and Q: The Teaching of Jesus and Its Earliest Records*. Edited by Michael Labahn and Andreas Schmid. Journal for the Study of the New Testament: Supplement Series 214. Sheffield: Academic, 2001.

————. "Jesus im frühen Christentum: Zur neueren Diskussion über kanonisch und apokryph gewordene Jesusüberlieferungen." *Verkündigung und Forschung* 51 (2006): 25-41.

Schulz, Siegfried. *Das Evangelium nach Johannes*. 12th ed. Das Neue Testament Deutsch 4. Göttingen: Vandenhoeck & Ruprecht, 1972.

Schürmann, Heinz. *Jesu ureigener Tod*. Freiburg: Herder, 1975.

————. *Gottes Reich — Jesu Geschick*. Freiburg: Herder, 1983.

————. *Jesus: Gestalt und Geheimnis*. Edited by K. Scholtissek. Paderborn: Bonifatius, 1994.

Schweitzer, Albert. *Das Abendmahl im Zusammenhang mit dem Leben Jesu und der Geschichte des Urchristentums, Zweites heft: Das Messianitäts- und Leidensgeheimnis: Eine Skizze des Lebens Jesu*. Tübingen: Mohr Siebeck, 1901. English: *The Mystery of the Kingdom of God: The Secret of Jesus' Messiahship and Passion*. Translated by Walter Lowrie. London: A. & C. Black, 1914.

————. *Von Reimarus zu Wrede: Eine Geschichte der Leben-Jesu-Forschung*. Tübingen: Mohr Siebeck, 1906. 2nd ed.: *Geschichte der Leben-Jesu-Forschung*. Tübingen: Mohr Siebeck, 1913. English: *The Quest of the Historical Jesus: A Critical Study of Its*

Progress from Reimarus to Wrede. Translated by W. Montgomery. London: A. & C. Black, 1910. New edition: London: SCM, 2000; Minneapolis: Fortress, 2001.

Sellin, Gerhard. "Textlinguistische und semiotische Erwägungen zu Mk 4,1-34." *New Testament Studies* 29 (1983): 508-30.

Shimazono, Susumu. "The Living Kami Idea in the New Religions of Japan." *Japanese Journal of Religious Studies* 6 (1979): 389-412.

————. *From Salvation to Spirituality: Popular Religious Movements in Modern Japan*. Melbourne: Trans Pacific Press, 2004.

Smith, D. E. "Table Fellowship and the Historical Jesus." Pages 135-62 in *Religious Propaganda and Missionary Competition in the New Testament World: Essays Honoring Dieter Georgi*. Edited by L. Bormann, K. Del Tredici, and A. Standhartinger. Novum Testamentum Supplements 74. Leiden: Brill, 1994.

Smith, D. Moody. *John Among the Gospels*. 2nd ed. Columbia, S.C.: University of South Carolina Press, 2001.

Smith, Morton. "The Dead Sea Sect in Relation to Ancient Judaism." *New Testament Studies* 7 (1961): 347-60.

————. "On the Wine God in Palestine." Pages 815-29 in *Salo Wittmayer Baron Jubilee Volume*. Edited by S. Lieberman. Jerusalem: American Academy for Jewish Research, 1975.

————. *Jesus the Magician*. San Francisco: Harper & Row, 1978.

Smith, Ralph L. *Micah-Malachi*. Word Biblical Commentary 32. Waco: Word, 1984.

Smitmans, Adolf. *Das Weinwunder von Kana: Die Auslegung von Jo 2,1-11 bei den Vätern und heute*. Beiträge zur Geschichte der biblischen Exegese 6. Tübingen: J. C. B. Mohr, 1966.

Stenger, Werner. "Sozialgeschichtliche Wende und historischer Jesus." *Kairos* 28 (1986): 11-22.

Stoesz, Willis. "The Universal Attitude of Konko Daijin." *Japanese Journal of Religious Studies* 13 (1986): 3-29.

Strack, Hermann Leberecht, and Paul Billerbeck. *Kommentar zum Neuen Testament aus Talmud und Midrasch*. 6 vols. Munich: C. H. Beck, 1922-61.

Strange, James F. "Cana of Galilee." Page 827 in vol. 1 of *The Anchor Bible Dictionary*. Edited by David Noel Freedman. New York: Doubleday, 1992.

————. "Tiberias." Pages 547-49 in vol. 6 of *The Anchor Bible Dictionary*. Edited by David Noel Freedman. New York: Doubleday, 1992.

Strauss, David Friedrich. *Das Leben Jesu*. Tübingen: C. F. Osiander, 1835-36. English: *The Life of Jesus Critically Examined*. Translated by Mary Evans, from the 4th German ed. 3 vols. New York: Calvin Blanchard, 1860.

Strecker, Georg. *Der Weg der Gerechtigkeit: Untersuchung zur Theologie des Matthäus*. Forschungen zur Religion und Literatur des Alten und Neuen Testaments 82. Göttingen: Vandenhoeck, 1962.

Stuhlmacher, Peter. "Vicariously Giving His Life for Many, Mark 10:45 (Matt. 20:28)."

Pages 16-29 in *Reconciliation, Law, and Righteousness: Essays in Biblical Theology.* Translated by Everett R. Kalin. Philadelphia: Fortress, 1986.

―――. "Spiritual Remembering: John 14.26." Pages 55-68 in *The Holy Spirit and Christian Origins: Essays in Honor of James D. G. Dunn.* Edited by Graham N. Stanton, Bruce W. Longenecker, and Stephen C. Barton. Grand Rapids: Eerdmans, 2004.

Suhl, Alfred. *Die Funktion der alttestamentlichen Zitate und Anspielungen im Markusevangelium.* Gütersloh: Mohn, 1965.

Sundermeier, Theo. *Was ist Religion? Religionswissenschaft im theologischen Kontext.* Theologische Bücherei 96. Gütersloh: Chr. Kaiser, 1999.

Tatum, W. Barnes. *John the Baptist and Jesus: A Report of the Jesus Seminar.* Sonoma, Calif.: Polebridge, 1994.

Taylor, Vincent. *The Formation of the Gospel Tradition.* London: Macmillan, 1933.

Teeple, Howard Merle. *The Mosaic Eschatological Prophet.* Philadelphia: Society of Biblical Literature, 1957.

Temple, Sydney. "The Two Signs in the Fourth Gospel." *Journal of Biblical Literature* 81 (1962): 169-74.

Tenri University's Oyasato Research Institute, ed. *The Theological Perspectives of Tenrikyô.* Tenri: Tenri University Press, 1986.

Tenrikyô Church Headquarters, ed. *The Doctrine of Tenrikyô.* Tenri: Tenrikyô Church Headquarters, 2002. Translation of Tenrikyô Kyoten, 1984.

―――. *Ofudesaki: The Tip of the Writing Bush.* Tenri: Tenrikyô Church Headquarters, 1993.

―――. *The Life of Oyasama, Foundress of Tenrikyô.* Tenri: Tenrikyô Church Headquarters, 1996.

―――. *Tenrikyô: The Path to Joyousness.* Tenri: Tenrikyô Overseas Mission Department, 1998.

―――. *Mikagura-uta: The Songs for the Service.* Tenri: Tenrikyô Church Headquarters, 1999.

―――. *Tenrikyô-Christian Dialogue.* Symposium held at the Gregorian University in Rome. Tenri: Tenri University Press, 1999.

Tenrikyô Overseas Mission Department, ed. *An Introduction to Tenrikyô: Its History and Teachings.* Tenri: Tenrikyô Church Headquarters, 1966.

Theissen, Gerd. *Urchristliche Wundergeschichten: Ein Beitrag zur formgeschichtlichen Erforschung der synoptischen Evangelien.* Studien zum Neuen Testament 8. 1974. 7th ed. Gütersloh: Gütersloher, 1998.

―――. "Frauen im Umkreis Jesu." 1993. Pages 91-110 in *Jesus als historische Gestalt.* Forschungen zur Religion und Literatur des Alten und Neuen Testaments 202. Göttingen: Vandenhoeck, 2003.

―――. *Die Religion der ersten Christen.* Gütersloh: Gütersloher, 2000.

―――. "Das Reinheitslogion Mark 7,15 und die Trennung von Juden und Christen." Pages 73-89 in *Jesus als historische Gestalt: Beiträge zur Jesusforschung: Zum 60. Geburtstag von Gerd Theissen.* Edited by Annette Merz. Forschungen zur Religion und Literatur des Alten und Neuen Testaments, 202. Göttingen: Vandenhoeck & Ruprecht, 2003.

————. *Die Jesusbewegung: Sozialgeschichte einer Revolution der Werte.* Gütersloh: Gütersloher, 2004. Rev. ed. of *Soziologie der Jesusbewegung.* Theologische Existenz heute 194. Munich: Kaiser, 1977.

Theissen, Gerd, and Annette Merz. *Der historische Jesus: Ein Lehrbuch.* 1996. 3rd ed. Göttingen: Vandenhoeck & Ruprecht, 2001. English: *The Historical Jesus: A Comprehensive Guide.* Translated by John Bowden. Minneapolis: Fortress, 1998.

Theissen, Gerd, and Dagmar Winter. *Die Kriterienfrage in der Jesusforschung: Vom Differenzkriterium zum Plausibilitätskriterium.* Freiburg, Switz.: Universitätsverlag/Göttingen: Vandenhoeck & Ruprecht, 1997. English: *The Quest for the Plausible Jesus: The Question of Criteria.* Translated by M. Eugene Boring. Louisville: Westminster John Knox, 2002.

Thyen, Hartwig. *Studien zur Sündenvergebung.* Forschungen zur Religion und Literatur des Alten und Neuen Testaments 96. Göttingen: Vandenhoeck & Ruprecht, 1970.

————. *Das Johannesevangelium.* Handbuch zum Neuen Testament 6. Tübingen: Mohr Siebeck, 2005.

Tilborg, Sjef van. *Reading John in Ephesus.* Novum Testamentum Supplements 83. Leiden: E. J. Brill, 1996.

Tiwald, Markus. *Wanderradikalismus: Jesu erste Jünger — ein Anfang und was davon bleibt.* Österreichische biblische Studien 20. Frankfurt: Lang, 2002.

Torrey, Charles Cutler. "The Translations Made from the Original Aramaic Gospels." Pages 269-317 in *Studies in the History of Religions: Presented to Crawford Howell Toy by Pupils, Colleagues and Friends.* Edited by David Gordon Lyon and George Foot Moore. New York: Macmillan, 1912.

————. *Our Translated Gospels: Some of the Evidence.* Cambridge, Mass.: Harvard University Press, 1916.

Tovey, Derek M. H. *Narrative Art and Act in the Fourth Gospel.* Journal for the Study of the New Testament Supplement Series 52. Sheffield: Sheffield Academic, 1997.

Uro, Risto. *Sheep Among the Wolves: A Study of the Mission Instructions of Q.* Annales Academiae Scientiarum Fennicae 47. Helsinki: Suomalainen Tiedeakatemia, 1987.

Vaage, Leif E. *Galilean Upstarts: Jesus' First Followers According to Q.* Valley Forge, Pa.: Trinity, 1994.

VanderKam, James C. "Messianism in the Scrolls." Pages 211-34 in *The Community of the Renewed Covenant: The Notre Dame Symposium on the Dead Sea Scrolls.* Edited by Eugene Ulrich and James C. VanderKam. Christianity and Judaism in Antiquity 10. Notre Dame: University of Notre Dame Press, 1994.

Vielhauer, Philipp. "Gottesreich und Menschensohn in der Verkündigung Jesu." 1957. Repr. pages 55-91 in *Aufsätze zum Neuen Testament.* Edited by P. Vielhauer. Munich: Chr. Kaiser, 1965.

Vogel, Manuel. *Herodes: König der Juden, Freund der Römer.* Biblische Gestalten 5. Leipzig: Evangelische Verlagsanstalt, 2002.

Brian Rhea

Vogt, J. *Aspekte erzählender Prosa*. Opladen: Westdeutscher, 1990.

Vögtle, Anton. "Exegetische Erwägungen über das Wissen und Selbstbewusstsein Jesu." Pages 224-53 in vol. 1 of *Gott in Welt: Festgabe für Karl Rahner*. Edited by J. B. Metz. 2 vols. Freiburg: Herder, 1964. Repr. pages 296-344 in *Das Evangelium und die Evangelien*. Kommentare und Beiträge zum Alten und Neuen Testament. Düsseldorf: Patmos, 1971.

————. "Jesus von Nazareth." Pages 3-24 in vol. 1 of *Ökumenische Kirchengeschichte*. Edited by Raymund Kottje and Bernd Moeller with Thomas Kaufmann and Hubert Wolf. 3 vols. Mainz/Munich: Matthias-Grünewald-Verl., 1970.

————. "Todesankündigungen und Todesverständnis Jesu." Pages 51-113 in *Der Tod Jesu — Deutungen im Neuen Testament*. Edited by Karl Kertelge. Quaestiones disputatae 74. Freiburg: Herder, 1976.

————. "Der verkündigende und verkündigte Jesus 'Christus.'" Pages 27-91 in *Wer ist Jesus Christus?* Edited by Joseph Sauer. Freiburg: Herder, 1977.

————. "Hat sich Jesus als Heilsmittler offenbart?" *Bibel und Kirche* 34 (1979): 4-11.

————. *Offenbarungsgeschehen und Wirkungsgeschichte*. Freiburg: Herder, 1985.

Wachsmann, Shelley. "Galilee Boat." Pages 377-79 in vol. 2 of *The Oxford Encyclopedia of Archaeology in the Near East*. Edited by Eric M. Meyers. 5 vols. New York: Oxford University Press, 1997.

Wahlen, Clinton. *Jesus and the Impurity of Spirits in the Synoptic Gospels*. Wissenschaftliche Untersuchungen zum Neuen Testament 2.185. Tübingen: Mohr Siebeck, 2004.

Weaver, Walter P. *The Historical Jesus in the Twentieth Century, 1900-1950*. Harrisburg, Pa.: Trinity, 1999.

Webb, Robert L. *John the Baptizer and Prophet*. Journal for the Study of the New Testament Supplement Series 62. Sheffield: Sheffield Academic, 1991.

Weder, Hans. *Die Gleichnisse Jesu als Metaphern*. Forschungen zur Religion und Literatur des Alten und Neuen Testaments 120. Göttingen: Vandenhoeck & Ruprecht 1980.

Weiser, Artur. *The Psalms: A Commentary*. Translated by Herbert Hartwell. Old Testament Library. London: SCM, 1962.

Weiss, Wolfgang. *"Eine neue Lehre in Vollmacht": Die Streit- und Schulgespräche des Markus-Evangeliums*. Beihefte zur Zeitschrift für die neutestamentliche Wissenschaft 52. Berlin: Walter de Gruyter, 1989.

Welker, Michael, and Michael Wolter. "Die Unscheinbarkeit des Reiches Gottes." Pages 103-16 in *Marburger Jahrbuch Theologie: 11: Reich Gottes*. Edited by Wilfried Härle and Rainer Preul. Marburg: Elwert & Meurer, 1999.

Wellhausen, Julius. *Einleitung in die drei erste Evangelien*. 2nd ed. Berlin: Reimer, 1911.

Wengst, Klaus. *Das Johannesevangelium*. 2 vols. Theologischer Kommentar zum Neuen Testament 4. Stuttgart: Kohlhammer, 2000-2001.

Westerholm, Stephen. *Jesus and Scribal Authority*. Coniectanea biblica: New Testament Series 10. Lund: Gleerup, 1978.

Wick, Peter. "Jesus gegen Dionysos? Ein Beitrag zur Kontextualisierung des Johannesevangeliums." *Biblica* 85 (2004): 179-98.

Wiefel, Wolfgang. *Das Evangelium nach Lukas.* Theologischer Handkommentar zum Neuen Testament 3. Berlin: Ev. Verlagsanstalt, 1988.

Wilcox, M. "The Denial-Sequence in Mark xiv.26-31, 66-72." *New Testament Studies* 17 (1970-71): 426-36.

Wilson, John F. "Archaeology and the Origins of the Fourth Gospel: Gabbatha." Pages 221-30 in *Johannine Studies: Essays in Honor of Frank Pack.* Edited by James Eugene Priest. Malibu, Calif.: Pepperdine University, 1989.

Wise, Michael O., Martin G. Abegg Jr., and Edward M. Cook. *The Dead Sea Scrolls: A New Translation.* San Francisco: HarperCollins, 1996.

Wolf, Peter. "Liegt in den Logien von der 'Todestaufe' (Mk 10.38f; Lk 12.49f) eine Spur des Todesverständnisses Jesu vor?" Ph.D. diss., Freiburg, 1973.

Wolff, Hans Walter. *Dodekapropheton 6: Haggai.* Biblischer Kommentar, Altes Testament 14.6. Neukirchen-Vluyn: Neukirchener, 1986.

Wolter, Michael. "'Gericht' und 'Heil' bei Jesus von Nazareth und Johannes dem Täufer." Pages 355-92 in *Der historische Jesus: Tendenzen und Perspektiven der gegenwärtigen Forschung.* Edited by Jens Schröter and R. Brucker. Beihefte zur Zeitschrift für die neutestamentliche Wissenschaft 114. Berlin and New York: de Gruyter, 2002.

―――. "Was heisset nu Gottes reich?" *Zeitschrift für die neutestamentliche Wissenschaft und die Kunde der älteren Kirche* 86 (1995): 5-19.

Wright, D. P. *The Disposal of Impurity: Elimination Rites in the Bible and in Hittite and Mesopotamian Literature.* Society of Biblical Literature Dissertation Series 101. Atlanta: Scholars Press, 1987.

―――. "Unclean and Clean: Old Testament." Pages 729-41 in vol. 6 of *The Anchor Bible Dictionary.* Edited by David Noel Freedman. New York: Doubleday, 1992.

Wright, Nicholas Thomas. *The New Testament and the People of God.* London: SPCK, 1992.

―――. *Jesus and the Victory of God.* Minneapolis: Fortress, 1996.

Zager, Werner. *Gottesherrschaft und Endgericht in der Verkündigung Jesu.* Beihefte zur Zeitschrift für die neutestamentliche Wissenschaft 2. Berlin and New York: de Gruyter, 1996.

Zeller, Dieter. "Prophetisches Wissen um die Zukunft in synoptischen Jesusworten." *Theologie und Philosophie* 52 (1977): 258-71.

Zerwick, Max. *Biblical Greek Illustrated by Examples.* English edition of *Graecitas Biblica,* adapted from the 4th Latin edition by Joseph Smith. Scripta Pontificii Instituti Biblici 114. 6th repr, 1994. Roma: Editrice Pontificio Istituto Biblico, 1963.

Zimmermann, Ruben. *Geschlechtermetaphorik und Gottesverhältnis: Traditionsgeschichte und Theologie eines Bildfeldes in Urchristentum und antiker Umwelt.* Wissenschaftliche Untersuchungen zum Neuen Testament. Second Series 122. Tübingen: Mohr Siebeck, 2001.

Brian Rhea

Cited Translations of Classical Authors

Apollodorus. *The Library with an English Translation.* Translated by J. G. Frazer. Loeb
    Classical Library. Cambridge, Mass.: Harvard University Press, 1921; repr. 1979.
Eusebius. *Eusebius' Ecclesiastical History: Complete and Unabridged.* Translated by C. F.
    Cruse. Peabody, Mass.: Hendrickson Publishers, 1998.
Ovid. *Metamorphoses, Books IX–XV.* Translated by F. J. Miller. Loeb Classical Library.
    Cambridge, Mass.: Harvard University Press, 1916; repr. 1976.
Pausanias. *Description of Greece.* Translated by W. H. Jones. Loeb Classical Library.
    Cambridge, Mass.: Harvard University Press, 1933; repr. 1966.
Pliny. *Natural History: Vol. 1: Praefatio, Books 1–2.* Translated by H. Rackham. Loeb
    Classical Library. Cambridge, Mass.: Harvard University Press, 1938; repr. 1967.
———. *Natural History: Vol. 8: Books 28–32.* Translated by W. H. S. Jones. Loeb Classi-
    cal Library. Cambridge, Mass.: Harvard University Press, 1963; repr. 1975.
Sophocles, *Fragments.* Edited and translated by H. Lloyd-Jones. Loeb Classical Library.
    Cambridge, Mass.: Harvard University Press, 1996.

Index of Modern Authors

Abegg, Martin G., Jr., 194n.36
Ahlbäck, T., 223n.106
Akazawa, Bunjirô (Bunji) (= Ikigami Konko Daijin), 238, 238n.25, 239, 240, 241, 242, 243, 244, 245, 246, 247, 248, 249, 249n.67, 250, 250n.69, 251, 252, 253, 254
Akazawa, Ieyoshi, 239
Allison, Dale, 15, 28n.41, 186, 187n.18, 188n.24
Alt, Albrecht, 10, 41
Anderson, Paul N., 75n.16
Aune, David E., 74n.10
Aus, Roger, 77n.25, 87, 87n.70, 88n.73, 88n.75
Aviam, Mordechai, 10n.7, 91n.87

Bäck, Sven-Olav, 223n.106
Barrett, C. K., 81n.41, 93n.96, 191n.30
Barth, Karl, 3, 4
Barthélemy, Jean-Dominique, 205n.32
Barton, Stephen C., 77n.23
Batey, Richard A., 91n.87, 107n.18
Bauckham, Richard J., 15
Baumgarten, Joseph M., 196n.42
Baur, Ferdinand C., 60, 60n.5, 73
Beasley-Murray, George R., 60n.7, 78n.30, 81n.41
Bebbington, David W., 21n.16

Becker, Jürgen, 77n.24, 80n.36, 98n.1
Becking, Bob, 201n.10
Belle, Gilbert van, 80n.38, 190n.28
Berger, Klaus, 82n.46, 166n.42, 199n.2, 210n.52, 227, 227n.117
Berger, Peter L., 128n.13
Berkey, Robert F., 184n.7
Betz, D., 74n.4
Betz, Otto, 192n.32
Billerbeck, Paul, 201n.12, 201n.13
Black, J. Sutherland, 26n.32
Black, Matthew, 32, 32n.56
Blackburn, Barry L., 200n.5
Blank, Josef, 157n.16
Blass, Friedrich, 214n.75
Bloedhorn, H., 74n.4
Blomberg, Craig L., 29n.45, 78n.28
Bock, Darrell L., 220n.96
Bolyki, János, 176n.18
Boobyer, G. H., 190n.27
Booth, Roger P., 213n.69, 215n.76, 217n.85
Borchert, Gerald L., 92n.91
Borg, Marcus J., 1, 179n.26, 199n.2, 210n.52
Borgen, Peder, 74n.10
Bormann, L., 216n.81
Bornkamm, Günther, 4, 39n.10
Bousset, Wilhelm, 60, 60n.6, 84, 84n.57

Bovon, Francois, 173n.10, 207n.38
Bowersock, Glen W., 86n.65
Braaten, Carl E., 17n.4, 74n.5
Braund, D. C., 43n.29
Bremond, Claude, 5, 129, 129n.14, 130, 131, 134
Broer, Ingo, 77n.24, 82n.47
Brooke, George J., 195n.42
Brown, Raymond A., 92n.89, 94n.104
Brox, N., 190n.27
Broyles, Craig C., 183n.2
Bruce, F. F., 192n.32
Brucker, R., 52n.57
Buchanan, George W., 152n.23
Bultmann, Rudolf, 3, 17, 17n.4, 17n.5, 21n.15, 26, 26n.33, 27, 27n.37, 29, 30, 30n.48, 30n.49, 39, 39n.8, 39n.9, 56, 60, 60n.7, 61, 70, 77n.24, 78n.30, 79, 80, 80n.39, 81, 93n.95, 140
Burchard, Christoph, 32n.56, 98n.1
Burkett, D. R., 33n.59
Burney, C. F., 32, 32n.56
Burridge, Richard A., 22n.20
Busse, Ulrich, 165n.38, 165n.41

Caird, George Bradford, 77n.25
Cancik, Hubert, 252n.77
Carmignac, Jean, 188n.23, 194n.40
Case, Shirley Jackson, 107n.18
Casey, M., 32, 32n.56, 189n.26, 190n.28, 191n.29
Ceroke, C. P., 190n.27
Chancey, M., 41n.16, 41n.20, 43n.27, 44n.34, 44n.35, 45n.36, 45n.37, 45n.38
Charlesworth, James H., 1n.1, 10n.7, 12n.9, 36n.1, 57n.2, 66n.12, 68n.14, 74n.10, 75n.16, 90n.83, 90n.84, 91n.87, 200n.5, 247n.58
Cheyne, Thomas K., 26n.32
Chilton, Bruce, 20n.12, 28n.39, 32, 32n.56, 37n.2, 75n.16, 183n.3, 184, 184n.6, 184n.9, 184n.10, 185n.11, 190n.28, 192n.32, 195n.42, 200n.2,

200n.4, 210n.54, 215n.77, 217, 217n.84, 222n.102, 223n.105, 225n.116, 226n.116
Christ, Felix, 116n.35
Claussen, Carsten, 10n.7, 12, 12n.10, 61n.9, 71n.16
Clemen, Carl, 81n.40
Clines, D. J. A., 211n.57, 225n.112
Coenen, Lothar, 149n.14
Cohen, O., 47n.43
Cohn-Sherbok, D., 18n.6
Collingwood, R. G., 23n.23
Collins, John J., 223n.106
Colpe, Carsten, 82n.46
Cook, Edward M., 194n.36
Cothenet, É., 194n.40
Court, J. M., 18n.6
Crossan, John Dominic, 1, 45n.38, 115n.34, 178n.22, 179n.26, 219n.93, 220n.95

Dalman, Gustaf, 31, 31n.53
Daniélou, Jean, 8, 8n.4
Dautzenberg, G., 159n.21, 160n.25, 161n.26, 163n.36, 164, 164n.37
Davies, Margaret, 81n.41
Davies, Philip R., 194n.37
Davies, W. D., 186, 187n.18, 188n.24
Deines, Roland, 74n.9, 89n.80
Deissmann, Adolf, 32n.55
Delbrunner, Albert, 214n.75
Del Tredici, Kelly, 216n.81
Dibelius, Martin, 29, 30n.48
Dodd, C. H., 75, 75n.14, 81n.41, 87n.69, 92n.92, 94n.103, 183, 183n.4
Downing, Francis Gerald, 115n.34, 179n.26
Dray, W. H., 23n.22
Dunderberg, Ismo, 48n.45
Dunn, James D. G., 18n.6, 20n.13, 23n.23, 27, 27n.36, 27n.38, 29n.47, 32, 32n.56, 36n.1, 37n.3, 42n.25, 73n.4, 77n.23, 77n.27, 122n.40, 200n.2, 201n.8, 203n.21, 211n.56, 215n.76, 215n.78, 217, 217n.84, 220n.94,

220n.96, 221, 221n.97, 223n.108,
229n.122
Dupont, J., 215n.78
Dupont-Sommer, André, 194n.40
Du Toit, David S., 18n.6, 28, 28n.40

Ebertz, Michael N., 99n.4
Ebner, Martin, 36n.1, 42n.25, 98n.1,
179n.26
Eco, Umberto, 128, 128n.12
Edwards, D. E., 45n.39, 51n.53
Edwards, Douglas R., 90n.84, 91n.87,
95n.109
Edwards, Sarah A., 184n.7
Egger, Wilhelm, 5, 129, 130n.15
Ego, B., 223n.107
Ehrensperger, Kathy, 15
Ehrman, Bart D., 75n.16
Eichholz, G., 127n.11
Ellis, E. Earle, 192n.32
Enroth, Anne-Marit, 213n.67
Enslin, Morton J., 174n.12
Erlemann, Kurt, 132n.18
Evans, Craig A., 5, 6, 7, 9, 28n.39, 37n.2,
60n.4, 183n.2, 184n.6, 191n.30,
192n.32, 196n.42, 200n.2, 200n.5,
204n.23, 210n.52, 215n.77

Fander, Monika, 120n.38
Fassbeck, G., 47n.43
Fiedler, Peter, 154, 154n.2
Fiensy, David A., 100n.6
Fine, Steven, 114n.32
Fischer, David H., 23n.23
Fitzmyer, Joseph A., 32n.57, 173n.11,
204n.23
Flint, Peter W., 15
Flusser, David, 1, 4
Foerster, W., 201n.10
Fortna, Robert T., 66n.11, 76n.19,
80n.36
France, R. T., 183, 183n.5
Fredriksen, Paula, 74n.11, 75n.16, 79,
79n.34, 79n.35, 97

Freedman, David Noel, 203n.20
Frey, Jörg, 73n.3, 74n.4, 78n.32, 92n.92,
97n.116, 97n.117
Freyne, Séan, 36n.1, 36n.2, 40n.13,
42n.23, 42n.24, 42n.26, 45n.40,
46n.41, 47n.44, 51n.52, 51n.55, 52n.56,
55n.60, 81n.44, 82n.44, 91n.87
Frymer-Kensky, Tikva S., 203n.20,
212n.61, 214n.72, 223n.104
Funk, Robert W., 182n.1, 215n.77
Furuya, Yasu, 234n.13

Gadamer, Hans-Georg, 78, 78n.32
Gal, Zvi, 10, 40, 41n.14, 41n.15, 41n.17
García Martínez, F., 205n.32
Gasper, Hans, 231n.5
Gathercole, Simon J., 18n.8
Gaventa, Beverly Roberts, 93n.98
Gemünden, Petra von, 116n.35
Georgi, Dieter, 216n.81
Gerhardsson, Birger, 122n.40
Giblin, Charles H., 97, 97n.115
Gibson, Shimon, 212n.60
Glasson, T. F., 20n.12, 20n.13, 21n.15
Gnilka, Joachim, 161n.29, 162n.33, 168,
168n.47, 169n.50, 177n.20
Graetz, Heinrich, 1
Grant, R. M., 192n.32
Grässer, Erich, 167n.43
Grenfell, Bernhard P., 207n.38
Grimm, Werner, 187, 187n.19, 192n.30
Guelich, Robert A., 197n.44, 199n.2,
201n.10, 202n.18
Guilbert, P., 188n.23
Gundry, Robert H., 188n.23, 201n.13
Gunkel, Hermann, 30n.48
Gutman, Shmaryahu, 114n.32

Haacker, Klaus, 7, 149n.14, 185, 185n.14
Häfner, Gerd, 156, 156n.13, 157, 157n.14,
157n.15
Hagner, Donald, 18n.6, 205n.35
Hahn, Ferdinand, 78n.32

Hane, Mikiso, 240, 240n.29, 240n.30, 240n.31, 242n.37
Hanhart, Karel, 76n.21
Härle, W., 137n.24
Hauck, F., 201n.11
Hawthorne, Gerald F., 192n.32
Hay, Lewis Scott, 190n.27
Heekerens, Hans-Peter, 80n.37
Heidegger, Martin, 3, 180n.30
Heininger, Bernhard, 131n.16
Heitmüller, Wilhelm, 26, 26n.32
Hendin, David, 15
Hengel, Martin, 73n.4, 74n.6, 74n.8, 75n.16, 77n.25, 79n.33, 81n.44, 89n.79, 92n.92, 109n.21, 109n.22, 112n.27, 113n.28, 116n.35, 150n.18, 151n.19
Higgins, A. J. B., 191n.30
Hoare, Rupert W. N., 60n.7, 78n.30
Hoegen-Rohls, Christina, 78n.32
Hoehner, Harold W., 45n.39
Hoffman, Paul, 111n.23, 111n.24, 162n.30, 165n.38, 165n.40, 190n.27
Hofrichter, P. L., 12n.12
Hollenbach, Paul W., 176n.17, 178n.22
Holmén, Tom, 6, 8, 28n.39, 184n.6, 199n.1, 212n.63, 213n.66, 213n.69, 215n.76, 215n.77, 215n.78, 216n.79, 221n.98, 223n.106, 224n.110, 224n.111, 225n.113
Hooker, Morna D., 184n.6, 192n.30, 199n.2
Hoover, Roy W., 182n.1, 215n.77
Hoppe, Rudolf, 7, 41n.18, 135n.22, 164n.38, 165n.38, 165n.39, 165n.41
Horn, Friedrich W., 141n.4
Horsley, Richard A., 41n.18, 91n.87
Horst, Pieter W. van der, 201n.10
Hübner, Hans, 215n.77
Humphrey, John H., 90n.84
Hunt, Arthur S., 207n.38
Hurst, L. D., 77n.25

Iburi, Izo, 238n.24
Illman, Karl Johan, 223n.106

Isler, Hans-Peter, 82n.50
Isson, Kino, 236, 250, 251

Jacob, Edmond, 116n.35
Jenkins, Philip, 39n.11
Jeremias, Joachim, 32, 32n.56, 87n.66, 123, 123n.1, 123n.2, 123n.3, 123n.4, 123n.5, 124, 124n.6, 125, 125n.8, 218n.88

Kähler, Christoph, 158, 158n.18
Kähler, Martin, 17, 17n.4, 73, 74n.5, 79
Kanda, Hideo, 236n.20
Kant, Immanuel, 57
Kanzo, Uchimura, 231
Käsemann, Ernst, 17, 17n.5, 26, 27n.34, 28, 28n.43, 61, 61n.8, 140, 215n.77
Kazen, Thomas, 201n.11, 202n.16, 207n.38, 207n.39, 212n.62
Kazmierski, Carl R., 171n.4
Kee, Howard Clark, 76n.21
Keener, Craig S., 92n.89, 94n.102, 94n.104
Kehrer, Günter, 252n.77
Kelber, Werner, 15
Kellermann, Diether, 208n.42, 209n.44
Kertelge, Karl, 154n.3, 168n.47, 190n.27
Kim, S., 192n.32
Kirk, Geoffrey S., 30n.51
Klauck, Hans-Josef, 159n.21, 160n.24, 161n.28, 163n.34
Klawans, J., 214n.71, 214n.72
Klinghardt, Matthias, 176n.18
Kloppenborg Verbin, John S., 103n.9, 165n.40, 196n.42
Knoblauch, Hubert, 231n.7
Koch, Dietrich-Alex, 216n.83, 217n.83
Koester, Craig R., 86, 86n.65
Koester, Helmut, 78n.30
Kohler, Kaufmann, 1
Kohler, Werner, 234n.14
Konko Daijin. *See* Akazawa, Bunjirô
Koselleck, Reinhart, 38, 38n.5
Kottje, Raymund, 154n.3

Kraeling, Carl H., 178n.23
Kruse, H., 214n.74
Küchler, M., 74n.4
Kuhn, Heinz-Wolfgang, 161n.25
Kuhn, Karl Georg, 140

Labahn, Michael, 18n.6, 77n.24, 81n.42, 82n.46, 115n.34, 189n.25
Lang, Manfred, 82n.46
Lange, A., 223n.107
Lapide, Pinchas, 92n.91
Laube, Johannes, 234n.14
Lausberg, Heinrich, 93n.97
Lauterbach, Jacob Z., 150n.15
Lefkovits, Etgar, 74n.7
Lessing, G. H., 2
Levine, Baruch A., 208n.42, 209n.43
Levine, Lee I., 45n.39, 48n.46
Lieberman, S., 81n.44
Lignée, H., 194n.40
Lindemann, A., 217n.83
Linnemann, Eta, 77n.24
Little, Edmund, 87n.69
Lohfink, Gerhard, 160n.22, 161n.29
Lohse, Eduard, 105n.13
Longenecker, Bruce W., 77n.23
Luck, Ulrich, 161n.27
Luckmann, Thomas, 128n.13
Lütgehetmann, Walter, 77n.24, 81n.41, 81n.42
Luther, Martin, 26n.31, 60, 231
Luz, Ulrich, 5, 165, 165n.41, 172n.8, 186n.16, 186n.17, 187n.21, 206n.35
Lyon, D. G., 32n.56

Mack, Burton L., 115n.34
Maegawa, Miki. *See* Nakayama, Miki
Manson, Thomas Walter, 191n.30
Marcus, Joel, 200n.2, 202, 202n.15, 202n.18
Martyn, J. Louis, 75, 75n.15
McArthur, Harvey K., 184n.7, 221n.98
McCane, Byron R., 197n.45
McCullough, C. Thomas, 91n.87

McDonald, Lee Martin, 15
McEleney, N. J., 221n.98
Meier, John P., 1, 28, 28n.44, 32n.58, 37n.4, 66n.11, 75n.16, 81n.41, 92n.93, 93n.95, 200n.4, 203n.19, 215n.78, 216n.81, 220n.96, 221n.99
Meister, Klaus, 85n.61
Mell, Ulrich, 77n.24
Mensching, Gustav, 230, 230n.1, 230n.2, 230n.3, 252, 252n.79
Merklein, Helmut, 155, 155n.6, 155n.7, 156, 156n.8, 156n.9, 156n.10, 156n.11, 156n.12, 157, 167n.44, 176n.16, 215n.76, 218n.88
Merz, Annette, 75n.12, 75n.16, 81n.41, 125, 125n.10, 135n.23, 141n.2, 172n.6, 174n.13, 182n.1, 215n.78, 221n.99
Metz, J. B., 154n.1
Meyer, Arnold, 31n.53
Meyer, Ben F., 27n.38, 222n.102
Meyers, Carol L., 203n.20, 208n.42
Meyers, Eric M., 45n.36, 91n.87, 114n.32, 208n.42, 212n.60
Michaels, Axel, 234n.15
Milgrom, Jacob, 206n.36, 225n.115
Milik, Józef T., 205n.32
Mödritzer, Helmut, 99n.4
Moeller, Bernd, 154n.3
Moloney, Francis J., 75n.16
Montanari, Franco, 83n.53
Moore, Carey A., 88n.71
Moore, George Foote, 32n.56
Moule, C. F. D., 146, 146n.10
Moulton, James Hope, 32n.55
Moxnes, Halvor, 54n.59, 91n.87, 100n.5
Müller, P. G., 157n.16
Müller, Ulrich B., 77n.24
Mullins, Mark R., 231, 231n.6, 233n.11
Mussner, Franz, 78n.32, 157n.16, 162, 162n.30, 162n.31

Nakayama, Miki (= Miki Maegawa), 237, 238, 238n.24, 240, 241, 242, 242n.36, 243, 244, 245, 246, 247, 248,

Index of Modern Authors

248n.62, 249, 250, 251, 251n.72, 252, 253, 254
Nakayama, Zenbei, 237, 238
Negev, Avraham, 212n.60
Neill, Stephen, 18n.8, 20n.13, 21n.16
Neirynck, Frans, 190n.28
Netzer, E., 43n.27
Neusner, Jacob, 205n.28, 210n.55
Newton, Michael, 211n.55
Nicol, W., 80n.36
Noetzel, Heinz, 77n.25, 81n.41, 84n.59, 87, 87n.66, 87n.68, 87n.69, 88n.76
Nolland, John, 186n.17, 196n.43
Nurmela, Risto, 223n.106

Oakman, Douglas E., 107n.16, 107n.17
Oberlinner, Lorenz, 154, 154n.2, 162, 162n.32, 167n.45
O'Conner, M., 203n.20
Oegema, Gerbern S., 15
Ogden, S., 26n.33
Okada, Kotama, 231
Olsson, Birger, 76n.21, 87n.69, 89n.77, 93n.96
Olyan, Saul M., 205n.29, 205n.30
Onuki, Takashi, 78n.32
Osten-Sacken, Peter von der, 105n.13
Ostmeyer, Karl-Heinrich, 47n.42

Pack, Frank, 74n.10
Perrin, Norman, 27, 27n.35, 190n.27, 215n.77, 221n.98
Pesch, W., 190n.27
Petersen, David L., 193n.34, 208n.41, 208n.42, 208n.43, 224n.110
Pilhofer, P., 223n.107
Poirier, J. C., 206n.36, 212n.60
Pokorný, Petr, 1, 6, 13, 13n.14, 15
Popper, Karl J., 21n.16, 27n.38
Porter, Stanley, 4, 5, 16n.1, 16n.2, 18n.6, 18n.7, 19n.10, 27n.38, 28n.42, 32n.58, 33n.60, 33n.61, 221n.98
Preul, Rainer, 137n.24
Priest, J. E., 74n.10

Rabin, Chaim, 194n.39
Rahner, Karl, 154n.1
Räisänen, Heikki, 48n.45, 213n.67
Ranke, Leopold von, 73n.1, 97
Rappaport, Uriel, 48n.46
Rau, Eckhard, 179n.27
Reed, Jonathan L., 11, 11n.8, 41n.19, 42n.22, 44n.33, 44n.34, 44n.35, 45n.37, 45n.38, 46n.41, 89n.80, 91n.87, 95, 95n.108, 95n.109, 95n.111
Regev, Eyal, 210n.54, 211n.55, 214n.71, 214n.72
Rehkopf, Friedrich, 214n.75
Reich, Ronny, 63, 74n.7, 212n.60
Reicke, Bo, 105n.13
Reiling, J., 201n.10
Reimarus, 2, 16n.3, 17n.3, 78n.32
Reiser, M., 32n.55, 179n.27
Renan, Ernest, 11, 18n.8, 38, 38n.6, 38n.7, 42
Rhoads, David M., 109n.22
Richardson, Peter, 13n.13, 90n.83, 90n.84, 91, 91n.85, 91n.86, 91n.87, 92n.88
Riches, John K., 60n.7, 78n.30, 215n.78
Riesner, Rainer, 47n.43
Rietz, Henry Morisada, 15
Risse, Günter, 231n.5
Ritmeyer, Leen, 12n.11
Rivkin, Ellis, 152n.24
Robertson, John M., 18n.8
Robinson, James M., 78n.30, 165n.40
Robinson, John A. T., 184, 184n.7
Roskovec, Jan, 15

Safrai, Shemuel, 222n.104
Salier, Willis Hedley, 86n.65
Sandelin, Karl-Gustav, 223n.106
Sanders, E. P., 1, 4, 30, 30n.50, 36n.1, 48n.45, 206n.36, 206n.37, 207n.38, 211n.59, 215n.78, 216, 216n.81, 216n.82, 217, 217n.84, 218n.88, 222n.102, 225n.116
Sarna, Nahum M., 209n.43

Sato, Migaku, 234n.15, 235n.16
Sauer, Joseph, 155n.3, 167n.43
Schenke, L., 41n.18, 159n.20
Schiffman, Lawrence H., 223n.107
Schleiermacher, Friedrich, 60
Schlosser, J., 221n.99, 224n.111
Schmeller, Thomas, 120n.39
Schmid, H., 156n.13
Schmid, J., 162n.30, 190n.27
Schmidt, A., 18n.6, 115n.34, 189n.25
Schmiedel, P., 26, 26n.32
Schnabel, E., 149n.14
Schnackenburg, Rudolf, 76n.22, 92n.92,
    96n.112
Schneider, Delwin B., 238n.25
Schneider, Gerhard, 105n.13
Schnelle, Udo, 80n.38, 81n.41, 82n.46
Scholtissek, K., 154n.3
Schottroff, Luise, 78n.30
Schröter, Jens, 10, 40n.12, 52n.57, 172n.7,
    189n.25
Schulz, Siegfried, 78n.30
Schürmann, Heinz, 154, 154n.3, 155,
    155n.4, 157, 158n.17, 158n.19
Schweitzer, Albert, 2, 3, 5, 16, 16n.3, 17,
    18n.8, 19, 20, 20n.12, 20n.13, 20n.14,
    21, 21n.15, 21n.16, 21n.17, 22, 22n.18,
    22n.19, 22n.21, 23, 23n.22, 23n.24, 24,
    24n.26, 24n.27, 24n.28, 24n.29, 25, 26,
    26n.30, 26n.31, 26n.33, 28, 29, 31,
    31n.52, 33, 34, 35, 39, 39n.8
Schwemer, Anna Maria, 116n.35
Schwienhorst, L., 205n.32
Segbroeck, F. Van, 190n.28
Seland, Torrey, 74n.10
Sellin, Gerhard, 159n.21, 160n.25,
    217n.83
Sevenster, J. N., 76n.21
Shimada, Katsumi, 234n.15, 242n.36
Shimazono, Susumu, 231n.6, 233n.10,
    234, 234n.12, 236, 236n.19, 236n.20,
    247n.59, 250n.71
Shukrun, Eli, 63, 74n.7
Smith, D. E., 216n.81

Smith, D. Moody, 73n.3
Smith, Joseph, 214n.75
Smith, Morton, 81n.41, 81n.44, 210n.54
Smith, Ralph L., 193n.34, 208n.42
Smith, William B., 18n.8
Smitmans, Adolf, 78n.29, 84n.58, 92n.92
Söding, T., 73n.3
Spinoza, Baruch, 57
Standhartinger, Angela, 216n.81
Stanton, Graham N., 77n.23
Stenger, Werner, 98n.1, 157n.16
Stern, Ephraim, 114n.32
Stern, M., 222n.104
Stoesz, Willis, 238n.25
Strack, Hermann L., 201n.12, 201n.13
Strange, James F., 44n.31, 90n.81
Strauss, David Friedrich, 2, 56, 60,
    60n.4, 73, 76, 76n.20
Strecker, Georg, 104n.12
Stuhlmacher, Peter, 77n.23, 192n.30
Suhl, Alfred, 193n.33
Sundermeier, Theo, 230, 231n.4
Swanson, Paul L., 231n.6
Syreeni, Kari, 48n.45

Tatum, W. Barnes, 171n.2, 171n.3
Taylor, V., 29, 30n.48
Teeple, Howard M., 153n.25
Temple, Sydney, 80n.37
Thatcher, Tom, 66n.11
Theissen, Gerd, 5, 7, 8, 11, 15, 19n.10,
    26n.31, 28n.39, 28n.41, 33, 33n.60, 57,
    57n.1, 75n.12, 75n.16, 76n.17, 81n.41,
    98n.1, 99n.3, 119n.37, 125, 125n.10,
    135n.23, 138n.26, 141n.2, 172n.6,
    174n.13, 182n.1, 201n.8, 215n.78,
    216n.79, 221n.98, 221n.99, 251n.73
Thumb, Albert, 32n.55
Thyen, Hartwig, 76n.21, 77n.26, 89n.78,
    171n.3
Tilborg, Sjef van, 82n.45
Tillich, Paul, 3
Tiwald, Markus, 104n.10
Toorn, Karel van der, 201n.10

Torrey, C. C., 32, 32n.56
Tovey, Derek M. H., 75n.16
Toy, C. H., 32n.56
Troeltsch, Ernst, 232n.8
Tsushima, Michihito, 235n.17
Tuckett, Christopher M., 48n.45, 190n.28
Tworuschka, Udo, 230n.3
Tyrrell, George, 3

Ulrich, Eugene, 194n.40
Ulrichsen, J. H., 74n.10
Uro, Risto, 111n.24

Vaage, Leif E., 115n.34
Vanderkam, James C., 194n.40
Venturini, Karl Heinrich, 1
Verheyden, J., 190n.28
Vermes, Geza, 4, 14
Vielhauer, Philipp, 137n.25
Vogel, M., 43n.27
Vogt, J., 133n.19
Vögtle, Anton, 154, 154n.1, 154n.3, 155, 155n.3, 155n.5, 157, 167n.43

Wachsmann, Shelley, 47n.43
Wahlen, Clinton, 201n.11, 202n.16
Weaver, Walter, 1n.1, 3, 3n.2, 4, 4n.3, 19n.9, 200n.5
Webb, Robert L., 15, 170n.1, 171n.5, 172n.6, 175n.15
Weber, Max, 232n.8
Wedderburn, A. J. M., 73
Weder, Hans, 159n.21, 163n.34
Weiser, Artur, 225n.115
Weiss, Johannes, 18

Weiss, Wolfgang, 215n.77
Welker, Michael, 137n.24
Wellhausen, Julius, 32n.56
Wengst, Klaus, 78n.31
Westerholm, Stephen, 206n.36, 211n.55, 214n.76, 218n.88
Whittaker, Thomas, 18n.8
Wick, Peter, 77n.24, 81n.42
Wiefel, Wolfgang, 105n.13
Wilcox, M., 193n.33
Wilson, Brian, 232n.8, 252n.76
Wilson, John F., 74n.10
Winter, Dagmar, 19n.10, 26n.31, 28n.39, 28n.41, 33, 33n.60, 57, 57n.1, 141n.2, 221n.98
Wise, Michael O., 194n.36
Wolf, E., 74n.5
Wolf, Peter, 154, 154n.2
Wolff, Hans Walter, 224n.109
Wolter, Michael, 5, 52n.57, 137n.24, 158n.18
Wrede, Wilhelm, 16n.3, 17n.3, 18, 18n.8
Wright, D. P., 203n.20, 203n.22, 206n.37, 214n.70
Wright, N. T., 18n.8, 20n.13, 27n.38, 29, 29n.45, 29n.46, 77n.25, 185n.12

Yamada, Shinji, 234n.15, 242n.39, 248n.65
Young, Richard F., 233n.11

Zager, Werner, 179n.27
Zeller, Dieter, 168n.49
Zerwick, Max, 214n.75
Zimmermann, Ruben, 94n.102

Index of Ancient Texts

**OLD TESTAMENT/
HEBREW BIBLE**

Genesis

1:1–2:4a	93
2:2-3	189
2:2	67
3	57
6–9	175
9:20	87n.66
12:7	148
13:15	148
15:7	148
15:18	148
23:13	197
24:7	148
26:3	148
28:4	148
28:13	148
35:12	148
48:4	148
49:11-12	87, 87n.66
50:5-14	197

Exodus

19:10-25	209n.47
19:11	96
19:16	96
20:10-11	189
21:17	196
29:37	208n.43
30:29	208n.43
32:13	148
32:27-29	196

Leviticus

5:1-6	206n.37
5:3	203n.20
6:11	208n.43
6:20	208n.43
13:1-46	204n.26
13:45-46	203n.20
14:20	203
15:19-24	203n.22
15:25-30	203
17:11-19	203
17:15-16	206n.37
18	213
18:5	185, 186
18:24	197
19:17	196
19:18	71
19:31	213
20:1-3	213
20:9	196
20:24	148
21	209n.46
21:1-2	209n.49
21:10-11	209n.50
26:1	225n.112
26:30	225n.112

Numbers

5:1-4	203n.22
5:3b	205n.30
6:5-12	209n.50
13:23-24	87n.66
14:11	150
14:23	148
14:24	148, 149, 150
14:27	149
14:30	148
14:31	148
15:27-31	225n.115
19	204n.25
19:2-9	204n.25
19:19	204n.25
20:12	150
20:24	148
27:12	148
31:24	204n.25
32:11-12	149, 150
32:11	148
33:51	148
33:53	149
35:33-34	214

Deuteronomy

1:8	147, 149
1:21	148, 149
1:32	150
1:35-38	149
1:35-36	150
1:35	148, 149
1:36	148
1:39	147, 149
2:29	147
3:20	148
3:25	148
4:5	148
4:22	148
5:31	147
6:1	147
6:18	147
8:1	147
9:5-6	147, 149
9:23	147, 150
10:11	147
12:29	147
16:20	147
18:15	153n.25
18:18	153n.25
19:8	148
21:20-21	175
23:2-5	9
26:15	148
27:2	148
28:26	209n.48
31:13	147
31:20	148
32:5	149
32:20	149

Joshua

1:11	147
2:9	148
2:14	148
2:24	148
3	152
5:6	148
18:3	147

23:5	148
24:13	148

Judges

6:9	148
14:12	92n.89, 94n.104
14:17	92n.89

1 Samuel

2:1-8	221n.100

2 Samuel

5:8	8, 205, 205n.30, 205n.35
5:11	107n.17

1 Kings

8:34	148
8:40	148
17:2-3	108
17:9-10	108
17:17-24	205n.28
18:1	108n.19
18:12	108n.19
19:3	108
19:19-21	108, 198
21:18	108n.19
22:22-23	201

2 Kings

1:8	175
4:18-37	205n.28
15:29	40

2 Chronicles

6:25	148
6:31	148

Nehemiah

9:8	148
9:15	147
9:35	148
13:19	209n.45
13:22	209n.45

Esther 80, 87, 88, 88n.70, 88n.75

1	77n.25
1:1-8	88
1:3-5	88
1:7	88n.75
2:18	88n.74
4:16	88
5:1	88
5:6	88
7:2	88
9	88

Job

14:4	211n.57

Psalms

2:7	192n.31
15	225n.115
24:3-5	219n.92, 225n.115
74:9	178
75:8	221n.100
78:7-8	150
78:8	149
78:21-22	150
78:32-33	150
95:10	149
106:24	150
110	192n.31
110:1	192n.31
113:7-9	221n.100

Proverbs

8	180n.29
20:20	196

Ecclesiastes / Qohelet

2:24	132n.17
3:12-13	132n.17
5:18	132n.17
8:15	132n.17

Isaiah 6, 51, 70, 80, 182, 188n.24

2:18	225n.112	36:25	219n.92	2:15		224
4:3-4	219n.92	36:29	219n.92			
5:1-7	195, 196n.42	37:22-28	219n.91	**Zechariah**		6, 183,
5:5	195	37:25	194n.41			192n.32, 193
5:7	195	44:31	209n.46	4:7		224
9:1-2	51n.54, 53	47:1	223	4:9		224
10:11	225n.112			11:7		193, 194
16:12	225n.112	**Daniel**	6, 183, 188	13		192, 195
19:1	225n.112	2	187, 188, 188n.24	13:1		223
21:9	225n.112	2:19-23	187	13:2		201n.11
26:19	182n.2	2:20-23	187	13:7-9		193n.34
29:14	186, 188n.24	2:21	221n.100	13:7		193, 194n.38,
29:18-19	182n.2	5:4	225n.112			194n.40
30:25	87n.66	5:23	225n.112	13:8-9		195
31:7	225n.112	6:28	225n.112	14:8		87n.66
33:14-16	225n.115	7	190, 190n.28, 191,			
35:5-6	182n.2		192n.31	**Malachi**		
35:8	219n.92	7:13-14	189, 191, 192,	3:1-7		176
40:3	171n.3		192n.31	3:1		171n.3
40:9	182n.2	7:13	191, 192n.31			
42:1-7	219n.91	7:14	191			
46:6	225n.112			**NEW TESTAMENT**		
52:1	205n.30, 219,	**Hosea**				
	219n.92	6:6	214	**Matthew**	2, 7, 49, 51, 53,	
52:7	182n.2				54, 60, 75n.11,	
53	155, 192	**Joel**			99n.2, 102, 104,	
56:2	190	3:13	163		105, 124, 145,	
61:1-2	182n.2	4:18	87n.66		152n.21, 194n.40	
				1:16		94n.100
Jeremiah		**Amos**		1:18		94n.100
7:22-23	214	9:13	87n.68	1:20		94n.100
7:33	209n.48			2:11		94n.100
8:1-2	209n.48	**Jonah**		3:2		152
23:5-6	219n.91	1:2	108	3:13-17		171
31:12	87n.68	3:2	108	4:12-16		53
		3:5	175	4:13		53, 104
Ezekiel		4:9-11	133n.20	4:15-16		51n.54
4:14	209n.46			4:17		152
6:5	209n.48	**Haggai**	208, 210	5:17-20		186
9:4	194	2:9	223, 224	5:20		142
17:24	221	2:10-14	224	5:21-22	244n.46, 253n.81	
21:27	221	2:11-13	208, 224	5:38		244n.46
29:5	209n.48	2:14	224, 224n.112,	5:42		244n.46
34:24	194n.41		225n.112	6:5		50

6:7-8	244n.46	12:42	149	21:12-14	205n.35
6:10	148n.13	12:43	201n.9, 202	21:31	142
6:12	51	12:45	149	21:32	219
7:21	142	13:1	104n.12	21:43	143
8:11-12	179, 220	13:33	135	22:1-14	94, 177
8:14	104, 104n.12	13:36	104n.12	22:1-10	164, 164n.28, 219
8:20	104	13:44	125n.8	22:2	96n.114
8:21-22	116, 197n.45	13:45-46	125n.8	22:16	98n.2
8:22	197	13:45	51	23:2-3	174
9:1	53	14:5	174	23:5	67
9:10	11, 103, 104,	14:36	67, 229n.124	23:8	99n.2
	104n.12	15:1	244n.46	23:25-26	214n.73
9:11	99	15:29-31	205n.34	23:37-39	223n.106
9:18-26	76n.18	16:4	149	24:23-26	151, 152
9:20	67, 229n.124	17:17	149	25:1-13	94
9:21	229n.124	17:24-27	104, 200n.3	25:31	244n.46
9:28	104n.12	17:24	99n.2	25:34	144, 149
9:32-33	202n.17	17:25	11, 103, 104n.12	26:29	167n.46
10:1	201n.9, 228n.120	18	134	26:73	48n.47
10:8	228	18:3	142	27:62	92n.94
10:13	111	18:8	142	27:63-64	92n.94
10:16	193n.35	18:9	143		
10:23	102n.8	18:12-14	127	**Mark**	2, 7, 49, 51, 60,
10:30	68	18:12	127, 193n.35		73, 74n.11,
10:39	244n.46, 220	18:23-35	51, 125n.8,		79n.34, 102, 104,
11:2-6	183n.2		226n.116		116n.36, 124,
11:5	7, 76n.18, 201n.6,	18:30	51		145n.9, 171, 174,
	201n.7, 202,	19:14	143		177, 193, 194n.40
	205n.34	19:16	98n.2, 144, 145,	1:2-8	171
11:16-17	177		145n.8	1:2	121, 171n.3
11:16	174	19:17	143	1:3	171n.3
11:17	177n.21	19:23-24	142, 143	1:4-5	175
11:18-19	172, 173	19:25	143n.5	1:6b	173
11:18	174	19:29	145	1:9-11	171
11:19	218n.88	20	134	1:14	53
11:25-27	186, 187n.19	20:1-15	132	1:15	7, 148n.13, 157,
11:25	186, 187n.20	20:2	132		158, 164, 180
11:28-30	102n.8	20:4	132, 133	1:16-20	106
12:11	67	20:8	133	1:19-20	47
12:22	205n.34	20:9	133	1:20	247
12:28	144n.7	20:10	133	1:22	99
12:39	149	20:15	133	1:23	201n.9, 202
12:41-42	253n.81	20:26	219	1:24	201n.13
12:41	149	20:28	192n.30	1:26-27	201n.9

1:29-31	120	4:16-20	159n.21	6:21	55
1:32-34	102	4:21-25	159n.21	6:32-44	200n.3
1:38	102	4:26-29	7, 135, 157, 158,	6:34	193n.35
1:39	54		159, 159n.21,	6:45-52	200n.3
1:40-45	7, 202, 203		160n.25, 161n.25,	6:53-56	102
1:41	201n.6, 202		163	6:56	67, 229n.124
1:42	203	4:28	135n.21, 163	7:1-23	221n.98
1:45	102, 104	4:30-32	7, 135, 157, 158,	7:3-4	95n.107
2:1-12	189		159, 159n.21,	7:15	197, 213, 213n.64,
2:10	190, 190n.27		160n.25, 161n.25,		213n.67, 214,
2:13-17	217n.83		164		215n.78, 216,
2:15	218n.88	4:35-41	200n.3		216n.79, 217n.87
2:16	218n.88	4:38	98n.2	7:19	197
2:17	124, 220, 218n.88	5	204, 205	7:24-30	120
2:19	96n.114, 177	5:1-20	229n.122	7:24	12, 103
2:21-22	120	5:1	12, 103	7:25	201n.9
2:23-28	189	5:2	201n.9, 202n.14	7:31	12, 103
2:25	184	5:7	201n.13	8:12	149
2:27-28	189	5:8	201n.9, 202	8:22-25	205n.34
2:28	190n.27	5:13	201n.9	8:27	12, 50, 103
3:1-5	205n.34	5:20	12, 103	8:28	99, 108
3:7-11	102	5:21-43	76n.18, 120	8:35	220
3:7-8	54	5:21-24	229n.122	8:38	149
3:11	201n.9, 201n.13	5:25-34	201, 229,	9:1	57, 145, 148n.12,
3:21	93, 100		229n.122		148n.13, 149,
3:22	11	5:27	229n.123		150n.16
3:29-30	201n.13	5:28	229n.123	9:9-13	171
3:30	201n.9	5:30	229n.123	9:12	184
3:31-35	93, 100, 118, 247	5:34	204n.23	9:17	98n.2
3:32	93	5:35-43	204n.24,	9:19	149
4:1-34	158, 159n.21,		229n.122	9:25	201n.9
	160n.25, 161n.26,	5:35	99	9:38	98n.2
	163n.36, 164n.37,	6:1-6	100	9:43-47	143
	166, 169	6:3	93	9:43	142
4:3-9	7, 135, 157, 159,	6:4	99, 100	9:45	142
	159n.21, 161n.25	6:7-13	210n.53	9:47	142, 143
4:3-8	160n.25	6:7	201n.9, 210n.53,	10:14	143, 149, 150n.16
4:3-7	161		228	10:15	142, 143
4:4	160	6:12-13	228	10:17	98n.2, 145
4:5	160	6:12	110	10:21	115
4:6	160	6:14-15	108	10:23-24	142
4:7	160	6:14	49, 99, 178	10:28-31	47
4:11-12	220	6:15	99	10:29-30	247
4:14-15	159n.21	6:17-29	49, 77n.25, 171	10:30	144, 145

10:31	220, 222	listed separately			201n.6, 201n.7,
10:35	98n.2	below]	2, 7, 51, 54, 60,		202, 205n.34
10:38	154n.2		73, 75n.11, 103,	7:24	174
10:45	191, 191n.30, 192,		105, 124, 145n.9	7:28	178
	192n.30, 192n.31,	1–2	94n.100	7:30	174
	195, 219	1:46-53	221n.100	7:31-35	116n.36
10:46-52	205n.34	1:54-80	171	7:31-34	177
11:12-14	200n.3	1:76a	171n.3	7:31-32	177
11:15-17	223n.106	2:41-52	240	7:31	174
11:20-21	200n.3	3:3	175	7:32	50, 175
11:23	244n.46	3:7-9	171	7:33-34	172, 174, 175, 178,
12:1-9	195, 196n.42	3:7	175		179, 180
12:10	184	3:8	175	7:33	173, 175
12:13-17	111, 114	3:9	175	7:34	175, 218n.88
12:26	184	3:10-14	170	7:35	180
12:35	184	3:15-16	171n.3	7:36-50	176, 201,
12:41	244n.46	3:16	172		226n.116
13:1-2	223n.106	3:17	171, 175, 176	7:40	98n.2
13:1	224	3:20	171	7:41-43	125
13:2	224	3:21-22	171	7:48	176
13:30	150n.16	4:14-16	90n.82	8:1-3	119
14:3-9	120	4:16-30	53	8:29	201n.9
14:3	201n.6	4:16-21	240	8:40-56	76n.18
14:22-25	176, 195	4:25-27	120	8:44	67, 229n.124
14:25	7, 87n.66, 157,	4:30	105	9:1-6	228n.120
	157n.16, 166, 167,	4:33	201n.9	9:27	145, 148n.12, 149
	168, 169, 176	4:36	201n.9	9:41	149
14:26-31	193n.33	4:42	105	9:42	201n.9
14:27	192	5:1-11	200n.3	9:51-53	105
14:28	169n.31	5:8	218n.88	9:51	105n.13, 105n.14
14:57-58	223n.106	6:18	201n.9	9:52-56	102
14:58	224, 225n.112	6:20-21	177	9:53	105n.14
14:62	192n.31	7:5	50n.50	9:56	105n.14
14:66-72	193n.33	7:6-11	105	9:57	105n.14
15:2-5	152n.22	7:11-17	76n.18, 201n.7,	9:58	54, 102
15:6-15	87n.70		204, 205,	9:59	247
15:26	152n.22		229n.122	9:60	197
15:40-41	118, 120	7:12-16	204n.24, 228	9:61-62	198
15:47	120	7:14	204n.24, 228	10:3	193n.35
16:1-8	120	7:18-35	172, 174	10:6	111
16:7	169n.51	7:18-23	183n.2	10:9	110
		7:19	172	10:10	50
Luke [list includes		7:22-23	181	10:13-15	179, 180n.28
references to Q, also		7:22	76n.18, 177,	10:14	12, 103, 121

10:21-22	186	13:29	121	18:10-14	219
10:25-37	184	13:31-33	102, 105n.13, 121	18:16	143
10:25	145, 185	13:31	49, 105n.14	18:17	142, 143
10:26	184	13:32	55	18:18	145
10:28	185	13:33-34	99, 105	18:24-25	142
10:30-37	125n.8, 219	13:33	105n.14	18:30	144, 145
10:38	105n.14	13:34-35	116n.36, 117,	19:1-10	176
11:5-8	120		223n.106	19:7	218n.88
11:14	202n.17	13:35	172	19:9a	176
11:20	138	14:7-11	219	19:11	103
11:24	202	14:12-14	219	19:23	51
11:27-28	94n.100	14:16-24	164, 164n.38,	19:28	105, 105n.13,
11:29-32	116n.36		169, 177, 219		105n.14
11:29	149	14:21	50	19:41-44	223n.106
11:30-32	149	14:26	196, 196n.43, 247	22:15-20	176
11:30	108	15	125	22:22	105n.13
11:31-32	119, 121, 179	15:3-10	120	22:29	144
11:39-41	214n.73	15:4-7	127	24:21	153n.26
11:43	50	15:4-6	193n.35		
11:45	98n.2	15:6	127	**John**	2, 12, 49, 53, 59,
11:49-51	99, 116n.36, 117	15:11-32	133, 219		60, 61, 63, 66,
12:7	68	15:17	133		72, 73, 74, 74n.11,
12:16-20	132	15:19b	133		75, 76, 77, 78, 79,
12:17	132	15:20-21	133		88, 88n.75, 89,
12:19	132	15:27	133		94, 96, 102, 144,
12:20	132	16:1-9	226n.116		146, 177
12:22-32	119	16:1-8a	131	1:1–2:11	93
12:22	180	16:3-7	51	1:1-18	89
12:25	180	16:3-4	131	1:14	63
12:27-28	180	16:7	87n.67	1:16-17	62
12:31	180	16:8a	131, 132	1:17	62
12:32	143, 149, 193n.35	16:16	138, 171, 178	1:19–2:11	93
12:35-36	94	16:19-31	219	1:24-28	171
12:49-50	178	17:11	105, 105n.13,	1:28	90
12:49	154n.2		105n.14	1:29-34	171
12:52	178	17:11-19	7, 16, 19, 201n.6,	1:35–4:54	76n.21
12:57-59	51		202	1:39	92
13:11-13	205n.34	17:14	203	1:43	92
13:11	202	17:15	202	1:44	90
13:18-19	119	17:17	202	1:45-46	89
13:20-21	119, 135	17:20-21	187	1:45	89
13:22	105n.13	17:21	138	2:1-11	76, 76n.22, 77,
13:26	50	17:34-35	119		77n.24, 77n.25,
13:28-29	177	18:1-8	120		78n.29, 79, 80,

	80n.39, 81,
	81n.41, 82,
	82n.46, 84, 86,
	87, 87n.66,
	87n.69, 88, 94,
	96, 96n.112, 97,
	97n.115, 200n.3
2:1-2	94
2:1	87n.69, 88, 89,
	90, 93, 94, 96
2:2	89
2:3-5	89, 93
2:3	94, 97
2:4	96, 97
2:5	94
2:6-10	94
2:6-7	13, 95
2:6	12, 13, 74, 76, 85,
	92
2:7-8	97
2:8-9	94
2:9-10	88
2:9	76, 82n.47, 85, 94
2:10	85
2:11	76, 87n.69, 88,
	90, 96
2:12	89, 93, 94
2:13	90
2:14-15	63
2:16	96n.114
2:19-20	96
2:19	96
2:23	90
3	57
3:1-21	96n.113
3:3	145
3:5	142
3:15	145
3:16	145
3:22	90
3:23	90, 121
3:29	96
3:36	145, 146
4:3-4	90

4:3	102
4:5	90
4:21	97
4:23	97
4:43-54	96n.113
4:43	102
4:46-54	80, 97
4:46	76, 90, 90n.82
5:1-9	62
5:1	74n.6
5:2-9	12, 74
5:2	61, 62, 90
5:16-18	67
5:24	144
5:25	97
5:28	97
5:39	144
5:40	144
6:1-15	87n.69
6:1	74n.6, 90
6:4	90
6:14-15	153
6:40	144
6:47	144
6:53	144
6:54	144
7:1	90
7:2-14	97n.115
8:3	11
9	12, 63
9:1-12	62
9:1	63
9:5	63
9:7	63
9:22	71
9:39	220
10:10	144
11:1-45	66n.11, 76,
	97n.115, 201n.7
11:1	66n.11, 90
11:17-44	204n.24
11:35	60
11:55	90
12:1-8	176

12:1	90
12:42	71
14:26	77n.23
15:1-8	87n.66
15:1a	96
16:2	71
18	65
18:1	64, 90
18:13	64
18:15-18	64
18:15	64, 96n.113
18:16	65
18:18	65
18:25-27	64
18:28	64
18:33-38	64
18:39-40	88n.70
19	65
19:6	64
19:13	12, 65, 74
19:17	90
19:25-27	94
19:25-26	94
19:26	94
19:29-30	94
19:41	90
20:13	94
20:15	94
20:31	144
21:1-14	80, 80n.37
21:2	76, 90
Acts	72, 102
1:4	146n.11
1:6	146n.11
3:1	67
3:2	205n.33
3:8	205n.33
3:10	205n.33
3:15	153n.25
3:22	153n.25
4:13	188
5:36-37	115n.33
5:37	109n.22, 110

6:13-14	223n.106	3:29	145	7:18-35	172, 174
7:37	153n.25	4:1	145	7:19	172
9:2	71	4:4	93	7:22-23	181
9:36-43	76n.18	4:7	145	7:22	177, 201n.6,
10:38	102	4:30	145		201n.7, 202,
11:26	71	5:21	145		205n.34
14:22	143			7:24	174
15	197	**Philippians**		7:28	178
18:8	71n.16	3:20	71n.18	7:31-35	116n.36
19:32	70			7:31-34	177
19:39	70	**Titus**		7:31-32	177
20:9-12	76n.18	1:15	227n.118,	7:31	174
21:26	67		229n.125	7:32	50, 175
21:38	151n.20			7:33-34	172, 174, 175,
22:4	71	**Hebrews**			178, 179, 180
22:17	67	3-4	149	7:33	173
24:5	71	3:12	150n.17	7:35	180
24:14	71	3:18-19	150n.17	9:34	218n.88
24:22	71	4:2-3	150n.17	9:58	54, 102
		10:32-33	101n.7	9:59	247
				10:3	193n.35
Romans		**James**		10:9	110
4:13	145	3:1	101	10:10	50
4:14	145	5:1-3	221n.100	10:13-15	179
6:9	229n.125			10:13	121
8:17	145	**1 Peter**		10:14	12
8:34	248	3:21	175	10:21-22	186
10:5	186			11:14	174, 202n.17
11:16	227n.118	**1 John**		11:20	138
		2:1	248	11:24	202
1 Corinthians		4:2	13	11:29-32	116n.36
1:19	187			11:31-32	119, 121, 179
6:9-10	145	**2 John**		11:39-41	214n.73
7:14	227	7	13	11:43	50
9:6	104			11:49-51	116n.36, 117
10:1-13	149	**Revelation**		12:22-32	119
11:23-26	176	19:7-9	96n.114	12:22	180
11:26	176			12:25	180
15:50	145	**Q, as found in Luke**		12:27-28	180
		3:7-9	171	12:31	180
2 Corinthians		3:7	175	12:57-59	51
3:1	104	3:8	175	13:18-19	119
		3:9	175	13:20-21	119
Galatians		3:16	172	13:28-29	177
3:12	186	3:17	171, 175, 176		
3:18	145	6:20-21	177		

13:29	121	50:5	219n.92	**Testament of Moses**	
13:34-35	116n.36, 117			5–7	222n.103
13:35	172	**Judith**			
14:16-24	169	8:18	225n.112	**Tobit**	188
14:26	247			1:16-19	209n.48
15:4-6	193n.35	**2 Maccabees**		1:18-20	197
16:16	138, 171, 178	5:10	209n.51	2:3-8	197, 209n.48
17:34-35	119	6:7	81n.43	4:3-4	197, 209n.51
19:23	51	14:33	81n.43	6:14	209n.51
		15:36	88n.72	6:15	197
				7:17 (Eng. 7:18)	188n.22
OLD TESTAMENT				11:19	92n.89, 94n.104
APOCRYPHA AND		**Odes of Solomon**	247	14:10-13	197
PSEUDEPIGRAPHA		42:6	247n.58	14:11-12	209n.51
2 Baruch	87	**Psalms of**		**Wisdom of Solomon**	
29:5	87n.67	**Solomon**	54, 70	12:24	186
		17	219n.91	14:8	225n.112
Bel and the Dragon		17:21-25	192n.31	15:14	186
1:5	225n.112	17:22-23	219n.92		
		17:26	219n.92		
1 Enoch	69	17:30	192n.31	**NEW TESTAMENT**	
10:19	87n.67	17:35	192n.31	**APOCRYPHA AND**	
19:1	201n.11	17:40-42	194n.41	**PSEUDEPIGRAPHA**	
42:1-2	117	17:40	193n.35		
62:12	101n.7	17:43	192n.31	**1 Clement**	
62:14	168			46:2	227n.118
89:54	223n.106	**Sibylline Oracles**			
89:56	223n.106	3.270-76	223n.106	**Didache**	
98:13	209n.51			11:8	104
		Sirach	116, 119		
4 Ezra		11:16-17 (LXX:		**Gospel of the Ebionites**	
2:22-23	209n.48	18-19)	132n.17	Frg. 3	171
		24:5-6	116		
Joseph and Asenath		24:7	116	**Gospel of Thomas**	39,
21.8 (21.6)	92n.89	31:3	132n.17		51, 102
		38:25-34	100	10	178
Jubilees				16	178
4:26	219n.92	**Testament of Benjamin**		64	177
10:1	201n.11	5.1-3	201n.11	86	102
11:4	201n.11				
23:7	209n.51			**Infancy Gospel of**	
36:1-2	209n.51	**Testament of Levi**		**Thomas**	
36:18-19	209n.51	15.1	223n.106	13	107n.16

Protevangelium of
James   107n.17
13:1   107n.17
15:1   107n.17

Pseudo-Clementine
Recognitions
1.60   170

DEAD SEA SCROLLS
AND RELATED
TEXTS

Cairo Damascus
Document   67, 68, 185,
                  193, 194, 195
3.15b-20   185
7.9-15   194n.37
19 (B = 1)   193
19.7-14 (B = 1.7-14)   194,
                    194n.37

1QpHab *(Pesher*
Habakkuk)   69, 71
7   69

1Q20 *(Genesis*
Apocryphon)   188
20.16   202
20.26   202
22.16   188n.22
22.21   188n.22

1QS *(Rule of the*
Community)
1.10 (= 4Q256
1:9)   196n.43
4.20-22   219n.92
8.4-10   223n.107
9.21-22 (= 4Q256
18:5)   196n.43

1QSa *(Rule of the*
Congregation)   8
2.2-10   223n.107

2.3-7   205
2.3-6   205n.32
2.3   205n.32
2.9b-10   8, 205
2.10   205n.32
2.11-22   168

1QM *(War Scroll)*
13.2-5   201n.13
13.5   201n.11

1QH[a] *(Thanksgiving*
Hymns)   9, 187n.20, 188
4.21   9, 188
6.19   9, 188
6.38   9, 188
15.29 [= 4Q428
frg. 9 line 1]   9, 188

3Q15 *(Copper Scroll)*   62

4Q174 *(Florilegium)*
Frgs. 1-2   9
Frg. 21 1.3-4   9

4Q196-99 *(Aramaic*
Tobit)   188n.22

4Q256
1.9   196n.43
18.5   196n.43

4Q285   192

4QMMT *(Some Works of*
the Torah)   71, 222n.103
Lines 39-42   9
Lines 55-57   205n.33

4Q428 [= 1QH[a] 15:29]
frg. 9 line 1   9

4Q500   195, 195n.42,
                    196n.42

4Q545
Line 6   94n.104

11QT[a] *(Temple*
Scroll)   8, 66n.11

45.12-14   8, 205, 205n.30,
                     205n.31

JOSEPHUS

Jewish Antiquities
3.262   206n.37
6.296   113n.29
6.298   113n.29
9:243   149n.13
10.277   112n.26
11.295   88n.72
13.318-19   42n.21
15.314   87n.67
15.328-30   43n.27
15.371   112
17   109n.22
17.66   149n.13
17.74   94n.99
17.152   109
18   109n.22
18.4   109, 109n.22, 112,
                       113
18.23   109n.22, 110, 112,
                       113
18.27   43n.30
18.36-38   217n.86
18.37-38   44n.32
18.116-19   49n.49, 170n.1
18.118-19   152n.22
18.117   175, 175n.14
19.32   112n.26
20.97-98   115n.33
20.97   113, 152
20.102   109n.22, 110
20.167-68   151
20.181   217n.87
20.206-7   217n.87

Jewish War
1.648   109
1.650   109
2.118   109, 109n.22, 113
2.143-44   217n.87

2.259	151	*On Planting (Plant.)*		**Talmud Babli**	
2.261-62	151	151	113n.30		
2.405	110			*b. Ketubbot*	
2.433	109, 109n.22,	*That Every Good Person*		2a	92n.90
	110, 113	*Is Free (Prob.)*		8b	92n.89
2.615	44n.31	75-91	114n.31		
2.618	44n.31	121-24	113n.30	*b. Megillah*	
2.641	44n.31			11b	88n.75
3.35-38	49n.48			12a	88n.75
3.377	209n.48	**RABBINIC**		13b	88n.73
3.506-21	49n.48	**LITERATURE**		14a	88n.73
4.1-83	114n.32			15b	88n.73
4.317	209n.48	**Mishnah**	95		
5.227	203n.22	*m. Berakot*		*b. Sanhedrin*	
5.545	209n.51	3.1	209n.51	11a	178
6.250	223n.106				
6.301	223n.106	*m. Demai*	217	**Targumic Texts**	
7.253	110	*m. Ketubbot*		*Targum Onqelos* 209n.43	
7.323	114	1.1	92n.90	*Targum Pseudo-*	
				Jonathan	209n.43
Contra Apion		*m. Parah*			
1.281	203n.20	3.3	95n.110	*First Targum of Esther*	
2.180	112n.26			9.26	88n.73
2.193-96	222n.103	*m. Qiddushin*		9.29	88n.73
		(Kiddushin)			
Life		4	9	*Second Targum of*	
12	112, 113	*m. Zabim*		*Esther*	
46	114n.32	5:6	203n.20	2.6	88n.73
64	44n.31			2.11	88n.73
86	90	**Tosefta**		4.13	88n.73
114	114n.32			6.11	88n.73
169	44n.31	*t. Berakot*		7.10	88n.73
179	114n.32	2.10	94n.104	9.26	88n.73
279	44n.31	*t. Me'ilah*		9.29	88n.73
284	44n.31	1.16	195		
				Targum at Zech	
		t. Sukkah		13:7	194n.38
PHILO		3.15	195		
				Other Rabbinic Works	
On the Life of Joseph		**Talmud Yerushalmi**			
(Ios.)		*y. Ketubbot*		*Mekilta of Rabbi Ishmael*	
5 §22-25	197	1.1, §1	92n.90	12.39	150n.18
		1.1, §6	92n.89	14.15	150n.18
Allegorical Interpretation				15.22	150n.18
(Leg.)		*y. Megillah*			
3.82	87n.69	4.4, §3	92n.89	*Midrash on*	
				Exodus	150n.18

306

Midrash on the Song of Songs   150n.18

Midrash on Psalms
2.9   192n.31

Lamentations Rabbah
1.7, §34   92n.89

Pesiqta de Rab Kahana
26.2   92n.90
28.9   92n.89

Pirqe Rabbi Eliezer
49   88n.75

Sipra Behuqotai pereq
5.266.1.7   92n.89

CLASSICAL SOURCES

Apollodorus
Library Epitome
3.10   83n.54

Athenaeus
Deipnosophistae
15.34a   86n.64

Augustine
Tractates on the Gospel of John
49.18-19   60

Diodorus Siculus
3.66.2   82n.47

Epictetus
Diatribai
2.19.25   101n.7
3.22.59   101n.7

Enchiridion
51.2   101n.7

Eusebius
Historia ecclesiastica
6.14.7   60, 73n.2

Horace
Carmina
2.19.9-12   82n.47

Jerome
Onomasticon   66n.11

Justin Martyr
Dialogue with Trypho
88   107n.16

Memnon of Heraclea 85
History of Heraclea
Books 9-16   85n.62
from *FGH* 434
frg. 1   85n.62

Nonnos
Dionysica
16.252-54   85n.63

Origen
Commentary on the Gospel of John
6.258-59   93n.96

Contra Celsum
1.65   104n.11

Ovid
Metamorphoses   82
13.650-54   83n.51

Pausanias   86
Description of Greece 86
6.26.1-2   86n.64

Photius
Bibliotheca
224   85n.62

Pliny the Elder
Natural History   83
2.231   84n.56
31.13   84n.60

Pseudo-Aristotle
Mirabilia 123   86n.64

Pseudo-Demosthenes
Erotici
7.27   95n.106

Seneca
Dialogi
1.2.8-9   101n.7

Epistulae morales
95.33   101n.7

Servius
Commentary on Virgil's Aeneid   83
3.80   83n.55

Silius Italicus
Punica
7.186-94   82n.47

Sophocles   82
Athamas
Frg. 5   82n.48

Xenophon
Cyropaedia
8.2.5   106n.15

INSCRIPTIONS AND PAPYRI

Corpus inscriptionum latinarum
I 2.381   83n.52
I 2.563   83n.52

Papyrus Oxyrhynchus
840   206n.38, 207n.38